THE BOOK OF
REVELATION

Pastor Chuck,

Keep living as an overcomer!

Matt Curly

THE BOOK OF
REVELATION

The Rest of the Story

Martin M. Culy

PICKWICK *Publications* · Eugene, Oregon

THE BOOK OF REVELATION
The Rest of the Story

Pickwick Publications
An Imprint of Wipf and Stock Publishers
199 W. 8th Ave., Suite 3
Eugene, OR 97401

www.wipfandstock.com

PAPERBACK ISBN: 978-1-5326-1718-8
HARDCOVER ISBN: 978-1-4982-4169-4
EBOOK ISBN: 978-1-4982-4168-7

Cataloging-in-Publication data:

Names: Culy, Martin M.

Title: The book of Revelation : the rest of the story / Martin M. Culy.

Description: Eugene, OR : Pickwick Publications, 2017 | Includes bibliographical references and index.

Identifiers: ISBN 978-1-5326-1718-8 (paperback) | ISBN 978-1-4982-4169-4 (hardcover) | ISBN 978-1-4982-4168-7 (ebook)

Subjects: LCSH: Bible. N.T. Revelation—Criticism, interpretation, etc.

Classification: LCC BS2825.52 C8 2017 (print) | LCC BS2825.52 (ebook)

Manufactured in the U.S.A.   10/05/17

Contents

Preface

ALMOST FORTY YEARS AGO, I had the privilege of teaching on Revelation and the end times to a group of fellow teens. Although I had a lot of zeal at the time, and those who attended were very appreciative, ultimately it was an exercise in the blind leading the blind. More than that, even as a teenager with limited familiarity with Scripture it did not take long to recognize that the end times charts and popular books of the day did not begin to do justice to the message of Revelation. In fact, numerous aspects of popular thinking seemed quite out of step with what I saw in the Bible. Ultimately, this left me wondering if the book of Revelation, in particular, was simply not intended to be understood. And so, for many years, though I continued to read Revelation, I did so with every expectation that it would remain impenetrable until the end of the age.

In early 1982, however, while I was studying in England, I was presented with a limited edition copy of William Ramsay's *The Letters to the Seven Churches*, and suddenly Revelation began to look very different, at least Revelation 2–3. Set in their historical context, these messages from Jesus to actual churches in the first century took on far greater significance. It wasn't until about a decade later, though, that I came to see that the seven "letters" of Revelation 2–3 could not be divorced from the rest of Revelation. The entire book is a message to followers of Jesus in first century Asia Minor, and to understand any part of it, it is critical to grasp how that part relates to the whole. Throughout this period I was still primarily stuck in the rut of reading Revelation as a book addressed to those suffering severe persecution. It wasn't until 1998 that I was introduced by Dr. Charles Talbert to the idea that Revelation was an example of "anti-assimilation literature." Whether or not such a label is legitimate at the level of genre, the notion that Revelation was written, at least in part, as a call to avoid compromising with and thus assimilating to the broader Greco-Roman culture was the missing part of the puzzle for me. Suddenly, the fact that only part of this marvelous book seems to address persecution made sense. What was still lacking, however, was how the book of Revelation fit together into a coherent whole.

In the almost two decades that have followed, I have had the privilege of teaching through the book of Revelation mostly in college and seminary contexts, but also in churches, almost twenty times. Each time through, I have been increasingly impressed not only with the profundity and relevance of Revelation's message for today, but also with its literary beauty and clarity. One does not usually speak of the perspicuity of Scripture and the book of Revelation in the same breath, but I hope that after you have read what follows the prior gulf between the two will have been bridged.

I am grateful to the one thousand or so students I have had the privilege of interacting with over the years as I have taught Revelation. Many of them have sharpened my thinking through insightful questions, and most of them have encouraged me to press on toward getting what follows in print as they have zealously embraced the message of Revelation to live as overcomers in a society where we do not belong and where allegiance to Jesus is often not appreciated.

I am also grateful to Dave Mathewson, Rob Godard, and Ed Watson for reviewing a full draft of the manuscript. Each of them provided helpful feedback, and their suggestions improved the book at several points. Finally, I am profoundly grateful to my wife, Jo-Anna, who more than anyone has encouraged me to press forward with this project year after year despite the constant delays as we chose to set the book aside and focus on other more urgent ministries. I dedicate this book to my family—Jo-Anna; Chris, Vanessa, and Thomas; Calvin, Rachel, and Wayland; and Charissa—and pray that God will help each of us and all who read this book to live increasingly as "those who keep the commandments of God and hold to the testimony of Jesus" (Rev 12:17).

Introduction

And though St. John the Evangelist saw many strange monsters in his vision, he saw no creature so wild as one of his own commentators.[1]

REVELATION, BY ANY MODERN standard, is a strange book. It has intrigued and perplexed readers down through the centuries, and all too frequently it has fallen victim to fanciful interpretations. Those who preach from the book of Revelation often spend an inordinate amount of time on chapters 2–3, followed by a quick sermon on chapters 4–5 before throwing in the towel or skipping to "the end of the story" in the last three or four chapters. This leaves Revelation 6–18 as some of the most neglected chapters in the New Testament. Two factors contribute to this state of affairs. On the one hand, the "letters" to the seven churches are messages we can readily identify with today. All of us have received letters ourselves and Jesus' words to each of the seven churches are for the most part straightforward. Most of the remainder of Revelation, on the other hand, is anything but straightforward; it is far removed from anything we have ever read or experienced. And the natural tendency is to gravitate to those portions of Revelation that are familiar and ignore those that are not. Unfortunately, by doing so we run the risk of missing out on much of what God is saying to us today through this final book of the Bible. We miss out on "the rest of the story."

I am convinced that, as with the other books of the New Testament, when God gave Revelation to the churches in Asia Minor he intended those early Christians to understand it—from beginning to end. This is clearly implied in the opening words of Revelation, as we will see. As we begin our study of Revelation, then, it is important to recognize that, although Revelation may seem quite mysterious and impenetrable to us today, God chose to reveal his message in language and imagery that was familiar to the original readers, language that they could understand. And he did so by weaving a beautiful tapestry of twenty-two interconnected chapters, each of which is a necessary part of the overall message. Indeed, Revelation can only be rightly understood when the parts are read in light of the whole. Thus, while some scholars have believed

1. Chesterton, *Orthodoxy*, 17.

that the seven letters were inserted into Revelation after the rest of the work had been written, almost as an afterthought,[2] and Ramsay goes so far as to claim that Revelation "would be quite complete without the seven letters,"[3] *the key to understanding the message of Revelation is actually found in the intricate relationship between the seven letters and the rest of the book.*[4] Although Ramsay's understanding of the relationship between the seven letters and what follows should be rejected, his overall thesis remains both compelling and vitally important for understanding Revelation. More than anyone before him, Ramsay highlighted the way in which each of the seven letters appears to play off of the history and/or physical characteristics of the city that is being addressed.[5] This should not surprise us since any competent communicator will make heavy use of what is familiar to those to whom he or she is writing in an effort to craft a message that is both intelligible and compelling.[6]

To understand Revelation we will need to determine how it would have been understood by the original readers.[7] A primary key to this end will be reading all of Revelation in light of the context set forth in the letters to the seven churches. As Swete points out,

> The book starts with a well-defined historical situation, to which reference is made again at the end, and the intermediate visions which form the body of the work cannot on any reasonable theory be dissociated from their historical setting. The prophecy arises out of local and contemporary circumstances; it is, in the first instance at least, the answer of the Spirit to the fears and perils of the Asian Christians towards the end of the first century. Hence all that can throw light on the Asia of A.D. 70–100, and upon Christian life in Asia during that period, is of primary importance to the student of the Apocalypse, not only in view of the local allusion in cc. ii-iii, but as helping to determine the aim and drift of the entire work.[8]

2. Ramsay, *Letters*, 25–27. R. H. Charles, who rightly emphasized the importance of Revelation's epistolary format, wrongly held that the letters of chapters 2–3 were written earlier, during the reign of Vespasian, only to be revised and then incorporated into Revelation during the reign of Domitian. Charles, *Revelation*, xciv, 43–46.

3. Ramsay, *Letters*, 27. Hemer differs from Ramsay on this point: "They appear quite distinct from the body of the Apocalypse, but prove on analysis to be intimately linked with it." Hemer, *Letters*, 14.

4. It will be obvious throughout that I owe an immense debt to Ramsay, Hemer, and Worth, in particular, for their incredibly helpful studies on the seven churches/cities of Asia Minor. Each of them significantly helps us to gain a clearer picture of the first-century circumstances and past history of the seven churches, and the ways in which this background information sheds light on how the original readers would have understood the seven messages.

5. Cf. Ramsay, *Letters*, 278; contra a few scholars who deny any local references in the seven letters; Hemer (*Letters*, xxn21) cites as examples Prigent (*L'Apocalypse*) and Sanders ("John on Patmos").

6. Thus, Ramsay (*Letters*, 37) rightly notes that "the letters were written to be understood by the Asian congregations," and were composed "in the current language familiar to the people of the time" (ibid., 38).

7. So ibid., 40.

8. Swete, *The Apocalypse*, ccxviii. Hemer (*Letters*, 51) closely follows Ramsay in terms of his overall

Beyond the historical context, however, it is also critical to recognize that Revelation is a literary work of astounding beauty and complexity, woven together with a series of threads that run from beginning to end and tie the entire work together into a coherent whole. *To understand any part, the whole must be taken into account.* To understand any given letter in chapters 2–3, one must read that letter in light of the rest of Revelation, while to understand the rest of Revelation one must also read it in light of each of the seven letters. It all works together as a package, a literary masterpiece whose overall force can only be grasped when it is read as a unified whole in light of its myriad of *intra*textual connections, i.e., parallel language and themes within Rev 1–22. Yes, we need to be cognizant of the frequent Old Testament allusions in Revelation (*inter*textual connections). Yes, we need to study the Greco-Roman context of Revelation. Yes, we need to be particularly aware of the characteristics and history of each of the seven cities of Revelation. But none of these, either individually or together, is sufficient. We must also recognize that *Revelation's message is integrally tied up in its carefully crafted inner-connections.*

As we read Revelation in this manner, we will discover that Jesus spoke loud and clear to the Christians living in Asia Minor in the first century; and that message in turn speaks just as loudly to us today. It is the same message that Jesus preached while he was on earth and that his followers have preached ever since. It revolves around the central question of human existence: Who is Lord? In the first-century Roman world, *everyone* knew the answer to that question: "Duh! Caesar is Lord! Who else?" Who else indeed? Paul was repeatedly thrown into prison for preaching that there was another Lord and his name was Jesus. While we may not be tempted to bow before an emperor, president, or prime minister today and worship a mere human being, the broad temptation to idolatry (giving our allegiance to someone or something other than God) is as rampant and as alluring today as it was two millennia ago.

Jesus' message to the church, which we know as "the book of Revelation," calls us to make a fundamental choice. Who is Lord? Whom will we serve? Will it be a human leader? Will it be a human system (including democracy or free market capitalism)? Will it be ourselves? Or will it be the only true King of kings and Lord of lords? The stakes are high, and our response has the most serious of all consequences. Jesus meant what he said about his message to the church at the very beginning of Revelation: "blessed are those who hear, and who keep what is written in it" (1:3). To respond appropriately is to enter into great blessing; to fail to keep the message is to come under the wrath of God.

---

thesis: "many things throughout Revelation may be illuminated by the assumption that local conditions and needs carried his thoughts back to the familiar Old Testament Scriptures, influencing his choice and directing his application of them." While we may reject the implicit view that John's own thinking drove the content and form of Revelation, the fact that Revelation speaks to real situations in real churches in late first-century Asia Minor should lead us to want to discover all we can about the circumstances the original readers would have been facing.

REVELATION AND THE LAST DAYS

Isn't Revelation, though, about the last days? Isn't it primarily designed to provide us with a roadmap of what to expect as the end of all things draws near? Actually, it is not. While it clearly supplies us with valuable information about the end times (eschatology), *shedding light on the future is only a fringe benefit of Revelation's overall purpose.* It is a means to an end, and that end is to exhort believers in first-century Asia Minor, and throughout the world today, to live in light of the reality that Revelation describes.[9] It is a forceful plea from the King of kings and Lord of lords for those who call themselves his followers to live as citizens of *his* kingdom, living lives that are shaped by *his* kingdom's values, not by the values of this world. Plain and simple, *Revelation is Jesus' call to radical discipleship.* It leaves no room for compromise, no room for sitting on the fence. Consequently, it is every bit as relevant, if not more so, than any other book in the New Testament for Christians today; and this relevancy extends not just from the beginning of chapter 2 to the end of chapter 3, but from 1:1 through 22:21. All twenty-two chapters of this remarkable book form one coherent message for the people of God . . . today. It is a message that has more often than not been utterly obscured by those who are more interested in making end times charts than hearing and responding to the clarion call to faithful and radical discipleship that Jesus makes to his people through this book.

It is my hope that as you read the chapters that follow you will appreciate anew—or perhaps for the first time—the profundity of what God has said to us through Revelation. I think you will find that Revelation makes sense! But those who have bought into a sugar-coated "gospel" that has more in common with the American Dream than with God's eternal purposes in saving us will not like what Jesus has to say in his message to the church. For, this message does not come from a cuddly Jesus, who resembles a teddy bear that can be picked up when comfort is needed, but is left in a corner most of the time. This message does not come from a Santa Claus Jesus, who exists for us, rather than we for him. Instead, the Jesus of Revelation is an awe-inspiring figure. There is no one in the entire universe who can begin to match his majesty. He has no equal. He is beyond compare. He is a Lion as well as a Lamb. He is Judge as well as Savior. No Christian should be able to read the only letter he wrote directly to the church without trembling as John trembled when he encountered Jesus on the island of Patmos. No true Christian can understand the message of Revelation without having his or her life dramatically changed.

So, continue reading at your own risk! Better yet, walk through the message of Revelation with me and pray that God will give you courage to respond appropriately. For the blessing that Jesus holds out for those who hear his message and keep it is

---

9. Murray Harris is reported to have reminded his students that "the purpose of prophecy was to receive encouragement to live faithfully and not 'to satisfy idle curiosity.'" Hess, "The Future Written in the Past," 24.

none other than an "abundant life" now and life forevermore in his presence in the age to come.

1

Revelation 1
This Book Comes with an Instruction Manual

THE FIRST CHAPTER OF Revelation serves at least three very important functions. First, it sketches out the setting for what follows, telling us something about both the sender and the recipients, as well as about the remarkable events that precipitated the writing of Revelation. Second, it introduces a number of key themes for the book as a whole. And third—and this point is often missed—Rev 1 provides us with a rather extensive series of reading instructions that serve as necessary lenses through which to read all that follows. Failing to make use of these reading instructions is like attempting to watch a 3D movie without 3D glasses. Everything is out of focus; nothing is clear. Put on the glasses, though, and the picture becomes so clear that you feel like you are part of the action. So it is when we follow the directions that God himself has provided for reading Revelation.

> *The revelation of Jesus Christ, which God gave him to show to his servants the things that must soon take place. He made it known by sending his angel to his servant John, ²who bore witness to the word of God and to the testimony of Jesus Christ, even to all that he saw. ³Blessed is the one who reads aloud the words of this prophecy, and blessed are those who hear, and who keep what is written in it, for the time is near.* (1:1–3)

The opening words of Revelation lead us to believe that what follows is going to be something remarkable. It is a revelation that God has given to his own Son, Jesus Christ, to pass on to his servants. Although God had given many messages over the centuries to his people, they typically came through a prophet or an angel. In this case, the revelation is delivered, first of all, to the Lord Jesus Christ himself. If there was ever a message to listen to, this is most certainly it.

It is also important to recognize the audience to whom Revelation is addressed. It is easy to assume that it was written to unbelievers and was intended to scare them into the kingdom. After all, the bulk of Revelation describes in vivid detail God's wrath being poured out on a world that is in rebellion against him. As we see in the opening verses, however, *Revelation was clearly intended as a message for God's own people.* And, as will become clear, every part of this marvelous book is intended to shape the way the people of God live in this world.

Reading Instruction #1: We must remember that Revelation is a message from God to his own people.

Once we recognize that Revelation is a message for God's people, we need to also be careful to hear it on its own terms. All too often, we miss the point of Scripture because we think we understand it, when in fact our long held interpretations are misguided. Consider the most well-known verse in Revelation: "Behold, I stand at the door and knock. If anyone hears my voice and opens the door, I will come in to him and eat with him, and he with me" (3:20). What does this passage mean? Many Christians tend to assume that Jesus is talking to those who do not know him and inviting them to enter into a relationship with him ("open the door of their hearts to him"). Consequently, Rev 3:20 is frequently used in evangelism. Christians who start with that prior understanding will tend to respond: "Been there, done that. This verse doesn't apply to me. I've already let Jesus in!" And they completely miss the point of this verse. Jesus addresses these words to *the church* in Laodicea, a church that has shut him out. He may, in fact, be speaking to us. When we come to Rev 3:20 below, we will need to stop and ask what the implications are for us today. For now, I would ask you to commit to trying to read Revelation anew, assuming that you may have misunderstood its message in the past.

Key Theme #1: Christians are God's Servants

In verse 1, notice how John refers to both himself and his audience: they are "servants" or "slaves" of God. The use of this title in both cases is not coincidental. Revelation reminds readers, right from the very beginning, that those who wear the name "Christian" *belong* to God. Jesus did not just purchase their salvation, he purchased them; and their calling now is to glorify God with their lives (1 Cor 6:20). John also models the life of a *faithful* servant by testifying to everything he saw, resisting the temptation to filter out the uncomfortable parts. Revelation will return many times to these themes in what follows, making it clear that they are central to Jesus' call to radical discipleship.

In verse 3, we have the first of seven beatitudes or "blessing statements" that are found in Revelation (see also 14:13; 16:15; 19:9; 20:6; 22:7, 14). We should not be surprised to find that there are *seven* beatitudes, since the number seven is all over Revelation. Here, a blessing is pronounced on the one who reads what follows aloud in the congregation. With literacy rates running very low in the ancient world, the role of Reader was very important in Christian congregations.[1] So, this is not a promise to all those, including us, who read Revelation. Our promise comes next, and it comes with a condition: "blessed are those who hear, and who keep what is written in it." To receive the blessing those who hear the message of Revelation must also "keep" or "take to heart" (NIV) what it says. The message that follows, then, is not simply intended to provide general encouragement to suffering believers. Nor is its primary purpose providing information regarding the future. Rather, it is intended to *shape* the lives of Christians in first-century Asia Minor.

Notice that Jesus promises those Christians living in Asia Minor a blessing, *if* they respond appropriately to what he is about to say to them. This clearly implies that he expected them to *understand* what he was saying, so that they could respond appropriately. It would have been heartless for Jesus to promise first-century Christians a blessing that no one would be able to receive until 2,000 years later "when the world had the advanced technology to make sense of the message."

Reading Instruction #2: We must determine what Revelation would have meant to Christians in first-century Asia Minor.

Jesus' promise of a blessing to those who keep the words of his prophecy is, in fact, central to the overall message of Revelation. This becomes obvious when we notice that he repeats the promised blessing in 22:7. The words "written in this scroll" (22:7) are not just those words written in Rev 2–3, but rather encompass all twenty-two chapters of Revelation. Although certain details of the symbolism in Revelation may well have remained obscure to some of the original readers, the overall message of Rev 1–22 would have been readily comprehensible. So, as we read Revelation from beginning to end, we need to continue asking ourselves: How would the original readers have understood "the words of this prophecy" (1:3)?

Key Theme #2: Jesus is Coming Soon

Finally, at the end of verse 3, we find another important theme in the message of Revelation. John urges his readers to sit up and pay attention to what follows "because the time is near." As we continue through Revelation we will repeatedly encounter Jesus informing us: "I am coming soon" (see 3:11; 22:7, 12, 20). He also tells us that God has "sent his angel to show his servants the things that must *soon take place*" (22:6). What exactly did Jesus mean when he said these things? After all, the majority of the events he describes have apparently not yet happened.

---

1. Ancient texts were generally read aloud, even when people were reading to themselves.

Without going into the range of explanations that scholars have offered over the centuries for this language, let me summarize what I think Jesus is *doing* with his "soon" language. First, we have to recognize that Revelation is not the only place in the New Testament where such claims are made. In fact, they are fairly common. For example, 1 Pet 4:7 tells us that "The end of all things is at hand." James 5:8 tells us that "the coming of the Lord is at hand," and James goes on to emphasize this by saying, "the Judge is standing at the door" (5:9). Why do we find such language in Revelation and elsewhere in the New Testament? The answer is actually quite simple: *The New Testament urges every Christian in every century to live with the belief that Jesus' return is imminent.* That belief is to shape our lives each and every day. However long Christians have been waiting for the return of Christ, all have been called to live in light of the fact that Jesus' coming is near. Just as John uses the phrase "the time is near" to motivate Christians to respond appropriately to Jesus' call to radical discipleship in Revelation, so Peter, James, and other New Testament writers use this important truth to spur every Christian of every age to live in light of the culmination of the ages. This, too, will be an important theme in what follows in Rev 1–22.

> *John to the seven churches that are in Asia: Grace to you and peace from him who is and who was and who is to come, and from the seven spirits who are before his throne,* [5]*and from Jesus Christ the faithful witness, the firstborn of the dead, and the ruler of kings on earth.* (1:4–5a)

Understanding the genre of a work is critically important if we are to avoid misinterpreting that work. When you hear the words, "Once upon a time there were three bears," you immediately, as a native speaker of English, have a certain set of expectations for the story that will follow. You know that you will be reading a fairy tale, rather than a factual account of a series of events. The expectations that you have for such a story, then, will be very different than the expectations for a text that begins, "On February 12, 1809, Abraham Lincoln was born in a one-room log cabin on the Sinking Spring Farm in southeast Hardin County, in the state of Kentucky." If we were to interpret the biography of Abraham Lincoln in the same way we interpret the story of the three bears, the result, of course, would be laughable. So, it is important to understand what type of text we are reading if we are going to rightly interpret it. What kind of expectations should we bring to Revelation? Well, that will depend on what genre we believe it to be.

After the first three verses, Revelation begins like a typical letter: "John to the seven churches that are in Asia" (1:4). So, Revelation is a letter, right? Perhaps, but almost any genre can be placed within the larger structure of a letter by adding a letter-style opening and closing; and the rest of Revelation does not follow the typical pattern of letters. Nevertheless, it is important to recognize that Revelation is framed like a letter for a reason. What might that reason be?

Think of the differences between a novel and a letter. A novel is written for whoever will buy it and is intended primarily to entertain. A letter is a more direct form of communication between two parties. Unlike with novels, which are more self-contained and include most of the information you need to follow the story, prior knowledge of the circumstances that are being addressed in a letter is critically important for understanding what that letter means, but those circumstances are typically not explicitly stated. Revelation as a whole is presented as a letter addressed to specific people, at a specific point of time, in a specific set of circumstances. So, to understand its message we must first gain some understanding of what circumstances were being addressed.

Revelation, though, is more than a letter. Although it is framed like a letter, it identifies itself as a prophecy (1:3). This genre identification is repeated in 22:7, 10, 18, and 19. Although prophecy is often predictive in nature, i.e., it tells something about the future, biblical prophecy is almost always concerned with calling God's people to live in conformity with his will. So, it is both letter and prophecy; but we are still not finished. Revelation also has all of the typical features of "apocalyptic." Scholars have noted common characteristics for this genre, which closely match what we find in Revelation:

- apocalypses are told like a story
- apocalypses record a revelatory vision that was given to a human being, most often through the intervention of an otherworldly being
- apocalypses depict cosmic transformation and divine judgment
- the visions of an apocalypse help the audience to make sense of their present circumstances
- apocalypses are most often addressed to those living in times of suffering, so desperate that they require direct divine intervention that will bring all to an end
- apocalypses tend to stress the impending judgment of the wicked and vindication of the righteous
- apocalyptic texts tend to employ a variety of literary techniques
- apocalyptic writings tend to urge readers to respond in a particular manner[2]

Reading Instruction #3: We must read Revelation in light of its complex genre.

We are clearly left, then, with an unusual literary work by any standard. *Revelation has all the features of apocalyptic literature, but claims to be a prophecy and is framed like*

2. See Collins, "Introduction," 1–20.

a letter. It thus has a triple genre; and its composite nature, in terms of genre, tells us something about how to interpret it. Revelation is a letter written to specific people at a specific point in time; it is a prophecy that tells something about the future and also calls its readers to live in a particular way; and it is an apocalypse that addresses people in dire circumstances who need to be reminded of a larger reality in order to remain faithful to God in their present and coming circumstances. In other words, the triple genre serves to emphasize the fact that Revelation is not simply or even primarily a road map to the future, but rather is first and foremost Jesus' call to radical discipleship addressed to a church facing both persecution and significant temptation.[3]

While Paul often includes co-senders in his letters, such as Timothy or Silas, John has the privilege of having the Trinity as his co-sender (vv. 4–5), though at first glance we might miss the Trinitarian reference. John could have simply written, "From the Father, Holy Spirit, and Jesus." Instead, he used distinctive titles for each member of the Trinity. He highlighted the fact that the Father is not only the Eternal One ("him who is and who was"); he is also the one who is coming to judge ("and who is to come").[4] He is the One who will most certainly bring all things to their culmination. The Holy Spirit, on the other hand, is described as "the seven spirits who are before his throne."[5] Since the number seven regularly symbolizes completeness in Jewish literature, here it likely points to the fullness of the Spirit. It is also possible that the frequent mentions of an unnamed voice in heaven elsewhere in Revelation are references to the Holy Spirit (see 9:13; 10:4; 16:17; 19:5).[6] For our purposes, though, it is the description of Jesus that is particularly important. Notice the three titles that he is given: "the faithful witness, the firstborn of the dead, and the ruler of kings on earth" (1:5). These three titles highlight central features of Jesus' role and provide a summary of the overall message of Revelation.

Key Theme #3: Christians are to Imitate Jesus, the Faithful Witness

The description of Jesus also subtly introduces what will be an important theme in Revelation. In his earthly ministry, Jesus was "the faithful witness." Though many say that the reference to Jesus as "the faithful witness" simply indicates that he is someone

3. Hemer (*Letters*, 12) rightly notes that "the connection of the Revelation with earlier works of this genre [apocalyptic] has been overestimated." Revelation is a genuine account of visions that John was given, visions that God revealed in an apocalyptic form, which unlike most apocalyptic texts were not only broadly prophetic in nature, i.e., hortatory, but also include predictive prophecy framed as a letter. John was writing as a prophet and conveying a prophetic message. Revelation is thus a letter whose primary content is a series of apocalyptic visions and whose primary function is a prophetic call to repentance and perseverance.

4. Divine "coming" is regularly associated with judgment in the Old Testament (e.g., Pss 96:13; 98:9; Isa 19:1; 26:21).

5. Not all see a reference to the Holy Spirit here.

6. It is unclear in 14:13 whether the reference to the Spirit identifies the referent of the "voice from heaven" or distinguishes the Spirit from that voice.

who speaks the truth and is reliable, this likely misses the point that is being made, which will serve as an important foundation for what follows. Jesus' title as "the faithful witness" is a reminder that Jesus remained faithful in following God's plan even when it led to his death. He is the one "who in his testimony before Pontius Pilate made the good confession" (1 Tim 6:13), that is, he is the one who did not shrink back or compromise to save his skin in the face of death. This choice of title, then, is far more than an appropriate description of Jesus; it also carries with it an important implicit exhortation that resonates from this point forward in Revelation: *be faithful in following Jesus even unto death.* As Jesus was and is the faithful witness, so he expects his followers to be faithful witnesses.

Key Theme #4: Death is Not the End of the Story

The second title introduces another important theme: "firstborn of the dead." Yes, Jesus' absolute faithfulness in bearing witness to the Father and to his own identity and mission led to his death; but death was not the end of the story. Jesus died, but as a faithful witness, God raised him from the dead. And as the "firstborn" from the dead he has set a precedent for the resurrection of his followers. Thus, where the first title would have carried an implicit *exhortation* to faithfulness, this title carries an implicit word of *encouragement* to the original readers: remain a faithful witness to the end, because death is not the end! When we seek to read Scripture through the eyes of those to whom it was originally addressed, we discover that there is far more there than mere information. Even titles can convey a powerful message. What, then, might the third title have communicated?

Key Theme #5: The Supreme Ruler of this World is Jesus, not Caesar

The description of Jesus as "the ruler of kings on earth," or better, "the ruler of the kings of the earth," is particularly significant in Revelation. You see, the Roman emperor was referred to as the *princeps regnum terrae* ("the ruler of the kings of the earth"), among other titles.[7] John, then, through his strategic choice of language, makes it clear that the supreme ruler of this world is not Caesar but Jesus. There is a man who claims to be the ruler of the kings of the earth (the emperor) and to have power over life and death, but he is a fraud. Jesus is the true King of kings and Lord of lords. Thus, from the very beginning, John models for his readers the radical devotion that Jesus is going to call the churches of Asia Minor to embrace and live out, no matter how dire their circumstances.

---

7. Greek writers used the same term that Revelation uses to refer to the *princeps*: ἄρχων (*archōn*). Elsewhere in Revelation, the phrase, "kings of the earth," is used seven times (6:15; 17:2, 18; 18:3, 9; 19:19; 21:24), in each case to refer to the corrupt rulers of this world.

THE PURPOSE OF THE BOOK OF REVELATION

Before we move on, let's pause for a moment and consider the overall purpose of the book of Revelation. Embedded within the titles of Jesus we find a hint of the two major issues that Revelation is intended to address. Traditionally, scholars have tended to argue that Revelation was primarily written to encourage Christians who were suffering under the reign of Domitian because they would not participate in the emperor cult, which demanded that the inhabitants of the Roman Empire worship the emperor. A message intended to steel the resolve of those facing persecution certainly fits well with the repeated references to the "blood of the saints" (16:5–7; 18:24; 19:2). Moreover, there is some evidence to suggest that persecution of Christians was occurring during the reign of Domitian (AD 81–96), though the extent of this persecution has recently been disputed.[8] The fact that Revelation only refers to one specific case of martyrdom (2:13) does not weaken this view.[9] After all, how many martyrs would there need to be from your congregation or city or region before you started fearing persecution? The main weakness of the persecution view, though, is that the focus of Revelation appears to be on a great persecution to come, rather than on present persecution (2:10; 3:10).

Most scholars today take a different view and believe that Revelation is primarily concerned with members of the seven churches who were advocating compromise with the pagan Roman culture. According to Howard-Brook and Gwyther, "the evidence of both historical documents and the text of Revelation itself suggests that it was seduction by the Roman Empire from within a context of relative comfort, rather than terrifying persecution, that more accurately describes the situation of the original audience of the book of Revelation."[10] A key strength of this view is that it fits what we know of the historical circumstances very well. Although the Roman Empire was a system of tyranny and exploitation, the author of Revelation was well aware that it was not resisted or opposed by most of its subjects. In the great cities of the province of Asia, where the seven churches were located, most people were very enthusiastic about Roman rule.[11]

---

8. See esp. Thompson, *Book of Revelation*, 15–17; cf. Collins, *Crisis & Catharsis*, 84–110.

9. Talbert, *The Apocalypse*, 10. While most now reject the persecution view, Schüssler Fiorenza has argued that given the fact that the elite historians, upon whom we are dependent, would have been unlikely to include references to such insignificant matters as occasional persecution of Christians, we should not be surprised that no external evidence exists to corroborate the persecution view. Schüssler Fiorenza, *Book of Revelation*, 9. Robinson, on the other hand, in an effort to account for the historical discrepancy, has argued that the book of Revelation should actually be dated to AD 68–70 so that it was addressed to an audience concerned with the recent Neronian persecution. Robinson, *Redating the New Testament*.

10. Howard-Brook and Gwyther, *Unveiling Empire*, xxii. As Keener notes (*Revelation*, 39), more of the churches in Asia Minor were "in danger of compromising with the world than of dying from it."

11. Howard-Brook and Gwyther, *Unveiling Empire*, 87–115.

Advocates of this view, which we might call the "anti-assimilation view,"[12] thus maintain that *the book of Revelation sounded a vivid call to radical Christian commitment and rejection of the dominant culture*. In the book of Revelation, Jesus does not allow his followers to remain neutral: either one shares Rome's ideology and values— "the view of the Roman Empire promoted by Roman propaganda—or one sees it from the perspective of heaven, which unmasks the pretensions of Rome."[13]

Here, we can see how the persecution view and the anti-assimilation view are actually closely related. The benefits that Rome had to offer exerted significant pressure on Christians to live like the culture around them (i.e., assimilate) either to avoid persecution or to enjoy the bounty of what society had to offer. In both cases, the temptation to compromise would have been overwhelming. Moreover, the anticipated persecution portrayed in Revelation makes it crystal clear that the clash between Greco-Roman (or the dominant cultural values in our society today) and Christian values will inevitably lead to conflict. The church can expect that the imperial powers, which are "in league with Satan,"[14] will be brought against them; but God nevertheless demands unfaltering resistance to the dominant culture.

In short, Revelation makes it clear to Christians in late first-century Asia Minor that many forms of participation in the larger culture would necessitate ratifying Rome's dominion and rejecting God's sovereignty.[15] Such a choice would be utterly foolish since—as Revelation affirms—in the end, the temporal forces of evil will be destroyed and Christ will prevail. As will be clear when we look at the letters to the seven churches, Jesus gives the message and visions of Revelation to John in order *both* to comfort those who are facing persecution *and* to warn those who are assimilating to or in danger of assimilating to a non-Christian worldview and lifestyle. We need to keep both of these purposes in mind as we read Revelation. Jesus is warning all Christians to beware of giving in to either the fear of persecution or the seduction of the surrounding culture.

Christians in Asia Minor, then, are not exhorted to oppose Rome simply because Rome persecutes Christians. Instead, it is precisely because Christians must dissociate themselves from the wicked Roman culture that they will likely suffer persecution. Let me reemphasize this point. If the original readers chose to respond positively to Revelation's call to resist assimilating to the culture around them, the *result* of that obedience would be persecution. That is precisely what we see reflected on a small scale in the churches of Asia Minor in Revelation. Those churches that had been resisting assimilation most steadfastly—in Smyrna and Philadelphia, and to a lesser extent Pergamum—were the churches that appear to be suffering the worst persecution. These

12. I was first introduced to this expression by Charles Talbert in the 1990s and am grateful to him for the many insights that have come as a result.

13. Bauckham, *Theology*, 35.

14. Howard-Brook and Gwyther, *Unveiling Empire*, 174.

15. Schüssler Fiorenza, "Revelation," 419.

Christians needed to be reminded of that reality so that they would press on and stand firm to the end. Christians in the rest of the seven churches, however, also needed to be reminded of that reality so that when they repented of their compromise and assimilation and faced subsequent persecution as a result they would "not be surprised at the fiery trial when it comes upon [them] to test [them], as though something strange were happening to [them]" (1 Pet 4:12).

To conclude this discussion, let's think for a minute about what the original readers were facing. If you've ever watched *Star Trek*, at least one of the later series, you will have encountered the Borg. The Borg are a race of beings composed of part flesh and part machine. There are no individuals; instead, all are part of the "hive," and as "drones" they are controlled by the "Borg Queen." The Borg travel the galaxy conquering other races, turning them into Borg, and incorporating them into the Borg "collective." When they encounter a new populated planet or an alien ship, they always say the same thing: "We are the Borg. You will be assimilated. Resistance is futile!"

I want to suggest that the message of the Roman Empire in the late first century was strikingly similar: "We are the Romans. You will be assimilated. Resistance is futile!" Rome "graciously" offered not to destroy those who willingly became a part of the Roman Empire. All they had to do was to swear allegiance to Caesar and worship Roman gods, and sometimes the emperor himself. Christians within the empire were faced with this do-or-die message, just like everyone else. The book of Revelation, though, sounds a very different note: Resistance is *not* futile! Indeed, it strongly warns readers that they must *not* be assimilated into the larger culture in which they live. They belong to the King of kings and Lord of lords. His kingdom is forever! The Roman Empire, on the other hand, is destined for certain and complete destruction.

> To him who loves us and has freed us from our sins by his blood ⁶and made us a kingdom, priests to his God and Father, to him be glory and dominion forever and ever. Amen. (1:5b–6)

In verses 5b–6, John inserts a doxology—a short statement of praise that ascribes glory to God. This one is directed to Jesus and provides a summary of the Good News of what Jesus has done for us. For our purposes, it is important to recognize that, more often than not, when the gospel is mentioned in the New Testament the writer makes it clear that we are not only set free *from* something but are also set free *for* something. Salvation is not just about heaven; it is about being set free to serve God. It is about becoming citizens of a new kingdom. Followers of Jesus Christ are no longer Americans, Canadians, Koreans, Kenyans, Spaniards, Russians, Chinese, Indians, or citizens of any other earthly nation. They are now citizens of the kingdom of heaven; and their values must come from *that* kingdom. They have been set free from sin (1:5) and thus must no longer pursue their selfish desires. They have become a kingdom and priests to serve their God and Father. He is to be their only Sovereign.

The description in verses 5b–6, thus, gets at the heart of the two-pronged Satanic attack on the churches of Asia Minor. Christians were being tempted to assimilate to the kingdom of Rome, to follow its values, worship its gods, and live by its standards. Revelation asks: How can a citizen of heaven dream of doing something so ridiculous? Some were being pressured to return to Judaism where there was a measure of safety and special rights under Roman law; but to do so would be to embrace the "synagogue of Satan" (2:9; 3:9). Priests of God could never stoop so low. They could never abandon service to the One who is both their God and Father in order to serve the evil one.

> *Behold, he is coming with the clouds, and every eye will see him, even those who pierced him, and all tribes of the earth will wail on account of him. Even so. Amen.* [8]*"I am the Alpha and the Omega," says the Lord God, "who is and who was and who is to come, the Almighty." (1:7–8)*

Here again, we encounter the theme of Jesus' return. The references to "those who pierced him" and the people wailing because of his coming make it clear that he is coming as judge. This theme will be developed extensively in what follows.[16] The sureness of the Second Coming is highlighted through reference to the character of God. He is the "Alpha and the Omega" (the first and last letters of the Greek alphabet). This same title is used of God in 21:6 and applied to Jesus in 22:13. There was nothing before him and nothing will exist after him. Consequently, nothing can happen outside of his awareness and plan. God is the one who began everything, and he will bring all things to completion.

To further emphasize this point, we are reminded that he is "the Almighty." What would using this title have said to the original readers? Why did he use this particular expression? What was he doing with his choice of language? Right from the beginning, God wants to remind Christians in Asia Minor that he is the Almighty One, not the Roman emperor. So important is this simple truth that this same title for God is used nine times in Revelation (1:8; 4:8; 11:17; 15:3; 16:7, 14; 19:6, 15; 21:22). Implicit in this title is the corresponding truth that those who belong to the Almighty One ultimately have nothing to fear in this world. God is in perfect control of the destiny of his children, and he can be trusted completely.

> *I, John, your brother and partner in the tribulation and the kingdom and the patient endurance that are in Jesus, was on the island called Patmos on account of the word of God and the testimony of Jesus. (1:9)*

It is no accident that John places "kingdom" in between "tribulation" and "patient endurance." John was not writing from a position of comfort. He knew what it was to pay a price for following Jesus, and he had remained faithful. He also knew that being "in Jesus"—i.e., in a relationship with Jesus as his Lord—and thus having the sure hope of sharing in his kingdom brought with it the promise of suffering to which,

16. Most agree that the statement here is an allusion to Dan 7:13.

by God's grace, he must actively choose to respond with patient endurance. By saying that he is their "partner" in tribulation, the kingdom, and patient endurance, John is making clear from the beginning what the whole message of Revelation will emphasize: following Jesus is not for wimps. Jesus calls for courage and resolve in the lives of his followers so that they will remain true to him even when the whole world is against them, or their lives or livelihood are on the line. John knew personally how high the cost was of following Jesus, and he was the vehicle through which Jesus was about to make that same point clear to Christians in first-century Asia Minor and throughout the coming centuries.

> *I was in the Spirit on the Lord's day, and I heard behind me a loud voice like a trumpet* [11]*saying, "Write what you see in a book and send it to the seven churches, to Ephesus and to Smyrna and to Pergamum and to Thyatira and to Sardis and to Philadelphia and to Laodicea." (1:10–11)*

On the first day of the week, the day when the Lord Jesus had risen from dead, John was "in the Spirit," likely meaning that he was in a state of prophetic inspiration.[17] The fact that the sound of the trumpet regularly occurs in passages describing an appearance of God (see, e.g., Exod 19:16; 20:18; Isa 18:3; Joel 2:1; Zech 9:14; Ps 47:5) suggests that the language is used here to help drive home the fact that John is about to have a close encounter with the risen and glorious Lord Jesus even as Moses had a close encounter with God on Mount Sinai.

Once again, we find an important reading instruction. In verse 11, we have a very clear indication of the setting of Revelation. The message that follows is directed to seven churches in the Roman province of Asia Minor—real people, facing real challenges in the first century.

Reading Instruction #4: We must read Revelation is light of the particular historical context to which it is addressed.

But why *seven* letters and why *these* seven churches? Given the frequent symbolic use of numbers throughout Revelation (the number seven is used 55 times), it is not inappropriate to ask such questions. We know that there were other churches in Asia Minor that Jesus did not address, including churches at Colossae, Hierapolis, and Troas. In fact, at no point in history were the seven churches of Revelation the only churches in Asia.[18] In Acts 19:10, we learn that while Paul was in Ephesus (roughly AD 54–56) "all the residents of Asia heard the word of the Lord, both Jews and Greeks." So, the gospel had been widely proclaimed to the people of this region roughly 40 years before Revelation was sent. Why are these other Christians not addressed as well?

17. This seems to be made clear in 4:2; 17:3; and 21:10.

18. Ramsay, *Letters*, 123.

Most likely, although Revelation is addressed to seven literal churches, the choice of seven churches (rather than eight or nine) has symbolic value. The number seven was regularly used to symbolize completeness in ancient Jewish contexts.[19] Consequently, the ancient church tended to see the seven churches as a symbol of the church universal. The Muratorian Canon (ca. AD 180) states that "John also, though he wrote in the Apocalypse to seven churches, nevertheless speaks to them all." Geographically, the order of churches fits with a natural circular route through Asia Minor, beginning with the church that is closest to Patmos, where John was located. The choice of the particular churches in Revelation may have been driven by the representative challenges they were facing or some other factors. What is important for us to grapple with, however, is the fact that these seven churches, with their particular circumstances, represent the primary context for understanding Revelation as a whole. If we are going to read Revelation rightly, we must read it against the historical context it was written to, not our own historical context.

> Then I turned to see the voice that was speaking to me, and on turning I saw seven golden lampstands, [13]and in the midst of the lampstands one like a son of man, clothed with a long robe and with a golden sash around his chest. [14]The hairs of his head were white, like white wool, like snow. His eyes were like a flame of fire, [15]his feet were like burnished bronze, refined in a furnace, and his voice was like the roar of many waters. [16]In his right hand he held seven stars, from his mouth came a sharp two-edged sword, and his face was like the sun shining in full strength. [17]When I saw him, I fell at his feet as though dead. But he laid his right hand on me, saying, "Fear not, I am the first and the last, [18]and the living one. I died, and behold I am alive forevermore, and I have the keys of Death and Hades. [19]Write therefore the things that you have seen, those that are and those that are to take place after this. [20]As for the mystery of the seven stars that you saw in my right hand, and the seven golden lampstands, the seven stars are the angels of the seven churches, and the seven lampstands are the seven churches. (1:12–20)

In verse 12, John turns and looks at the One from whom the voice was coming. And so begins our plunge into the sea of images and symbols that covers much of the remainder of Revelation. The first thing John sees is seven golden lampstands. Fortunately, in verse 20 he is told the meaning of this symbol, along with the meaning of the seven stars. Thus, Rev 1 clearly contains another important reading instruction.

---

19. See, e.g., Davis, *Biblical Numerology*, 119.

Reading Instruction #5: We must recognize that Revelation makes use of symbols and symbolic uses of numbers.

Jesus makes it clear that features of this vision are symbolic, rather than literal representations of reality. "Stars" here stand for angels. "Lampstands" stand for churches. If this is the case, we should beware of reading Revelation as if John were simply using language from his time to describe things from the future that he was not familiar with. We find the same clear indication of the presence of symbolic language, with John identifying the significance of an image, elsewhere in Revelation: "and before the throne were burning seven torches of fire, which are the seven spirits of God" (4:5); "each holding a harp, and golden bowls full of incense, which are the prayers of the saints" (5:8).[20]

One could also point to a seven-headed dragon, a lamb with seven horns and seven eyes, and a seven-headed beast that comes out of the sea. Clearly, not all of Revelation is intended to be taken literally. In fact, Rev 1 should lead us to expect that the visions that follow are typically—though not necessarily always—symbolic in nature. Sometimes the symbols operate on more than one level. For example, the "seven spirits" in 1:4 are almost certainly a symbolic reference to the Holy Spirit; but in 4:5 this symbolic notion ("seven spirits") is itself symbolized as "seven torches of fire," and then as "seven eyes" on the Lamb in 5:6. If, then, we are going to read Revelation rightly, we will need to determine how the original audience would have understood the symbol it utilizes.

Ramsay maintained that "the most dangerous kind of error that can be made about the Apocalypse is to regard it as a literal statement and prediction of events."[21] While it is difficult to take the language of Revelation seriously and not see it involving predictions, Ramsay's statement about the danger of reading Revelation literally is important. In a fascinating biography of Nero, Champlin ably demonstrates how skilled the Romans were in identifying double meanings in plays and other performances: "from the late Republic onward, an abundance of evidence shows that Roman theatrical audiences were extraordinarily quick to hear the words spoken and to see the actions presented on stage as offering pointed commentary on contemporary public life."[22] This appears to be precisely what Jesus is doing throughout the book of Revelation through the visions and messages he gives to John to convey to the churches of Asia Minor. In other words, the indirect commentary on life as they knew it in the Roman Empire through the use of conventional symbols would have been familiar to first-century Christians in Asia Minor.

---

20. Passages like 9:1–12 also support the view that Revelation is full of symbols. There the "star" is clearly some sort of person rather than a literal star.

21. Ramsay, *Letters*, 80.

22. Champlin, *Nero*, 95.

In verse 17, the speaker identifies himself as "the first and the last"—a title that is equivalent to "the Alpha and the Omega," which was applied to God the Father in verse 8. The following verse leaves no doubt as to the identity of the speaker. Jesus is the true "living one"; only he was dead, but now lives, and will continue to live forever. And he reminds the readers, from the very beginning, of an important truth: *he* holds the keys of Death and Hades. In other words, no one can stand against his sovereign control over their lives and their deaths. He is omnipotent; after all, by laying claim to the keys of Death and Hades Jesus is clearly taking authority that Jews associated with God alone.[23] The fact that Jesus himself is God will be reiterated repeatedly throughout Revelation. Here, as we ask how the original readers would have understood the details of Revelation, we dare not fail to note that Jesus' reminder that he alone is in control of death would have provided strong encouragement to those who were suffering, afraid, and facing the possibility of martyrdom. There is no need to fear for those who belong to the true King.

Reading Instruction #6: We need to recognize that Revelation often communicates using Old Testament language and imagery.

Finally, we should also note that to determine what Revelation is saying through the details of its visions, we often need to look beyond the New Testament. At the end of Rev 1, we find Jesus revealed in language that would have sounded very familiar to Christians acquainted with the Old Testament. Readers of Revelation would have already perhaps noticed the allusion to Dan 7:13 in 1:7. Now, in 1:14–15 they would have been exposed to striking similarities between the description of Jesus and the description of the Ancient of Days in Dan 7:9–10. In Dan 7:14, the "one like a son of man" "was given dominion and glory and a kingdom, that all peoples, nations, and languages should serve him; his dominion is an everlasting dominion, which shall not pass away, and his kingdom one that shall not be destroyed." This is clearly consistent with the description of Jesus in the book of Revelation. Much of the description of Jesus also closely parallels Daniel's description of an angel in Dan 10:5–12. These parallels here would have made it clear to the original readers that John is having an encounter with a heavenly being. The parallel with the description of the Ancient of Day's hair and Jesus' hair may have also suggested that this is more than an angel. This would have been strongly affirmed when John heard the words, "I am the first and the last" and "I have the keys of Death and Hades"—both of which are implicit claims to deity—and the words, "I died, and behold I am alive forevermore"—which could only be spoken by the resurrected Jesus. At this point, then, the intertextual connections to the Old Testament primarily add further "color" to the already magnificent depiction of Jesus' appearance to John. Elsewhere in Revelation, we will find that the Old

---

23. Keener, *Revelation*, 98.

Testament helps us to understand the actual meaning of particular symbolic language in Revelation.

HOW TO READ THE BOOK OF REVELATION

So, what have we learned from Revelation itself about how this magnificent book is supposed to be read? First, we have learned that we need to recognize that whatever message it intends to communicate, it is a message that is directed to the people of God, the church. Second, we have learned that Jesus expected his followers living in Asia Minor during the late first century to understand Revelation—all of it. That should give us great hope as we seek to understand this final book of the Bible today. Third, we have learned that the genre of a book is important; and the genre of Revelation, we might say, is important three times over. We dare not read Revelation as a simple historical narrative when it has clear features of an ancient letter, a prophecy, and apocalyptic literature, each of which is important to keep in mind. Together they lead us to expect a specific message to specific people at a specific point in time; they lead us to expect insights into the future that are intended to exhort the listeners to live a particular way in the present; and they lead us to expect visions of cosmic upheaval that serve to broaden the readers' view of reality so that the visions of what is to come give them hope and courage in the midst of severe current and imminent challenges. Fourth, we have learned that the particular readers to whom Revelation was addressed lived in first-century Asia Minor. It is their historical context that necessarily forms the crucial grid through which Revelation must be read. Fifth, we have learned that Revelation itself instructs us to expect symbolic language in what follows. To read all the symbols of Revelation "literally" is to go against the clear instructions that Jesus has given us in the text itself. And sixth, we have learned that the Old Testament will serve as a crucial guidebook in sorting out the significance of some of the language and much of the imagery that is found in the book of Revelation.

Each of these six reading instructions will be important to keep in mind as we work our way through Revelation. There is, however, one final reading instruction that is more important than all the rest. It is more important not because it will unlock all of the puzzles in Revelation, but rather because it is the most neglected. Only with this final reading instruction can we understand "the rest of the story" of Revelation.

Our final reading instruction is introduced in Rev 2, but for the sake of organization, we will examine it here. The way that Jesus introduces himself to each of the seven churches in Rev 2–3 in each case parallels language that was used in reference to him in Rev 1:

"him who holds the seven stars in his right hand, who walks among the seven golden lampstands" (2:1)	"In his right hand he held seven stars" (1:16), "in the midst of the lampstands" (1:13)

"The words of the first and the last, who died and came to life" (2:8)	"I am the first and the last, 18and the living one. I died, and behold I am alive forevermore" (1:17–18)
"The words of him who has the sharp two-edged sword" (2:12)	"from his mouth came a sharp two-edged sword" (1:16)
"The words of the Son of God, who has eyes like a flame of fire, and whose feet are like burnished bronze" (2:18)	"His eyes were like a flame of fire" (1:14), "his feet were like burnished bronze" (1:15)
"The words of him who has the seven spirits of God and the seven stars" (3:1)	"In his right hand he held seven stars" (1:16)
"The words of the holy one, the true one, who has the key of David, who opens and no one will shut, who shuts and no one opens" (3:8)	"and I have the keys of Death and Hades" (1:18)
"The words of the Amen, the faithful and true witness, the beginning of God's creation" (3:14)	"Jesus Christ the faithful witness, the firstborn of the dead, and the ruler of kings on earth" (1:5)

These very obvious connections *within* the text of Revelation (thus, "*intra*-textual") make it clear that what follows will not be a hodge-podge of different visions and prophetic utterances that have been cobbled together into a single work. Quite the contrary, there is a careful Craftsman behind this message; and he is once again giving us an important reading instruction so that we will not miss the message he is seeking to communicate.

Reading Instruction #7: We must notice and carefully consider Revelation's intratextual connections.

From beginning to end, Revelation is a carefully crafted message with later parts continually building on earlier parts. Not only do the descriptions of Jesus in the messages to the seven churches in Rev 2–3 build on the vision of Jesus in Rev 1, but more importantly *the remainder of Revelation constantly builds on, fleshes out, and drives home each of the messages to the churches in Rev 2–3*. Recognizing these regular intratextual connections between the seven messages and the rest of Revelation is a primary key for understanding Revelation as whole. As we watch for these inner-connections we will discover that the message of Rev 4–22 would have spoken loud and clear to the original audience.

Now that we have identified seven reading instructions—and since there are seven we must be "completely" ready to proceed!—let me say a word about the format of the remaining chapters. In what follows, I will model several different ways the message of Revelation can be processed, or several different vantage points from which Revelation can be examined. We begin with seven sets of chapters relating to the seven churches. In the first chapter of each set, we will carefully examine the message that Jesus gives to a particular church in Rev 2 or 3. Then, in a companion chapter we will examine "the rest of the story," i.e., what the remainder of Revelation likely would have meant to Christians in that particular church. By carefully examining Revelation's message in terms of how each of the seven churches would have understood John's visions we will, in the end, arrive at what Revelation means for the church today.

We could go about our examination, however, in at least two different ways. We could go verse by verse through the messages to the seven churches and in each case look *forward* and think about how the rest of Revelation would have spoken to that particular church in light of Jesus' initial message to them in Rev 2 or 3. Or, we could study Rev 4–19 chapter by chapter, or passage by passage, in each case looking *backwards* to Rev 2–3 and asking ourselves how the chapter or passage we are studying would have spoken to the churches in Asia Minor in light of Jesus' initial message to them. Since both reading strategies are appropriate and fruitful I will model each of them with several of the seven churches. Then, for the final three chapters of Revelation we will examine how these chapters would have spoken to all seven churches. I invite readers to practice reading Revelation in these ways in order to discover how the fullness of its message becomes more and more apparent. Keep in mind that the features of Revelation's message that are highlighted in what follows are illustrative, not exhaustive. I encourage readers to apply the reading instructions we examined in Rev 1 and flesh out for themselves what I have only sketched in this book.

So then, with our reading instructions firmly in hand let's set off on our journey through Revelation. We start, of course, with the first of the seven messages to the seven churches, where Jesus begins to provide us with far more historical context (Reading Instruction #4) and set the direction for the message of Revelation as a whole.

2

Jesus' Message to the Church in Ephesus

To the angel of the church in Ephesus write: (2:1a)

READERS OF THE MESSAGES to the seven churches in Rev 2–3 are quickly faced with a perplexing question: Who are the angels that the messages are addressed to? While some have attempted to associate the seven "angels" with the leaders or bishops of each church, or with the "messengers" who carried the letters,[1] the fact that John elsewhere in Revelation always uses the Greek term ἄγγελος (*angelos*) to refer to supernatural beings subordinate to God suggests that angels are in view here.

Why then are the messages addressed to angels rather than to the churches themselves? Throughout Revelation we regularly find angels serving as intermediaries through whom God conveys his messages. Likewise, we are told elsewhere in the New Testament that the Law itself was given "through angels" (Acts 7:53; Gal 3:19) and "spoken by angels" (Heb 2:2). This suggests that when God wanted to further highlight the importance of his message to his people he used angels as his intermediaries. Here, then, the messages to the seven churches are not only coming from the holder of the seven stars; they are also being conveyed by God's most important emissaries. Just as Moses had a close encounter with God at Mount Sinai and then was given the Law to present to the people of Israel—law that was given "through angels"—so John is now having a close encounter with Jesus on Patmos and is given this new revelation to present to the people of God living in Asia Minor—a revelation that is also to be mediated by angels. This, then, is another example of how God has constructed Revelation to play off features of the Old Testament.

---

1. Both "angel" and "messenger" are possible translations of the same Greek word: ἄγγελος (*angelos*).

The first of the seven messages is addressed to followers of Jesus living in Ephesus, the city that was closest to the island of Patmos. Ephesus was described by Strabo as the largest commercial center in the region[2] and was one of the greatest cities in the Roman province of Asia, along with Smyrna and Pergamum. Ephesus had a large market, with very impressive gates and marble roads. Most historians maintain that it had a population of around 200,000, though this estimate is based on very limited data.[3] At any rate, it was likely one of the five largest cities in the Roman Empire.[4] Ephesus had an impressive theater, which seated about 24,000 people, and was home to the Temple of Artemis, one of the seven wonders of the ancient world. The massive platform on which the temple was built was more than 100,000 square feet in area. Ephesus was also a "temple-keeper," a prestigious role that included responsibility for temples dedicated to Artemis, and the emperors Vespasian, Domitian, and Hadrian. Although there is some debate as to whether the imperial temple was constructed during the reign of Vespasian or Domitian, it "contained a 'four times life-size' statue of Domitian."[5]

This brief summary of the background of the city is not mere trivia that is of no ultimate use for understanding Revelation. Instead, it highlights two important realities that shed light on the message to the church in Ephesus. First, the dedication of the temple to Domitian, in particular, showed that the citizens of Ephesus in general had a *positive* attitude toward the current emperor. How could the Ephesians like Domitian, a man who was described as a tyrant by some writers from the period (after he was dead and could no longer retaliate, of course!)? Quite simple: Domitian, and the Roman Empire, brought the inhabitants of Ephesus wealth and the good life. This leads to a second point: As we read the message written to Christians living in Ephesus we have to recognize that we are dealing with a very prosperous city where the citizens were generally quite pleased with the life that the Roman Empire had made possible for them. Although persecution is certainly an issue for Christians in some of the cities in Asia Minor at the time, many of the churches were faced with an altogether different kind of pressure: the pressure to assimilate to the culture around them in order to enjoy what it had to offer.

> *The words of him who holds the seven stars in his right hand, who walks among the seven golden lampstands.* (2:1b)

As we come to the actual message to the Christians in Ephesus, we need to notice how the message is introduced. The phrase, "The words of him" is a translation of the Greek phrase Τάδε λέγει (*tade legei*). These are the same words that the KJV translates, "Thus saith the Lord," throughout the Old Testament, the exact same Greek

---

2. Strabo, *Geogr.* 14.1.24.

3. See Worth (*Seven Cities*, 11) for more details on population views.

4. Ibid., 12. The other largest cities would have been Rome, Alexandria, Antioch, and Pergamum.

5. Ibid., 51.

expression that is used more than 250 times in the Greek Old Testament to introduce prophecies from the Lord. The fact that this phrase was obsolete by the time the New Testament was written—as obsolete as the expression "thus saith" is today—makes it clear that Jesus chose these words to draw a link in the minds of the readers between his words and the prophetic words of the Old Testament. Once again, God is about to speak to his people.

To his followers in Ephesus, Jesus introduces himself as the One "who holds the seven stars in his right hand, who walks among the seven golden lampstands." We have already been told (1:20) that the seven stars represent the seven angels and the seven golden lampstands represent the seven churches. Thus, in the first part of the title that he adopts here, Jesus makes it clear that he is both in control of (or sends) the seven angels. In the second part of the title, he makes it clear that he is present among them and intimately aware of what is going on in their church. As with the other six messages to the churches in Asia Minor, the title that Jesus chooses for presenting himself to Christians in Ephesus is handpicked for this particular church. As we will see, the Ephesian Christians had fallen to the temptation to live as "stealth Christians" in Ephesus. They thought they could hide their light and focus on other areas of faithfulness to Jesus; but Jesus makes it clear that they are not hiding anything from him. He himself walks among the lampstands.

> I know your works, your toil and your patient endurance, and how you cannot bear with those who are evil, but have tested those who call themselves apostles and are not, and found them to be false. (2:2)

In the case of the Ephesian Christians, Jesus begins with a wonderful commendation. First, he reminds them that he, the one who knows all things, is well aware of how they are doing. He has been observing them and is pleased with the fact that they had continued serving him in spite of their circumstances. They had patiently endured the challenges that came from being Christians in a pagan city. Describing life in the cities of Asia Minor, Worth points out that a "central responsibility of the [local] government was to offer sacrifice to the deities worshipped in the city, who were believed to protect the community. Just as the medieval Catholic Church had a saint's day for every day of the year, there was a civic calendar of gods in ancient Ephesus. One was honored each and every day."[6] This raised important questions regarding community involvement for early Christians. As Worth notes, "so pervasive was polytheism that *some* involvement of *some* type was inevitable in the very act of service to the community."[7] In most parts of Asia, religion and public life were closely intertwined. To participate in the life of the city Christians would almost invariably be faced with the temptation to compromise and be involved in honoring pagan gods. Such expectations, of course, made Christians particularly conspicuous when they

6. Ibid., 13–14.
7. Ibid., 14.

chose not to participate, which in turn invited persecution from neighbors and civil authorities who could easily blame Christians when the city faced problems of any sort; the gods were responding to Christians' lack of piety.

Nevertheless, we find that Christians in Ephesus had apparently not given in to such temptations. They had continued to work hard in serving the Lord and had patiently endured when the city turned against them. More than that, as we see in the second half of verse 2, they had also vigorously defended the purity of their congregation by guarding against false teaching. To appreciate Jesus' commendation here, it is helpful to remember the history of the Ephesian church. According to Acts 20, Paul spent approximately three years ministering in Ephesus. At the end of that time, he shared some parting words with the elders of the church. For our purposes, verses 29–31 are particularly important:

> I know that after my departure fierce wolves will come in among you, not sparing the flock; [30]and from among your own selves will arise men speaking twisted things, to draw away the disciples after them. [31]Therefore be alert, remembering that for three years I did not cease night or day to admonish every one with tears. (Acts 20:29–31)

Jesus' words in Rev 2:2 suggest that the Ephesians had taken Paul's words decades earlier to heart and had been very careful not to allow heresy to creep into their church. They had not tolerated wicked men. This is one of several places in the seven messages where it is apparent that there was some competition within the early Christian communities for authority. There were false apostles and teachers as well as genuine apostles and teachers; and both were active in the churches of Asia Minor and elsewhere. It is likely that the "apostles" that Jesus refers to here were itinerate teachers who claimed a certain amount of authority.

Lest we fail to recognize the seriousness of false teaching, notice that Jesus does not simply say that these individuals' theology was "a bit off here and there." Instead, those who were traveling around spreading false teaching are labeled "evil." Jesus recognizes the dire consequences of allowing false teachers within the church. This will be highlighted in some of the other messages.

Whatever the specific nature of the false teachings that the Ephesian Christians successfully resisted—some of the other messages will likely shed some light here— these Christians were particularly careful to guard against false teaching from outside. This persistent vigilance apparently led Ignatius, only ten to fifteen years later, to declare, "all of you live according to the truth and . . . no heresy dwells among you" (*Eph.* 6.2, my translation). He later states, "I know some who passed by from there who hold to evil teaching, whom you did not allow to sow among you, plugging your ears so that you would not receive what was sown by them" (*Eph.* 9:1; my translation). This was clearly a church that was unyielding in its vigilance against false teaching, and Jesus was pleased with them. He is not finished, however, commending them.

I know you are enduring patiently and bearing up for my name's sake, and you have not grown weary. (2:3)

It is striking that Jesus mentioned the Ephesians' patient endurance, using the exact same word (ὑπομονήν, *hupomonēn*), twice in two verses (vv. 2–3). Here, he adds to the description the expression "bearing up." Together, this language suggests that the Ephesian Christians had been paying a significant price for their faith ("for my name's sake"). As those who had been clearly identified as followers of Jesus who would not participate in the idolatry around them, there is little question that these early Christians would have faced reprisals in various forms. Even so, they had patiently endured and had not grown weary of following Christ.

In the West, Christians do not typically think or talk about patiently enduring hardships for Jesus' sake. Although the negative consequences for Christians in the West are clearly on the rise, they still pale in comparison to what Christians face daily in many countries around the world. A few years ago as I was preparing to teach a course on Revelation, three itinerant missionaries in Asia were severely beaten and then tied to a sacred tree in the village they had entered to share the gospel. Their captors told them that they would be sacrificed to their gods if they did not pay a ransom within 48 hours. That is hardship; and it is a hardship that is not uncommon in other parts of the world. In this case, God intervened and the missionaries were released; but that is not always the way the story ends. Christians in Ephesus had learned this firsthand, and their response had consistently been admirable and God-honoring.

But I have this against you, that you have abandoned the love you had at first. (2:4)

Having read the glowing report in the preceding verses, Jesus' words in verse 4 are all the more striking. Despite all that they were consistently doing right over the long term, the Ephesian Christians had forsaken their first love. Among many North American Christians, Jesus' initial words here raise serious questions: How can Jesus hold anything against his own people? Haven't they been saved? Aren't they free from condemnation? How could Jesus say, "I hold this against you"? Isn't Jesus always supposed to encourage when he speaks to us?

Such questions may well indicate that Western Christians have embraced a warped view of the gospel, a view where Jesus is obligated to always be happy with us, a view where God is blind to our sin, rebellion, and apathy, or forsaking of our first love, since "when he looks at us he sees Jesus." Here, though, Jesus clearly does not see a perfect church, though he is writing to Christians who have been washed in the blood of the Lamb. He sees a serious problem, a problem that he "holds against" them; and he is about to strongly warn them of the consequences of failing to deal with this problem.

While Jesus has something against them, though, it is not initially clear what exactly that something is. What was the "first love" that the Ephesian Christians had abandoned? Have they ceased to *love one another* in their effort to guard their doctrinal purity? Has their *love for God* grown cold in the midst of the battle against false apostles? Two things are important to keep in mind in responding to these types of questions. First, it is likely that Jesus intentionally communicated in a somewhat vague manner so that Christians of all ages will read "first love" in a variety of ways depending on their particular circumstances. In other words, Jesus' rebuke of the Ephesian Christians for abandoning their first love invites us to ask ourselves whether or not we have lost our first love; and that first love may be our earlier devotion to the Word and to prayer, our earlier commitment to serving God's people, our earlier contentment and satisfaction in God's glorious character, our earlier commitment to regular fellowship with the people of God, or something else.

Although this ambiguity is important to acknowledge, I believe that more can be said about the specific nature of the Ephesian Christians' first love. It is unlikely that Jesus would have commended them for their "hard work" if they were not still actively serving one another in love. It is unlikely that Jesus could have commended them for patiently enduring, bearing up for his name's sake, and not growing weary if all of that did not flow out of a profound love for God. Thus, while one might argue that the vagueness of Jesus' language is intended to leave the precise nature of "first love" an open question, given the broader context of Revelation we may be able to pinpoint what abandoning their first love entailed for the Ephesian Christians.

Remembering that there are intratextual connections throughout Revelation can be helpful here. Thus far, we have seen that followers of Jesus, who have been made into a priestly kingdom (1:6), need to expect to suffer and to patiently endure (1:9). When we look at the description of the Christians in Ephesus, we find that they were doing outstanding in this very area. Jesus was well aware of their deeds, which were characterized by hard work and perseverance. Indeed, the same word that John had used in 1:9 (ὑπομονή/*hupomonē*) is used twice in Jesus' commendation of the Ephesian Christians (2:2, 3).[8] Notice the combination here of suffering and patient endurance. The very marks of a devout follower of Jesus that were used in 1:9 are the marks of the church at Ephesus. So, what could possibly be wrong? With these two marks of a true disciple, what could Jesus possibly have against them?

If we look at what constitutes an "overcomer" in Revelation we find something important that is not mentioned in Jesus' commendations of the Ephesian Christians. Key passages include the following:

> And they have conquered him by the blood of the Lamb and by the word of
> their testimony, for they loved not their lives even unto death. (12:11)

8. The NIV has obscured the intratextual connection here by translating the same word "patient endurance" in 1:9 and "perseverance" in 2:2, 3.

Then I fell down at his [the angel's] feet to worship him, but he said to me, "You must not do that! I am a fellow servant with you and your brothers who hold to the testimony of Jesus." (19:10)

Then I saw thrones, and seated on them were those to whom the authority to judge was committed. Also I saw the souls of those who had been beheaded for the testimony of Jesus and for the word of God, and those who had not worshiped the beast or its image and had not received its mark on their foreheads or their hands. They came to life and reigned with Christ for a thousand years. (20:4)

Each of these passages highlights followers of Jesus serving as his faithful witnesses through their active testimony. There is, in fact, a major focus throughout the book of Revelation on being a faithful witness of Jesus. This theme is first introduced in 1:2, where John says that he testified to "all that he saw" (1:2). Then, in 1:5 Jesus is described as "the faithful witness." We learn in 1:9 that proclaiming "the word of God and the testimony of Jesus" led to John's exile. We also find that the churches are symbolized by lampstands, a symbol that is used later to represent witnesses (see 11:4). In fact, after Rev 1 the only place where the word "lampstand" is used, besides in reference to the two witnesses in 11:4, is in the letter to the church at Ephesus; and it is used twice in this letter (2:1, 5). What does all of this mean?

The Christians in Ephesus have had to bear up (ἐβάστασας, *ebastasas*) under difficult circumstances on account of Jesus' name (διὰ τὸ ὄνομά μου, *dia to onoma mou*), but it appears that they had ceased to be *active* witnesses for Jesus.[9] They had been doing a great job playing defense, but their offensive role had been scaled back to almost nothing. Thus, Jesus calls on them to "repent, and do the works you did at first" (v. 5). This reading, it seems to me, is perhaps the only way to make sense of how Jesus describes these Christians. They have been exemplary in many ways in their deeds, but they were no longer *doing* something (v. 5). It also makes good sense of what Jesus threatens them with: He warns them that he will remove their lampstand if they do not repent and do the things they had done at first. A lampstand provides a handy symbol for a witness, as is made explicit in Rev 11. Jesus has already said in 1:20 that the lampstands represent the seven churches, but we still need to ask why he chose that image to symbolize this particular church. Using the lampstand as a symbol of the church almost certainly highlights the fact that the central role of the church is to testify about Jesus. Thus, for the Ephesian Christians to forsake their first love—and the language is quite strong (ἀφῆκες, *aphēkes*)—was to abandon their *raison d'être*. This is why, despite the overwhelmingly positive assessment of how they were doing in 2:2–3, Jesus can speak of them falling from some higher place (2:5), an apparent reference to these Christians having excelled in their witness earlier in their history. Jesus is about to make it clear that to choose to abandon this central calling is to plunge over a cliff to

9. For another scholar who holds this view, see Beale, *Book of Revelation*, 230–32.

ruin. It is simply not an option for the people of God, no matter how bleak the future may look for those who advertise their allegiance to Jesus in a hostile society through actively spreading the gospel.

One other argument for this interpretation of "first love" should be mentioned. As we will see in the chapters that follow, there is abundant evidence supporting the central thesis of this book: Revelation 4–22 consistently builds on, fleshes out, and drives home each of the messages to the churches in Rev 2–3. With all of the other components of the various messages to the seven churches we find a significant amount of material in the remaining chapters of Revelation serving this purpose. If by referring to abandoning their first love Jesus was communicating that the Ephesian Christians had ceased loving one another, we would have expected subsequent parts of Revelation to drive home this message; but we find nothing of the sort. In fact, there are no obvious references or allusions to Christians loving one another in Rev 4–22. This alone should be sufficient to lead us to conclude that Jesus' concern did not relate to their failure to love one another; but when we add this to the other arguments above, it becomes even more unlikely. We are left with forsaking their central call to be Jesus' witnesses as the most likely specific referent of abandoning their first love.

Most of us can readily sympathize with the apparent reticence among the Ephesians to maintain an overt witness to their city. Witnessing their beloved pastor's arrest and banishment to Patmos may have had been a significant motivating factor for the church to shrink back from spreading the gospel and just "show God's love through acts of kindness." Paul wrote 1 Corinthians while he was staying in Ephesus (1 Cor 16:8–9) and mentions that he "fought wild beasts" there. While it is not completely clear what he meant by this language, it is very likely that he is speaking metaphorically of the intense opposition he faced as he sought to proclaim the Good News of Jesus Christ. Writing about the historical context of the letters to the seven churches, Ramsay notes that Ephesus "was already, or shortly afterwards became, known as the highway of the martyrs, 'the passageway of those who are slain unto God,' as Ignatius called it a few years later, i.e., the place through which must pass those who were on their way to Rome to amuse the urban population by their death in the amphitheater."[10] Living in Ephesus as a follower of Jesus Christ was not easy. It would have been natural to draw back into a defensive posture, continuing to guard the church against false teaching, continuing to care for one another, continuing to do a variety of good works, but refraining from explicitly proclaiming that Jesus is Lord.

How true is this of many churches today, where doing nice things for our community has all but replaced a verbal witness to the Good News of Jesus Christ? In our culture, going mute with respect to the gospel is a natural response to the intense pressure to accommodate our culture's demand for tolerance; but it is also a deadly response. To choose this option is to forsake our first love; and Jesus does not mince words for churches or individuals who make such a choice.

10. Ramsay, *Letters*, 174.

Remember therefore from where you have fallen; repent, and do the works you did at first. If not, I will come to you and remove your lampstand from its place, unless you repent. (2:5)

Verse 5 brings us to Jesus' solution to their problem. We in the West, in particular, need to realize that it is not just unbelievers that God calls to repentance. The church, as well, frequently needs to repent if she is to remain pure and pleasing to God. What was true of Israel is true of us, as much as we hate to admit it: our hearts are prone to wander. And sometimes, like the church in Ephesus, it is not minor changes that need to take place. Jesus' words in verse 5 make it clear that a drastic change in the spiritual health of the Ephesian church had occurred; and that drastic change called for a drastic response. They had been model servants of God, but they had abandoned their lofty position. Their fall came not through seduction by false teachers or through letting blatant sin get a foothold in their congregation. They had done well in avoiding evil, but they had failed to pursue their central calling. Their initial devotion to Jesus had expressed itself in active witness; but now they had sunk into a defensive stance that held off the enemy, but gained no ground for the Kingdom of God. The solution Jesus presents is both simple and obligatory: repent. He calls them to change their lives, and to embrace afresh their calling as his ambassadors. They are not given a new command, but instead urged to remember what God had called them to be in this world.

Failure to respond appropriately to Jesus' admonition to repent will bring serious consequences. Jesus does not simply try to cajole the Ephesians into having their devotion to him rekindled. He does not say, "Resisting false teaching is great; now try to get more serious about spreading the Good News as well." Instead, he threatens them with their very existence. Ramsay, Hemer, and others have noted that over the centuries Ephesus had been a victim of "remarkable changes in . . . [its] physical geography,"[11] with the city undergoing several changes of site over the centuries. Jesus may well be drawing in his choice of language ("I will remove" or "I will move," κινήσω, *kinēsō*) on the fact that the city had been forced to move as its harbor was filled up with silt. The history of the city would have been well known to the readers and such a connection would have been naturally made.[12] What is important for our purposes

---

11. Hemer, *Letters*, 35.

12. See Ramsay, *Letters*, 178. Strabo (*Geogr.* 14.1.20), writing around AD 20, described Ephesus as a coastal city. The river Cayster, however, had caused the gulf on which Ephesus was located to slowly fill with silt, ultimately resulting in the ancient great seaport becoming a city located several miles from the sea (Hemer, *Letters*, 35). Indeed, Ramsay (*Letters*, 169) suggests that Paul's choice to sail past Ephesus on his way to Jerusalem may reflect a growing tendency at the time to avoid the harbor at Ephesus due to increasing problems caused by silting. This continued in the years that followed. Hemer (*Letters*, 35) notes that "the relation of sea and land has changed in quite unusual fashion: the broad level valley was once a great inlet of the sea, at the head of which was the oldest Ephesus, beside the temple of the goddess near where the modern village stands." By the fourth century, the harbor, now full of silt, was becoming a swamp, and the Ephesian economy was suffering as a result (Worth, *Seven Cities*, 16–17).

is how Jesus makes strategic use of features of each city's history or circumstances (Reading Instruction #4).[13] Here and elsewhere in Rev 2–3, Jesus is creating what I like to call a "rhetorical hotspot," that is, he is using features of the seven cities' physical characteristics and/or history to help capture the attention of the specific readers he is addressing at this point. Each message, then, carries a distinctive label: "Custom made for you." We are still left, however, with the question of how the Ephesian Christians would have heard Jesus' threat to "remove" or "move" their lampstand.

The Old Testament may be of help here (Reading Instruction #6). When God wanted to speak of the permanence of something in the Old Testament, he often described it as not subject to being moved/removed, for which the Septuagint uses the same Greek verb (κινέω, kineō).

> Behold Zion, the city of our appointed feasts! Your eyes will see Jerusalem, an untroubled habitation, an immovable tent, whose stakes will never be plucked up (LXX: μὴ κινηθῶσιν, mē kinēthōsin),[14] nor will any of its cords be broken. (Isa 33:20)

> The craftsman strengthens the goldsmith, and he who smooths with the hammer him who strikes the anvil, saying of the soldering, 'It is good'; and they strengthen it with nails so that it cannot be moved (LXX: "they will not be moved," οὐ κινηθήσονται, ou kinēthēsontai). (Isa 41:7)

The Septuagint translation of Isa 22:25 uses similar language:

> On that day, thus saith (τάδε λέγει, tade legei) the Lord of hosts: The man who was firmly established in a secure place will be (re)moved (κινηθήσεται, kinēthēsetai) and will fall, and the glory that was on him will be taken away, because the Lord has spoken.[15]

Perhaps most striking, however, is the language of Bar 2:35:

> And I will establish an eternal covenant with them so that I will be their God and they will be my people. And I will not remove (οὐ κινήσω, ou kinēsō) my people Israel from the land which I have given to them anymore.[16]

---

13. I have occasionally drawn attention thus far to the fact that Reading Instruction #4 is in view. In reality, much of this book is highlighting ways in which knowledge of the historical circumstances of the seven churches serves as a crucial backdrop against which to interpret this book. As we read Revelation in this way, we are also consistently following Reading Instruction #2 and seeking to determine how the original readers would have understood the narration, dialogue, and visions of Revelation.

14. The full clause in the LXX reads "nor will the pegs of its tent be moved forever," οὐδὲ μὴ κινηθῶσιν οἱ πάσσαλοι τῆς σκηνῆς αὐτῆς εἰς τὸν αἰῶνα χρόνον (oude mē kinēthōsin hoi passaloi tēs skēnēs autēs eis ton aiōna chronon).

15. My translation.

16. My translation.

Here, we find the verb κινέω (*kineō*), coincidentally in the same exact form as in Rev 2:5 (κινήσω, *kinēsō*), clearly being used to refer to exile, the judgment for apostates. The Septuagint's use of this verb, then, suggests that (1) it was frequently used, in its negative form, to speak of permanence; and (2) it could be associated with severe judgment, i.e., exile, for lack of faithfulness. It is likely appropriate, then, to view the warning to the church in Ephesus as far more serious than a simple loss of influence, as if the "light of their influence" would merely be dimmed if they went on in their present state. Rather, since the church in Ephesus has abandoned its central calling to be a light to the nations, Jesus is pronouncing the imminent loss of their existence as a church should they fail to repent.[17] One need only look briefly at the history of the church to see that this has happened to many churches in many countries over the centuries.

> *Yet this you have: you hate the works of the Nicolaitans, which I also hate.* (2:6)

Jesus follows his strong rebuke and warning of judgment with a softer tone, reminding the believers in Ephesus that he recognizes the good work of God among them as well as their problems. He commends them for resisting heresy not only by rejecting false apostles, but also by rejecting the practices/teachings of the Nicolaitans. The language here suggests, though we cannot be sure, that while the unmasking of the false prophets was a past event that Jesus commends them for (v. 2), the Nicolaitans were a continuing threat that the Ephesians were currently dealing with. Paul's prophecy to the Ephesian elders likely sheds light on the challenges the Ephesian Christians were facing, with the "fierce wolves [who] will come in among you, not sparing the flock" (Acts 20:29) representing the false apostles (itinerate teachers) who came from the outside seeking to deceive (2:2), while Paul's warning that "from among your own selves will arise men speaking twisted things, to draw away the disciples after them" (Acts 20:30) refers to the Nicolaitans (2:6), who were heretical *insiders*.

So who were the Nicolaitans, who are mentioned here and in 2:15? No one knows for sure, but there are a couple of things that we can say with confidence.[18] In 2:14–15, it appears that the Nicolaitans' teachings were parallel to the teachings of Balaam. Balaam's teachings consisted of promoting the eating of meat that had been sacrificed to idols and engaging in sexual immorality. The latter could be literal sexual immorality or refer to idolatry (as is common in the OT). We will talk more about the teachings of the Nicolaitans when we look at the message to the church at Pergamum; for now, two points should be kept in mind. First, the Nicolaitans were libertarians, that is, they preached "freedom" to indulge in activities that others recognized as being an offense to God.[19] This is not to say, however, that they were necessarily motivated

---

17. Cf. Swete, *The Apocalypse*, 27; contra Hemer, *Letters*, 52.

18. The view that the Nicolaitans were followers of Nicolaus, one of the seven "deacons" of Acts 6:5, is as old as Irenaeus (*Haer.* 1.26.3), but even Irenaeus provides no evidence for this view.

19. Hemer (*Letters*, 94) concludes that "Nicolaitanism was an antinomian movement whose

by self-indulgence. This brings us to our second point. It is likely during this period that there was increased pressure from Rome for Christians to engage in emperor worship, pressure that was amplified by the establishment of a "pretentious temple" to Domitian in Ephesus.[20] The Nicolaitans apparently responded to such pressure by advocating accommodation to imperial demands "wherever possible." What seemed reasonable to the Nicolaitans, however, evoked the hatred of God and of his followers in Ephesus. The church in Ephesus thus excelled at maintaining both doctrinal purity by guarding against false teachers from the outside and ethical purity by separating themselves from practices in the surrounding culture that were an offense to a holy God, even when there were likely prominent "Christian" teachers encouraging them to do otherwise. It is worth noting that Jesus commends these Christians for their hatred! In a church culture that sometimes overemphasizes that God is a God of love, we would do well to remember that there are things that God hates, and there are things that we should hate as well.

> *He who has an ear, let him hear what the Spirit says to the churches.* (2:7a)

This statement, which occurs at the end of each of the seven messages, is a strong call to pay attention to what has just been said. While some of the strikingly similar statements by Jesus in the Gospels in conjunction with parables may lead us to think that he is pointing to a deeper meaning in Rev 2–3, that is not the function here.[21] Jesus' refrain at the end of each message is a call to obedience; it builds on the promise that he made in 1:3 to those who hear and "keep" what is written in this book. Once again, the Old Testament provides critical guidance for understanding the book of Revelation (Reading Instruction #6). The use of very similar language in Ezek 12:2 ("Son of man, you dwell in the midst of a rebellious house, who have eyes to see, but see not, who have ears to hear, but hear not, for they are a rebellious house.") suggests that "He who has an ear, let him hear what the Spirit says to the churches" essentially means, "Don't rebel against what the Spirit is saying to the churches! Obey!" And the call here to obey the message is not simply for the Ephesians; Jesus and the Spirit are calling the churches of Asia Minor (and followers of Jesus today) to pay attention to this message.

> *To the one who conquers I will grant to eat of the tree of life, which is in the paradise of God.* (2:7b)

Finally, as in each of the other messages, Jesus concludes with *a promise* to "him who overcomes" (NIV 1984). Throughout what follows I will repeatedly refer

---

antecedents can be traced in the misrepresentation of Pauline liberty, and whose incidence may be connected with the special pressures of emperor worship and pagan society."

20. Ibid., 40.

21. Indeed, it is quite possible that the typical understanding of the similar expression in the Gospels has been misread, with Jesus' words there also functioning as a call not to rebel rather than a call to pay attention and think about what he was saying in the parables.

to "overcomers" and "overcoming," simply as a personal preference relating more to my familiarity with this language than an exegetical decision or preference based on translation theory. The ESV's "the one who conquers" is a perfectly good translation, as is the NIV 2011's "the one who is victorious." Both of these renderings highlight the fact that Jesus is using language of warfare, and followers of Jesus must win the battle. The verb "overcome," on the other hand, points to the need to successfully get beyond or surmount a significant obstacle, or to prevail in a struggle or conflict. All of these ideas are closely related and reflect the idea behind the Greek term that is used by Jesus. Jesus is calling Christians in Ephesus to be victorious by conquering or overcoming. What precisely, though, would it mean for Christians in Ephesus to "overcome"? In the context of 2:1–6, Jesus is issuing a promise to those who will re-embrace their role (their first love) to be his visible ambassadors carrying the gospel to their city. Those who "overcome" in this way will be given "the right to eat from the tree of life, which is in the paradise of God."

Jesus' promise to the Ephesian Christians unmistakably turns our attention back to the Garden of Eden (a.k.a. "the paradise of God"),[22] where the right to eat from the tree of life was lost due to the sin of Adam and Eve (Gen 3:24). Jesus is offering to over-comers in Ephesus something that human beings ever since Adam and Eve had been longing for: for God to reverse the effects of the Fall. For those who overcome, Adam's sin will be undone! But more needs to be said here. In quite a number of Jewish texts from outside the Bible, which can provide a helpful window into the way people may have thought in the early centuries of the church, eating from the tree of life appears at times to be used as a metaphor for salvation (1 *En.* 24–25; *T. Levi* 18:10–11; *Apoc. Mos.* 28; *Apoc. El.* 5:6). The same is true in at least one other Christian writer (*T. Jac.* 7:24).[23] Access to the tree of life, then, is another way of pointing to eschatological salvation. Indeed, as we will see, at the end of each of the messages to the seven churches, those who "overcome" are all promised the same reward using different language: They will enter fully into all the blessings of living forever in the presence of God. (The term "paradise" is frequently used to refer to the very presence of God.)[24] In Chapter 18 we will consider how salvation can be offered as a reward to overcomers if it is a gift of God. For now, it is crucial to recognize that Jesus is using a picture of this wonderful reward as a means of motivating Christians in Ephesus to make the right choice about being his witnesses to the world around them.

22. The Greek word for "Paradise" (παραδείσος, *paradeisos*) is actually a loan word from Persian (*paridaida*) meaning "park" or "garden."

23. The phrase "tree of life" is often used metaphorically as well (see, e.g., Prov 3:18; 11:30; 13:12; 15:4). Attempts to connect the "tree of life" with the tree/cross of Christ are unconvincing. For further discussion, see Hemer, *Letters*, 43–44.

24. See, e.g., 2 Cor 12:2–4. And as Hemer (*Letters*, 41) notes, "the ideas of paradise and the heavenly city tend to merge" in Jewish literature (see 2 *Bar.* 4; *T. Dan* 5:12).

Finally, with Jesus' reference to the tree of life he may once again be playing off of local realities in order to capture the attention of the specific audience to which this message is directed. A sacred tree associated with the cult of Artemis was a primary symbol in Ephesus, a symbol that regularly appears on coins from both the pre-Roman and Roman periods. All inhabitants of Ephesus would have been very familiar with this key civic symbol. This is not to say that the presence of such a tree in the Ephesian mind is the necessary background information needed to understand Rev 2:7. On the contrary, the phrase "which is in the paradise of God" makes the reference to Genesis quite obvious, and any lingering doubts would have been removed by the descriptions in Rev 21–22. What the sacred tree of Ephesus provides for Jesus is a ready point of contact, a rhetorical hotspot that allows his message to resonate in a particularly effective way for Christians in Ephesus (Reading Instruction #4). In other words, the communicative point of Jesus' reference to the "tree of life" is to be found in the Jewish notion of such a tree described in Gen 1–3, while the communicative tool used to arrest the attention of the Ephesians was their familiarity with a sacred tree within their own cultural context.

EPHESUS: PROFILE OF A CHURCH

To conclude this chapter, it is important to summarize what we can know about this church from both Jesus' message that is addressed to these Christians and from other sources that shed light on the characteristics of the city of Ephesus that may be relevant. This information allows us to construct a profile of this particular church, which will help us to understand how Christians in first-century Ephesus would have understood the other parts of the book Revelation, which in its entirety was addressed to them. So, what would a profile of the Christians in Ephesus include?

This particular group of Christians lived in a city that was devoted to the Emperor and to the Roman Empire, and had reaped the benefits of that devotion. There would have been intense pressure for Christians to go along with the program for the good of their neighbors and the city. In the midst of this pagan city, we find Christians who had not only begun well, but had persevered in serving the Lord. They had not given up on their faith, even when they faced great hardships because they followed Jesus. The reference to enduring hardships "for my name's sake" makes it clear that these believers had chosen to resist the temptation to bow to pressures to participate in the frequent ceremonies honoring the gods of the city, and had paid the price for doing so. They had lived as visible Christians within their city. Furthermore, they had carefully guarded the doctrinal purity of the church by actively watching for false teaching and rejecting it whenever it raised its ugly head. In many ways, they were a model congregation. Unfortunately, although they had rightly circled the wagons to protect against false teaching either from outside or from within, they appear to have shrunk back from being an overt witness to the society around them. They had not bowed to the pressure to conform to the pattern of life around them, but they *had* bowed to the pressure to stop shining the light in the darkness. Perhaps they had reasoned that since everyone around them knew that they were Christians, that was sufficient "witness." No need to "cram the gospel down their throats. We'll just let our lives be our witness!" Jesus, though, reminds them that to shrink back from verbally testifying about him was to abandon their reason for existing. He, therefore, calls for repentance, commanding them to go back to what they were doing at first—actions that no doubt led to the hardships they had endured earlier. If they do not listen to his admonition, he will "remove their lampstand" and they will cease to exist as a church. If they *do* repent and "overcome" or "conquer" the temptation to try to live as stealth Christians in their city, Jesus will reward them with the life that God intends for those who love him: They will live forever in God's presence, eating from the tree of life in the paradise of God.

As we come to understand the characteristics of the church in Ephesus, and the characteristics of the other churches, we will be better equipped to address the foundational questions that must be answered before we can grasp what God is saying to Christians today through Revelation: What would all of Revelation have meant to Christians in Ephesus? What would all of Revelation have meant to Christians in Smyrna? And so forth. What we have in Rev 1, then, is an introductory chapter that sets the stage, introduces some of the key themes of the book, and provides fairly extensive reading instructions. This is followed by seven messages in Rev 2–3; but the messages to the seven churches do not end at Rev 3:22. Instead, they represent the beginning of Jesus' specific message to each church. What follows provides the rest of the message, "the rest of the story" for each church. And once we have read Revelation through this lens, asking what the book as a whole would have meant to each of the seven churches, we will then be prepared to answer the final question: What is Jesus' message to the church today in the book of Revelation?

3

Jesus' Message to the Church in Ephesus
The Rest of the Story

As we think about what the rest of Revelation would have meant to Christians in Ephesus, we need to recognize, first of all, that they would have also heard the messages to the other six churches; and some parts of those messages would have resonated. We will limit our discussion here to just one example. If the analysis above concerning the referent of "first love" is correct, the Ephesian Christians would have been struck, in particular, by the example of Antipas from Pergamum who remained a faithful witness even when it cost him his life (2:13). This example, and the fact that life for overt Christians may have been even more difficult in places like Pergamum, would have helped to steel the Ephesians' resolve to take up their role as heralds of the gospel of Jesus Christ.

We have learned much about the church in Ephesus through the message that Jesus sent them in 2:1–7 and from what is known about the background of the city. Keeping the key features of the profile in mind, we will now consider how Rev 4–22 intersects with that profile to strengthen and drive home the message Jesus has for these particular Christians. As we look at "the rest of the story," our strategy will be to go chapter by chapter through the remainder of Revelation and attempt to read it through the eyes of the original readers in Ephesus. The reflections on each chapter of Revelation will be illustrative only, and readers are invited to discover more of the rest of the story for themselves by making use of the reading instructions from Rev 1. Some comments here and in subsequent chapters of this book will also apply to other churches who were facing similar circumstances, but they will not been repeated to avoid redundancy. As you proceed through the comments below that sketch "the rest of the story" for Christians in Ephesus, you will gain the most benefit by reading through the relevant portions of Revelation first.

REVELATION 4–5: THE MESSAGE TO EPHESUS

As the Ephesian Christians encountered the amazing throne room scene in Rev 4–5, it would have quickly helped to put things in perspective. The pressures of living in such a wealthy city, where every citizen was expected to be a loyal team player would have been considerable. To proclaim Jesus as Lord in a land where Caesar's absolute lordship went without question would have been dangerous. How much easier it was to retreat to the relative safety of quiet Christian worship and fellowship, and avoid rocking the boat. When these Christians caught a glimpse of God on the throne, however, and were reminded that the Lamb who was slain had "ransomed people for God from every tribe and language and people and nation" (5:9), suddenly what seemed like prudence and wisdom would have been seen for the folly that it was. They had been made "a kingdom and priests to our God" (5:10); they were the ones who will "reign on the earth" (5:10); and yet they had abandoned their holy calling in order to protect their way of life. No wonder Jesus tells them that they had fallen so far! They had followed conventional wisdom rather than following the Lamb. They had neglected their role in spreading the message that by his blood Jesus had decisively dealt with sin so that people can be reconciled to God. These chapters, then, among other things would have reminded them that they, like John the Baptist before them, were called to be heralds proclaiming in their city for all to hear: "Behold, the Lamb of God, who takes away the sin of the world!" (John 1:29).

REVELATION 6: THE MESSAGE TO EPHESUS

To embrace the call to be overt witnesses for Jesus in Ephesus would have been sobering. Such a call carried more than a little likelihood of danger and suffering; and like the readers of Hebrews, the Ephesian Christians had been there and done that. They knew what their city did to Jesus' ambassadors. As they read through the following chapter of Jesus' message to them, they would have found a sobering affirmation of their fears. Hardships were on the horizon. God's people could expect to live in a world of increasing conquest, widespread wars, famine, and plagues (the first four seals). Worse yet, they could expect to be martyrs (the fifth seal). What would have been particularly sobering about the fifth seal (6:9–11) is the clear indication that God's *plan* for at least a significant number of his people was for them to die for their faith.

The call to be overt witnesses for Jesus, then, did not carry with it a promise that if they did, all would go well. Instead, it was accompanied by a revelation from God that if they "heard" and "kept" (i.e., obeyed) the message Jesus was sending them (1:3) they very well might end up like Antipas (2:13). Nevertheless, live as a lampstand in Ephesus they must; and to bolster their resolve Jesus shows them that the very ones who are pressuring them to keep quiet, the very ones who can bring great hardship and even death to those who choose to proclaim the Good News that Jesus is Lord, will one day soon find themselves facing the wrath of the Lord and longing to hide from it (the sixth seal; 6:12–17). While that should inspire thanksgiving for the coming justice that will be doled out to their opponents in Ephesus, it should also inspire a sense of urgency to reach those who are about to face the wrath of the Lamb with the gospel. They knew very well that they themselves were "by nature children of wrath, like the rest of mankind" (Eph 2:3), but God in his great mercy had rescued them by his grace. How can those who have been shown mercy not do everything in their power to offer that very mercy to other "children of wrath"?

We should also note, however, that there is a striking parallel between the earlier warning to the church in Ephesus ("If not, I will come to you and *remove* your lampstand *from its place*, unless you repent," 2:5) and the description of destruction in 6:14 ("The sky vanished like a scroll that is being rolled up, and every mountain and island was *removed from its place*"). These are the only places in Revelation where this expression is used,[1] effectively driving home Jesus' warning to the Ephesian Christians and helping to make clear that "removal" points to destruction.

REVELATION 7: THE MESSAGE TO EPHESUS

As Christians in Ephesus came to Rev 7, the question at the end of Rev 6 would have still been ringing in their ears: "for the great day of their wrath has come, and who can stand?" (6:17). Conquest, bloodshed, famine, plagues, wild beasts, martyrdom, and a huge earthquake— these were not things to look forward to. Who, indeed, can stand in the midst of such utter destruction? The beginning of Rev 7 answers that question: There are *some* who can stand, those who are not the objects of God's wrath, but instead have been sealed so that his wrath will never touch them. In Rev 7, before the final seal and the sounding of the seven trumpets, God graciously interrupts the scenes of judgment to convey some beautiful promises to those whose allegiance belongs to the Lamb. Yes, the evil one can have God's people put to death. Martyrdom is to be expected; it is God's plan for some (6:9–11). But it is only those who are willing to face the wrath of the evil one who will avoid the wrath of God! Servants of God are sealed by him and will not be touched by his wrath, any more than the Israelites were touched by the plagues that God poured out on Egypt. This would have been encouraging to those who were afraid of becoming too visible in their city and thus facing the wrath of the authorities or their neighbors. We will examine the significance of the sealing of the 144,000 more fully in Chapter 5.

---

1. Both verses use the same verb and prepositional phrase: κινήσω . . . ἐκ τοῦ τόπου αὐτῆς (2:5, *kinēsō ek tou topou autēs*); ἐκ τῶν τόπων αὐτῶν ἐκινήθησαν (6:14, *ek tōn topōn autōn ekinēthēsan*).

As Ephesian Christians came to the next vision in 7:9–17, several things would have stood out. First, God makes it clear that his saving purposes will come to pass. People from every ethnic group in the world will hear the Good News of Jesus and be saved (7:9–10). The question for the Ephesian Christians is whether or not they will be part of God's plan for bringing the Good News to the nations. Again, getting on board with God's plan does not imply that hardships will cease. Quite the contrary, the vision speaks of "the ones coming out of the great tribulation" (7:14), an expression that almost certainly implies martyrdom. Martyrdom, however, is not the end of the story. Instead, the end for overcomers is a place before the throne of God, where they will serve him night and day forever, enjoying his absolute protection, and never again facing hunger, thirst, scorching heat, or sorrow (7:15–17).

We should also note that there are other biblical passages that help us to understand the nature of this great tribulation. We find this period of suffering described in Daniel and in Jesus' words in the Gospels:

> And there shall be a time of trouble, such as never has been since there was a nation till that time. (Dan 12:1)

> For then there will be great tribulation, such as has not been from the beginning of the world until now, no, and never will be. [22]And if those days had not been cut short, no human being would be saved. But for the sake of the elect those days will be cut short. (Matt 24:21–22)

> in those days there will be such tribulation as has not been from the beginning of the creation that God created until now, and never will be. [20]And if the Lord had not cut short the days, no human being would be saved. But for the sake of the elect, whom he chose, he shortened the days. (Mark 13:19–20)

All of these passages make it clear that a time of unprecedented tribulation is coming, and this certainly fits with Rev 6, which describes the beginning of that period of tribulation. The cataclysmic upheaval will be so great that humanity will be on the brink of utter extinction; but for the sake of the elect, God's own people, God will bring an end to the destruction before that takes place. Jesus' words in Matthew and Mark point to the presence of God's elect during this time period (we will return to this question later), as do his words in Luke:

> But watch yourselves lest your hearts be weighed down with dissipation and drunkenness and cares of this life, and that day come upon you suddenly like a trap. [35]For it will come upon all who dwell on the face of the whole earth. (Luke 21:34–35)

"That day" is coming, and Jesus urges his followers to be vigilant and to be prepared in Luke 21; and he is doing the same thing, in pictorial form, in the book of Revelation. The point of this part of Revelation, then, is relevant to all Christians regardless of their location in history. Although some attempt to correlate the "great tribulation" with the whole period of church history, during which God's people suffer tribulation (see, e.g., John 16:33; Acts 14:22; 2 Tim 3:12), this fails to grapple with the specific nature of the prophecies in Dan 12:1, Matt 24, and Mark 13. In each case, these passages clearly point to a period of unparalleled future suffering, just as Jesus does in Rev 3:10. Having said that, listening to Jesus' words for how to prepare for that suffering is critical for every Christian of every era; for we can all expect to suffer, and we are all called to be faithful to the end. The focus here on these particular martyrs who endure the wrath of the beast when it is directed full force against the people of God encourages the people of God at all times and in all places to resist the temptation to cave in or fail to stand firm in their faith when they face a choice between life and faith in Jesus.

REVELATION 8–9: THE MESSAGE TO EPHESUS

Revelation 8–9 paint a horrific picture of divine judgment on those who reject God. The section begins by striking an ominous tone with half an hour of silence in heaven as the seven trumpets are about to be blown (8:1). The blowing of the first six trumpets brings widespread destruction to the earth. The fact that the descriptions here are not pointing to periodic global catastrophes throughout history, but rather are concerned with a series of catastrophes that are distinctively horrifying, is driven home by the strong declaration of woe that follows the first three trumpet blasts: "Woe, woe, woe to those who dwell on the earth, at the blasts of the other trumpets that the three angels are about to blow!" (8:13). The suffering that people face will be so intense that they will long to die (9:6). Their lives will be filled with terror and agony. Yet despite their suffering, those who survive the destruction will still refuse to change their ways (9:20–21).

Two things need to be noticed here as we think about how the Ephesian Christians would have heard this part of Revelation. First, the mention of the refusal by the inhabitants of the earth to repent suggests that part of the purpose of the trumpets is to motivate repentance. God is still giving people a chance to turn from their wicked ways and avoid destruction. Second, anyone with an ounce of compassion in Ephesus would have longed for their neighbors, the merchants they bought goods from, and even city officials to avoid the fate being described in these chapters. The trumpet visions are, in part, intended to move the Ephesian Christians to action and create a sense of urgency to be heralds who warn their fellow citizens of the coming destruction and show them how they can be saved. Far too often Christians today read Revelation and think, "Wow, I'm glad I won't be here to go through that suffering!" without a hint of concern for their neighbors or family members who will face the full force of God's wrath if they do not hear the gospel and repent.

REVELATION 10: THE MESSAGE TO EPHESUS

The sense of urgency evoked by the six trumpets would have only increased as the Ephesians read in Rev 10 that "there would be no more delay, [7] but that in the days of the trumpet call to be sounded by the seventh angel, the mystery of God would be fulfilled, just as he announced to his servants the prophets" (10:6–7). God's purposes are about to reach their culmination. Time is short. Therefore, time is of the essence for those being called to do the work they did at first as Christ's ambassadors in Ephesus.

The message all ambassadors of Christ bring, however, carries a dual outcome that is vividly portrayed in the "sweet and sour scroll" (10:8–11). The scroll tastes sweet to John, but it turns his stomach sour. In this passage, John's taking of the scroll (message from God) and his commission to proclaim it far and wide is generally consistent with the call of all believers to "go and make disciples" (Matt 28:19). The message Christians carry, however, though it is sweeter than honey—it is truly the best of news—often also brings discomfort to the messenger. The vision of John eating the scroll thus affirms the very thing that the Ephesian Christians feared. They would suffer if they heed Jesus' call to return to their first love and spread the good news of what he had done for the people of Ephesus through his death and resurrection. But, as with John, the call of God on their lives remained: They must testify about Jesus to "many people" (10:11) in their city.

The parallel actions in Ezek 3:1–3 (Reading Instruction #6) help us to understand that the eating of the scroll symbolizes the reception of a message from God that is to be passed on to others. This is made clear in both Ezek 3:1 and Rev 10:11. John ingests God's Word in preparation to proclaim it to others; and his actions would have reminded the Ephesian Christians that they have received the Good News of Jesus Christ not just for their own benefit but also so that they can pass it on to others—others who are still enemies of God and objects of his coming wrath, which has already been described in great detail. Although the dual nature of the scroll (bitter and sweet) could relate to the fact that it promises both blessing (for overcomers) and wrath (for those who refuse to repent), the image more likely points to the fact that the message from Jesus will taste sweet but turn stomachs sour *for John and the people of God*.[2] Yes, the Good News promises a wonderful reward for those who repent and embrace it. Indeed, as we will see, it promises the "sweetest" of all endings to the story; but throughout the New Testament, and in Revelation in particular, God makes it clear that the path to eternal life runs straight along the Via Dolorosa—"the way of suffering."[3] God, through Paul, tells Timothy that "all who desire to live a godly life in Christ Jesus will be persecuted" (2 Tim 3:12); and he reminds the Philippians, "it

2. This becomes clearer as the same vision continues into Rev 11, where we encounter the two witnesses, their message, and their fate.

3. "Before the final triumph (sweetness), believers will pass through a great ordeal of suffering (7:14, bitterness)"; Smalley, *Revelation*, 268.

has been granted to you that for the sake of Christ you should not only believe in him but also suffer for his sake" (Phil 1:29). This is why Jesus can say, "whoever would save his life will lose it, but whoever loses his life for my sake and the gospel's will save it" (Mark 8:35), and actually mean it. He expects those who profess his name to live as overcomers; and "overcoming" for those in Ephesus means embracing a willingness to lose their life for Jesus and the gospel.

REVELATION 11: THE MESSAGE TO EPHESUS

This message is driven home in even starker terms in Rev 11. The account of the two witnesses would have particularly caught the attention of the Ephesian Christians due to the use of the lampstand image. The Ephesians were being threatened with the removal of their lampstand; here in Rev 11 they are reminded how a proper lampstand is supposed to function. The clothing of the two witnesses, sackcloth (11:3), suggests a message of repentance. The fact that they are invincible (11:5) during the time they are serving as God's witnesses would have reminded the Ephesian readers that God is sovereign; he is more than able to protect his people as they serve as his witnesses in the world. There really is no need to fear man when God is in control. Their faithful witness, however, does not ensure indefinite protection by God. Quite the contrary, Rev 11 makes it clear that God has ordained a particular number of days for the two witnesses to carry out their role, and the same is true for all followers of Jesus, whether their end comes from a quiet, peaceful death or through a martyr's violent death. At the end of the time that God has allotted for his two witnesses, his hand of protection will be lifted and they, like the martyrs under the altar described in the fifth seal (6:9–11), will be killed by the beast (11:7).

What is critical for fearful believers in Ephesus to remember as they consider Jesus' call to return to their first love and do the work of evangelism as they had done at first is that although God has ordained that more of Jesus' followers will die for their faith before the end (6:11), death is not the end of the story for the two witnesses, nor will it be the end of the story for Jesus' faithful witnesses in Ephesus. Like the two witnesses (11:11), they will be raised from the dead. Like the two witnesses (11:12), they will be caught up to meet Jesus in the air and so they will be with him forever (1 Thess 4:13–17). And those who persecuted them will face God's justice (11:13). All of this would have helped remind the Ephesian believers that when they followed the Lord Jesus faithfully and faced painful consequences as a result, they could rest assured that nothing was happening by chance. They were safe and secure in the sovereign hand of God, and until *he* decided that they were to face the cruel hand of the enemy the evil one would not be able to touch them. For now, they needed to live in light of the fact that God was about to begin his reign (11:17). His purposes would be accomplished.

REVELATION 12: THE MESSAGE TO EPHESUS

After the announcement in Rev 11 that God has begun to reign, we encounter a flash-back in Rev 12 that provides a fuller picture of what brought about that reign and what it will look like for the people of God as they wait to enter into the fullness of his kingdom. The description of the child in verse 5 makes it very clear that this is a symbolic description of the birth of Jesus Christ and his ascension. He alone is the one who will rule with an iron scepter; but he does not presently rule unopposed. The image of the enormous dragon waiting to devour the child (12:3–4) fits with the Satanic attempt to devour Jesus by killing all the young children in Bethlehem (Matt 2:16). The dragon's seven heads with seven crowns and ten horns speak of his current universal authority (seven crowns) over this world and his overwhelming power (ten horns). As the apostle John writes elsewhere, "the whole world lies in the power of the evil one" (1 John 5:19). This same reality is stated in Rev 12:9, where the Ephesian Christians are reminded that Satan is "the deceiver of the whole world."

For the Ephesian Christians, perhaps the most important features of this vision relate to Satan's current activities. He is not only actively deceiving the world, so that the Good News of Jesus Christ will sound like foolishness (1 Cor 1:18), he is also actively making war against the people of God, who are defined as "those who keep the commandments of God and hold to the testimony of Jesus" (12:17). The Christians in Ephesus have been called upon in no uncertain terms to repent and return to their first love. They need to obey God's command and embrace their central calling to hold to the testimony of Jesus by actively proclaiming it to the city around them. To do so, however, will inevitably make them a target of the dragon. Plain and simple, such opposition from the evil one cannot be avoided by those who are devoted to the Lord Jesus. Christians are called to serve the Lord Jesus by bringing the light into the darkness, recognizing, as we will see in Rev 13, that their adversary the devil and his emissary the beast are not to be taken lightly.

So how are Christians to stand in the face of such terrifying and powerful opposition? Jesus makes the way to overcome the dragon quite clear: "they have conquered him by the blood of the Lamb and by the word of their testimony, for they loved not their lives even unto death" (12:11). Their lives, indeed, may well be on the line; but the *only* path to victory is the path of an active testimony. They have been washed in the blood of the Lamb; now they must testify to their pagan neighbors what Jesus has done for them too.

REVELATION 13: THE MESSAGE TO EPHESUS

Having gone back to the death, resurrection, and ascension of Jesus in Rev 12 to explain the nature of the battle the people of God were facing, the visions in Rev 13 return to the present and future to paint a clearer picture of how the dragon will make war against the saints. The account of the two beasts makes it clear that those who oppose the dragon by refusing to worship the first beast and by the word of their testimony can expect a dramatic increase in the challenges they will face in this life. The dragon will give the beast his power and authority, symbolized by ten horns with ten crowns (13:1); and the beast will not only make war against the saints, but will also "conquer them" (13:7). We see that the dragon, who leads the whole world astray (12:9), does so in part through impressive miracles (13:3, 13–15). But those who do not believe the miracles will still be left with little choice in how to respond to the beast. The beast will rule with an iron fist; and the choice will ultimately be quite simple: If you want to live, give your allegiance to the beast. If not, you will die (13:15). If you think you can hide from his might, know that you will not even be able to buy food or earn a living if you have not first given your allegiance to the beast by taking his mark.

Although we will say more about the mark of the beast later, at this point it is worth reflecting briefly on what it would have meant to Christians in Ephesus. The fact that the mark is to be placed on the right hand or forehead is important. This echoes the exhortation from the Old Testament (Reading Instruction #6) in what was perhaps the most familiar passage to Jews:

> Hear, O Israel: The Lord our God, the Lord is one. ⁵You shall love the Lord your God with all your heart and with all your soul and with all your might. ⁶And these words that I command you today shall be on your heart. ⁷You shall teach them diligently to your children, and shall talk of them when you sit in your house, and when you walk by the way, and when you lie down, and when you rise. ⁸You shall bind them as a sign on your hand, and they shall be as frontlets between your eyes. ⁹You shall write them on the doorposts of your house and on your gates. (Deut 6:4–9)

This passage, known as the *Shema*, was the central confession of the old covenant people of God. As straightforward as it sounds in English, if you look at the footnotes in your Bible you will see that the precise sense of the first sentence is not clear. In my view, the most likely understanding of the passage is this: "Hear O Israel: Yahweh is our God, Yahweh alone!" It is thus *a declaration of absolute allegiance to God.* No other gods allowed! That absolute allegiance is then spelled out in what follows, including verse 8, a verse that led to the practice of Orthodox Jews tying phylacteries (small leather boxes containing this and other passages from the Torah) around their hands and foreheads. God's instructions in Deut 6 were likely originally intended in a figurative sense;[4] by calling for these "marks" on their hands and foreheads God was making it clear that their allegiance to him was to be patently obvious to all around them. There were to be no closet Jews, just as there are to be no closet Christians (see, e.g., Matt 10:32; 1 John 2:23).

---

4. See also Prov 3:3; 6:21; 7:3.

The beast requires public, overt testimony by those who belong to him. What the Ephesian Christians need to be reminded of is that Jesus requires no less. The discussion of the mark of the beast would have reminded them that everyone will be marked as belonging to either Jesus or the beast. The choice was theirs, but there would be no way to go unnoticed by avoiding a mark altogether. Therefore, they needed to repent of their sin of forsaking their first love and shrinking back from being an overt witness to their city. They had been models of patient endurance in other areas, now they needed to heed Jesus' call to "patient endurance and faithfulness" (13:10, NIV) by re-embracing their role as his ambassadors in Ephesus regardless of the consequences.

REVELATION 14: THE MESSAGE TO EPHESUS

As the visions of Revelation leave the terrifying power of the beast behind in Rev 13 we encounter a beautiful reminder of what Jesus has in store for those who refuse to bow to the beast's demands for worship and instead give their allegiance to him alone. The full measure of those who have been sealed to protect them from God's wrath can now sing the song of God's redemption and walk with Jesus forever (14:3–4). With such a future in store for those who are faithful, the response for those awaiting that end is obvious: "Fear God and give him glory, because the hour of his judgment has come, and worship him who made heaven and earth, the sea and the springs of water" (14:7). The temptation is to fear men, to fear the power of Rome/Babylon/this world; but Babylon, God reminds them, is about to come crashing down (14:8), and those who give in to the temptation to give their allegiance to the beast will meet the same fate (14:9–11).

While some Christians are prone to bask in their security before God, God himself is eager to warn Christians then and now to be sure to patiently endure in the face of pressure to shrink back from following Jesus, and to remain faithful to him, carefully obeying God's commands (14:12). Like the rest of Revelation, this section emphasizes that being a follower of Jesus is not for the faint of heart. Jesus never promises anyone that if they just "ask him into their heart" or "ask him to be their personal Savior" or "ask him into their life" they are good to go whatever subsequent choices they make in this life. Christians are expected to endure to the end; Christians are *required* to endure to the end.

More than that, Rev 14:1 would have reminded Christians in Ephesus that overt identification with Christ is not optional. Jesus' followers have "his name and his Father's name written on their foreheads." There is no mistaking to whom they belong. Their allegiance is readily apparent. Every follower of Christ is called to live a life that obviously displays who his or her master is.

Standing firm in the faith by hiding in the shadows and waiting for Jesus' return simply does not qualify as "enduring to the end." Once again, the revelation that Jesus gives the saints in Asia Minor returns to the central calling of all believers: the proclamation of the gospel. In 14:6, we find a vision of an angel carrying "an eternal gospel to proclaim to those who dwell on earth, to every nation and tribe and language and people," as he flies through the air. God's purpose remains the same right to the end. He desires his people—including the Christians in Ephesus who had abandoned their first love and central calling—to go and make disciples of all nations. But what is that eternal gospel? We might expect the angel to announce the finished work of Christ in verse 7, but instead we find him shouting out, "Fear God and give him glory, because the hour of his judgment has come, and worship him who made heaven and earth, the sea and the springs of water." Has something changed with the gospel message? In reality, the gospel has always been a call to turn from sin and rebellion and bow the knee to the true Lord of the Universe. It is a call to worship God and him alone. It is a call to repent of idolatry and live a life of fearing the Lord. This gospel message is summarized in Paul's description of the Thessalonians: "you turned to God from idols to serve the living and true God, [10]and to wait for his Son from heaven, whom he raised from the dead, Jesus who delivers us from the wrath to come" (1 Thess 1:9–10). These words are a vivid picture of the Thessalonians' belief in Jesus and their transfer of allegiance to him. This is what God has always demanded of those who would be saved. It has always been that way; and this will always be the gospel. If you would be saved, you must "believe in your heart that God raised [Jesus] from the dead" *and* you must "confess with your mouth that Jesus is Lord" (Rom 10:9). Anything else is another gospel (see Gal 1:8–9). God does not call anyone to some vague "trust Christ for your salvation." He calls people to a complete change of existence and allegiance. He calls people to recognize their dire need for a Savior, believe what Jesus has done for them through his death and resurrection, turn from their sins, and give their allegiance to him. That is the only way anyone can "fear God and give him glory."

For the Ephesians, in particular, Rev 14:6–7 would have been a reminder to make sure they were preaching a biblical gospel. Even as they call on their neighbors and others in Ephesus to embrace what God has done for them in Jesus Christ, so that they can avoid the wrath that is coming and be reconciled to their Creator, they dare not downplay the fact that this requires repentance, obedience, and single-minded devotion to God alone. Today, there are far too many habitually immoral individuals who are "trusting Christ alone for their salvation." They know that they cannot save themselves. They believe that salvation is a "free gift" that comes by grace alone through faith alone in Christ alone. They "believe" that and carry on with their lives of sin. They have embraced another gospel, a gospel that cannot save anyone.

As if he were anticipating the natural response the Christians in Asia Minor would have had to this section, God adds some important words in 14:13. Hearing about the fury of the beast that God's people would be facing and Jesus' corresponding exhortation for the saints to patiently endure, the natural response would have been: "But what if we are tortured for our faith?" "But what if we face death unless we renounce our faith? What then?" Jesus responds, "Blessed are the dead who die in the

Lord from now on" (14:13). In other words: Stop looking at death as the worst thing that could happen to you. To die in the Lord, to die for being a witness for Jesus in this world, is actually a blessing! God will reward you if you die for him. So, what are you worried about? If you die for your faith, you will enter into the wonderful rest that God has in store for you, and your faithful obedience to him will be rewarded: Your deeds will follow you (14:13). Stop living as if this world were all there is. This world and this life are merely a prelude to true life in God's presence for eternity.

For the Ephesian Christians, all of this would have helped once more to bolster their courage to be the lampstand in Ephesus that God had intended them to be, a beacon that drew others to Jesus even as it drew unwanted attention to itself, attention that may result in their death, but would also certainly result in great eternal rewards. And Jesus' language in 14:12 would have helped bolster the courage of those who had already been excelling in patient endurance in other areas of their devotion to him: "This calls for patient endurance on the part of the people of God who keep his commands and remain faithful to Jesus" (NIV).

The message is clear. The hour is late; there is no time to lose when it comes to serving as Christ's ambassadors. The earth is ripe for harvest; and God will soon harvest his people from this world (14:14–16)—many through a violent death during the great tribulation—and harvest the wicked to be crushed under his wrath (14:17–20). An overwhelming number of people will perish because of his wrath, filling the land with a river of blood. They need to hear the Good News of Jesus Christ. The need, then, for Christians in Ephesus to return to their first love and do the things they had done at first was urgent.[5]

REVELATION 15: THE MESSAGE TO EPHESUS

To reinforce both the urgent need and the promise of eternal rewards our attention is drawn once again in Rev 15 back to heaven. We first see seven angels bearing the seven last plagues of Revelation. God's outpouring of wrath is on the verge of being completed. The opportunity for the gospel to go out and people to repent is almost past. In the presence of God an important group of people are singing a new song. These people are "those who had conquered the beast and its image and the number of its name" (15:2). This is what God has in store for all of those who overcome; and overcoming, broadly speaking, involves refusing to give one's allegiance to the beast. These are God's faithful servants who have been redeemed from the earth—again, many through their deaths—and now can sing the song of deliverance, much like the Israelites sang the Song of Moses when God rescued them at the Red Sea from the Egyptians (Exod 15). For the Ephesians, the question was whether or not they would heed Jesus' call to stop compromising their witness by becoming mute in the

5. The words of Keith Green from his powerful song, "Asleep in the Light," aptly illustrate Jesus' call to the Ephesian Christians through the book of Revelation.

face of the pressure of Ephesus and Rome. To drive this point home, Jesus offers them a critical question in 15:4 in the song of the overcomers: "Who will not fear, O Lord, and glorify your name?" Will they fear God, or fear people? Will they glorify God by completing the works he has given them to do (cf. John 17:4), or will they continue to hide their light under a basket (see Matt 5:14–16).

REVELATION 16: THE MESSAGE TO EPHESUS

As the reality of the seven last plagues unfolds in Rev 16, the urgent call to be faithful witnesses to a world on the brink of destruction would have been driven home yet again for Christians in Ephesus. The seven bowls of God's wrath are not something to wish on anyone. They represent God's undiluted judgment (16:5–6); and Christians who are called to love their enemies should want God's grace for unbelievers, not his justice. The majority will continue to respond to God's wrath by cursing him and refusing to repent (16:11, 21), despite the agony that they face (16:10). God's people in Ephesus have already been told that God will seal his people to protect them from his wrath that is poured out on the earth. In the midst of the outpouring of wrath, though, followers of Christ are to live as faithful, overt witnesses to what he has done for the world. Jesus is coming soon and his followers need to be vigilant to be about his business so that they are not ashamed when they stand before him (16:15). God is about to judge the world and destroy those who oppose him (16:16–20). Will the Ephesians fear for their lives and shrink back from their role as Christ's ambassadors, or will they fear God and choose to obey him who alone deserves their absolute allegiance? Will they sound the clarion call in Ephesus that God's judgment is coming, or will they continue to be mute to save their own skin even when countless people around them are on the brink of destruction?

REVELATION 17–18: THE MESSAGE TO EPHESUS

Near the end of Rev 16, we are told: "and God remembered Babylon the great, to make her drain the cup of the wine of the fury of his wrath" (16:19). Now, in Rev 17–18 Jesus gives us a fuller picture of what the fury of God's wrath will look like. He had already given a brief glimpse of Babylon's downfall with the announcement of the second angel in 14:8. Now, he fleshes out the picture more fully, much like the pattern we have been seeing throughout Revelation. While the message conveyed through the imagery of the seducing prostitute of Rev 17 is primarily directed at many of the other churches in Asia Minor, there are features of the visions of Rev 17–18 that would have driven home the message to the Christians in Ephesus in important ways.

First, the great prostitute is blasphemy personified (17:3). She represents a world that refuses to fear God and give him glory (see Rom 1:21), and that does the opposite of worshiping him who made the heavens and the earth and all that is in them (14:7).

In a world of such blasphemy, God's people are called to intentionally and visibly live as God designed them to live. They are to "proclaim the excellencies of him who called [them] out of darkness into his marvelous light" (1 Pet 2:9). Like the two witnesses of Rev 11, they are to call people to repentance even as the great prostitute is seducing them to idolatry and blasphemy.

Second, a battle is coming between the beast with his followers and the Lamb. The Lamb is the King of kings and Lord of lords, and there is no doubt that he will prevail (17:14). The prostitute, on the other hand, will meet a gruesome end (17:16). All of this would have driven home the point that Christians in Asia Minor must avoid at all costs associating with the prostitute in any way, a point that is further strengthened by the brief clause that is tacked on at the end of 17:14—"and those with him are called and chosen and faithful." For Christians in Ephesus, being *faithful*—overcoming—meant returning to their first love, a choice that would carry with it significant cost. That brings us to our final point here.

The Ephesian Christians' motivation to keep quiet about their faith might have been driven by their desire not to draw attention to the fact that they were not participating in pagan rituals in their city. "On the day each year when the port officially opened after its winter closing, the priests of Artemis carried her statue to the waterfront. There they dipped it into the water as a sign of her blessing upon the merchant vessels that brought prosperity to the city and as a symbol of her protection upon the vessels' sailors during the following year."[6] For those of us who live in a culture dominated by a worldview that is heavily driven by consumerism the danger of looking to a false god for our comfort and wealth is perilous. In the wake of the recent economic travails, it has become commonplace for people to celebrate when "consumer confidence" is high and become anxious when it is low. In other words, our culture has become dominated by the need to maintain the façade of a wealthy society by spending money we do not have. The Economy has almost been deified, and professing Christians seem to be rushing headlong, like everyone around them, to grab all they can get from the society they live within, often compromising their testimony to participate in the excessive luxury of "Babylon."

Finally, it is worth noting that a small detail of this vision may have been particularly pertinent for those living in Ephesus. We are told in 18:11–13 that "the merchants of the earth weep and mourn for her, since no one buys their cargo anymore, [12]cargo of gold, silver, jewels, pearls, fine linen, purple cloth, silk, scarlet cloth, all kinds of scented wood, all kinds of articles of ivory, all kinds of articles of costly wood, bronze, iron and marble, [13]cinnamon, spice, incense, myrrh, frankincense, wine, oil, fine flour, wheat, cattle and sheep, horses and chariots, *and slaves, that is, human souls.*" Ephesus was the largest business center in Asia, with a wide range of commodities passing through it and an unrivaled banking system. More than that, Worth notes that "in the lamentable trade in humans, the city had a long-established reputation. It had been a

---

6. Worth, *Seven Cities*, 17.

major regional slave market for hundreds of years before the Roman ascendancy over Asia."[7] This reality would have helped the earliest readers of Revelation, particularly those in Ephesus, to look closer to home for a reference to Babylon. The temptation to get on board with the booming economy of Ephesus by assimilating to the culture— even if by only keeping quiet about their faith in their daily dealings with outsiders— would have been extreme. Such temptation, writes Jesus, must be weighed against the sure reality that the Babylons of the world will soon be destroyed. Those who indulge in the benefits of such a sick society that is opposed to the lordship of Jesus Christ and gain wealth through exploiting others cannot expect to escape the wrath of the Lamb. Followers of Jesus can have no commerce with those who trade in (lit.) "the bodies and souls of men." Jesus, our gracious Redeemer, gives us the solution: "Come out of her, my people, lest you take part in her sins, lest you share in her plagues; [5] for her sins are heaped high as heaven, and God has remembered her iniquities" (18:4–5). For the Ephesians, "coming out" means ceasing to muzzle their witness in an effort to maintain their lifestyles.

REVELATION 19: THE MESSAGE TO EPHESUS

There are a number of things in the visions of Rev 19 that would have captured the attention of readers in Ephesus. First, although they may face the wrath of the beast if they heed Jesus' strong admonition to repent and embrace their call to be his ambassadors in Ephesus, in the end their blood and suffering will be avenged (19:2).

Second, they would be reminded that servants of God are those who fear *him* (19:5). There is no room to give in and let fear of the beast shape how they live, let alone continue to let their behavior be shaped by what they might lose if they are intentional witnesses for Jesus.

Third, they, like the rest of those who represent the bride of Christ, needed to make themselves ready (19:7). They needed to live in such a way now that they would be prepared to meet the Lord Jesus when he returns or when they enter his presence through their death. That readiness involves being properly attired for the wedding, and the only suitable attire is "the righteous deeds of the saints" (19:8). In other words, to be prepared to meet Jesus, the Bridegroom, they must be sure to repent and do the works they had done at first (2:5), making sure that their lives again came to reflect Jesus' priority of making disciples of all nations (Matt 28:19–20).

To drive home this last point, God has the angel remind John and the readers of Revelation that it is those who are invited to the wedding supper of the Lamb who are blessed (19:9), not those who shirk their duty to their Lord in order to guard what they have or save their skin. While the New Testament often emphasizes God's prerogatives in saving people and the amazing nature of his grace, throughout Revelation we find

7. Ibid., 16.

a strong focus on human responsibility. Yes, God will save his people; but he makes it clear to his people in great detail that they are not to be passive recipients of his salvation, but rather persevering and conquering saints who overcome not only by the blood of the Lamb but also by the word of their testimony.

SUMMARY: JESUS' MESSAGE TO CHRISTIANS IN EPHESUS

I hope that you are beginning to see just how interconnected the book of Revelation is from beginning to end. For the church in Ephesus, Rev 4–19 would have both further encouraged them in their hard work and perseverance and further admonished them in their neglect of that which is of first importance for all Christians: bearing witness to who Jesus is and what he has done to redeem sinners. The visions of these chapters would have spurred them on to continue enduring right to the end, knowing the inestimable value of the reward that will belong to overcomers. It would have also served to reignite their commitment to the testimony about Jesus, the eternal gospel, and highlighted the urgency of their situation. The need for repentance was urgent because judgment was imminent—judgment for those who had not yet heard the gospel, and judgment for those vested with the responsibility of taking the gospel to all nations, beginning with their neighbors. The fact that overcomers are faithful witnesses is driven home through reference to Jesus the faithful witness in 1:9, Antipas the faithful witness in 2:13, the martyrs under the altar in 6:9 who had lost their lives due to their testimony, the example of the two witnesses in Rev 11, the reference in 12:11 to the saints overcoming through the word of their testimony, the reference to the servants of God being those who hold to the testimony of Jesus in 19:10, and the reference to those who had died for their testimony for Jesus in 20:4. This consistent theme of Revelation, developed in these passages and others, is designed to arrest the attention of those in Ephesus, in particular, so that they will grapple with their urgent need to repent and embrace their first love once again.

4

Jesus' Message to the Church in Smyrna

And to the angel of the church in Smyrna write: The words of the first and the last, who died and came to life. (2:8)

As was the case with Ephesus, as we consider what Jesus had to say to Christians in Smyrna in the late first century, we need to recognize that we are dealing with a major city, not a backwoods hick town. Smyrna (modern Izmir) had a developed culture and all the comforts of the first-century world. It was a large port city of approximately 100,000 people and was located about forty miles north of Ephesus. "During the Roman period, Smyrna was a center for science and medicine . . . and renowned for its fine wine, its beautiful buildings and its wealth."[1] Indeed, "under the Roman government Smyrna enjoyed . . . an almost unbroken career of prosperity."[2] It was known for its beautiful streets that were carefully paved,[3] and for the groves of trees that made the suburbs a pleasant place to live.[4]

Smyrna had been the first city in Asia Minor to build a temple for the goddess Roma (in 193 BC). Later, a temple was built in honor of the Emperor Augustus, his wife Livia, and the Senate, and in AD 26 Smyrna became a "temple-keeper" making it an important center for the imperial cult.[5] For our purposes, it is important to recognize that Rome's willingness to grant this distinctive honor to Smyrna highlights

1. Aune, *Revelation 1–5*, 160.

2. Ramsay, *Letters*, 193.

3. Strabo, *Geogr.* 14.1.37.

4. Ramsay, *Letters*, 185–86. Ramsay also notes (185) that Smyrna, like Ephesus and Pergamum, claimed the title "First of Asia" (on its coins), sometimes more specifically claiming to be "First of Asia in beauty and size."

5. Hemer, *Letters*, 69. The temple was dedicated to Tiberius.

the close relationship between Smyrna and Rome, and the very positive sentiment that the inhabitants of Smyrna had toward the Roman Empire. Indeed, in the eyes of Rome, Smyrna was "the city of our most faithful and most ancient allies,"[6] known for its extraordinary loyalty to Rome.[7] This devotion to Rome was illustrated in the famous story of the citizens of Smyrna around AD 130 responding to the suffering of Roman soldiers during an unusually cold winter by stripping off their own garments and offering them to the soldiers.[8] Not surprisingly, the city's faithfulness to Rome appears to have been a fairly common motif in patriotic speeches.[9]

As we consider what Jesus has to say to the church in Smyrna, then, we need to recognize the challenge that Smyrna's historic loyalty to Rome would have posed for believers living in this city. Children would have been brought up with stories of the extreme commitment of their city to Rome, and Rome's generous benefaction that they enjoyed in return, thus creating a deep sense of loyalty to Rome from a young age. To be a citizen of Smyrna was to be loyal to Rome, plain and simple. Hemer maintains that "in view of the evidently liberal policy of Smyrna in granting its citizenship, there is no reason to doubt that converts to Christianity included many citizens, or that they continued to share the characteristic attitude of a citizen to his *polis*."[10] How, though, were Christians to respond when loyalty to Jesus came into conflict with loyalty to Rome? The answer to that question is a significant focus of Jesus' message to Christians in Smyrna.

To begin, Jesus once again handpicks a title that speaks a loud and clear message to this particular church: He introduces himself as "the first and the last, who died and came to life." The phrase "the first and the last" is used three times in the book of Revelation (1:17; 2:8; 22:13), always in reference to Jesus, and is a clear allusion to the divine title found twice in Isaiah (Isa 44:6 and 48:12). By using this distinctive title of Yahweh from the Old Testament Jesus is unabashedly portraying himself as God. Why, though, does he use this particular title here? "The first and the last" appears to point to Jesus' eternal nature. From everlasting to everlasting he is God, and there is no other. Within the context of Isaiah, the use of the phrase likely helps highlight the fact that God alone is worthy of devotion and loyalty. He is the one who created all things by the power of his word. Inherent in this title, then, are strong connotations of power and sovereignty. Jesus is in absolute control of all things, including the lives of his followers.

For Christians in Smyrna, this would have served as a vivid reminder to keep their relationship to Rome in perspective. Yes, their city was known for its intense devotion to Rome; but Christians are to be known—even Christians who live in

---

6. Cicero, *Phil.* 11.5.

7. *Chios quoque et Zmyrnaeos et Erythraeos pro singulari fide*; Livy, *History of Rome* 38.39.

8. Dmitriev, *City Government*, 249.

9. See Hemer, *Letters*, 71.

10. Ibid., 57.

Smyrna—for their intense devotion to Jesus. Roman emperors come and go, and so will the Roman Empire itself, as Revelation later makes clear, but Jesus is the first and the last, the Eternal One to whom all must give an account.

But there's more to Jesus' title; he also introduces himself in a way that carries an important implicit promise for the church in Smyrna: Jesus is the one "who died and came to life." While in popular thinking the death of Jesus is often highlighted as the culmination of the eternal plans of God, Scripture tends to place at least as much focus, if not more, on the resurrection. It is through the resurrection that God puts his stamp of approval on Jesus' perfect sacrifice, vindicates him before his enemies, and exalts him to the place of highest authority and honor. It is his resurrection that serves as the promise that we too will live again. Indeed, without his resurrection we are utterly lost; without it we are the most pitied people on the planet (1 Cor 15:19); without it our faith is useless and futile (1 Cor 15:14, 17), and we are still dead in our sins (1 Cor 15:17). But, Jesus *has* been raised from the dead! And the implicit contrast between appearance (dead is dead) and reality (he came to life again) will be used to set up similar contrasts in what follows. With Jesus' death it appeared that it was all over; the reality was another story altogether. And that reality has profound implications for what Christians in first-century Smyrna were facing.

It is quite possible that Jesus' choice of title was also driven by the Christians in Smyrna's particular context. Strabo tells us that after the ancient city of Smyrna was destroyed by the Lydians, the inhabitants lived for about four hundred years in villages.[11] The city was finally reestablished around 290 BC,[12] but centuries later it would have to be rebuilt again after being severely damaged by an earthquake. Through such events Smyrna came to have the local reputation of being like the mythical phoenix that rose from the ashes back to life.[13] If these ideas were woven into the fabric of Smyrnaeans' identity, as some scholars suggest, then Jesus' title would have created another rhetorical hotspot. He was the one who, on an individual and even more dramatic level than the city of Smyrna, had died and come back to life (Reading Instruction #4).

> *I know your tribulation and your poverty (but you are rich) and the slander of those who say that they are Jews and are not, but are a synagogue of Satan.* (2:9)

The paradox of Jesus' death and resurrection sets up the paradoxical statement in 2:9. Appearances can be deceiving. Outwardly, the Christians in Smyrna were oppressed and impoverished; but that was not the full picture. Jesus reminds them that they are, in fact, rich. There is nothing in this passage that offers any insight into why they were poor. They may simply have been converts from the lower classes, though most early Christian communities seem to have come from a variety of backgrounds. More likely, these Christians had already suffered economically because of their faith.

11. *Geogr.* 14.1.37.

12. Ramsay, *Letters*, 196–97; Hemer, *Letters*, 61.

13. Hemer, *Letters*, 63, citing Aristides.

Given their city's loyalty to Rome, the pressure to remain faithful to Rome and to the imperial cult may have been even more intense in Smyrna than elsewhere. Allowing treasonous refusals to worship the emperor in the city most renowned for its loyalty to Rome would be very bad politics indeed. Rome could not allow it; Smyrna could not allow it. Christians, then, needed to be rooted out and brought into conformity or destroyed before their loyalties to another King were allowed to corrupt the city known for being a friend of Rome.

Being a Christian and an inhabitant of Smyrna was thus likely a very dangerous combination. It was the path to poverty and suffering; and those who walked it could easily be discouraged by what they had lost or what they were missing out on. Jesus, though, reminds them that their true wealth and true life are found in him; and neither of those can ever be taken from them. His brief comment would have served to lift some in Smyrna from despair over all that they had lost by reminding them that they have "an inheritance that is imperishable, undefiled, and unfading, kept in heaven for . . . [those], ⁵who by God's power are being guarded through faith for a salvation ready to be revealed in the last time" (1 Pet 1:4–5).

In the second half of verse 9, we learn that some of the problems facing the beleaguered Christians in Smyrna stemmed from mistreatment by members of the Jewish population in town. The believers were being slandered by those who came from the "synagogue of Satan," the chief slanderer and accuser of the people of God (Rev 12:10; cf. Zech 3:1). The fact that the Christians in Smyrna were being bothered by Jews at all suggests that at least some, and perhaps many of them were ethnic Jews, since Jews were unlikely to be concerned with Gentiles converting to Christianity.[14] The fact that Paul's ministry, while he was based in Ephesus, reached "all the Jews and Greeks who lived in the province of Asia" (Acts 19:10) supports this view, though we cannot be certain of how many Jewish converts were among the Christians in Smyrna. Whatever the number, having Jews embracing Jesus as Messiah would have certainly created tension between local Jewish leaders and the church in Smyrna, likely leading to slander and persecution of various sorts. The Jews in Smyrna would certainly not want the attention of the authorities drawn to the synagogue because some of their members were now giving their allegiance to another King. This had to be stopped. Hemer argues that "probably, in Smyrna, the unbelieving Jews had become active in instigating persecution of the church or denouncing to the authorities those Jews who were also Christians,"[15] much like we find in both the Gospels (Matt 27:22–23; Mark 15:12–14; Luke 23:20–23; John 19:6–7, 14–15) and Acts (18:12–17). Jewish hatred for Christians became so intense in Smyrna that not many years later (likely on February 23, 155) the Jews of the city were so overcome by their rage that they gathered wood *on the Sabbath* to burn Polycarp.[16]

14. Ramsay, *Letters*, 198.

15. Hemer, *Letters*, 67; see also Aune, *Revelation 1–5*, 162.

16. *Mart. Poly.* 21.

Tension with the Jewish population in Smyrna would thus have been not only uncomfortable for Jewish Christians, but also extremely dangerous. While there was safety in being part of the Jewish community due to the legal rights afforded to Jews by Rome, those identified as followers of Jesus Christ forfeited those rights when they separated (or were forced to separate) from the synagogue.[17] Part of the temptation for Christians in Smyrna, then, would have been to go back to Judaism where they would be "safe." Jesus, though, makes it very clear that what appears to be a safe haven is in reality "a synagogue of Satan," a group of people who belong to the one who will be thrown into the lake of fire along with all his followers. Any perceived "safety" would be temporary at best.

Synagogues were places where Yahweh was supposed to be worshipped. So, as we encounter the shocking reference to "a synagogue of Satan," we need to be careful to ask what such a label might be intended to communicate. At its core, Jesus is using this label to make it clear that certain Jews in Smyrna were unwittingly acting as Satan's agents and doing his work, much like Saul of Tarsus had done decades earlier when his misguided zeal for God led him to attempt to destroy the church (Acts 8:3). For Jews in Smyrna who had fallen into this same trap, Jesus announces that they are in league with Satan. We cannot know for certain, but it is quite possible that some of the Jewish believers in Smyrna had been driven out of the synagogue and told that they were no longer God's people, much as had happened with the blind man who was healed in the Gospel of John (see 9:22, 34). Any temptation to give in to pressure and return to the synagogue would have been challenged by Jesus' revelation that their Jewish opponents represented "a synagogue of Satan." They were not true Jews, the kind of Jews Paul calls "circumcised in the heart" (Rom 2:28–29). They were deluded, and their delusion ran so deep that they had failed to recognize that they no longer belonged to God and were no longer doing his work.

Before moving on, we dare not fail to ask a key question: If superficially pious Jews could unwittingly become "a synagogue of Satan," is it possible for superficially pious Christians to unwittingly become "a church of Satan"? If so, what would it look like in our context? We may find some hints as we look at the messages to the following churches and the rest of Revelation.

> *Do not fear what you are about to suffer. Behold, the devil is about to throw some of you into prison, that you may be tested, and for ten days you will have tribulation. Be faithful unto death, and I will give you the crown of life.* (2:10)

To those living in Smyrna, Jesus' words would have been quite sobering, to say the least. He does not tell them, "Don't worry about what *could* happen to you because it won't!" Instead, Jesus tells them, "Yes, you are going to suffer, and it will involve prison and may even lead to death; but don't be afraid anyway." Jesus can tell them, "Do not fear what you are about to suffer," precisely because he is the first and the last.

---

17. Hemer, *Letters*, 68.

He can say it because he is the one who died and came to life again. He is in control of their lives and he is the resurrection and the life for those who follow him.

It is important to realize that Roman prisons were not like prisons in the West today.[18] You could not count on a warm bed, a flush toilet, three square meals a day, medical care, and regular opportunities for exercise. And you certainly could not work toward a college degree in prison. Prison was a place for prisoners awaiting trial, a place where the authorities tried to compel prisoners by torture to confess to a crime, and a place for those awaiting execution.[19] Prisons were places of despair, disease, and hunger, where all you had to look forward to was more misery and torture the next day and your eventual execution. It was into such a "hell hole" that the devil was going to put some of them. In telling them this, Jesus does not downplay the enormity of what Christians in Smyrna had on their near horizon. They were facing a major trial that would cost some of them their lives.

A famous letter that Pliny the Younger (AD 61–112) wrote to the Emperor Trajan (AD 98–117) while he was serving as the Roman governor of Bithynia-Pontus (AD 110–112) will help us to gain a clearer picture of what Christians in Smyrna may have been facing, though it was written nearly two decades after the time of Revelation. It is worth reading the entire letter:

> To the Emperor Trajan
>
> It is my invariable rule, Sir, to refer to you in all matters where I feel doubtful; for who is more capable of removing my scruples, or informing my ignorance? Having never been present at any trials concerning those who profess Christianity, I am unacquainted not only with the nature of their crimes, or the measure of their punishment, but how far it is proper to enter into an examination concerning them. Whether, therefore, any difference is usually made with respect to ages, or no distinction is to be observed between the young and the adult; whether repentance entitles them to a pardon; or if a man has been once a Christian, it avails nothing to desist from his error; whether the very profession of Christianity, unattended with any criminal act, or only the crimes themselves inherent in the profession are punishable; on all these points I am in great doubt. In the meanwhile, the method I have observed towards those who have been brought before me as Christians is this: I asked them whether they were Christians; if they admitted it, I repeated the question twice, and threatened them with punishment; if they persisted, I ordered them to be at once punished: for I was persuaded, whatever the nature of their opinions might be, a contumacious and inflexible obstinacy certainly deserved correction. There were others also brought before me possessed with the same infatuation, but being Roman citizens, I directed them to be sent to Rome.

18. See Rapske, *Book of Acts*, 195–225.

19. Cf. Ramsay, *Letters*, 199. "Prison" is thus likely a synecdoche for the whole range of suffering that included incarceration, torture, and execution.

But this crime spreading (as is usually the case) while it was actually under prosecution, several instances of the same nature occurred. An anonymous information was laid before me containing a charge against several persons, who upon examination denied they were Christians, or had ever been so. They repeated after me an invocation to the gods, and offered religious rites with wine and incense before your statue (which for that purpose I had ordered to be brought, together with those of the gods), and even reviled the name of Christ: whereas there is no forcing, it is said, those who are really Christians into any of these compliances: I thought it proper, therefore, to discharge them. Some among those who were accused by a witness in person at first confessed themselves Christians, but immediately after denied it; the rest owned indeed that they had been of that number formerly, but had now (some above three, others more, and a few above twenty years ago) renounced that error. They all worshipped your statue and the images of the gods, uttering imprecations at the same time against the name of Christ. They affirmed the whole of their guilt, or their error, was, that they met on a stated day before it was light, and addressed a form of prayer to Christ, as to a divinity, binding themselves by a solemn oath, not for the purposes of any wicked design, but never to commit any fraud, theft, or adultery, never to falsify their word, nor deny a trust when they should be called upon to deliver it up; after which it was their custom to separate, and then reassemble, to eat in common a harmless meal. From this custom, however, they desisted after the publication of my edict, by which, according to your commands, I forbade the meeting of any assemblies. After receiving this account, I judged it so much the more necessary to endeavor to extort the real truth, by putting two female slaves to the torture, who were said to officiate in their religious rites: but all I could discover was evidence of an absurd and extravagant superstition. I deemed it expedient, therefore, to adjourn all further proceedings, in order to consult you. For it appears to be a matter highly deserving your consideration, more especially as great numbers must be involved in the danger of these prosecutions, which have already extended, and are still likely to extend, to persons of all ranks and ages, and even of both sexes. In fact, this contagious superstition is not confined to the cities only, but has spread its infection among the neighbouring villages and country. Nevertheless, it still seems possible to restrain its progress. The temples, at least, which were once almost deserted, begin now to be frequented; and the sacred rites, after a long intermission, are again revived; while there is a general demand for the victims, which till lately found very few purchasers. From all this it is easy to conjecture what numbers might be reclaimed if a general pardon were granted to those who shall repent of their error.[20]

Several things are important in this letter. First, Christians are punished simply for being Christians. Giving your allegiance to Jesus was a crime in the Roman Empire of

20. Pliny the Younger, *Ep.* 10.96.

that day. Second, Christians could be anonymously reported by their neighbors and then forced to either affirm or deny their allegiance to Jesus. Third, denying allegiance to Jesus involved repeating an invocation to the Roman gods, worshiping idols, and worshiping before Caesar's statue. Some of those who capitulated also slandered the name of Christ. Fourth, true Christians were known to be willing to pay the ultimate price for their faith rather than deny Jesus. Fifth, there were apparently some Christians who had renounced their faith, some as early as shortly prior to the writing of Revelation ("a few above twenty years ago"). Sixth, at least under Pliny's government Christians were forbidden to gather together in groups for worship. Seventh, Christians, including women, were tortured for their faith. Finally, despite all of these forms of persecution Christianity was spreading widely to all kinds of people in all kinds of places. When Jesus warns Christians in Smyrna that suffering, prison, and death are coming, then, they likely would have had a frame of reference through stories they had heard of what was happening to Christians elsewhere. This was a frightening time and place to be a follower of Jesus.

Two features of Jesus' message in 2:10, however, offer hope. First, the persecution will only last for "ten days." Once again, we almost certainly have a symbolic use of a number (Reading Instruction #5). Although some point to Domitian's persecution of Christians, which is said to have lasted ten years (AD 81–91), and point out that "day" is often used for "year" in prophetic passages in the Old Testament, the fact that Revelation was likely written after this period makes it unlikely. More likely is the view that "ten days" symbolizes an indefinite but short period of time—more than a day, less than a month. The brief nature of the period is supported both by the context and by the reference to this period of time in Dan 1:12–13.[21] By referring to the length of their coming persecution, Jesus is thus reminding them that yes they will suffer, but the suffering will be short-lived.[22] The fact that it will be short-lived, however, does not mean that they can expect to get back to life as usual after a short period of suffering. On the contrary, the end point of their suffering may well be the end of life itself. This is implied by the fact that Jesus calls on them to "Be faithful unto death."

When we read the message to this church with our modern notion of prisons in mind, we tend to assume that some will be thrown into prison—where they will be treated humanely—and there is a chance that some of that group may end up being executed. Thus, we read Jesus' exhortation as, "be faithful *even if you happen* to face

---

21. This does not mean that the original readers would have recognized a reference to Daniel here. The passage in Daniel simply helps us establish the probability that "ten days" would have been understood as a brief period of testing.

22. It is also possible that it is the number "ten" rather than the phrase "ten days" that is being used in a non-literal manner here. Ten tends to symbolize completeness. "Ten days" would then be a reference to the full number of days that God had ordained. This reading would certainly be consistent with the strong emphasis on God's sovereign control of things throughout Revelation. The context, however, seems to point to an effort by Jesus to soften the blow through reference to a limited period of time.

the ultimate threat, death." In reality, Jesus is promising that some will be imprisoned, and given the nature of Roman imprisonment it is likely that many of those who are imprisoned will face death.[23] Furthermore, all those who are thrown into prison will suffer in profound ways that any normal human would be eager to avoid. They would not just be losing their freedom; they would be subjected to all sorts of cruel and unusual punishment.

So, how are they to "not fear what [they] are about to suffer" and remain faithful in such dire circumstances? How can they stand firm in the face of torture and death? To answer these obvious questions, Jesus draws their attention to the fact that death is not the end of the story for his followers, a point that was first introduced in 1:5 and has already been reemphasized in 1:18, earlier passages that would no doubt have particularly caught the attention of believers in Smyrna. The reward for those who are faithful even to the point of death will be a "crown of life." The obvious paradox helps make Jesus' promise that much more striking: Death will bring a reward of life. Therefore, it is not something that you need fear.

Just as Jesus used the language of being "(re)moved" and the tree (of life) imagery to create rhetorical hotspots by playing off of local realities in Ephesus, so here the use of "crown of life" may well have served as a particularly powerful way of capturing the attention of the church in Smyrna (Reading Instruction #4). Ramsay points out that the city was built on Mount Pagus with beautiful buildings on its rounded top and on its sides, giving it the appearance of a crowned head and leading to the expression "the crown of Smyrna."[24] He goes on to point to Aristides (fifth cent. BC) who compared Smyrna to "the crown of Ariadne shining in the heavenly constellation" at one point, and specifically refers to Smyrna as the crown of Ionia elsewhere.[25] The crown (or wreath) motif appears regularly in pre-Imperial coins from Smyrna, even appearing three times on the same coin in numerous cases.[26] By referring to the reward of life using "crown" language, then, Jesus creates a rhetorical hotspot for this particular church that would have helped the promise to resonate all the more.

> He who has an ear, let him hear what the Spirit says to the churches. The one who conquers will not be hurt by the second death. (2:11)

Along with the same exhortation to pay careful attention to what has been said and to respond accordingly comes a promise expressed in very emphatic terms (with the double negative οὐ μὴ, *ou mē*): "The one who overcomes will *absolutely not* be hurt by the second death." The nature of this second death will not be fleshed out until the

---

23. Ramsay, *Letters*, 200. The likelihood of death flows out of an understanding of the function of prisons in the first-century Roman world, rather than from the use of the preposition ἄχρι (*achri*) rather than ἕως (*heōs*); contra Hemer, *Letters*, 71.

24. Ramsay, *Letters*, 186. Hemer (*Letters*, 59) notes that the beauty of Smyrna was found in its buildings and their careful arrangement, rather than in its natural surroundings.

25. Ramsay, *Letters*, 186–87.

26. Hemer, *Letters*, 59–60.

end of Revelation. For now, it is sufficient to note that the Jews of Smyrna who were persecuting the believers may well have harangued them with the threat that they would face God's judgment in the end, since they were not the people of God. If so, this promise would have served as a powerful reminder that quite the opposite was true. One should fear the second death, not the first death. Or, in the words of Jesus in Luke 12:4–5: "I tell you, my friends, do not fear those who kill the body, and after that have nothing more that they can do. [5]But I will warn you whom to fear: fear him who, after he has killed, has authority to cast into hell. Yes, I tell you, fear him!"

The promise, however, is directed to those who overcome, not to all professing followers of Jesus. For Christians living in Smyrna, what would it mean to overcome? Within the context of this letter, overcoming seems to relate to the need to stand firm in the faith in the face of persecution, even to the point of death. Despite the fact that they had apparently remained true to him—unlike every other church except the church in Philadelphia they are not rebuked in any way—Jesus tells them that suffering is coming, and that suffering may culminate in their lives being violently wrenched from them; but even this does not give them license to shrink back. Those who follow him, deny themselves and take up their cross. Walking in the footsteps of Jesus will often involve walking the *Via Dolorosa*. The irony, of course, is that the road of suffering culminates in both death and a crown of life.

SMYRNA: PROFILE OF A CHURCH

Once again, we conclude the chapter by briefly highlighting the key characteristics of the church in Smyrna. This is a suffering church. They had suffered the loss of possessions and livelihood (thus their "poverty") and they had suffered persecution ("tribulation"). The primary instigators of their pain and suffering were Jewish opponents in their city. Jesus reveals to them that their suffering is actually about to get worse. They are on the verge of being thrown into prison. This intensification of their suffering will not last long ("ten days"), but it may well end in their death. So, with the revelation comes an exhortation ("be faithful unto death") and two promises: "I will give you the crown of life" and you "will not be hurt by the second death."

The message to Smyrna is thus the most ominous of the seven messages. These apparently faithful and devoted believers are informed of intense suffering on their near horizon. Jesus' words were no doubt very sobering for the original readers in Smyrna. What about us? How would we respond if we had been faithfully following Jesus, to the point that he had nothing against us, and when he chooses to speak to us he reveals that his plan is for us to be thrown into prison very soon where some or many of us will face death. Talk about God having "a wonderful plan" for our lives! In a culture obsessed with comfort and with avoiding suffering, these are hard words to swallow. After all, doesn't Jesus want us to be happy? Doesn't Jesus bless those who are faithful to him? Such questions reveal the tendency in modern hearts to recreate

Jesus in our own image, to embrace a warped picture of him that implies that he exists for us rather than vice versa. The Bible teaches that Jesus is far more concerned with our holiness than our happiness. He is far more concerned with our faithfulness than our freedom. God's chief goal in our lives is to conform us to the image of his Son, "who, though he was in the form of God, did not count equality with God a thing to be grasped, ⁷but emptied himself, by taking the form of a servant, being born in the likeness of men. ⁸And being found in human form, he humbled himself by becoming obedient to the point of death, even death on a cross" (Phil 2:6–8). How did Jesus do it? Jesus, "for the joy that was set before him endured the cross, despising the shame, and is seated at the right hand of the throne of God" (Heb 12:2). He recognized that this life is not all there is, and he focused on the reward to come. This is precisely what Jesus is calling his followers in Smryna to do. He calls them to submit to his purposes for their life (which may include their death). He calls them to trust him and obey him, regardless of how hard things appear, regardless of how difficult life gets. We got a hint of this with the message to the church of Ephesus, but it comes through loud and clear here: Following Jesus is not for wimps! Being his disciple is serious business; it may well cost you your life.

5

Jesus' Message to the Church in Smyrna
The Rest of the Story

JESUS MAY HAVE ADDRESSED only four short verses to the impoverished Christians in Smyrna in 2:8–11, but the rest of Revelation would have had much to say to them as well. In this chapter we will take a different approach than what we did with Ephesus. Rather than walking through each of the subsequent chapters of Revelation and asking what that chapter would have said to the church in Smyrna, we will instead walk through the four verses of the message to Smyrna again and ask how the rest of Revelation would have fleshed out and driven home the points of each verse. The purpose of this alternative approach is simply to illustrate for readers an alternative way of reading Revelation in light of what we are learning. The approach modeled with Ephesus involves carefully developing a picture of the church through studying the message Jesus sent it and what can be known about the church from other sources, and then asking how each subsequent chapter of Revelation would have spoken to that church. The approach modeled here involves carefully studying the rest of Revelation and then rereading the message to Smyrna in light of everything that follows. Both approaches are fruitful, and the more one reads and internalizes the entire book of Revelation, the more one will naturally read the messages to the seven churches in light of what follows.

Before we look at that question, however, we should also ask how the other six messages would have spoken to the church in Smyrna. If any church would have been tempted to seek to lower their profile in order to avoid the coming persecution, it would have been the church in Smyrna. The message to the church in Ephesus, however, makes it clear that to abandon their overt witness to their city would inevitably result in Jesus having something against them. The message to Ephesus, therefore, served as a reminder that having their city against them, and having the devil against them, was vastly preferable to having the King of kings and Lord of lords who was coming on a white horse to judge the world (Rev 19:11–21) against them. The only reasonable response is to persevere as faithful followers of Jesus despite what is coming.

The message to the church in Pergamum would have reminded Christians in Smyrna that their situation was not unique. There were actually some Christians who were living in Satan's headquarters on earth, and Jesus nevertheless expected them to stand firm in the faith. Jesus' message to the church in Pergamum would have helped remove any sense of isolation that Christians in Smyrna would have felt. They were not alone in their struggle against the evil one, and just as Jesus called those living in Satan's city to persevere in the faith, so he was calling them to stand firm even unto death.

Finally, Jesus' message to the church in Philadelphia would have been a great encouragement to Christians in Smyrna. They, like the Christians in Smyrna, had little power, but they had not abandoned their faith. Jesus' commendation to the Philadelphian Christians would have reminded the church in Smyrna what they had to do in the coming trial: "yet you have kept my word and have not denied my name" (3:8). The temptation to deny Christ would be great, but if those with "little power" could persevere and keep Jesus' word, so could they.

How, then, would the remainder of Revelation have strengthened and driven home the message to the church in Smyrna in 2:8–11? As we will see, the careful divine craftsmanship of Revelation is once again readily evident as the final nineteen chapters address the unique situation of Christians in Smyrna in the late first century, and in so doing address Christians today as well.

> And to the angel of the church in Smyrna write: The words of the first and the last, who died and came to life. (2:8)

Jesus writes to the Christians in Smyrna as "the first and the last, who died and came to life." As we have seen, the titles Jesus uses to describe himself are specifically chosen for each church as an important part of his message to that church. There is a repeated emphasis in Revelation on the fact that Jesus and the Father are the first and the last (1:17; 2:8; 22:13), the Alpha and the Omega (1:8; 21:6; 22:13), the beginning and the end (21:6; 22:13); and it is no coincidence that these titles are used as bookends, at both the beginning and end of Revelation. They effectively frame all that is contained in these pages with the reality of the sovereignty of the Eternal One who is in absolute control of history from beginning to end. This truth would have been particularly important for Christians who were about to face the rage of the devil firsthand. The theme of God's sovereignty is vividly driven home in the imagery and symbolism of Rev 4–5, as the first thing Jesus does after addressing messages to each of the seven churches in Asia Minor is to give them a good reality check. As he pulls back the curtains on the heavenly realm, they would have looked with mouths agape at what was currently happening at the center of all things. This would have been particularly important for Christians in Smyrna. They had no doubt heard of the awesome throne room in Rome from which the Roman Emperor exercised his power. Now, they are given a glimpse of true power, true authority, true majesty. All that follows in Jesus' message to them must be understood and responded to in light of the heavenly scene that Jesus reveals in these chapters.

In Rev 4–5, all attention is directed at the One who is seated on the throne and the Lamb. The word for "throne" occurs nineteen times in these two chapters alone. It is used a total of forty-seven times in the book of Revelation, compared to fifteen times in all the rest of the New Testament combined. Revelation 4–5, then, along with the rest of the book, were clearly intended to remind God's people that it is God who is seated on the throne; he is reigning supreme; he is in control. And as fearsome as Caesar may seem, with his apparently irresistible power, such power is nothing compared to the power and authority of the One enthroned in heaven. The message to the church in Smyrna is plain: As they face the even greater challenges ahead, to overcome they must remember that *God alone is in control of their fate.* Like Job, they were being attacked by the evil one, perhaps preeminently through the fierce opposition of Jewish leaders in the city, but they must remember that the evil one can only act when given permission to do so by the true Sovereign of the universe (Job 2:6).

Jesus, however, is not only the first and the last, he is also the one "who died and came to life" (2:8). Jesus is going to tell Christians in Smyrna that they are about to face suffering and death (2:10), but before he does that he graciously reminds them that he has been there and done that. What's more, just as death was not the end for him, neither will it be the end for them. On the contrary, death will usher in something infinitely better, with the story they are now living being merely a prelude to what is to come.

Christians in Smyrna would have seen this implicit promise supported in various ways as they listened to the rest of Revelation. First, they would have encountered the Lamb who had been slain in 5:6 and been reminded that Jesus' death was neither a mistake—it was the means by which he redeemed a vast people for himself (5:9–10)— nor was it the end. Jesus is now worshiped by the host of heaven; his shame has been turned to the highest of honors (5:11–14). Up until now, Christians in Smyrna had only heard that they must be among those who overcome. Now they are shown that Jesus himself has overcome, and he has done it through his death and resurrection. Perhaps most vivid, though, would have been the account of the two witnesses in Rev 11. These two wonder-working ambassadors of Christ would ultimately be killed for their testimony (11:7) and humiliated in their deaths (11:8–10), like some in Smyrna, but they would then be gloriously raised to life (11:11) and welcomed into the presence of God (11:12). Death and rejection by this world is thus set in the larger context of a promised resurrection and eternal life in God's presence.

The encouragement to press on in the face of terrifying circumstances is driven home in the final portion of Rev 11. The chapter concludes with an important vision-ary scene that redirects attention back to where it belongs: to the One who is seated on the throne. Loud voices in heaven remind Christians in Smyrna that God is about to institute his absolute reign in this world. His reign will not be short-lived like that of a Roman emperor; the Lord Jesus will reign forever and ever (11:15). To bow to the pressure of a ruler whose authority is temporary at best is to forget the One who truly reigns and whose kingdom will have no end. It is to forget the One who alone is worthy of absolute worship and devotion (11:16–17), the One to whom everyone must ultimately give an account (11:18). It is to forget that those who fear the name of the Lord will be rewarded (11:18), while those who fear men and follow the ways of this world will face judgment.

> *I know your tribulation and your poverty (but you are rich) and the slander of*
> *those who say that they are Jews and are not, but are a synagogue of Satan.* (2:9)

In the brief words in the first part of this verse, Jesus again helps those in Smyrna to put their current situation in context. Yes, they are suffering and poor. After all, those who refuse to give their allegiance to the beast can expect to suffer financially. They will ultimately not be able to buy or sell like their non-Christian neighbors (13:17). They will be squeezed out of the economy. The believers in Smyrna had already begun to experience this on a smaller scale and were thus living in poverty. But Jesus reminds them that this is not the full picture. In reality, they are the richest people in their city! These riches, of course, are fleshed out in all sorts of ways in the book of Revelation, but most fully in Rev 21–22, which we will look at later.

When God pulled back the curtain on the world beyond their natural senses (Rev 4:1) and gave them a glimpse of things as they are in heaven, he was reminding Christians in Smyrna just how rich they really are. Look at the majesty, grandeur, and beauty of the triune God described in Rev 4 and 5. How magnificent he is! No one can compare to him. No one else is worthy of worship. And this is the one to whom *they* belong! Are they then poor? Certainly not! Christians in Smyrna, as faithful followers of Jesus Christ, were richer than anyone on earth could ever be. They were children of the King; and all of his resources were their inheritance.

Jesus thus calls on the Christians in Smyrna to reassess their status. The world may view them as poor, as pitiful folk who are missing out on the "good things of life" because of their misguided piety and devotion to God. But Jesus assures them that it is the world that is misguided. And he does this not only by showing them what true wealth is, but also by describing the ultimate fate of the rich and famous. Being a king or a general, being rich or mighty, being famous or influential will ultimately profit nothing when the wrath of the Lamb is poured out (see Rev 6:15–17). In that moment, those who are most highly esteemed in this world will recognize that their riches were not only fleeting but were also glaring evidence of a poverty of spirit that has now left them utterly helpless before the One to whom they must give an account. Their only recourse is to cry out for their own destruction in the hope that their death might hide them from the wrath that they are due, wrath that extends far beyond physical death.

This point is further driven home in Rev 18 where the "excessive luxuries" (18:3, NIV) of this world that entice many are destroyed, and "the kings of the earth, who committed sexual immorality and lived in luxury with her, will weep and wail over her when they see the smoke of her burning" (18:9). Those who trust in the riches of this world will first see that wealth evaporate and then face the lake of fire; but whoever loses his life for Jesus and the gospel will save it (Mark 8:35), and the one who hates his life in this world will keep it for eternal life. Jesus thus calls believers in Smyrna to guard against letting "the cares of the world and the deceitfulness of riches and the desires for other things enter in and choke the word" (Mark 4:19). Instead, they need to live now in light of a larger reality where they are truly rich and will reign with Jesus.

Apparently, followers of Jesus living in Smyrna were not only suffering under the burden of poverty, but were also the target of verbal abuse (2:9b). No one enjoys being slandered, and being slandered by the local religious leaders, who had likely formerly been the trusted leaders of the Jewish followers of Jesus in Smyrna, would be particularly difficult for those doing their best to follow God. It would be difficult for them not to question their status. "Maybe we're just a bunch of misguided, worthless followers of a crucified leader, like we're being told. Maybe we have given up our opportunity to be true members of the people of God and a part of the local synagogue where he is worshiped. Maybe we've got it wrong after all." Jesus' response, though, makes it clear that they have actually been getting it quite right. "These Jews who have been haranguing you," he reminds them, "are only masquerading as my people. They are actually imposters who have been deluded into thinking that they are serving God and his purposes when in fact they are serving the purposes of Satan."

Jesus goes on to reinforce this message in a variety of ways throughout Revelation. One of the most important ways is introduced in Rev 1 and reiterated in Rev 5 and 11. The members of the "synagogue of Satan" were telling Christians in Smyrna that they were not the true people of God. Both John and Jesus respond by reminding them just who they are. John reminds them that Jesus has "made us a kingdom, priests to his God and Father" (1:6)! They were not members of a dusty little synagogue that was actually serving Satan. They were citizens of the kingdom of heaven! They served the true and living God and related to him as their Father. In case they did not catch this important truth, it is reiterated by the twenty-four elders in 5:10 ("you have made them a kingdom and priests to our God"), who go on to remind them that "they shall reign on the earth" (5:10). Ultimately, then, no one will be able to view them as downtrodden, impoverished outcasts. For the day is coming—and Jesus has told them that it is coming soon—when they will enter into their inheritance and reign with the King of kings and Lord of lords! When the seventh angel sounds his trumpet, and loud voices in heaven declare, "The kingdom of the world has become the kingdom of our Lord and of his Christ, and he shall reign forever and ever" (11:15), they will reign with him. A day is soon coming when the twenty-four elders, who are seated on their thrones before God, will fall on their faces and worship God, saying:

> We give thanks to you, Lord God Almighty, who is and who was, for you have taken your great power and begun to reign. [18]The nations raged, but your wrath came, and the time for the dead to be judged, and for rewarding your servants, the prophets and saints, and those who fear your name, both small and great, and for destroying the destroyers of the earth. (11:17–18)

Yes, the nations are angry and fight against God and his people; but God's wrath is coming. The time for judging the dead is coming; and no one will ultimately get away with anything. God is well aware of every action and every thought of every person who has ever lived; and all will be judged "according to what they had done" (20:12). Moreover, the time for rewarding the servants of God is also coming (11:18). So, Christians in Smyrna need to stand firm in the midst of slander by those who only claim to be servants of God. The end is sure, both for the true people of God and for those masquerading as servants of God.

For Christians in Smyrna suffering under attacks from Jewish opponents—especially those Christians who had come out of the synagogue because of their faith in Jesus—the reference to the Ark of the Covenant in 11:19 would have brought encouragement: "Then God's temple in heaven was opened, and the ark of his covenant was seen within his temple." The Ark was off-limits to virtually all Jews. It was not something they were typically allowed to see, let alone touch. Its placement in the Holy of Holies reinforced the sense of distance between God and them. Those in the synagogue of Smyrna would have placed a high value on the Ark of the Covenant, which had been lost following the destruction of the temple a couple of decades earlier; but what they could *never* do—lay their eyes on this important symbol of God's covenant presence among his people—followers of Jesus are *invited* to do in Revelation. Barriers between God and man have been stripped away by the blood of Jesus Christ; and followers of Jesus currently possess something that those of the synagogue of Satan will never have: direct access to God.

To further encourage them, Jesus reminds the suffering Christians in Smyrna that they are not alone in being slandered. First they read that fellow Christians in Philadelphia are facing the same opponents (3:9). Then they read in 13:5–6 that Satanic opposition is far broader than their city and Philadelphia, or even Asia Minor; and they were not the only ones who would be slandered. God himself puts up with the slander of his own name . . . for a time (13:5–6). In fact, even when those who are facing God's judgment obstinately refuse to repent (9:20–21) and choose to curse God's name instead (16:9, 11), he does not immediately strike them down as he could. He knows their time is coming; meanwhile he astoundingly still gives them an opportunity to repent. These passages would have reinforced both the reality that suffering is to be expected, and also the reality, introduced in 2:10, that slander and suffering will only be for a time ("ten days"). Christians should not be surprised when they are slandered. After all, Jesus had already warned, as the Apostle John himself recorded: "If they persecuted me, they also will persecute you" (John 15:20). They should, then, count themselves blessed and rejoice that they share God's slander (see Matt 5:11–12). They should follow the example of the apostles, who had faced the same harsh treatment from "the synagogue of Satan" (see Acts 5:41).

Jesus, of course, also reminds believers at Smyrna of the judgment that is coming upon the enemies of God. One day soon, there will be none who stand in defiance against God Almighty or who presume to slander his people. None will be left to persecute Jesus by persecuting his people (see Acts 9:6). One day soon, the vision recorded in Rev 5:13 will be a reality: "And I heard every creature in heaven and on earth and under the earth and in the sea, and all that is in them, saying, 'To him who sits on the throne and to the Lamb be blessing and honor and glory and might forever and ever!'" As the seal judgments (6:1–17), the trumpet judgments (8:6—9:21), and the bowl judgments (16:1–21) make infinitely clear, the enemies of God are destined for imminent and ultimate destruction.

In contrast, though the people of God suffer now under the oppressive hand of the evil one, they are marked with the seal of God and are protected from his wrath that will be poured out on all mankind (7:3–4; 9:4). How, though, do we get from the sealing of the 144,000 from the tribes of Israel to *Christians in Smyrna* being protected from God's wrath? There are several things that point to the 144,000 representing both Jewish and Gentile followers of Jesus—preeminently those Jewish and Gentile Christians who will face the wrath of the beast when he is revealed, but by application all Christians throughout history.

That Jewish believers are in view is obvious; after all, Jesus spells out a detailed list of the "144,000, sealed from every tribe of the sons of Israel" (7:4) in 7:5–8. That seems to settle things; these must be ethnic Jews who are sealed. But Jesus has done something that would not have been missed by Christians in Asia Minor. He has intentionally altered the list of tribes, much like Matthew alters the genealogy of Jesus at the beginning of his gospel, in order to signal to the reader that he intends to communicate something more than first meets the eye. The fact that he refers to "every tribe of the sons of Israel" and then does *not* include every tribe in his list serves as a clear literary gesture to the reader that would have been no less obvious than the explicit statement in 13:18: "This calls for wisdom: let the one who has understanding calculate the number of the beast."

In the listing of the tribes making up the 144,000 two things are vitally important: (1) which tribes are excluded; and (2) which tribes are included. The two tribes that are excluded are Dan and Ephraim. This is not coincidental. When the biblical writers described wicked kings in the Old Testament, they often wrote that such kings walked in the way of Jeroboam son of Nebat. What was Jeroboam's sin? It was leading the Israelites into idolatry (see 1 Kgs 12:25–33). And where did Jeroboam set up the detestable idols? In Bethel and Dan (1 Kgs 12:29). The city of Bethel was originally located in the tribe of Benjamin's territory, but by Jeroboam's time it had been incorporated into Ephraim and came to be associated with that tribe. "Ephraim" also became an alternative designation for the northern kingdom of Israel, which plunged head first into conforming to the ways of the nations around them (assimilation).

All of this suggests that as Jesus provides a vivid picture of who will be sealed from the wrath of God, he makes it clear that simply bearing the right ethnicity (Jewish) will not be sufficient. He has already characterized some Jews as "a synagogue of Satan" (2:9; 3:9), ethnic Jews who only claim to be "real" Jews, but are liars (3:9). Here in Rev 7, we have a picture of *real* Jews being sealed by God. Those Jews who have been cut off (Rom 11:13–24), on the other hand, those who have assimilated to the nations around them, will not be sealed. To think that God would seal the synagogue of Satan is absurd. Equally absurd is the notion that ethnic Jews are sealed from God's wrath, but Gentile Christians are not. How would that have encouraged the believers in Smyrna and the rest of Asia Minor to whom Revelation was addressed?

That brings us to the question of why Jesus includes the tribes that he does in the listing of the 144,000. With Dan and Ephraim being intentionally left out, in order to have twelve tribes some tribes needed to be added. In dividing the land of Israel among the tribes of Israel, recall that the tribe of Levi was not given a land inheritance; God himself was to be their inheritance (see Num 18:20–24). The land was still divided into twelve tribal allotments, however, with the tribe of Joseph being split into two half-tribes (Ephraim and Manasseh). In Rev 7 Jesus both includes the tribe of Levi and also lists Joseph as a distinct tribe in order to fill the gap left by Dan and Ephraim. By including Levi, Jesus adds a priestly component to those who are sealed. Jesus had already told the Christians in Asia Minor that he has "made us a kingdom, priests to his God and Father" (1:6). This is reiterated by the four living creatures and twenty-four elders in 5:10. In the broader context of what has preceded, then, we recognize that when Jesus includes the priestly tribe of Levi in the 144,000, he has already made it clear that the priests of God now come from every tribe, language, people, and nation. In other words, the "Israel of God" (note that this expression in Gal 6:16 clearly refers to all believers regardless of ethnicity) now *excludes* those ethnic Jews who have been cut off (Rom 11:17) because of unbelief (Rom 11:20) and *includes* those ethnic Gentiles who have been grafted into the Jewish tree (Rom 11:19). This should not surprise us at this point in Revelation since Jesus had already begun to redefine what it means to be a "Jew" in Rev 2–3, and he will later portray all of his followers as Israel's offspring (12:17).

Let's return for a minute to the imagery that Paul uses in Rom 11 to describe the gathering in of Gentiles into the nation of Israel. There we see a recognition that many ethnic Jews had been cut off because of unbelief, effectively making room for many ethnic Gentiles to be grafted in. But Paul also makes it very clear in Rom 11:23–24 that God is not yet finished with ethnic Jews. And he goes on to say that we should expect a mass turning of ethnic Jews to Christ at some point before the creation of the new heavens and the new earth (see Rom 11:25–26). This very well may take place through the preaching of the two witnesses described in Rev 11, since the location of their preaching is Jerusalem, at least at the end of their ministry (11:8). The success of their mission to Israel may be alluded to in the final words of 11:13.

The listing of the 144,000 in staunchly Jewish terms, but with a significant twist, then, is intended to point to the protection of ethnic Israel (ultimately recognizing and embracing the Lord Jesus as their Messiah en masse) *and* Gentile followers of Jesus from the wrath of God during this period of great tribulation. The fact that including Joseph as well as Manasseh in the listing does not make sense serves to urge the reader to recognize that "Israel" is being redefined. That some have unexpectedly been excluded from Israel and some have unexpectedly been included reinforces the overall message of Revelation and the message to the church in Smyrna. They are not rejected by God, as the synagogue of Satan claims; they are sealed by him; they belong to him. Beyond that, while the inclusion of Levi highlights the priestly function of the 144,000 and stands in stark contrast to the idolatry that characterized Dan and Ephraim, the inclusion of Joseph is likely meant to provide a vivid contrast between one who steadfastly followed God even while living and suffering unjustly in a foreign land (see Gen 37, 39–50) and those who choose to assimilate to the culture around them.

This reading of the 144,000—including both Jewish and Gentile followers of Jesus among those sealed—is supported by perhaps the most obvious indicator of the identity of the 144,000. This elite group is described in 7:3 as "the servants of our God." Once again, we have an important connection to what has come earlier. In the very first verse of Revelation we are told to whom the book is addressed. Later the addressees will be further specified as the members of the seven churches of Asia Minor, but in 1:1 they are simply called "his servants." It is very natural then to associate the very ones addressed in Revelation with the 144,000 who are sealed in Rev 7.[1] This interpretation is reinforced by the next appearance of the 144,000 in 14:2–3. Two details are important there—the 144,000 are playing harps, and they are singing a new song. These details come up again in 15:2–3 where the parallels in language suggest that we are reading a description of the same group of people in Rev 14 and 15. In Rev 14, the group is identified as the 144,000 and they are singing a new song that only they know accompanied by harps, or playing the harps themselves. In 15:2, the singers/harpists are also identified as "those who had conquered the beast." Their victory is defined as not having taken the mark of the beast. This time, though, the nature of the new song

---

1. This does not mean that the 144,000 does not ultimately have a more specific referent. For readers in first-century Asia Minor those sealed from the coming wrath of God would have included them, as it includes all Christians at all times. Ultimately, however, the 144,000 specifically refers to all Jewish and Gentile Christians who are alive at the time of the beast's reign of terror.

is specified; it is "the song of Moses, the servant of God, and the song of the Lamb" (15:3). The "song of Moses" draws our attention back to Exod 15, which celebrated God's mighty deliverance of Israel from Egypt; and indeed "singing a new song" is associated with a new mighty deliverance throughout Scripture. So, in Rev 14–15, the 144,000 are singing a song of praise to God for delivering them. This is why "No one could learn that song except the 144,000" (14:3). For only they have experienced God's amazing redemption from the beast. What is important here for our purposes is the nature of the new song that is sung by the 144,000: it is the song of Moses and the song of the Lamb. It is both a song associated with ethnic Israel and a song associated with all those who have been redeemed by the blood of the Lamb. It is a song sung by the Israel of God, which includes believing Jews and believing Gentiles who have been added to Israel.

Why, though, does Jesus use the number 144,000? This number is made up of three components: 12 x 12 x 1000. Given how many tribes made up Israel, the number twelve naturally came to symbolize the people of God (Reading Instruction #5).[2] The fact that there are two twelves likely represents the combination of the twelve tribes of Israel (old covenant people of God) with the twelve apostles (new covenant people of God). In other words the number 144,000 stands for the full people of God in which a great mass of Gentiles from every ethnic group has been incorporated into Israel. By multiplying the two twelves by 1000, Jesus is simply referring to the great multitude of the people of God. And although the 144,000 may be viewed as the full people of God from every century, the focus in Revelation is more specifically on the full number of the people of God who go through the great tribulation and do not compromise their allegiance to Jesus.

As we conclude our discussion of the 144,000, for now, we need to recognize that all of this strongly suggests that when Christians at Smyrna heard about the sealing of this group (7:3–4), they would have breathed a sigh of relief knowing that although they would face the wrath of the devil, all the true people of God are under his watchful and all-powerful care. The outpouring of his wrath, which is infinitely worse than anything Christians will ever face, will not touch them. They belong to God, and he takes care of his own. Salvation is found in him alone, and the multitudes who follow Jesus will ultimately not be disappointed (see 7:9–10).

In fact, they will see the day when their enemies, who refuse to repent and follow the Lamb, are judged for persecuting the saints of God (18:20). The evil powers of this world, empowered by the evil one himself, will not get away with anything in the end. They will not be able to hide their wicked deeds, as is made clear in Rev 18–19, where the great prostitute, in whom "was found the blood of prophets and of saints, and of all who have been slain on earth" (18:24), at last meets her fate. A day will come when a great multitude in heaven will shout out their hallelujahs to God, for he will have "judged the great prostitute who corrupted the earth with her immorality, and

2. See, e.g., Keener, *IVP Bible Background Commentary*, 783.

... avenged on her the blood of his servants" (19:2). Indeed, the ferocity and finality of his wrath will be astounding. No one will be able to withstand him; no one will escape (see 19:11–21).

Among those who will face the wrath of the Lamb were leaders in the synagogue of Satan who were oppressing God's true people in Smyrna. This is highlighted in the account of the two witnesses in Rev 11, where the location of the death of the two witnesses is striking: "and their dead bodies will lie in the street of the great city that symbolically is called Sodom and Egypt, where their Lord was crucified" (11:8). Jerusalem, the city of God, was now firmly opposed to the true people of God, those who bear witness to Jesus and his resurrection. Jerusalem had killed the prophets in centuries past and had recently put to death the Lord Jesus. In doing so, it had gone from being the city at the center of worshiping the Lord to being a "city of Satan." The city of Satan would put the two witnesses to death just as the synagogue of Satan would bring about the death of faithful witnesses in Smyrna. Both the city (11:13) and the synagogue of Satan, though, would face the wrath of the Lamb. Justice would certainly come, in time.

> *Do not fear what you are about to suffer. Behold, the devil is about to throw some of you into prison, that you may be tested, and for ten days you will have tribulation. Be faithful unto death, and I will give you the crown of life.* (2:10)

Jesus had made it clear that suffering was imminent for Christians in Smyrna. It was just over the horizon, and it would be serious. The believers in Smyrna were people, just like you and I, struggling to follow Jesus in an environment that often made that very difficult. Jesus' words here are clearly not what they would have wanted to hear. Along with the exhortation to be faithful in 2:10, though, Jesus also provided substantial encouragement throughout the entire book of Revelation to help these harassed Christians keep things in perspective. John had already reminded them that grace and peace come from God the Father, God the Son, and God the Holy Spirit (1:4); now Jesus conveys that grace and peace to them through some gracious reminders. Suffering will soon be upon them, but Jesus reminds them with the very first words of Revelation that suffering is not all that is coming soon (1:1). "The earth-shattering events that are depicted in this book are also imminent; and they will usher in your reward and the righting of all wrongs," Jesus assures them. And he does it not just once at the beginning of Revelation, but repeatedly throughout the book to make them absolutely certain that things are not going to remain as they are or as they are about to be. Their end (death) will not be *the* end.

Look at how many times Jesus returns to this theme in his message to the church. In 1:3, he says, "Blessed is the one who reads aloud the words of this prophecy, and blessed are those who hear, and who keep what is written in it, *for the time is near.*" So, in the span of three verses at the very beginning of this book, Jesus twice makes it clear that the end of all things (for the enemies of God) is at hand and the beginning of all things (for the people of God) is also at hand. Then, in 4:1, at the beginning of the extended visions that make up Rev 4–22, Jesus again reiterates that what is coming, what is going to take place "soon" in the words of 1:1, is something that God has decreed must take place: "And the first voice, which I had heard speaking to me like a trumpet, said, 'Come up here, and I will show you what *must* take place after this.'" The language used here is strong (δεῖ/*dei* plus an infinitive) and comes from the divine voice of one who sounds like a trumpet. There is no question left lingering about the outcome. What God says *must* happen *will* happen.

Jesus' words of encouragement are further buttressed with John's own reminder of his circumstances: "I, John, your brother and partner in the tribulation and the kingdom and the patient endurance that are in Jesus, was on the island called Patmos on account of the word of God and the testimony of Jesus" (1:9). John recognized the truth of God's Word spoken through the apostle Paul, who had the audacity to preach a message to brand new Christians that sounds very strange to our ears—ears that have been infected by our tendency to embrace the American Dream as the right of believers:

> When they had preached the gospel to that city and had made many disciples, they returned to Lystra and to Iconium and to Antioch, ²²strengthening the souls of the disciples, encouraging them to continue in the faith, and saying that *through many tribulations we must enter the kingdom of God.* (Acts 14:21–22)

As Paul reminded the believers in Lystra, Iconium, and Antioch, so John reminds believers in Asia Minor: suffering is part and parcel of the life of the Christian. It is normal, and it is to be expected. All who follow Jesus Christ must be prepared to face tribulations and persecution (2 Tim 3:12). How, though, can one face persecution and death and yet not be afraid, as Jesus' words indicate in 2:10? Part of the answer, we will see in the rest of Revelation, comes from the reminder of where fear should be directed. The Christians in Smyrna need not fear the fury of the evil one or what they will suffer at his hands. After all, he and those who do his bidding can merely kill the body. There is Another, though, "who can destroy both soul and body in hell" (Matt 10:28). He is the One they should fear (see 14:6–7 and 15:3–4). For there will come a day when all those who do not belong to him, whose names have not been written in the book of life, will be thrown into the lake of fire (20:15). In comparison, the pain and even death that the enemy can inflict are only temporary and therefore not worthy of our fear.

Reading the ominous words in 2:10, the believers in Smyrna could have been left with the impression that the devil exercised control over their lives, that he was sovereign. When placed within the context of Revelation as a whole, however, it is clear that nothing could be farther from the truth. Jesus makes it clear later in his message to the church that the power of the devil and his emissary the beast is granted by God (see 6:2, 4, 8; 7:2; 9:1, 3, 5; 11:2; 13:7). They have no power on their own. Although the ESV uses "was given," "was allowed," and "was permitted" in its translation of these passages, in each case it is the same word in the Greek. In fact, this same exact form of the verb (ἐδόθη, edothē, lit. "it was given") is used twenty-one times in Revelation[3] as one of many ways of driving home the point that God is in absolute control. The passages above, and many others, are particularly focused on the fact that the power of the devil, who will persecute them for a time, is derivative. He can only do what God allows him to do. The fate of Christians in Smyrna, then, is not in the hands of Jewish or Roman authorities, nor is it in Satan's hands; it is in God's hands. It is Jesus who is really "the ruler of kings on earth" (1:5), the "King of kings and Lord of lords" (19:16).

What's more, the devil's end is sure. Currently, he is like an injured lion backed into a corner. He is fighting for his life, now that he has lost the battle in heaven. In his graciousness, Jesus provides a vivid picture in 12:7–9 of what has taken place in the spiritual realm to help readers in Smyrna understand why the battle is so intense at times.

The enemy of the saints, who began his wicked work in this world as the serpent in the Garden, continues to attempt to thwart God's plan and to lead the world astray. Having been banished from heaven, he and his minions now inhabit the earth. He can no longer accuse God's people day and night (12:10), but he has not yet been destroyed. And he is not at all pleased with his situation: "But woe to you, O earth and sea, for the devil has come down to you in great wrath, because he knows that his time is short!" (12:12). Once again, we see an emphasis on the temporal nature of Satan's battle against God and God's people. This would have helped the Christians in Smyrna to persevere, being reassured that their suffering would soon be over. But we also find in Rev 12 that Satan's inability to destroy the Son of God has only increased his fury, and he has redirected it at the followers of Jesus: "Then the dragon became furious with the woman and went off to make war on the rest of her offspring, on those who keep the commandments of God and hold to the testimony of Jesus" (12:17). So, there is both comfort here for Christians in Smyrna and a call to brace themselves for the onslaught of the evil one.

The might of the evil one, however, and the evil world system that is opposed to them is about to be destroyed: "As she glorified herself and lived in luxury, so give her a like measure of torment and mourning" (18:7). For those who had been forced into poverty, daily seeing the luxury surrounding them would have been like rubbing salt in a wound; but Jesus reminds them that the luxury of Babylon (and Smryna) is about to go up in smoke: "her plagues will come in a single day, death and mourning and famine, and she will be burned up with fire; for mighty is the Lord God who has judged her" (18:8). Justice is coming to those who have oppressed the saints of God in Smyrna and elsewhere. Christians in Smyrna should then take heart, despite their

---

3. 6:2, 4 [2x], 8, 11; 7:2; 8:3; 9:1, 3, 5; 11:1, 2; 13:5 [2x], 7 [2x], 14, 15; 16:8; 19:8; 20:4. Plural forms of the same passive verb occur in 8:2 and 12:14.

current and imminent circumstances. For one day soon they would be rejoicing in God's coming justice: "Rejoice over her, O heaven, and you saints and apostles and prophets, for God has given judgment for you against her!" (18:20).

We should also note that the various statements of imminency, which are clustered at the beginning and end of Revelation (2:16; 3:10, 11; 22:6, 7, 10, 12, 20), frame the whole prophecy as something that will soon come to pass. This would have brought great hope to those who were about to suffer for "ten days." Particularly important is Jesus' repeated reminder: "I am coming soon!" (3:11; 22:7, 12). This wonderful promise would have helped reinforce his call to Christians in Smyrna to cling to their devotion to him in the midst of the coming persecution because they can rest assured that their trial will be short lived ("ten days").

The end of verse 10, however, makes it clear that the short-lived nature of their coming trial did not mean that life would quickly return to normal. On the contrary, the brief trial, at least for some of them, would end with their death. Even for those who have no fear of what comes after death, the *process* of death can be a significant source of trepidation. Nobody enjoys pain; and the Christians in Smyrna were likely not facing a quick and painless execution. Torture, as we are all too aware from the account of Jesus' passion, was a regular part of the execution process in the ancient world. And as they read through the rest of Jesus' message to the church, the reality of what was facing them would have become even more apparent.

In vivid color, they would have been confronted as they read about the fifth seal (6:11) with the fact that many faithful ones who proclaimed the word of God and maintained their testimony as followers of Jesus would be killed for their faith. In fact—and this was of crucial importance—their deaths were part of God's plan. God had set a specific number of servants of Jesus, brothers and sisters of those in Smyrna, who were to be killed. Not until all those faithful martyrs had glorified God through their deaths would God's final judgment come.

The picture in heaven in Rev 7, where it is a great multitude that no one could count (7:9) who come out of the great tribulation (7:14) almost certainly through their deaths, makes it clear that we should not be thinking that only a few Christians will be martyred for their faith. This is the calling of all Christians, a calling that Jesus had made clear in the Gospels: "If anyone would come after me, let him deny himself and take up his cross and follow me" (Matt 16:24). While "taking up one's cross" has been domesticated by Western Christians so that it includes all sorts of trivial things, early readers of the New Testament would have recognized that it is an image of death.

Jesus' call to lay down one's life to follow him and the vivid pictures of martyrdom in Revelation, however, do not mean that he did not care about the Christians in Smyrna who were about to suffer severe persecution. In Rev 8, Jesus shares a powerful reminder that God will bring justice in the end. The chapter begins with a dramatic period of silence that lasted about half an hour (8:1). As we wait to hear about the seven trumpets, our attention is drawn to an eighth angel who is holding a golden censer. This censer does not just contain incense; it also contains "the prayers of all the saints" (8:4). For those suffering or about to suffer persecution and death in Smyrna, it would have been easy to become discouraged and wonder if God was really hearing their prayers. They have heard that Jesus walks among the lampstands/churches; he must, then, know what they are facing. But did God really hear their cries for help? For those who might have felt like their prayers were being blocked by some kind of spiritual force field, Jesus reminds them, with a beautiful picture, that their prayers are actually reaching the ears of the One who is in control of the entire universe. In fact, "the prayers of *all* the saints" were going up before the throne. Not one was being missed or ignored. More than that, the connection between the prayers of the saints and the censer being hurled to earth (8:5), followed by the trumpet judgments, provides a vivid reminder that there will come a time when God will act dramatically and decisively against the enemies of his people in response to his people's cries for justice. The cry of the saints under the altar in 6:10 ("How long?") will be answered.

As readers in Smyrna encountered the interludes in Rev 7 and Rev 10–11, they would have been encouraged by the reminder that the end of the story was not in doubt. A time was coming when "there would be no more delay" (10:6). Yes, God at times seems slow in bringing his purposes to pass, but ultimately he will do everything that he has promised through his prophets (10:7). His mysterious purposes will eventually be fully realized, and the time is surely coming when the people of God will be

> before the throne of God, and serve him day and night in his temple; and he who sits on the throne will shelter them with his presence. [16]They shall hunger no more, neither thirst anymore; the sun shall not strike them, nor any scorching heat. [17]For the Lamb in the midst of the throne will be their shepherd, and he will guide them to springs of living water, and God will wipe away every tear from their eyes. (7:15–17)

Some Christians today struggle with the content of the martyred saints question: "O Sovereign Lord, holy and true, how long before you will judge and avenge our blood on those who dwell on the earth?" Didn't Jesus say that vengeance is wrong? Actually, the Scriptures portray taking vengeance into our own hands as sin. Godly people leave vengeance to the Lord (Deut 32:35; Rom 12:19; Heb 10:30), just as we see the martyred saints doing here. And God's vengeance is both righteous and appropriate. More than that, God's judgment on the wicked reveals his holy character through his righteous acts. As Isa 5:13–16 makes clear, when God pours out his judgment on his enemies, he glorifies himself. For, he is a God of justice. When he takes vengeance on the wicked, he demonstrates his holiness. If he were not holy, the injustice of the wicked could go unanswered.

As the vivid scenes of Revelation moved toward the end of the cycles of judgment—the pouring out of seven bowls of God's wrath—Christians in Smyrna would have encountered the One who loved them to the point of death bringing wrath on the ones who had murdered his followers who had faithfully loved him to the point of death in 16:4–6. Those who shed the blood of God's saints and prophets would drink the full measure of his wrath. God's justice will be meted out on those who persecute his people; but this realization of his ultimate justice does not mean that his people will not suffer and die for bearing his name now. The great prostitute of Rev 17 would be judged, but only after she has killed many of God's people (17:6). That is the grim reality; but Jesus mixes the reality of persecution and death with an even heavier dose of encouragement and hope throughout the book of Revelation.

> *He who has an ear, let him hear what the Spirit says to the churches. The one who conquers will not be hurt by the second death.* (2:11)

In the initial part of his message to Christians in Smyrna (2:8–11), Jesus offers strong encouragement from the promise that he gives to those who overcome, a promise that speaks loudly to their particular circumstances. Yes, death may be part of their immediate future, but the *second* death will never touch them. In fact, it will not be able to hurt them at all. The reality of what this means, of course, is vividly brought out toward the end of Revelation, which we will examine in more detail later. For now, it is enough to note that the way Jesus has chosen his language makes Rev 20:11–14 a particularly poignant part of the message to Christians in Smyrna:

> Then I saw a great white throne and him who was seated on it. From his presence earth and sky fled away, and no place was found for them. ¹²And I saw the dead, great and small, standing before the throne, and books were opened. Then another book was opened, which is the book of life. And the dead were judged by what was written in the books, according to what they had done. ¹³And the sea gave up the dead who were in it, Death and Hades gave up the dead who were in them, and they were judged, each one of them, according to what they had done. ¹⁴Then Death and Hades were thrown into the lake of fire. *This is the second death, the lake of fire.*

In Rev 20 no question is left regarding what the second death refers to. The lake of fire is a fate that no one would aspire to. To his followers in Smyrna Jesus gives the promise that this fate will not impact them in any way . . . if they overcome. Not only will they be free from the fiery judgment that awaits the enemies of God, but they will also enjoy the wonderful privilege of serving as priests of God and Christ and reigning with him for a thousand years (20:4). Thus, contrary to what their opponents in the synagogue of Satan were telling them, *they* will be priests, *they* will reign, and *they* will not be touched by the lake of fire, that second death that all the enemies of God will ultimately face.

All of this, of course, leaves us asking: What would it have meant for Christians in Smyrna to "overcome"? If they are to avoid the second death, what must they do? The answer is quite clear. For Christians in Smyrna to overcome they must avoid at all costs the temptation to save their own skins at the expense of their devotion to Jesus; for to "save" their life would be to lose it. This pattern of overcoming through death is reiterated throughout Jesus' message to the church.

First, we find sporadic examples of others who overcome through losing their lives as a faithful witness. There is the case of "Antipas my faithful witness, who was killed" in their sister city of Pergamum (2:13). It is highly likely that believers in Smyrna would have been well aware of what had happened to Antipas. The same would be the lot of the "two witnesses" described in Rev 11. They will serve as God's spokesmen for a significant period of time, and will be impervious to attempts to harm them. A time will come, though, when God's purposes will be best served through their deaths (see 11:7–10). The agent of Satan who comes up from the Abyss will not only attack them, but will overpower and kill them—just as the devil will be allowed to throw some of the believers in prison in Smyrna and put some of them to death (2:10). The two witnesses will face the ultimate humiliation of not only having their bodies lie unburied for all to see, but also having the inhabitants of the earth celebrate their deaths and the shameful treatment of their bodies. It will appear that the beast has triumphed, but the end of the story remains to be told. In 11:11–13 Christians in Smyrna would have clearly seen that that the apparent end of the two witnesses would not be their end at all. God will raise them, as he raised Jesus, and usher them into his presence and glory where none will be able to deny that they belong to him and serve him. Moreover, their exaltation will be accompanied by the judgment of those who persecuted them (11:13).

The two witnesses and Antipas, though, are not the only examples of those who overcome through death in Revelation. Jesus' message to the church universal is full of descriptions of the ultimate Overcomer, who triumphed in the very same manner. To make the connection between dying as a faithful witness and overcoming, Jesus includes multiple references to his own example in this regard at both the beginning and end of the visions of Revelation. In Rev 5, he is repeatedly referred to as the one who willingly gave his life to accomplish God's purposes. Jesus is the Lamb looking "as though it had been slain," who now stands in the center of the throne of heaven (5:6) and is the object of worship (5:8). He is worthy of the worship of the twenty-four elders (5:8), worthy of the worship of thousands upon thousands, and ten thousand times ten thousand angels (5:11), and worthy of the worship of "every creature in heaven and on earth and under the earth and in the sea, and all that is in them" (5:13), because he was slain and with his blood "ransomed people for God from every tribe and language and people and nation" (5:9) and made them to be a kingdom and priests who serve God (5:10). Jesus has overcome by his own blood!

This connection between his death and his exaltation—which is also beautifully highlighted in Phil 2:6–11—is picked up again in Rev 19 and 20. In 19:11–16, we have a remarkable picture of the coming King. The rider on the white horse, of course, is none other than Jesus himself—the Word who was with God in the beginning and was God (John 1:1), the only legitimate king, who commands the army of heaven and who will himself strike down his enemies and rule the nations. Within this jaw-dropping description of Jesus, though, are two features that would have likely stood out to Christians in Smyrna.

First, Jesus is described as the one who is Faithful (19:11). He did not shrink back in the face of death; he did not save his own life when it was on the line, as much as he would have liked to (Matt 26:39–43 || Mark 14:35–36 || Luke 22:42–44). He was obedient to God to the point of death, even a brutal death on a cross (Phil 2:8). And second, Jesus' attire, though it includes "many crowns" on his head (19:12), surprisingly also includes "a robe dipped in blood" (19:13). Perhaps, though, it should not be surprising to find the King of kings and Lord of lords modeling for his followers how they ought to live. He is the coming King precisely because he has overcome by his blood. Blood and crowns are inexorably linked together in the fathomless mind of God.[4] And the same is to be true of Jesus' followers (cf. 1:9, where "kingdom" is surrounded by "tribulation" and "patient endurance"). A time is coming when they will reign with their Lord, but for now they must remain faithful even to the point of death. For that is how they will overcome:

> And I heard a loud voice in heaven, saying, "Now the salvation and the power and the kingdom of our God and the authority of his Christ have come, for the accuser of our brothers has been thrown down, who accuses them day and night before our God. [11]And they have conquered him by the blood of the Lamb and by the word of their testimony, for they loved not their lives even unto death." (12:10–11; cf. 20:4)

Faithful witnesses cannot expect to escape the first death. Jesus' followers dare not love their lives and thus abandon their faith in the face of death. For what Jesus says to the church at Smyrna when he promises, "The one who conquers will not be hurt by the second death" (2:11), he also says to every one of his followers: "Whoever finds his life will lose it, and whoever loses his life for my sake will find it" (Matt 10:39); and "whoever would save his life will lose it, but whoever loses his life for my sake will find it" (Matt 16:25; see also Mark 8:35; Luke 9:24; 17:33). We dare not domesticate these passages so that they merely are thought to mean that we need to be willing to give up our extra stuff for Jesus, which we don't really need anyway. Jesus *is* talking about life and death here. To fail to be faithful or to shrink from the threat of death that comes from being faithful both represent a failure to overcome.

As those in Smyrna came to Rev 13, Jesus' words directed at them at the end of their message in Rev 2 would have no doubt still been ringing in their ears: "He who has an ear, let him hear" (2:11). In 13:9, we find the exact same words repeated,

---

4. We will consider an alternative way of interpreting the image of Jesus' robe being stained with blood in chapter 9 as we examine Jesus' message to Christians in Thyatira. For now, it is enough to say that by its very nature symbolic language sometimes lends itself to more than one way of reading it. This is likely the case here.

marking what follows as particularly important for all of the churches in Asia Minor, and indeed for the church universal. What is the message that Jesus wants to emphasize? It is not a message that things are going to get better: "If anyone is to be taken captive, to captivity he goes; if anyone is to be slain with the sword, with the sword must he be slain." (13:10). For Christians in Smyrna these words would have been yet another sobering reminder. Suffering is on their doorstep; death is looming large. "Pay attention!" Jesus reminds them, "for the days will be very dark indeed." And then he makes clear why he is telling them this: "Here is a call for the endurance and faith of the saints" (13:10). In case they might have not heard this exhortation in the midst of all the terrifying visions of Rev 13, Jesus repeats this message in the very next chapter: "Here is a call for the endurance of the saints, those who keep the commandments of God and their faith in Jesus" (14:12). Revelation is not a message intended to scare unbelievers in the kingdom; it is a message to believers to urge them to endure as members of Jesus' kingdom. Jesus expects his followers to remain faithful until the end, even to the point of death (2:10). To do so will require patient endurance. One cannot expect to be faithful for a moment, to testify that Jesus is Lord for a moment, only to give up in the face of more intense suffering. He had told them before, and he implies it again here: "and you will be hated by all for my name's sake. But the one who endures to the end will be saved" (Matt 10:22 || Mark 13:13).

SUMMARY: JESUS' MESSAGE TO CHRISTIANS IN SMYRNA

For Christians in Smyrna Jesus' message is clear: suffering and even death are coming, but death will not be the end of the story. He who died and was raised from the dead guarantees a glorious resurrection to those who overcome. Yes, they are poor; and the evil one, through his emissary the beast, is only going to push more followers of Jesus into poverty as they refuse to take his mark (13:16–17). But they should not think that they are facing something new. After all, the dragon has been in a rage and trying to destroy the people of God ever since Jesus' ascension (12:17). The temporary suffering that is coming to them will be intense. It will bring about the death of all his servants whom God has ordained to die as his witnesses (6:11). Such suffering, however, is not the end of the story. God will bring justice to those who have opposed him and his people, and he will spectacularly reward those who overcome. That reward, as the message to the church in Smyrna makes clear, is eternal life itself (2:10). How then could God's people not persevere? They, like the Lord Jesus before them, must for the joy set before them endure the trial, despising the shame (Heb 12:2), so that they may enter into the joy of their Lord forever.

6

Jesus' Message to the Church in Pergamum

And to the angel of the church in Pergamum write: The words of him who has the sharp two-edged sword. (2:12)

THE RECIPIENTS OF JESUS' third message to the churches of Asia Minor lived in the northernmost of the seven cities in the region known as Mysia. Pergamum was a major cultural and political center with medical facilities, temples, and one of the largest libraries in the ancient world, having 200,000 volumes and rivaling the famous library of Alexandria.[1] It also had an impressive theatre with 80 rows of seats that could accommodate 10,000 people. We know from historical texts that a number of Christians were fed to wild animals in this very theatre. More important for our purposes, though, was the fact that Pergamum had been the capital of the province of Asia since 133 BC. It was thus the seat of authority for the entire region. Like Ephesus and Smyrna, it claimed for itself the title, "First of Asia." In fact, Pergamum was the first city in Asia to build a provincial temple for the imperial cult in honor of Rome and Augustus in 29 BC,[2] and thus the first city in Asia to be a "temple-keeper." Once again, this highlights the long history of devotion to Rome of which Pergamum could boast, a history that no doubt would have put additional pressure on Christians living there to conform to the values of the society around them.

One of the temples in Pergamum—actually more of a sanctuary—was dedicated to Asclepius, the god of healing. It was located outside of the city, but was connected to the city by a sacred pathway. As many may be aware, thanks to the American Medical

---

1. The city was so famous for book production that the English word "parchment" actually was derived from the name of the city.

2. Ramsay, *Letters*, 207.

Association, the snake, which was associated with Asclepius, became a common symbol of healing.[3]

Part of Pergamum, which had a population of about 120,000, was built on a huge hill that rose one thousand feet above the plains.[4] It was an impressive sight, with many of the city's public buildings perched on terraces that had been built into the side of the hill. At the summit of the hill was an acropolis with a massive altar to Zeus.

The message to the church in Pergamum, then, is addressed to Christians living in another major city with a rich history. It was a thriving city of great importance, and its success would have been attributed, in large part, to its devotion to Rome and the gods of the Roman Empire. To serve a lord other than Caesar would have been dangerous in such a context, to say the least.

Jesus addresses himself to these Christians as the one "who has the sharp two-edged sword," repeating the image of 1:16. Readers of Scripture will quickly think of two passages where God's word is compared to a sword: Eph 6:17 and Heb 4:12. In these passages, however, the Greek word (μάχαιρα, *machaira*) refers to a different type of sword, a short sword or dagger. In Rev 2:12, on the other hand, we are dealing with a broad sword (ῥομφαία, *romphaia*), the type of sword one would take into battle.[5] The focus of this symbol, then, is on power and judgment. The latter becomes clear in 2:16, and will be driven home later in the book. For now, let's think about the rhetorical force of Jesus identifying what follows as "The words of him who has the sharp two-edged sword." At the very least, this imagery suggests the gravity of the message that follows. Jesus' words are to be taken seriously, for they are powerful; and failure to respond will have dire consequences. Jesus is not someone to trifle with or to take lightly. But there's more.

The title that Jesus uses here would have especially resonated with these particular Christians who were living in a city that was the seat of Roman power in Asia. As will be made infinitely clear in the remainder of Revelation, true authority is not found in the Roman emperor or in any other earthly power; Jesus is the King of kings and Lord of lords. He alone holds the power of life and death. Everyone in Pergamum and throughout the entire region understood very well that it was the proconsul of Asia, ruling from Pergamum, who wielded the "power of the sword" or "right of the sword" (*ius gladii*), which meant that he had the "power of life and death."[6] That pow-

---

3. The proper symbol for Asclepius is a staff without wings and only one snake. It is just a touch ironic that the symbol used by the American Medical Association (with wings and two snakes) is actually based on the staff of Hermes, who among other things was the god of thieves, merchants, and commerce!

4. Hemer, *Letters*, 78.

5. Although Isa 11:4 and 49:2 show conceptual similarities, the lack of correspondence in actual language makes an allusion to either unlikely; contra ibid., 85. The MT for Isa 11:4 refers to "the rod of his mouth," while the LXX reads "the *word* of his mouth." In 49:2, the LXX uses μάχαιρα (*machaira*) rather than ῥομφαία (*romphaia*).

6. Ramsay, *Letters*, 214.

er, following the policy of the Roman government, could be directed at anyone who refused to worship the emperor. This was a frightful reality for not only Christians in Pergamum, but also Christians elsewhere in the province of Asia who would be sent to Pergamum to face the proconsul if they were identified as followers of another King. Jesus, though, wants to shift their attention from that reality to the bigger picture. So, he creates another rhetorical hotspot that drives home the truth of the matter: the proconsul was a very small man with no power at all compared to him whose words are a sharp, double-edged sword (Reading Instruction #4). Jesus is the One before whom every last person will stand, not a proconsul, and not the Roman emperor.

> *I know where you dwell, where Satan's throne is. Yet you hold fast my name, and you did not deny my faith even in the days of Antipas my faithful witness, who was killed among you, where Satan dwells.* (2:13)

As Jesus begins his message to these Christians, we find that once again he is well aware of the situation they are facing. While the believers in Smyrna were being slandered by Jews from the "synagogue of Satan," the church in Pergamum was living in "Satanville." It is striking that Jesus emphasizes this fact twice in a single verse. Pergamum was the place where Satan both lived and had his throne. It was not a place that any Christian would want to visit, let alone make their home. Notice that once again Jesus does not downplay in any way the seriousness of the challenges these Christians were facing. In fact, he does just the opposite. He acknowledges that they are living in a city where Satan is on the prowl in a particularly aggressive and oppressive manner.

Many scholars have wrestled with the precise nature of Jesus' reference to "Satan's throne." There are plenty of worthy candidates for what Jesus may be referring to. After all, this was the city that built a temple for Augustus and the goddess Roma in 29 BC, the first imperial temple in the Roman province of Asia and one of the more important centers of the imperial cult. This was the city with the massive throne-like altar of *Zeus Soter* ("Zeus the Savior"), which was located on the same acropolis as the temple of Augustus and Roma. This was the city that founded the cult of Asclepius, whose symbol was the snake or serpent, a symbol also associated with Satan (see 12:9, 14, 15; 20:2). And this was the city in Asia Minor where the judge's bench or tribunal was located, where Christians could be condemned to death for their faith.

Although scholars often debate which of these is in view here, it is probably best simply to recognize that Jesus' language is intended to portray Pergamum as a place where Satan's work was particularly effective, as was evident in all of the above realities. As in some other cases, then, we may well err by trying to be too narrow in identifying the referent of a particular symbol in the book of Revelation. What we can say with some level of confidence is that, given the focus of Revelation as a whole and the specific content of the rest of 2:13, the reference to Satan's throne alludes in part

THE BOOK OF REVELATION

to the fact that Pergamum was the place where Christians faced the evil one's ultimate temptation: worship idols or die. It was in Pergamum "that the Christian faced the actual threat of Roman execution."[7] The fact that it was the original seat of the imperial cult in Asia and still a prominent center for emperor worship likely also plays into the equation. The massive altar to Zeus, who is blasphemously called "Savior," and the flourishing cult of Asclepius simply support the contention that Satan is particularly active in this city.

Both Jesus' words and what we know about first-century Pergamum make it crystal clear that Pergamum was the last place where you wanted to be a narrow-minded, intolerant, monotheistic Christian. If, however, believers in Pergamum lived in Satanville, a place where the evil one's reign and influence were particularly evident, and they remained true to Jesus in that oppressive context, what does that say to Christians living elsewhere? If the Christians in Pergamum could remain faithful in the city where Satan was most active, then there is no environment in this world that would provide any excuse for a follower of Jesus to give in to the pressure to turn their back on him. Jesus expected Christians in Pergamum to remain faithful; and he expects the same of Christians in all places at all times, whether they live where Satan's activities are very subtle or where they are far more obvious (e.g., Nazi Germany).

Jesus' words also make it clear that believers in Pergamum had already suffered significant persecution, with one of their fellow Christians losing his life because of his testimony as a follower of Jesus. It is interesting that Antipas, the martyr, is given the title "faithful witness"—the same title that Jesus himself bears (1:5; 3:14). Being a faithful witness involves a willingness to persevere in accomplishing God's purposes even to the point of death, as both Antipas and Jesus himself exemplified. What is particularly striking in Jesus' words is the level of devotion to the Lord that Christians in Pergamum had so clearly demonstrated. They had "remained true" to him, or "held fast" to his name. This suggests that unlike Christians in Ephesus who appear to have retreated from public witness, these courageous Christians living in the heart of Satan's activity on earth had refused to hide their faith in an effort to avoid persecution or even death. The further acknowledgement that they had not "denied" their faith in him again suggests that visible allegiance to Jesus is in view. These Christians embraced the fact that Jesus' followers are called to be "the light of the world" (Matt 5:14); and they went on living like Christians even when one of them was killed because of his witness. They appear to have exemplified the boldest of witness in the harshest of environments.

While Christians sometimes use the idea of trying to preach the gospel at Mecca as an example of the need to combine common sense with boldness, Christians in Pergamum appear to have favored faith and boldness over conventional wisdom. It was *their* city—even though Satan lived there—and they viewed themselves as Jesus' appointed ambassadors who were responsible for bringing the gospel to Pergamum.

7. Hemer, *Letters*, 85.

Given their example, is there anywhere in the world, where God would call Christians to keep quiet? I do not mean to be insensitive by posing this question. I have personally known followers of Jesus who were killed for their faithful testimony. Facing such danger as a Christian is extremely difficult, especially for those with children. Jesus here, however, invites us to wrestle with the nature of his calling on our lives whatever our circumstances happen to be.

> *But I have a few things against you: you have some there who hold the teaching of Balaam, who taught Balak to put a stumbling block before the sons of Israel, so that they might eat food sacrificed to idols and practice sexual immorality.* (2:14)

Although there is much for which to commend Christians in Pergamum, all was not well. Despite the incredible devotion that Jesus affirms in verse 13, we find in verse 14 that he has "a few things" that he holds against them. Jesus' description here makes it clear that the church in Pergamum had the opposite problems of the church in Ephesus. The Ephesian Christians had done an outstanding job of guarding the theological integrity of the church. The front door of the church in Ephesus had a sign tacked to it that read, "No false teachers allowed!" Christians in Ephesus, however, had failed to maintain an overt witness to their city. Christians in Pergamum, on the other hand, had done an outstanding job of being a vibrant witness for Jesus in their city, and had paid the price for doing so, but they had failed at the task of keeping false teaching out the church. There were some among them who held to "the teaching of Balaam," who was infamous for leading the Israelites into sexual immorality and idolatry.

We have here, then, an important link to the Old Testament (Reading Instruction #6). The biblical account of Balaam is found in Num 22–24, where we read about the efforts of Balak, king of Moab, to get Balaam to curse the Israelites. Although Balaam ultimately cooperated with the king's messengers and traveled to Moab, God would not let him curse the Israelites. Instead, he ended up blessing the Israelites four times, much to the chagrin of Balak. The only negative commentary on Balaam that is recorded in the account relates to him having to be corrected by his donkey, which he had abused. He certainly does not come out of the story as the villain he is later portrayed as (see 2 Pet 2:15; Jude 11). What happened? As we read through Numbers, we eventually learn in Num 31:15–16 that Balaam was responsible for advising the Israelites to indulge in sexual immorality with Midianite women, worship their gods, and feast on idol sacrifices (see also Num 25:1–3, though Balaam is not mentioned there). Tradition held that Balaam thought that the quickest route to Israel's destruction was to have them so pollute themselves that God would be moved to destroy them.[8] Balaam was not willing, or perhaps able, to curse them in the name of the

---

8. In other Jewish texts (Philo, *Mos.* 1.294–99; Josephus, *Ant.* 4.126–30; *y. Sanh.* 28cd) Balaam advises Balak to trick the Israelites into having relations with prostitutes and participating in pagan worship.

Lord, but he appears to have been quite willing to use other means to try to bring about Israel's destruction.

So, why were the false teachings that were infecting the church at Pergamum called the "teachings of Balaam," an individual who had lived many, many centuries earlier? It was not uncommon for writers in the ancient world to disparage their opponents by associating them with infamous characters from the past.[9] Balaam became the stereotypical wicked man or false teacher who leads God's people into sin, particularly sins of sexual immorality and idolatry. He also, as King Jeroboam after him, became infamous for leading the people of Israel to assimilate to the ways of the nations around them.

Like Balaam before them, false teachers in Pergamum were leading some Christians to eat food sacrificed to idols and engage in sexual immorality. While Jesus' reference to sexual immorality is relatively straightforward,[10] his reference to eating food sacrificed to idols could mean a number of things. We have to keep in mind that meat was not nearly as common at meals in the ancient world as it is today. The average person tended to rely more on grains made into porridge, bread, etc., than on meat, which was mainly eaten or available in relation to religious rituals, unless one was wealthy. "Eating food sacrificed to idols" could indicate taking part in sacred meals at a temple, simply accepting sacrificial meat distributed during a public religious festival, eating meat purchased from the marketplace that had been used in pagan sacrifices, or taking part in meals that were a part of various associations or guilds. Whichever specific interpretation is correct, it is very clear that the readers were under intense pressure to compromise in this area and assimilate to the society around them by somehow eating food that had been sacrificed to idols. This is the key to understanding the reference to Balaam. Balaam was not simply a "worldly" prophet who liked to have his cake and eat it too. Instead, Balaam represented the stereotypical false prophet who leads the people of God astray by encouraging them to compromise their devotion to God by assimilating to the culture around them. In Pergamum, there were influential teachers who taught that Christians should participate widely in the surrounding culture. "It's really not that bad!" might have been their motto. Jesus, however, makes it clear that it really *is* that bad.

So also you have some who hold the teaching of the Nicolaitans. (2:15)

---

9. Balaam is also used this way in 2 Pet 2:15, Jude 11, and in rabbinic literature such as *'Abot* 5.19.

10. I am aware of the view that "sexual immorality" could refer to spiritual adultery here, as is often the case in the Old Testament. At points in Revelation, it is likely that this language does carry a dual reference to both literal sexual sin and spiritual unfaithfulness as well. Given what we know of the historical context, however, it is best in my view to treat the references to sexual immorality and eating food sacrificed to idols here as two separate literal sins rather than a single sin of spiritual unfaithfulness.

As I have already mentioned, this verse appears to draw a link between those promoting the teaching of Balaam and the Nicolaitans. A better translation of verses 14–15 might be: "But I have a few things against you: you have some there who hold the teaching of Balaam, who taught Balak to put a stumbling block before the sons of Israel, so that they might eat food sacrificed to idols and practice sexual immorality. 15 *Thus*, you also have those who hold the teaching of the Nicolaitans." The language suggests that we are not dealing with two problems, but with a single problem that is given two names. Scholars tend to agree that the Nicolaitan's distinctive doctrine was the doctrine of accommodation (assimilation to Greco-Roman culture). As Ramsay notes, the teaching of the Nicolaitans

> was evidently an attempt to effect a reasonable compromise with the established usages of Greco-Roman society and to retain as many as possible of those usages in the Christian system of life. It affected most of all the cultured and well-to-do classes in the church, those who had most temptation to retain all that they could of the established social order and customs of the Greco-Roman world, and who by their more elaborate education had been trained to take a somewhat artificial view of life and to reconcile contradictory principles in practical conduct through subtle philosophical reasoning.[11]

This description, like the social context to which Revelation is addressed, finds close parallels in the church in the West. Followers of Jesus in the West are often rich and are enjoying the American Dream like their neighbors, but at what cost? Have they followed the teaching of the Nicolaitans like some of those in Pergamum had done before them?

> *Therefore repent. If not, I will come to you soon and war against them with the sword of my mouth.* (2:16)

Jesus calls the church in Pergamum to stop allowing Nicolaitans to spread their poison among them. He makes it clear that he expects them to take immediate action; false teaching is not to be tolerated. What was implied in the first verse of this letter through the imagery of the sword coming out of his mouth is here made explicit in Jesus' warning of imminent judgment if repentance is not forthcoming. In this case, the fact that Jesus is "coming soon" does not speak of the benefits for believers of entering into his presence. Instead, it points to looming judgment if they do not repent, with the sword of his mouth likely referring to words ("mouth") of judgment ("sword") that he will pronounce.

Notice that Jesus clearly calls on the church to repent and change their behavior, as he had done with the Ephesian Christians. The church today has become far too reticent to think of its own need to repent, preferring to associate repentance almost solely with those who have not yet surrendered to Christ. Jesus' repeated reminder in

11. Ramsay, *Letters*, 219.

Revelation that he has something against many local churches, though, should be a sober wake up call for his followers today to do some corporate self-introspection to seek to discover if Jesus has anything against us for which we need to repent. The fact that Jesus rebukes five out of the seven churches he addresses in Revelation should tell us that the odds are that he has something against us as well.

Notice also that the call for repentance is directed at the church as a whole, rather than just at the Nicolaitans among them. Jesus wants his Bride to be pure and undefiled, and for that to happen the spread of this spiritual cancer must be ended. Tolerance of false teaching is dangerous. And the danger is not just for those who "sit in the pews." Church leaders will be held accountable for how well they have protected the sheep under their care, as well as how effectively they have nurtured and helped the sheep to grow. Here, though, the language suggests that the focus is not simply on guarding the sheep who may succumb to the false teaching of the Nicolaitans, though it is clear from other Scriptures that that is required of church leaders (Acts 20:28–29). Instead, the focus is also on the need for the church to repent for the sake of those who are promoting the false teaching. Jesus warns them to repent so that he will not have to come and fight "against them," i.e., the Nicolaitans and their followers. He is thus calling those who lead to confront false teaching and so save those within their church who are being led astray or leading others astray from coming under judgment.[12] Being "intolerant," then, can be redemptive! "The believers are being given a choice: go to war against the heretics or else God will do so for them, but with far more drastic results."[13]

> He who has an ear, let him hear what the Spirit says to the churches. To the one who conquers I will give some of the hidden manna, and I will give him a white stone, with a new name written on the stone that no one knows except the one who receives it. (2:17)

Jesus follows his powerful warning by first repeating the same exhortation to pay careful attention to what he has said and respond appropriately, and then by offering a promise to those who do repent. In fact, the believers at Pergamum are given two promises if they overcome. Those promises, however, make use of symbols that can be difficult to decipher: hidden manna and a white stone. Once again, we need to look to the Old Testament (Reading Instruction #6). We know from passages like Exod 16:4–36 that God used manna to feed the Israelites while they were in the wilderness. Manna is also referred to as "bread from heaven" in both the Old Testament (Neh 9:15; Ps 105:40) and the New Testament (John 6:31–33, 50–51). It is thus something nourishing and necessary for life that comes from God. We also know that the return of manna was frequently associated with the coming eschatological age in Jewish literature from around the time of the New Testament: "And it will happen at that time

12. See also Jas 5:19–20 and 1 Tim 4:16.
13. Osborne, *Revelation*, 146.

that the treasury of manna will come down again from on high and they will eat of it in those years because these are they who have arrived at the consummation of time" (2 *Bar.* 29:8). Manna is referred to as "the bread of the age to come" in *Gen. Rab.* 82.8 on Gen. 35:17, and the "bread of angels" in Ps 78:25. It is likely, then, that being given manna is simply another way of saying that overcomers in Pergamum will partake of the blessings of the age to come. This interpretation is reinforced by referring to it as "*hidden* manna."

Three factors may be in view here. First, manna was kept in a jar as a reminder to later generations—but it was kept before the Lord where God's people did not actually have access to it (Exod 16:32–36). It was thus "hidden" from the people of God. Second, spiritual manna could be viewed as "hidden" in that only those who enter the age to come would have access to it. This way of thinking is reflected in the quote from 2 *Baruch* above. And finally, the jar of manna was hidden by Jeremiah with the ark before the destruction of Jerusalem according to 2 Macc 2:5, and Jewish tradition held that it would not be recovered until Israel was restored (2 *Bar.* 6:7–10). All of this suggests that the point of using "hidden manna" as a symbol here in Jesus' promise to these Christians is to direct their attention to the long awaited eschatological blessing that would be theirs, if they remained true to him. That blessing was not something they could currently see; it was still "hidden." But they could rest assured that there was a wonderful inheritance in store for all those who lived as overcomers during their temporary stay in Satanville.

Fixing their minds on things above (Col 3:1–2) would have been particularly important given the economic consequences of following Jesus in Pergamum.[14] We will consider these in more detail when we look at the message to Thyatira. For now, we should note that for Christians to refuse to blend in with their community, or for them to refuse to enter in to the idolatry that was a part of everyday life in the first-century Roman world would have led to poverty. They would have experienced deprivation and hunger. Their existence in the prosperous and comfortable city of Pergamum would have become a desert experience, where they may not have known where their next meal would come from. In these circumstances, Jesus urges his followers to persevere knowing that God will eventually give them his hidden manna. Though they are hungry now, they will ultimately be nourished with food that fully satisfies. Indeed, it is only those who abstain from the food of idols that was a regular part of life in the Roman Empire who will ultimately enjoy the sumptuous fare of the heavenly feast.[15]

Now that that is "clear," what about the "white stone, with a new name written on the stone"? And why would the name on it be known only to "the one who receives it"? Scholars have suggested a number of possible explanations for the white stone. First, it could simply refer to a costly reward. Beryl, for example, which is used in the

14. Cf. Hemer, *Letters*, 92.
15. Ibid., 95.

foundation of the New Jerusalem (21:20), was a white stone of great value. Second, white stones were used to indicate a vote of acquittal in the Greco-Roman world (as opposed to black stones for condemnation), suggesting that the focus might be on being declared innocent before God. Paul speaks of casting his stone against Christians before his own conversion (Acts 26:10). Third, white stones were given as tokens that people could use to gain admission to special events in the Greco-Roman world or to obtain free bread. Some scholars argue that awarding victors at games with a white stone that would allow them to attend a special feast was a well-established custom. The white stone with one's name on it in Revelation would then serve as a personalized verification of entry rights into God's kingdom and the great feast to come. The problem with this view is the lack evidence that stones were used in this way.[16] Finally, the white stone could simply be used to emphasize the permanence of the new name/identity/status (it is not written on papyrus or parchment), with the real emphasis being on the new name rather than the material it was written on.[17] In the end, certainty is impossible and it may be best to recognize with Beale that "there may be no single background for the 'white stone.' It could be intentionally allusive and suggest diverse but compatible historical associations."[18]

It is worth noting, however, that Jesus may have once again specially chosen his language to create a rhetorical hotspot for this particular church. Hemer points out that the buildings at Pergamum tended to be made of "very dark brown granite," with the numerous inscriptions that have been found on the lower terraces being written on white marble that contrasted with the dark granite.[19] Jesus may well be taking something familiar from their environment and using it to communicate notions of both permanence and visibility (Reading Instruction #4). Indeed, Hemer points out that "honorific decrees of the city repeatedly stipulate that the record of its benefactors shall be engraved on λευκὸς λίθος [leukos lithos, 'white stone']."[20] The point, then, would be that overcomers will permanently bear a new name that all will see as they enjoy the benefits of the messianic kingdom.

What, then, would the "new name written on it" be? Some point to 3:12, where Jesus states: "The one who conquers, I will make him a pillar in the temple of my God. Never shall he go out of it, and I will write on him the name of my God, and the name of the city of my God, the new Jerusalem, which comes down from my God out of heaven, and my own new name." This seems to suggest that the new name in 2:17 may be the name of God, Jesus, and/or the new Jerusalem. There are also, however, two interesting parallels in Isaiah, both of which point to a future day when the servants

16. Ibid., 98n96.

17. Ramsay, *Letters*, 222–23.

18. Beale, *Revelation*, 252. Osborne (*Revelation*, 149) appears to agree and prefers a combination of the feast token view and the vote of acquittal view.

19. Hemer, *Letters*, 102.

20. Ibid., 102n108.

of God will receive a new name: Isa 62:1–2 and 65:12–15. Given the eschatological nature of these texts, it is quite possible that the "new name" language serves to connect what Jesus is saying to the church at Pergamum with the promises that God gave through Isaiah many centuries earlier. We should also remember, though, the common practice in the early church and in many churches today (outside of the West) of a person being given a new name at the time of his or her baptism.[21] As with that custom, the function of the new name is to identify the person's new status as one who belongs to Christ and shares in his kingdom (see 2 Cor 5:17). Indeed, "name" is frequently associated with identity and status. This may well be the case here, with the secret nature of the name emphasizing the invulnerability of the believer's identity in Christ.

Finally, one other bit of information may potentially shed some light on this passage. Within the very recent memory of readers at Pergamum, the center of Roman power in Asia, was the dramatic events surrounding the founding of the Roman Empire. Octavius had almost miraculously restored order to the Roman republic. In order to honor Octavius the Roman Senate took an old word that had primarily been used by priests and was not used of any human being, and applied it to Octavius. As the founder of the Roman Empire, he was given the title, "Augustus."[22] This "new name" served to remind all those who heard it of Octavius's new and exalted status. For Christians in Pergamum, who were being tempted to enter into the "blessings" of the Roman Empire by simply burning a little incense to the emperor, Jesus tells them that if they resist this temptation, they will be given a new name, just as Octavius had been; but their status would be infinitely higher than a puny Roman emperor could ever imagine,[23] not to mention that their new status would last forever. "So," Jesus implies with his promise, "don't trade your eternal inheritance for the cheap trinkets that the Roman Empire has to offer! Don't compromise!"

PERGAMUM: PROFILE OF A CHURCH

As we have seen, Christians living in Pergamum in the late first century were living in a place where Satan was extremely active. As the seat of Roman power in Asia Minor, Pergamum was the place from which the proconsul of Asia wielded the sword and thus had the power of life and death. This was not some distant reality for Christians living in Pergamum; they had experienced the terror of Satan's power firsthand in the martyrdom of one of their very own: Antipas. Despite this traumatic experience these

---

21. Cf. Ramsay, *Letters*, 223.

22. Ibid., 226–27.

23. The fact that Christians only receive a new name when they overcome, then, does not pose a problem, since the focus is not on receiving a new character, but rather on having their character as "overcomers" recognized through the granting of a new and appropriate name; contra Hemer, *Letters*, 103.

Christians had refused to retreat from being visible witnesses of Jesus in their city. They were, in fact, model Christians in this respect. Even with death on the line, they had remained true to Jesus' name. Where they had failed, though, was in carefully guarding the church from false teaching. Unlike the church in Ephesus, the church in Pergamum was guilty of harboring false teachers (Nicolaitans). As a result, there were some in the church who had chosen assimilation over purity; they had compromised with the surrounding culture, becoming willing to eat food that had been sacrificed to idols and to engage in sexually immoral activities. So Jesus calls upon the church to take urgent action to deal with these false teachers so that those who are being deceived by them (and the false teachers themselves?) do not face his imminent judgment. Within the context of the message to the church in Pergamum, then, "overcoming" involves repenting of their laziness and "tolerance" in failing to guard the purity of the church from false teaching. Doing well in not renouncing their faith in the face of persecution was admirable, but it wasn't enough. They needed to take more seriously the call to keep that faith pure. Only then would they enjoy the rich food and new status that God had in store for his faithful followers.

7

Jesus' Message to the Church in Pergamum
The Rest of the Story

AS CHRISTIANS IN PERGAMUM reflected on the other six messages, perhaps most striking would have been the message to the church in Ephesus. Like their neighbors in Ephesus, Christians in Pergamum had a problem with an infestation of Nicolaitans who were peddling "the teaching of Balaam." But in contrast to the Ephesians, who had applied the appropriate eradication formula to rid themselves of Nicolaitans, the church in Pergamum had apparently taken a "live and let live" approach to the problem. They were more tolerant than those at Ephesus, perhaps focusing on the positive things the Nicolaitans brought to the church. They may have even established a "Nicolaitans and Christians Together" dialogue to celebrate their common beliefs and discuss how they could collaborate together for "the cause of Christ," forgetting that Jesus' hates the practices of the Nicolaitans (2:6).

Also important would have been Jesus words to those in Smyrna who were likewise suffering under Satan's oppressive hand. Christians in Pergamum had read that their brothers and sisters in Smyrna were facing imminent imprisonment and even death. This would have bolstered their own resolve to persevere, knowing that they were not the only ones whom Satan had singled out as targets of his wrath. And however powerless they may have felt living at the center of Satan's work in this world, they apparently have more "power" than their fellow Christians in Philadelphia, who had nevertheless remained faithful to Jesus and refused to deny his name (3:8).

REVELATION 4–5: THE MESSAGE TO PERGAMUM

For Christians in Pergamum who were staying true to Jesus' name in the midst of incredible adversity, the reminder of who is on the throne would have been very comforting. Yes, they were living where Satan had *his* throne, but look at who is sitting on the Throne of thrones! The impressive nature of the acropolis at Pergamum and the superficially absolute power that the Roman governor had over the lives of people in Asia Minor paled in comparison to the picture of God and his throne in Rev 4–5. The powers that be may be arrayed against the people of God currently, but they ultimately had only temporary authority over a small patch of land in a world that God created and controls. It was only by God's will that these authorities even existed (4:11). Satan may be running the show in Pergamum—indeed, his control may well extend to the ends of the earth (1 John 5:19)—but that control is limited, derivative, and temporary. While God was currently allowing Satan to rage against his people, particularly in places like Pergamum, Satan's power was not absolute. It was power that God had allowed him to have for a time; but a day was soon coming when his power would be undone, and God's people—including those suffering in Pergamum, Satan's city—would reign with him on the earth (5:10). In short, Rev 4–5 repeatedly draw the attention of those living where Satan has his throne to the One who is sitting on the only throne that really matters.

Furthermore, these chapters remind Christians in Pergamum over and over again that God and the Lamb are the only ones who are worthy of their faithful devotion. Look at who God is and what he has done. To even consider denying the faith would be utter insanity. Look at whom you would be denying! Ultimately, "every creature in heaven and on earth and under the earth and in the sea, and all that is in them" will cry out with loud voices, "To him who sits on the throne and to the Lamb be blessing and honor and glory and might forever and ever!" (5:13). Believers in Pergamum should, therefore, continue to live out a life of visible praise to God and continue to call others to do so as well.

REVELATION 6: THE MESSAGE TO PERGAMUM

The vision of the four horsemen of the apocalypse would have quickly reinforced what it meant for Jesus to come and fight against those who had chosen assimilation over pure devotion to him (2:16). Conquest, bloodshed, famine, plagues, and even death by wild animals were coming to those who refused to glorify God (6:1–8). To be lured into compromise by the Nicolaitans in order to save their skins or enjoy as much as possible of what their city had to offer neglected a very plain fact: Avoiding the wrath of a hostile society controlled by Satan *now* would lead to facing the wrath of the Lamb *later*. There is no question that refusal to compromise may lead to death, as it had with Antipas. God did not promise that after the one martyr in their city he would prevent any further deaths. In fact, the vision of the fifth seal would have made it clear to Christians in Pergamum that there would be many more who would face the fate of Antipas. It was God's plan for others to be his witnesses even at the cost of their lives. This reminder would have helped strengthen the resolve of those in Pergamum who were beginning to weaken under the onslaught of the evil one and the seductive teachings of the Nicolaitans. Fear of the unknown can be debilitating; so God removes the unknown and makes it clear that some of them will indeed likely also be put to death.

Christians in Pergamum would have also been comforted by the vivid reminder that justice was coming. Those who held the reins of Roman power in Pergamum and had persecuted them would ultimately face the wrath of God. Although Satan and those in league with him may seem to be winning now, a time was soon coming when God would right all wrongs and bring his enemies to justice. This, though, is only part of the story. As believers in Pergamum came to the sixth seal (6:12–17), they would have come face to face with language drawn right out of the Old Testament (Reading Instruction #6). Two passages are particularly important:

> Samaria's king shall perish like a twig on the face of the waters. [8]The high places of Aven, the sin of Israel, shall be destroyed. Thorn and thistle shall grow up on their altars, and they shall say to the mountains, "Cover us," and to the hills, "Fall on us." (Hos 10:7–8)

> Enter into the rock and hide in the dust from before the terror of the Lord, and from the splendor of his majesty. (Isa 2:10)

It is far too easy to read the seal judgments and focus on—and perhaps even celebrate—the fate awaiting God's enemies. As with the rest of Revelation, though, we need to remember that this portion of the book is addressed to Christians (Reading Instruction #1). That does not mean that it is describing the fate of followers of Jesus. Quite the contrary, we find that throughout Revelation the horrors that God ordains are targeted at those who reject him. By using language right out of the Old Testament, however, Jesus is intentionally calling his people to think more carefully about what the passage is saying to *them*.

If we look at the context of the passages from Hosea and Isaiah, who do we find needing to hide from God's wrath? In Hosea, it is the northern kingdom of Israel. In Isaiah, it is the southern kingdom of Judah. In other words, we are dealing with God warning *his own people* of coming judgment if they do not repent. Why in the world did God's own people need to hide from him? Isaiah 2:19–21 is particularly enlightening:

> And people shall enter the caves of the rocks and the holes of the ground, from before the terror of the Lord, and from the splendor of his majesty, when he rises to terrify the earth. [20]*In that day mankind will cast away their idols of silver and their idols of gold, which they made for themselves to worship,* to the

moles and to the bats, [21]to enter the caverns of the rocks and the clefts of the cliffs, from before the terror of the Lord, and from the splendor of his majesty, when he rises to terrify the earth.

Here we see not only the judgment repeated, but also its cause identified: idolatry (a.k.a. assimilation). That broad assimilation is in view is even clearer earlier in the chapter:

For you have rejected your people, the house of Jacob, because *they are full of things from the east and of fortune-tellers like the Philistines, and they strike hands with the children of foreigners.* [7]Their land is filled with silver and gold, and there is no end to their treasures; their land is filled with horses, and there is no end to their chariots. [8]Their land is filled with idols; *they bow down to the work of their hands, to what their own fingers have made.* (Isa 2:6–8)[1]

What does all of this mean for our understanding of Rev 6? It is likely that given circumstances in Asia Minor and the strategic use of language from these particular Old Testament passages, the original readers would have heard the sixth seal as a warning not to fall prey to the temptation to assimilate. For, those who profess to be God's people but follow the teachings of the Nicolaitans or the teaching of Balaam will be judged severely along with those with whom they have chosen to associate, just as the nation of Israel was in the Old Testament for the same lack of faithfulness.

REVELATION 7: THE MESSAGE TO PERGAMUM

For Christians living in Satanville, the visions of Rev 7 would have provided deep encouragement and hope. Revelation 7:1–8 would have reminded them that God's servants will be protected from his wrath. This would help drive home the importance of what they had just heard in Rev 6. God is about to pour out his wrath on a world where Satan is not only active, but also has the allegiance of the vast majority. Those who serve him or his emissaries (e.g., Rome) will face a dreadful fate, but God's people will be spared. They are marked as his own precious possession. The sealing of the 144,000 would have reminded Christians in Pergamum that "The Lord knows those who are his" (2 Tim 2:19).

As they read 7:9–10, their courage would have been bolstered. They had remained true to Jesus' name and had not renounced their faith in him, and they could continue to do so, knowing that "Salvation belongs to our God who sits on the throne, and to the Lamb" (7:10). The temptation, of course, was to think that they had to take matters into their own hands to save themselves from the evil one, whose throne was located in their hometown. Quite the contrary, Jesus reminds them in this vision that they must look to the one who is on the Throne of thrones, for "there is salvation in no

---

1. "Striking [or clasping] hands with the children of foreigners" likely refers to alliances with pagans, which would necessitate significant compromise, often including worship of foreign gods.

one else, for there is no other name under heaven given among men by which we must be saved" (Acts 4:12). Yes, they may pay the ultimate price for their faith—as Antipas had—and their death may be the way they come "out of the great tribulation" (7:14), but a day is soon coming when God will take away their hunger, thirst, and pain, and they will dwell in his presence forever (7:15–17).

REVELATION 8–9: THE MESSAGE TO PERGAMUM

Jesus' message of hope to Christians living in Pergamum is strengthened further in Rev 8–9, where they would have been reminded that God is attentive to their prayers for justice (8:3–4) and would soon bring the wrath that is due to Satan's followers. In Rev 2:13, we learned that Satan lived and ruled from Pergamum, his Jerusalem. Now we read that his kingdom is going to be utterly decimated as God pours out his wrath on the land (8:7), sea (8:8–9), rivers and springs (8:10–11), sun, moon, and stars (8:12), and "those who dwell on the earth" (8:13), i.e., those who follow the evil one and are not sealed by God (9:4). Those who had tortured and killed Antipas and others in Pergamum would face unthinkable torture as God poured out his wrath on them (9:5–6). The demonic hordes of hell, apparently led by Satan himself (9:11), would have free rein to torment the unsealed inhabitants of the earth, much as Satan had been allowed to torment, but not kill, Job.

The vivid description of the fifth trumpet in 9:7–11 is intended to heighten the horror of what is going to happen. This is further compounded in the account of the sixth trumpet in 9:15–16, where we find an unthinkably large army that is released to kill a third of all mankind. John makes it clear that he heard a specific number (9:16), and that number was off the charts. But it gets worse. This was clearly no ordinary army. Where Elisha asked God to open his servant's eyes so that he would see that "the mountain was full of horses and chariots of fire all around Elisha" (2 Kgs 6:17), here we see another type of supernatural army, a terrifying army of riders on fire-breathing horses that have heads like lions.

This is the type of judgment that those who cavort with the evil one will face. Remember, Jesus had warned the faithful majority in Pergamum to repent and deal with those in their midst who had chosen assimilation over faithfulness. Why should they repent? Jesus makes it perfectly clear that if they fail to repent he—the one "who has the sharp two-edged sword" (2:12)—will come and "war against them with the sword of my mouth" (2:16). Revelation 6, 8, and 9 paint a stark picture of what having Jesus pronounce judgment against you might look like, a picture that would have spurred Christians in Pergamum to repent quickly in order to rescue those among them who had been ensnared by false teaching.

REVELATION 10-11: THE MESSAGE TO PERGAMUM

Christians in Pergamum had beautifully represented what it looked like to live as Jesus' witnesses in a hostile environment. Although they struggled with the temptation to let false teaching go unchecked within their congregation, they had been prepared to lose their lives for the sake of the gospel. The vision of the "sweet and sour" scroll in 10:9–11 would have communicated two important things to this particular church. First, it would have reminded them that their experience—the abundant life of living for Jesus that was coupled with the stark reality of torture and death—was to be expected. It was ordained by God. The message of the gospel was one that carried not only a delightful sweetness but also a sharp sour note. As we saw with our discussion of the message to the church at Ephesus, the sweetness comes from the fact that what is being consumed was truly Good News, and those consuming it were recipients of all that Good News announced through the person and work of Jesus Christ. The sourness, on the other hand, stemmed from the fact that those who partake of the Good News are also called to pass on the Good News. They are called to be faithful witnesses, just as Antipas was. Jesus was not exaggerating when he talked about people losing their life for him (Matt 16:25); he was not being melodramatic when he spoke of the requirement for his followers to "take up their cross" (Matt 16:24). He expects his followers to be willing to put their lives on the line as they embrace his call to be his ambassadors in their context.

The fact that the sourness of the scroll is connected to bearing witness to Jesus is made clear in 10:11 and reinforced in the vision of the two witnesses recorded in Rev 11, which is presented not as a new vision but rather as a continuation of the vision in Rev 10.[2] The two witnesses provide another example to Christians in Pergamum of what it looks like to live as faithful witnesses. They faithfully carry out the role that God has given them, protected from the evil one until they have finished their job. Christians in Pergamum had been faithful thus far. Jesus encourages them through these visions to press on as his witnesses, knowing that though they too may be hated and killed, God will raise his faithful witnesses from the dead (11:11) and call them home to his presence (11:12). He will also bring judgment upon the city where they were killed for their testimony (11:13).

Revelation 10:9—11:10 has something very important to say to a generation of Western Christians who are committed to proving to the society around them that they are citizens who should be valued. Conventional wisdom is increasingly urging Christians to establish credibility with their city through acts of benevolence and through getting involved in the things that matter to the people of their city. We are told that we can become "a church of irresistible influence," a church whose ministries that target the physical needs of the city will eventually win over the hearts of our

---

2. The two chapters are linked with a καί (*kai*), which indicates continuity rather than a new development in the discourse.

fellow citizens, drawing them to God. The message to Christians in Pergamum—in Rev 2 and the rest of Revelation—tells a very different story. A world where Satan rules is never going to be won over by the things of God. A true community of believers will never become a church of irresistible influence. We may win our community's friendship by doing things that appeal to its fleshly desires or genuine physical needs—and followers of Jesus should be the most compassionate and generous people on the planet—but when we bring out the message that we are called to carry to our neighbors and the nations, the response will not always, or even usually, be positive. We have been commissioned to call others to repentance. This is symbolized in the attire of the two witnesses in Rev 11 (sackcloth). When we carry out that commission, we can expect the same response that Paul received when he acted as a faithful witness to Jesus: "Away with such a fellow from the earth! For he should not be allowed to live" (Acts 22:22). The question that the message to Pergamum calls us to ask ourselves is not "How do I win the trust and affection of the city in which I live?" but rather, "Will I continue to faithfully proclaim the Good News of Jesus Christ to a city that hates those who bear that message?"

The final portion of Rev 11, which records the sounding of the seventh trumpet, reminds Christians in Pergamum that Jesus Christ is going to reign forever and ever. Yes, the nations are currently angry and, incited by Satan, they are fighting against God and his purposes in this world; but God's wrath is coming. They will be judged, and God's faithful servants will be rewarded (11:18). Therefore, they should continue to fear him (the definition of a "saint" in 11:18) rather than fearing the authorities in Pergamum.

REVELATION 12: THE MESSAGE TO PERGAMUM

The account of earlier events that led to Satan's current activities in this world would have been particularly attention-grabbing for Christians in the city where Satan lived and had his throne. What in the world had led to Satan having such a powerful presence in their city? Jesus reveals through the visions of past events that Satan had first attempted to destroy the Messiah when he was born (12:1–5); but he had failed. He had then turned to pursuing the nation of Israel, from whom the Messiah had come; but he failed again. So, at last, he turned on followers of Jesus, "the rest of her offspring" (12:17).

Jesus wants to make it clear to those living in Satan's city, that although Satan is not a minor adversary, he is an adversary who will ultimately be destroyed. So, he reveals to them, through the visions that John saw, a mighty battle in heaven, with Satan and his angelic followers fighting against Michael and other angels loyal to God (12:7). Satan lost, and he was thrown out of heaven with his followers (12:8). It is important to note how he was defeated. He did not engage in a colossal battle with God himself in which God was barely able to defeat him. Not at all! Although some

Christians today think Satan is an adversary that God has to fight against, this is not a biblical perspective at all. Compared to God, Satan has no power at all. He cannot even begin to resist God's purposes. He can only do what God allows him to do. Here in Rev 12, the fact that Satan and his angels/demons lose a fight with Michael (who is an angel himself) and the angels under his command makes it clear that Satan is far from invincible. If Satan can be defeated by another angel, what will happen when God finally passes judgment on him?

As Christians in Pergamum read Rev 12, they would have noticed that Satan was defeated in the past, but he was not destroyed. Instead, both he and his angels/demons were sent down to earth (12:9), where he unfortunately established his base of operations in Pergamum; and he was not at all happy about being thrown out of heaven. He is the same evil one who has been leading the world astray ever since the beginning when he appeared as a serpent and deceived Adam and Eve (12:9); and he continues to attempt to undermine God's work in this world, furiously fighting against God's people, knowing that his time is quickly running out (12:12). Unfortunately for those in Asia Minor, some of the most effective soldiers in his army in the first century were the Nicolaitans.

Christians in Pergamum are reminded that they are to continue overcoming him in the same way that they have been doing all along: "they have conquered him by the blood of the Lamb and by the word of their testimony, for they loved not their lives even unto death" (12:11). They cannot shrink back from their habit of spreading the word of their testimony throughout their city. They must follow the example of Antipas, and not give in to the temptation to be mute even when their lives are on the line. Jesus' message to them here in Rev 12, then, is, "Keep on doing what you've been doing! That's how you will overcome!"

There is more, though, in the visions of Rev 12 for Christians in Pergamum. Notice how the rest of the offspring of the woman, the true people of God, are described in 12:17. They are "those who keep the commandments of God and hold to the testimony of Jesus." Readers in Pergamum would not have missed the fact that the description here of holding to the testimony of Jesus was precisely where they had been excelling: "you hold fast my name, and you did not deny my faith ['your faith in me'] even in the days of Antipas my faithful witness, who was killed among you, where Satan dwells" (2:13). But there is more to the description of the true people of God. God's people also obey his commands; they take God's Word seriously. They find out what pleases the Lord (Eph 5:10) and act on it. Among those commands are these reminders: "But sexual immorality and all impurity or covetousness must not even be named among you, as is proper among saints" (Eph 5:3) and "flee from idolatry" (1 Cor 10:14). The church in Pergamum would have known that the sexually immoral and idolatrous will not inherit the kingdom of God (Gal 5:19–21). Therefore, it was critical to repent of looking the other way and warn those who had embraced the teaching of Balaam to repent now, while there was still an opportunity.

REVELATION 13: THE MESSAGE TO PERGAMUM

For Christians in Pergamum, the vision of the beast in Rev 13 would have hit very close to home. Satan (the dragon) is powerful, and so are his emissaries. The description here would have particularly helped Christians in Pergamum to understand the nature of Satan's power in their city. They had heard in 12:3 that the dragon, Satan, had seven heads with seven crowns. This spoke of his overwhelming authority, authority that appears to be absolute (Reading Instruction #5). Now in Rev 13 they learn that his emissary, the beast, carries a huge amount of authority himself (symbolized by the ten crowns on his ten horns). The additional imagery makes it clear that something else is at work in the symbol of the ten-horned beast. In addition to having ten horns, the beast also "was like a leopard; its feet were like a bear's, and its mouth was like a lion's mouth" (13:2). These four symbols draw our attention back to Dan 7 (Reading Instruction #6), where we find four separate beasts matching these descriptions. The vision of the beast that Jesus gives his followers in Rev 13, then, combines the four beasts of Daniel into one Superbeast. The allusions to Daniel, perhaps especially in Rev 13, are likely intended to draw attention back to four men (Daniel, Shadrach, Meshach, and Abednego) who would not compromise or assimilate even when their lives were on the line.[3]

Like the dragon, the beast is evil personified. This is symbolized by the fact that both have seven heads. Leviathan, one of the common images of evil in the Old Testament, was thought to have seven heads, though the number is not specified in the Old Testament (see the reference to "heads" in Ps 74:13–14). What makes the connection even more likely is the fact that the Greek term δράκων (*drakōn*), here translated "dragon," is used to translate "Leviathan" in Job 3:8; 41:1; Ps 104:26; and Isa 27:1 in the Septuagint.[4] Jesus is thus using common symbols of evil and power (Reading Instruction #5) to paint a picture of the ultimate adversary of God and his people in Rev 12–13. The picture of the beast in Rev 13 would have made clear to the original readers that although incredibly powerful evil rulers have come on the scene in the past, they were nothing in comparison to the beast that was to come. That Superbeast will institute a reign of terror with the unprecedented power and authority that he receives from Satan himself (13:2).

For Christians in Pergamum, the point would have been particularly sobering. Satan has his throne in Pergamum, but he has given that throne to the beast, his emissary. It is hard to believe that the Christians in Pergamum would not have connected

---

3. Indeed, the book of Daniel and the book of Revelation function in an analogous manner. Whereas Revelation establishes the context for interpreting its apocalyptic imagery through the seven messages in chapters 2–3, however, Daniel does the same thing through the narrative of chapters 1–6. In each case, the first part of the book sounds a clarion reminder that compromise is not an option, while the second part of the book reinforces and fleshes out that call through its apocalyptic visions.

4. Osborne, *Revelation*, 459; see also *Odes Sol.* 22:5, written around the same time as Revelation, which also refers to a seven-headed dragon.

this derived authority with the power that Rome wielded in their city. Remember, the citizens of Pergamum worshiped the goddess Roma because she had given Rome authority over the nations (cf. 13:4a). They also worshiped Rome and Augustus, asking, "Who is like Rome? Who can make war against Rome?" (cf. 13:4b). And they worshiped Zeus on the great altar atop the acropolis, who was praised with the words "Zeus was, Zeus is, Zeus will be; O mighty Zeus."[5] This, of course, suggests that the words in 1:8 may well have created another rhetorical hotspot for Christians in Pergamum in particular (Reading Instruction #4): "I am the Alpha and the Omega," says the Lord God, "*who is and who was and who is to come, the Almighty.*"

With the fate of Antipas, Christians in Pergamum had seen firsthand that the beast had been "allowed to make war on the saints and to conquer them" (13:7). They saw their fellow citizens worshiping the beast (13:8). It would have been terrifying to stand out from their neighbors and those they had to do business with. Jesus subtly reminds them, though, that they should not look with longing on the easier life of those "whose name has not been written before the foundation of the world in the book of life of the Lamb who was slain" (13:8). He also reminds them that the fate of Antipas was not going to be out of the ordinary for those who bear the name of Jesus. He first strongly gets their attention ("If anyone has an ear, let him hear," 13:9) and then sets forth the sober reality plainly: "If anyone is to be taken captive, to captivity he goes; if anyone is to be slain with the sword, with the sword must he be slain" (13:10). God's people will be killed.[6] Antipas was not the first to die for his faith, and he would not be the last (6:9–11).

How are his people to respond to all of this? "Here is a call for the endurance and faith of the saints" (13:10). There is no indication of a free-ride or a get-out-of-tribulation-free card here for the people of God. They are in the thick of things in Revelation, facing the wrath of the beast; and God expects them to exhibit patient endurance and faithfulness. These were the two areas where Christians in Pergamum had been excelling; and Jesus, through his portrayal of the beast, urges them to be prepared to continue in their faithfulness and perseverance as the days get darker.

This message is reinforced in the final portion of Rev 13. Christians in Pergamum had already come face to face with martyrdom and had almost certainly faced persecution in a variety of forms, some of which affected their livelihood. In 13:11–18, Jesus makes it clear to them that things are only going to get worse for the people of God. There is coming a time when Satan will give his power and authority to an emissary

---

5. Pausanias 10.12.10; cited by Aune, *Revelation 1–5*, 31.

6. Revelation 13:10 probably operates on two levels. First, it reminds Christians that death and captivity are coming, and then exhorts them to endurance and faithfulness. Second, it is likely that some of the original readers would have noticed the similarity between the language here and the language in Jer 15:1–2, which announces God's judgment on those professing to be his people for their refusal to repent as is clear in what follows (see Jer 15:7). This intertextual connection would have reminded readers of Rev 13 that they dare not give in to the persuasion of the Nicolaitans. The path of compromise had always led the people of God to divine judgment.

who will be a messianic figure ("It had two horns like a lamb," 13:11a) serving the purposes of the evil one ("it spoke like a dragon," 13:11b). This figure, portrayed as a second beast, will promote and compel the worship of the first beast (13:12) and do miracles on behalf of the first beast (13:13–14). He will have power to kill any who refuse to worship the first beast (13:15), and will make it impossible to work or buy the necessities of life for those who do not give their allegiance to the beast by taking his mark (13:16–18). The picture, then, is one of intense pressure to assimilate. Go along with the beast, or starve and die. Christians in Asia Minor were already experiencing this on a smaller scale, but things were going to get much worse.

Revelation 13 then concludes with the intriguing puzzle of the number of the beast: 666. In both Greek and Hebrew, each letter of the alphabet had a corresponding numerical value. Thus, every name also had a numerical value that was determined by adding up the numbers associated with each letter of the name. Here, we are told that the beast's number is man's number, a number representing fallen man in all his imperfection. The beast, then, is fallen man par excellence (Reading Instruction #5). It is very likely that the original readers would have associated the number six hundred and sixty-six with Nero. The fact that this relies on the numerical value of "Nero Caesar" as it would have been written in Hebrew rather than Greek (the language of Revelation) does not seriously undermine this view. After all, the Apostle John explicitly tells the readers that they are going to have to think about it carefully if they are going to catch what he is saying (13:18).

It is very interesting that only on two occasions does John say that understanding what he is saying "calls for wisdom." The first place is here in 13:18, where John records the number of the beast; the second is in 17:9, where the angel interprets the seven heads as seven hills/seven kings. The vast majority of scholars views 17:9 as a not so subtle reference to Rome, "the city built on seven hills." The reference to seven kings, five of whom have fallen, one who was currently reigning, and one who would reign in the future, but only for a short time (17:10), works well—and only works well—as a reference to the first century, when Julius Caesar, Augustus, Tiberius, Caligula, and Claudius had died, Nero was reigning, and Nero's successor Galba was to reign only a few months. The beast in 17:11 is identified as an eighth king. The connection with Nero is thus strongly reinforced by the visions in Rev 17.

The beast is distinguished from Nero, the sixth emperor, and yet connected to him by the number he bears. He is a new emperor, a revived Nero. Nero committed suicide on June 9, AD 68 by thrusting a sword through his throat, and that was the end of him. The beast, on the other hand, seems to have a fatal wound and then lives. It is quite possible that Jesus is playing off both what was known of Nero and the legend that developed after his suicide that he would come back and retake the throne. What is clear is that the beast in Rev 13 is being cast in the image of Nero—much like the two witnesses in Rev 11 are cast in the image of Moses and Elijah, and the prophetess in 2:20 is cast in the image of Jezebel—in order to give the original readers a fuller picture *through association* of what he would be like. In other words, Jesus is telling readers that the beast will be a Nero-like figure, just as the two witnesses will be Moses-like and Elijah-like figures.

The Christians in Pergamum had already faced the fury of Satan in their city. A day was coming, though, when that fury would increase. A day was coming when a figure would be so powerful and so deceptive that he would lead the whole world astray and seemingly exercise absolute power. While many readers would have likely thought Jesus was describing their current circumstances under the Roman Empire, John appears to speak of the same beast in one of his letters in future rather than present terms (1 John 2:18). He recognized that there were all sorts of antichrists in this world, i.e., those who oppose or try to supplant the true Christ either through usurping his role or spreading false teachings; but there was also a preeminent Antichrist who was on the horizon as John wrote his letter, presumably sometime after writing Revelation.

So, Rev 13 should not be read as merely a reference to the fact that evil rulers will periodically rise up throughout history, or simply as a reference to the Roman emperor at the time. Such readings fail to recognize that the passage is concerned with the bad guy, par excellence, who will come at the culmination of the ages. For Christians in Pergamum, whom Jesus is calling to overcome, Rev 13 is a heads up that things are going to get worse before they get better. The key question they need to continue to ask themselves is: "Whom will I worship?" Everyone worships either God or the beast. There is no middle ground.

REVELATION 14: THE MESSAGE TO PERGAMUM

As with Christians living in Smyrna, the visions of Rev 14 would have been a strong reminder to those in Pergamum to persevere in the midst of suffering, and even death, choosing to fear God (14:7) rather than the one who had his throne in Pergamum. Satan, and his city—here identified as "Babylon"—will come to utter ruin (14:8). The same will be true of all who give their allegiance to the beast (14:11). The obvious response, which resounds with great force because of the repeated language from 13:10, is to be vigilant to avoid shrinking back from following the Lord Jesus: "Here is a call for the endurance of the saints, those who keep the commandments of God and their faith in Jesus" (14:12). For the faithful, like Antipas, death that comes for following the Lord is a blessing (14:13a), in part, because God will reward such people for their deeds (14:13b). Jesus reminds his followers in Pergamum that their faithfulness in remaining true to his name and not renouncing their faith in him (2:13), even in the face of death, will be visible for all to see and richly rewarded when they stand before him. The end of all things is near—a time when God will separate the sheep from the goats, harvesting the earth. The faithful will be harvested, like cherished first fruits from the world (14:14–16), while the faithless and rebellious of the world will be trampled under the force of God's wrath (14:17–20).

REVELATION 15–16: THE MESSAGE TO PERGAMUM

The vision at the beginning of Rev 15 would have been particularly encouraging for the church in Pergamum, which had remained true to Jesus (2:13). Those who press on in their faithfulness and conquer "the beast and its image and the number of its name" will one day soon stand "beside the sea of glass with harps of God in their hands" (15:2). Victory will come through continuing to stand firm, and the victorious (overcomers) will worship before God with great joy (15:2–4). That will be their fate, while the fate of the enemies of God will be the seven bowls of his wrath (15:5–8), which are described in detail in Rev 16. Those who renounce their faith in Jesus and give their allegiance to the beast will suffer horribly (16:2). Those who have shed the blood of the saints—saints like Antipas of Pergamum—will get what they deserve (16:6), and the martyred saints who had been crying out from under the altar (6:9–11) will finally be able to rejoice in God's just judgment (16:7).

In the midst of the description of God's wrath being poured out, Jesus pauses to address his people directly, including those in Pergamum: "Behold, I am coming like a thief! Blessed is the one who stays awake, keeping his garments on, that he may not go about naked and be seen exposed" (16:15). The language here is the language of preparation for battle. It is reminiscent of the situation described in Neh 4 (Reading Instruction #6). The people of God were facing significant opposition as they began to rebuild the wall around Jerusalem. Nehemiah summed up how he led the people to respond in verses 21–23. The language he uses, particularly in verse 23, paints a picture of constant vigilance and readiness; and this is precisely what Jesus was calling his followers to. They are to be like Nehemiah and his men, always dressed and armed for battle. They are to get up each morning recognizing that they are at war. Jesus' warning in Rev 16:15 reminds them in no uncertain terms that if they do not take the battle seriously, they will be put to shame like prisoners of war who are stripped and forced to march away to exile or execution.

REVELATION 17–18: THE MESSAGE TO PERGAMUM

The vivid portrayal of the downfall and destruction of Babylon in Rev 17–18 would have been particularly poignant for Christians in Pergamum for a variety of reasons. First, they lived in "Satanville," a place where the evil one was particularly active, the seat of his power on earth. This is precisely what Babylon represents. Although it is clearly a cipher for Rome—Rome was known as the city on seven hills (17:9)—it also represents the center of Satan's influence in this world. Whatever Jesus meant precisely by referring to Pergamum as the place "where Satan's throne is" (2:13a) and the city "where Satan dwells" (2:13b), it is very much on par with the description that we find of Babylon in Rev 17–18. There, Babylon is personified as the greatest of prostitutes who is opposed to God and stands against all that he stands for. Babylon is "full of blasphemous names" (17:3). Perhaps most striking, however, would have been the description of the prostitute as "drunk with the blood of the saints, the blood of the martyrs of Jesus" (17:6). Pergamum was the seat of Roman power in Asia Minor, the city from which the sword of Rome was wielded, the place where Christians would be put on trial for their lives. Implicit in all of this is the question of how Christians in the church in Pergamum could possibly compromise their faith and align themselves with the teachings of the Nicolaitans by associating with or benefiting from the prostitute who was gleefully murdering their fellow servants of Christ.

Jesus makes it clear to Christians in Pergamum that although the beast and his allies will continue to fight against God, his purposes, and his people, their doom is imminent. Yes, they "will make war on the Lamb," but "the Lamb will conquer them, for he is Lord of lords and King of kings" (17:14a). More than that, the Lamb will not be alone. The description of those who accompany the Lamb in his triumph should not be missed: "those with him are called and chosen and faithful" (17:14b). Christians in Pergamum had been faithful thus far in the midst of the most challenging of circumstances. Even when one of their number—Antipas, the *faithful* witness—was martyred, they did not give in to fear. As Jesus describes the destruction of the beast in 17:14, he subtly reminds them of the need to remain faithful to the end and so be at his side when the beast is destroyed.

Just as Jesus' characterization of Pergamum as "Satanville" would have encouraged Christians in Pergamum neither to compromise in the face of intense pressure nor to be seduced by what Pergamum had to offer those who gave their allegiance to the city, so Jesus' description in Rev 18 of the downfall of mighty Babylon would have reminded them of the temporary nature of any earthly benefits that unfaithfulness to him might bring. Like Babylon, the mighty Pergamum was destined to become a wasteland, a ghost town (18:2). The only wise response for Christians living there was to separate themselves carefully from the sins of the city they inhabit (18:4), since those sins were well known to God (18:5) and they will bring harsh judgment in the end (18:6–8, 21–24). A day is soon coming when the people of God will be able to rejoice in the justice God will bring to this evil city where Satan lives and has his throne (18:20), and where the people of God have been oppressed and put to death (18:20, 24).

REVELATION 19: THE MESSAGE TO PERGAMUM

The same theme continues into Rev 19. Christians in Pergamum can rest assured that a day will come when God avenges the blood of his people (19:1–3). Like Christians elsewhere in Asia Minor, they would have been reminded that God's servants fear him

(19:5). They recognize him for who he is (in contrast to feeble earthly rulers) and they live in obedience to him regardless of the personal cost. As those living in the most oppressive of all cities in Asia Minor, Christians in Pergamum would have stood and cheered with the great multitude in heaven at the thought of the coming wedding feast of the Lamb (19:7a, 9). At the same time, they would have been reminded of the need to be ready for that feast (19:7b), and readiness required faithfulness to the end.

The center of attention in Rev 19, however, is on the triumphant appearance of the rider on the white horse. There is no question concerning his identity. Only one bears the title "Word of God" (19:13), and only one has been described as having a sword coming out of his mouth (19:15; 1:16; 2:12, 16). This is Jesus; and just as he is the Faithful One (19:11), so he expects his followers to be faithful as well, regardless of which city they live in. Perhaps most striking for those in Pergamum would have been Jesus' words in verses 11, 15 and 21. Jesus had not only appeared to John as one with a sword coming out of his mouth (1:16), but had also presented himself to the Christians in Pergamum as the one "who has the sharp two-edged sword" (2:12); and he had gone on to strongly warn them that if they did not repent and deal with the false teaching among them, he was going to come and "make war" against those who were leading his people astray "with the sword of [his] mouth" (2:16). Now, what Jesus threatened is portrayed in vivid terms. Jesus is not a cuddly lamb; he is a terrifying warrior with eyes of blazing fire (19:12), the King of kings and Lord of lords (19:16), whose justice no one will escape. He is not a pacifist Jesus; he is coming to judge and "make war" (19:11). Through him God's fury and wrath will finally be executed to their fullest (19:15). None will escape the fate that is due them; whether one is a king, proconsul, or the emperor himself, all who have opposed Jesus will become buzzard food (19:17–21). All who willingly or under pressure take the mark of the beast and associate themselves with the enemy will perish when Jesus returns. Indeed, the seemingly omnipotent beast himself (13:4) is really nothing at all; he will be thrown into the lake of fire alive (19:20). This passage, in fact, responds to the people of the world who "worshiped the beast, saying, 'Who is like the beast, and who can fight against it?'" (13:4).[7] Jesus, the King of kings and Lord of lords, can and will make war against the beast; for the beast is nothing compared to his majesty and power. Although things may look bad for the people of God living in Pergamum, then, their suffering cannot compare to what is coming for the enemies of Jesus.

SUMMARY: JESUS' MESSAGE TO CHRISTIANS IN PERGAMUM

To Christians living in the city where Satan had his throne, Jesus makes it clear beyond a shadow of a doubt that this temporary reality must be understood and responded to in light of the fact that there is Someone infinitely greater seated on the only Throne

7. Regrettably, the ESV's inconsistency in translation once again obscures the connection. Both 13:4 (ESV: "fight against") and 19:11 ("makes war") use the same Greek verb (πολεμέω, polemeō).

that really matters. And while he has temporarily allowed Satan to exercise control in this world, he is still actively bringing about his eternal purposes. Among those purposes is the sobering reality that he will not only bring his wrath full force upon this world, but he has also ordained that Antipas of Pergamum will not be a lone martyr. There will, in fact, be many more (6:9–11).

Those living in the seat of Roman power in Asia Minor, however, could rest assured that those who persecuted God's people would be brought to justice in the end. God would hear their prayers (8:3–4) and respond decisively, utterly decimating the world over which Satan currently exercises control (Rev 6, 8–9, 16–18). The frightful pictures of God's wrath being poured out drive home the danger of having Jesus come to "war against" those within the church who are in rebellion against him through their false teaching or assimilation to the culture around them. They must continue to embrace the reality that following Jesus is a "sweet and sour" experience (10:9). The pain that comes from being Jesus' ambassadors, however, rests firmly under the umbrella of the sovereignty of God, where they are not only sealed from his wrath (7:3), but also completely protected from the wrath of Satan until God decides their work for him is done (11:7). At that point, they will enter into God's presence where the suffering they now face will forever be a thing of the past (7:15–17).

Therefore, God is the only One that they should fear (11:18). Fearing anyone else was a sure path to destruction. Yes, Satan is raging against both God and his people, furious that he has lost his place in heaven and been forced to relocate to Pergamum (Rev 12). His power in this world is profound, and it is directed against all those who will not submit to his rule and worship him (Rev 13). Those who refuse to capitulate will lose their livelihoods and likely their lives as well, but they will be richly rewarded by the King of kings and Lord of lords for their endurance, obedience, and faithfulness (14:12–13) when God comes and separates the wheat from the chaff (14:14–20). Therefore, absolute vigilance is called for (16:15).

Followers of Jesus in Pergamum dare not give in to the toxic teaching of the Nicolaitans and so compromise their faith by cavorting with a prostitute who is about to be destroyed (Rev 17–18). They, above all others, know firsthand that the prostitute is "drunk with the blood of the saints, the blood of the martyrs of Jesus" (17:6), among whom Antipas was only one. How, then, could they consider any sort of commerce with her? How could they consider assimilating in any way to the lifestyle that she promoted? The only sane response was to "come out from her" (18:4) and separate themselves from her sins by living a life that is clearly in line with the values of the kingdom and the King to whom they belong. That is the only way they can be properly clothed for the wedding supper of the Lamb (19:7–9). And if, despite all of this, Christians in Pergamum were still wavering in their resolve to repent of tolerating Nicolaitans in their midst, they need only look at the terrifying image of the one who had warned them already that there were some among them in danger of having him "war against them with the sword of [his] mouth" now coming on a white horse

(19:11) with the armies of heaven (19:14) and a sharp sword protruding from his mouth (19:15). Compromise of any sort was simply not worth it.

8

Jesus' Message to the Church in Thyatira

And to the angel of the church in Thyatira write: The words of the Son of God,
who has eyes like a flame of fire, and whose feet are like burnished bronze. (2:18)

JESUS IDENTIFIES HIMSELF TO the Christians in Thyatira as the "Son of God." As we have seen earlier, the titles Jesus chooses for himself are important, and go well beyond simply linking him to the One who appeared to John in Rev 1 (see 1:14b). Although this title occurs forty-six times in the New Testament, in Revelation it is used only here.[1] On the one hand, it is likely, particularly given the reference to Psalm 2 later in this letter, that Jesus is identifying himself with the "Son" of Psalm 2 who will exercise authority over the nations (see Ps 2:7–9). He alone is the promised Messiah who will one day rule without opposition. But there is likely more at work in his choice of titles. Today, we often view "Son of God" as a unique title that is distinctively associated with Jesus as the unique Son of God. The original readers, on the other hand, would have known very well that Roman emperors often claimed to be a "son of god" (Reading Instruction #4). It would thus have been very natural for them to hear Jesus contrasting himself with the interloper emperor in Rome through his choice of titles. By identifying himself as the "Son of God," a title that legitimately belongs to him alone, Jesus effectively called Christians in Thyatira to think twice about any level of allegiance to the feeble emperor in Rome who had been usurping his title.

The description of Jesus as one "who has eyes like a flame of fire, and whose feet are like burnished bronze" again sets him apart from the Roman emperor who relies on outward grandeur to bolster his image. In contrast, Jesus' very being (his eyes and his feet) radiates his unparalleled glory. Which "Son of God" will they fear? To which

---

1. God is also referred to as Jesus' Father in a number of places (1:6; 2:27; 3:5, 21; 14:1); Charles, *Revelation*, 68.

"Son of God" will they give their allegiance? By highlighting his eyes being "like a flame of fire" Jesus is likely symbolizing his piercing vision that sees beyond the surface. When he says in the next verse "I know . . .," he really means it. He is well aware of all of the good in the church at Thyatira; but Jezebel has not escaped his notice. So what does Jesus have to say to this group of believers?

> *I know your works, your love and faith and service and patient endurance, and that your latter works exceed the first.* (2:19)

In contrast to the church in Ephesus, which had lost its first love, the church in Thyatira had matured since its inception and was currently a more effective witness than it had been in its early years. Jesus' knowledge of their deeds indicates his awareness of the life of the church over the years. The four things that are listed are all specific examples of their "works" or behavior. The church at Thyatira is characterized by love (for one another and toward God), faith toward God (though faithfulness/dependability may be in view), service that expresses the reality of their relationship with God by doing his will, and patient endurance despite their circumstances. This is an extremely positive assessment of how Christians in Thyatira were doing. Unfortunately, Jesus still has something "against" them.

> *Nevertheless, I have this against you: You tolerate that woman Jezebel, who calls herself a prophetess. By her teaching she misleads my servants into sexual immorality and the eating of food sacrificed to idols.* (2:20)

Don't forget the glowing affirmation in the preceding verse. The problem for the Christians in Thyatira was not that they had ceased being about their Lord's business. They had actually grown in their devotion to God. Their problem was not a lack of love or a lack of faith. They excelled in those areas. Their problem was not that they had stopped serving the Lord or had grown weary of living in a hostile world. Service and patient endurance characterized this congregation of believers. Their one problem was that they were tolerant when they should have been intolerant. In direct contrast to the Ephesians, the Christians in Thyatira were great at spiritual offense, but were failing in one area of spiritual defense.

Within the church in Thyatira was a self-styled prophetess who was leading God's people into sin. Again, it is unlikely that a particular doctrine was being promoted that encouraged Christians to participate in pagan worship, as if pagan worship were a good thing. Instead, this was probably a case of a particularly influential person advocating Christian accommodation to the larger culture, just as the Nicolaitans were doing elsewhere. This time, though, those teachings were perhaps even more appealing due to the prevalence of trade guilds in Thyatira. Although it was a smaller city than many of the vast metropolises found in Asia Minor at the time, Thyatira was home to a regional slave market and a wide range of trade guilds, including guilds for bakers, tanners, potters, linen workers, wool merchants, garment makers, slave traders, shoemakers, dyers, and copper smiths, at the very least. Little else is known of life in ancient Thyatira, but what is known of the trade guilds is extremely important for understanding what was likely going on in Thyatira among the Christians there when Revelation was written.

Asia Minor at the end of the first century had a robust and diverse economy. Unfortunately, almost everyone involved in economic enterprises of any kind was required to be a member of one of the trade guilds. In Thyatira, in particular, attempting to operate independently in any trade without attracting considerable attention would have been very difficult. People tended to live and work in guild communities, with particular blocks housing particular trades.[2] The challenge for Christians was that participation in the trade guilds inevitably included a religious dimension of some sort. Indeed, the regular feasts that were part of guild life had a strong religious flavor and were typically held in the temple of Apollo Tyrimnaeus, the patron god of the guilds.[3] Being a Christian, who was called to reject any form of idolatry, could thus have drastic implications. To withdraw from the guilds was to be denied access to the marketplace, where goods could be sold and fortunes could be made.[4] Beyond the issues raised by the guilds was the fact that life in a Roman city at the time revolved around idolatry. "A meeting of the citizens of a city for political purposes was always inaugurated by pagan ritual, and . . . the citizens in this political assembly were all united in the worship of the patron national deity in whose honor the opening ceremonies were performed."[5] It was simply not possible to be a "normal" citizen of the city without engaging in idolatry.

While this may seem strange to Westerners today, it is not unusual in many parts of the world. Years ago, I was asked to speak at a translation conference in a country in Southeast Asia where ceremony is very important. One of the royal princesses came to give her blessing to the conference and, as is the case with most important events there, there was a Buddhist ceremony at the beginning of the conference. They brought out a large Buddha statue along with all sorts of flowers and incense as I watched from my seat in the front row of the large auditorium. We were all asked to stand as the ceremony began. Then, when a senior monk gave the signal, the entire audience (minus one) began to bow down to the idol. I could almost feel the pressure

2. Hemer, *Letters*, 109.

3. Ibid. Ramsay's description of the life of a Roman soldier provides a good illustration of this reality: "The Roman soldier, marching under the colors of his regiment, was marching under the standard of idolatry, for the standards (*signa*) were all divine, and worship was paid to them by the soldiers as a duty of the service, and all contained one or more idolatrous symbols or representations. Moreover, he was frequently required, standing in his place in the ranks, to take part in idolatrous acts of worship" (*Letters*, 252). Thus, even if an early Christian were able to justify military service as a suitable vocation for a follower of Jesus, the idolatry that was required of soldiers would have made such service unthinkable.

4. Lydia herself may have faced these types of challenges after becoming a believer. Hemer, *Letters*, 121.

5. Ramsay, *Letters*, 253.

of the hundreds of people behind me bowing to the idol. The urge to assimilate was great! Who wants to stand out? Who wants to fail to show respect to one's host? It would have been easy to go with the flow.

Christians in Thyatira, and likely throughout the seven cities Jesus addresses, would have faced such pressures on a daily basis, and to a much greater degree: "it was to the ancient mind an outrage and almost inconceivable thing that people could be fellow citizens without engaging in the worship of the same city gods. The bond of patriotism was really a religious bond."[6] A city and its religion were two sides of the same coin;[7] to be a Thyatiran was to worship the gods of Thyatira. Moreover, "there were numerous societies for a vast variety of purposes, the condition of membership in which was professedly and explicitly the willingness to engage in the worship of a pagan deity."[8] This, of course, included the trade guilds. In such a climate, those who chose not to engage in public acts of worship to the local deities or to the emperor were readily visible and easy targets for persecution. They were viewed as unconcerned with the welfare of the city, people who refused to be "team players."

Added to the tremendous pressure from society to conform was the added pressure from within the church. Where the Nicolaitans promoted compromise in other cities, in Thyatira the same teachings were presented as prophetic utterances from the Lord, making them perhaps even more tempting. Beyond that, any other course of action was simply not practical, since it would have been virtually impossible for anyone engaged in a trade to continue to do business in Thyatira without maintaining their membership in the appropriate guild.[9] Such membership, however, required participation in guild feasts, which were likely contexts where both eating food sacrificed to idols and sexual immorality were commonplace. What could a follower of Jesus do in such a context. Jezebel's message was simple: "It's not that bad! Idols are really nothing anyway! Sex of whatever sort is no big deal when you are already seated with Christ in the heavenly realms! Besides, if you don't go with the flow, you're going to be out of a job!"

Whatever the precise nature of her message, Jezebel appears to have been the local advocate of the Nicolaitan's libertine teachings. It is likely that, as in the case of Balaam, the name Jezebel is used as a rhetorical device to characterize the guilty prophetess in a highly negative way by associating her with a notorious figure from the past. In the Old Testament (Reading Instruction #6), Jezebel was the daughter of Ethbaal, king of Tyre and Sidon, who was famous for marrying Ahab, king of Israel (1 Kgs 16:31; Josephus, *Ant.* 8.317), and enticing Israel to worship Canaanite gods (1 Kgs 16:32–33). Much of her story is recorded in 1 Kings 18–21, including her campaign

---

6. Ibid., 105.

7. Cf. ibid., 147.

8. Ibid., 253.

9. "At Pergamum the Christian's *life* was directly threatened by the pervasiveness of the imperial cult, here his *livelihood* by the issues involved in membership in the guilds." Hemer, *Letters*, 123.

to kill the prophets of Yahweh (1 Kgs 18:4), her support for 450 prophets of Baal and 400 prophets of Asherah (1 Kgs 18:19), her attempt to kill Elijah (1 Kgs 19:1–3), her instigation of the murder of Naboth (1 Kgs 21:1–16), and so forth. Ultimately she meets a terrible fate—she becomes dog food—in fulfillment of Elijah's prophecy (1 Kgs 21:23; 2 Kgs 9:30–37). Not a good person to get your nickname from! Jesus is thus identifying the false prophetess as a vicious enemy of the people of God by linking her to an historical figure who epitomized what it means to be an enemy of God and deceiver of God's people.

Now we need to be careful not to miss something very important in verses 19–20. Jesus makes it clear that false teaching was being tolerated in the church at Thyatira and he is about to pass judgment on it. What do we find along with the false teaching? An abundance of good works! In the ancient world, many people would have rightly pointed to "all the good" the Roman Empire was doing in the world. The Roman emperors generously contributed to the rebuilding of cities destroyed by earthquakes. Many of them were generous in helping people during famines. The Roman Empire was known to have brought peace and security and a higher standard of living to countless people. To use modern language, many might have even argued that terrorism was being kept at bay by the might of Rome. And the trade guilds themselves were devoted to good works![10] Despite all this, John, writing under the direction of Jesus, portrays Rome as a whore and the epitome of all that is contrary to God and his purposes. And he portrays the teachings promoted by the prophetess of the church in Thyatira as being on par with what Queen Jezebel had done to God's people in the past.

Lest we miss the obvious connection, let me make it clear: We need to be very careful today that we not look at the "good" our country is doing and use that to conclude that our country is doing the work of God. And the same is true of our church. As Jesus reminds us, "On that day many will say to me, 'Lord, Lord, did we not prophesy in your name, and cast out demons in your name, and do many mighty works in your name?' [23]And then will I declare to them, 'I never knew you; depart from me, you workers of lawlessness'" (Matt 7:22–23). Just as Jesus was full of grace *and truth*, so also we must live lives overflowing with grace but never compromising the truth in any way. Both are non-negotiable for followers of Jesus Christ.

> *I gave her time to repent, but she refuses to repent of her sexual immorality.*
> [22]*Behold, I will throw her onto a sickbed, and those who commit adultery with*
> *her I will throw into great tribulation, unless they repent of her works, [23]and I*
> *will strike her children dead. And all the churches will know that I am he who*
> *searches mind and heart, and I will give to each of you according to your works.*
> (2:21–23)

10. Ibid., 123.

The first words of 2:21 are striking: "I gave her time to repent." Keep in mind whom Jesus is talking about, a false prophet. Jezebel is an enemy of God and is seeking to lead God's people astray; and yet in his amazing grace Jesus had given her time to repent. Apparently, this was not the first warning this "prophetess" had been given. She had had ample opportunity to turn from her wicked ways but had refused. Now, time had run out; and Jesus pronounces imminent judgment. The expression, "to cast/ throw someone on to a bed," was likely an idiom meaning "to punish with serious sickness of some kind." Many Western Christians today have a hard time accepting the fact that God sometimes disciplines his people with sickness even though it is clear from Scripture that he does. In Corinth, Christians were abusing the Lord's Supper by not treating each other appropriately. Paul tells them, "That is why many of you are weak and ill, and some have died" (1 Cor 11:30). In Acts 5, Ananias and Sapphira were struck dead for lying to the Holy Spirit. While not all sickness is the result of sin in the life of the Christian, the New Testament clearly teaches that sickness is one of God's ways of disciplining his people.

Suffering is also promised to all those who do not repent of Jezebel's ways. It is clear that "her children," who will be struck dead, are those who have followed her teachings. Jesus says that he will, literally, "kill her children with death." Although this could simply be an emphatic way of saying that he is going to strike them dead, the same expression is used in the Septuagint to translate the Hebrew, "they will die by plague" (Reading Instruction #6).[11] The sense here, then, is likely something like, "I will kill them with a deadly disease."[12] It may sound a bit harsh in the tender ears of many Christians today, but these are the words of the Son of God recorded in the Bible.

This judgment that Jesus pronounces is also presented as imminently fair. Jesus reminds believers in Thyatira that they will be judged based on what they have done. Again, we need to remember to whom Jesus is talking. These are Christians! Many modern Christians have largely banished from their minds the fact that "we must all appear before the judgment seat of Christ, so that each one may receive what is due for what he has done in the body, whether good or evil" (2 Cor 5:10).[13] A day of accounting is coming; a day that Christians must face. Each follower of Jesus will be evaluated by their Master, who will determine whether they have been good and faithful servants or something far less noble.

> *Now I say to the rest of you in Thyatira, to you who do not hold to her teaching and have not learned Satan's so-called deep secrets (I will not impose any other burden on you):* [25]*Only hold on to what you have until I come.* (2:24–25)

---

11. Ibid., 121.

12. Cf. Louw and Nida 23.158; BDAG, 443.3, s.v. θάνατος.

13. To think that a person can become a Christian and have no obligation to live a life of devotion to Christ is simply out of step with the consistent teaching of the New Testament (see also Matt 16:27; Rom 2:6; 2 Tim 4:14; 1 Pet 1:17).

Fortunately, those who followed Jezebel in Thyatira appear to have been in the minority. The rest Jesus simply exhorts to continue to resist false teaching from the Jezebel's of the world until his return. They do not need any new instructions. They simply need to maintain vigilance in doing what they already know to be right. If the words, "I will not impose any other burden on you," sound familiar, they should. When the apostles met with Paul, Barnabas, and other leaders in Jerusalem about forty-five years earlier to consider whether Gentile Christians needed to be circumcised and follow the Law of Moses, those leaders summarized their verdict in a letter to the Gentile churches: "For it has seemed good to the Holy Spirit and to us to lay on you no greater burden than these requirements: [29]that you abstain from what has been sacrificed to idols, and from blood, and from what has been strangled, and from sexual immorality. If you keep yourselves from these, you will do well" (Acts 15:28–29). Two things are important here. First, at least two of the four requirements clearly relate to the teachings of Jezebel and the Nicolaitans: abstaining from food sacrificed to idols and sexual immorality. Second, the language "not impose any other burden on you" is very similar to the apostolic decree's "lay on you no greater burden" (Acts 15:28).[14] Jesus is thus likely reminding believers in Thyatira that they need to continue to follow the commands that were given earlier by he himself and his apostles. In this case, it should have been obvious that Jezebel's teaching violated the apostolic decree, but it sounded so convincing![15]

The fact that Jesus refers to these convincing arguments as "what some call the deep things" or "the so-called 'deep things'" suggests that this was the way that the prophetess was marketing her teachings. Jezebel was purporting to teach "deep truths" of the faith, truths that allowed Christians to survive in a hostile world. "It may appear to be a problem to attend the guild feasts, given all of their idolatry and sexual immorality, but when you understand the deep things of God you will see that you are free to participate," she might have said. But Jesus makes it clear that just as those who claimed to be a synagogue of God's people had actually become a synagogue of Satan, so here, the one who claimed to teach the "deep things of God" was actually teaching the "deep things of Satan."

> *The one who conquers and who keeps my works until the end, to him I will give authority over the nations, [27]and he will rule them with a rod of iron, as when earthen pots are broken in pieces, even as I myself have received authority from my Father. [28]And I will give him the morning star. [29]He who has an ear, let him hear what the Spirit says to the churches. (2:27–29)*

14. So, e.g., Ramsay, *Letters*, 249; Hemer, *Letters*, 18. Compare Jesus' language here (οὐ βάλλω ἐφ' ὑμᾶς ἄλλο βάρος, *ou ballō eph' humas allo baros*) with the language of the Apostolic Decree in Acts 15:28 (μηδὲν πλέον ἐπιτίθεσθαι ὑμῖν βάρος πλὴν τούτων τῶν ἐπάναγκες, *mēden pleon epitithesthai humin baros plēn toutōn tōn epanagkes*).

15. As Hemer (*Letters*, 123) points out, "membership [in the trade guilds] necessarily involved contradiction of the Apostolic Decree and the needed repentance must necessarily involve repudiation of the guilds."

With the first three churches, we have needed to look more carefully at the message as a whole to determine what it would have meant for those particular Christians to "overcome." Here, Jesus defines "overcoming" for us: keeping his "works" to the end. This expression is not used elsewhere in the New Testament, and we might have expected Jesus to say "keeps my words" or "obeys my commands," but not "keeps my *works*." It is likely that this phrase is essentially synonymous with keeping Jesus' words or commands, but has more emphasis on the actual outworking of the obedience. Overcomers are those who actually *do* Jesus' will. Overcomers are those who are consistently and actively about their Father's business in this world.

The one who overcomes in the church in Thyatira is also given a double promise. He or she will be given authority over the nations and also be given the morning star. What do these two promises mean? Verse 27 clearly alludes to Ps 2:9, where the Messiah is promised victory over his enemies. The overcomers at Thyatira are promised a share in that victory, a victory that the Father had granted to the Son. The language of violence makes the absolute nature of the victory crystal clear. It also highlights what will happen to those who, like Jezebel, insist on resisting the lordship of Christ.

It is worth noting that the particular promise that is given to this specific church would have sharply contrasted with their local reality (Reading Instruction #4). Thyatira was one of the least important of the seven cities,[16] a small city with no authority in the province and no claim to being the "*Seventh* of Asia," let alone the "First of Asia" (like Ephesus, Smyrna, and Pergamum). Thus, although these believers came from an insignificant city, they would be granted authority over all the nations, including the great Roman Empire, if they "overcame."

Second, Jesus will also give overcomers in Thyatira the morning star. The "morning star" (τὸν ἀστέρα τὸν πρωϊνόν, *ton astera ton prōinon*) was one way of referring to the planet Venus, which was viewed as the largest star and the star that heralded the new day. Venus was also often viewed as an emblem of authority in the ancient world.[17] In Greek, its name was Φωσφόρος (*phōsforos*), which is used in 2 Pet 1:19. In Latin, its name was *Lucifer*. A similar word, ἐωσφόρος (*eōsphoros*), is used in the Septuagint translation of Isa 14:12 to speak of the fall of the "Day Star." In Job 38:7, it is used in the plural ("stars of the morning") and then fleshed out with the further designation "sons of God."[18] Jesus clearly uses the title for himself in 22:16. So what does the giving of the morning star represent in 2:28? When Christians in Thyatira heard Jesus' words in Rev 22:16, they may have realized that part of the promise here is that Jesus will give them himself as a reward. This would be similar to what Jesus promises his disciples

---

16. Ramsay, *Letters*, 243–44.

17. Hemer, *Letters*, 126.

18. Hemer (ibid., 126) notes that the reference to a "scepter" (or rod) and a "star" both appear in Balaam's prophecy in Num 24:17, a passage that was widely viewed as messianic in reference. It is quite possible that Jesus is referring to these same authority motifs (rod and star) in this passage. See also Collins, *Sceptre*.

who obey him in John 14:21, 23. His words there promise intimacy with him and the Father to all those who keep his words and obey his commands (overcomers). But there is probably more in Jesus' use of "morning star" language in 2:28. Jesus' words likely point to a new eschatological day that will dawn for those who overcome, with the brightness of that day heralding the future glory that overcomers will share with their Lord. This is consistent with the picture painted in Dan 12:3: "And those who are wise shall shine like the brightness of the sky above; and those who turn many to righteousness, like the stars forever and ever."

THYATIRA: PROFILE OF A CHURCH

As with the other "letters," the message to Christians in Thyatira serves as a foundation on which Jesus builds the rest of his message to this church in the remainder of Revelation.[19] As we prepare to examine "the rest of the story" for the church in Thyatira in the next chapter, it is important to have a clear sense of what appears to be at the heart of the temptations facing Christians in this city. In a city where one's livelihood often depended on membership in trade guilds, we find a group of believers facing a daunting dilemma. What do you do when your source of livelihood itself becomes incompatible with following Christ? What do you do when refusing to compromise could result in economic ruin? At a point in history when many in the Western world have recently lost their homes to foreclosure, some modern readers might be able to begin to understand what Christians in Thyatira were facing. What would you do if you were told to renounce your faith or lose your job? What would you do if refusal to renounce your faith meant that you would be blacklisted from ever working again in your field?

Added to this pressure from "the world out there" was the fact that some within the church were strongly encouraging compromise. One self-proclaimed prophetess, in particular, was advocating continued engagement in the trade guilds and other civic activities, even though they involved idolatry and sexual immorality. "Go along to the party! You can just play along without really participating. Just make it look like you're one of the gang. What's the real harm in eating food that's been sacrificed to idols? Idol sacrifices are just superstitions anyway. What's the harm in pretending to enjoy the ribald entertainment at the party? Laugh along with the rest! Tell a dirty joke or two and nod your head when fellow guild members make lustful comments about the dancers at the party. It's no big deal! You'll be able to keep your job and in the long run even have a good spiritual impact on your fellow guild members. Hey, you're building relationships and planting seeds! You have to go where people live to reach them with the gospel!"

---

19. Contra Hemer (ibid., 127) who finds connections with the rest of Revelation elusive.

We do not know what specific form Jezebel's appeals would have taken, but we do know that there would have been intense pressure to compromise the clear teaching of Scripture. Jesus warns that not only Jezebel but also all those who follow her teachings will be severely disciplined if they do not repent. A painful death by disease awaits those who compromise. So, how does Jesus support and flesh out the message to Thyatira in the remainder of Revelation?

9

Jesus' Message to the Church in Thyatira
The Rest of the Story

As was true for other Christians in Asia Minor, the pressures that the church in Thyatira was facing centered on temptations to compromise either to save their skin or simply to protect their way of life. The specific temptation for those in Thyatira seems to have focused on maintaining their ability to earn a living. The economic benefits of the Roman system were likely more evident in Asia Minor than anywhere else in the civilized world in the first century, with the exception of Rome itself. Prosperity ruled supreme. Given Jesus' strong commendations of this church, though, Christians in Thyatira likely would have been less concerned with the loss of their prosperity than with the loss of their ability to feed their families. Should a father not be willing to compromise his faith a little in order to carry out his God-given responsibility to take care of his family? In what follows in Rev 4–22, Jesus reminds these Christians that his followers must look to God to take care of their needs, not to any world system or even to one's own hard work.

Jesus' message to Christians in Smyrna would have been particularly important support for his message to those in Thyatira. It would have been very easy to rationalize the need to compromise in order to care for their families. The message to the church in Smyrna, however, makes it clear that faithful followers of Jesus can expect far worse than economic deprivation. Similarly, if calling the false prophetess of Thyatira Jezebel and threatening her with death were not enough to convince these Christians that compromise was not an option, they had the message to the church in Ephesus to remind them that Jesus hated the practices of the Nicolaitans, who taught the same things that were being peddled by Jezebel. They were not something to be permitted within the church, as Jesus makes eminently clear in his message to the church in

Pergamum. These themes, and other features of the initial message to the church in Thyatira in 2:18–29 are driven home and reinforced in a wide variety of ways in the remainder of Revelation where we encounter the rest of the story for those in Thyatira.

REVELATION 4–5: THE MESSAGE TO THYATIRA

While Jesus' description of himself as one "who has eyes like a flame of fire, and whose feet are like burnished bronze" (2:18) gives Christians in Thyatira a hint of his majesty, and should have inspired reverent fear in them, what we find in Rev 4–5 would have taken that fear to a whole new level. The Thyatirans were afraid of what might happen to them if they did not compromise with the society around them. What they should really fear is the One who is seated on the throne and the mighty Lamb who is about to open seals that will unleash judgment on the enemies of God. And they should pay attention to the beautiful promise Jesus gives them that those who overcome will be given authority over the nations. This is reiterated with the song of the twenty-four elders in 5:10, which reminds them that the ransomed people of God "shall reign on the earth." As they wrestled with the challenge of not having access to the necessities of life because of their commitment to Jesus, they needed to avoid becoming like Esau "who sold his birthright for a single meal" (Heb 12:16), trading what was of great value for that which was almost worthless. Christians in Thyatira needed a perspective check; they needed to be reminded that as frightening as it is to lose your livelihood, compromising your allegiance to the One who reigns in glorious splendor in heaven must be avoided at all cost.

These two chapters of Revelation set in stark contrast the worth of the things that Christians in Thyatira were being tempted to cling to, even at the expense of their faith, and the worth of the One who sits on the throne and the Lamb. All the host of heaven, any single one of whom is more glorious than the Roman emperor will ever be, worship the One on the Throne and the Lamb. They incessantly cry out in adoration and praise. They cannot help but do so given the majestic character of God. To compromise, as Jezebel was suggesting, would be to turn one's back on the glorious God described in Rev 4–5. The repeated reference to the worthiness of the Lamb in these chapters makes it very clear that abandoning allegiance to the Worthy One for the sake of one's livelihood, or even life itself, is not even close to being "worth it."

REVELATION 6: THE MESSAGE TO THYATIRA

The details of the seal judgments in Rev 6 would have starkly reminded Christians in Thyatira that Jesus' warning of coming judgment should not be downplayed. He is not someone to trifle with. The earth is on the verge of Judgment Day. War, death, famine, and destruction are coming. And all of it will reflect only the beginning of the outpouring of the wrath of the Lamb (6:16). He who threatens Jezebel and her followers with judgment, sickness, and death is a just Judge whose wrath cannot be avoided by those who have spurned him. If the fact that many of those who are faithful to Jesus and do not compromise will be killed for their faith (6:9–11) does not give them license to compromise, what basis can those who are "merely" being threatened with a loss of their livelihood have for compromising their faith? Jesus' call to all who would be his disciples to deny themselves, take up their cross, and follow him still stands. His vivid description in the fourth seal of the inhabitants of the earth being struck down "with pestilence" recalls the language of 2:22, where the sense of the expression that has been translated "I will strike her children dead" is likely "I will kill her children with a deadly disease." Christians in Thyatira who had just been warned of Jesus' impending judgment on Jezebel and her followers would not have been quick to relegate the seal judgments of Rev 6 only to "the world out there." All who associate themselves with the world, whether they outwardly wear the name of Christian or not, will have to face the wrath of the One on the throne and the wrath of the Lamb.

REVELATION 7: THE MESSAGE TO THYATIRA

As we come to Rev 7 and the sealing of the 144,000, we find a vision that would have been particularly striking for Christians in Thyatira, as well as others in the churches of Asia Minor who were wrestling with the pressure to assimilate. You will recall from Chapter 5 that both intertextual and intratextual connections are important for understanding the vision of the 144,000. First, at an intratextual level (connections within Revelation itself) we noticed that those who are sealed in Rev 7, "the servants of our God" (7:3), appear to be the very ones to whom Revelation is addressed (see 1:1). Thus, it is natural to conclude that those who are sealed in Rev 7 include those, at the least, among the readers who respond appropriately.

Second, at an intertextual level (connections between Revelation and the Old Testament) there is striking similarity between the sealing of God's servants here and the sealing of God's servants in Ezek 9:3–6, which helps clarify the significance of the sealing of the 144,000 (Reading Instruction #6). We know that sealing symbolizes protection from the wrath of God, but there is more that needs to be said. Ezekiel 9 shows us that this is not the first time God has sealed his people prior to bringing judgment. Christians in Thyatira would have naturally been drawn to the identity of those who were being judged in Ezekiel. In Ezek 9, God was pronouncing judgment not on the world, but on those who were masquerading as the people of God, while living like the world around them. Judgment was being pronounced on Jerusalem, which was supposed to be the place where the one true God was worshiped. Likewise, in his initial message to the church in Thyatira (2:18–29), Jesus pronounced judgment on those in Thyatira who profess to be his people, but whose duplicity makes it clear that such is not actually the case. This is driven home in part by the fact that the time of severe suffering that is coming as God's wrath is poured out is described as a "great tribulation" in 7:14, and the only other place that this expression is used in Revelation is in 2:22, where Jesus strongly warns those in Thyatira who persist in following Jezebel's wicked teachings and refuse to repent that he will "throw [them] into great tribulation." Thus, Christians in Thyatira would have been strongly encouraged by the visions in Rev 7 to make sure they were among those who were sealed and not among those who would be thrown into great tribulation, i.e., face the wrath of God.

There is much more here, however, that is relevant for the Christians in Thyatira (and for us today). Notice who receives the mark on their forehead in Ezek 9; it is "those who grieve and lament over all the detestable things that are done in it" (Ezek 9:4, NIV). It is the ones who rather than compromising and assimilating to the nations around Israel, were deeply distressed by the idolatry all around them in Jerusalem and in the temple itself. The others would face the full brunt of God's wrath; and that wrath would begin with those who were performing their duties in the sanctuary itself and with the leaders of the people (Ezek 9:6). What had brought about such wrath? We are told in Ezek 11:12: "And you will know that I am the LORD, for you have not followed my decrees or kept my laws but have conformed to the standards of the nations around you" (NIV). God's people, whom he had called to be separate and distinct from the nations of Canaan, had instead become just like those nations. In fact, in God's eyes they had become worse (see Ezek 5:5–9). The obvious connection between the sealing of the 144,000 and the sealing of "those who grieve and lament over all the detestable things that are done in it" (Ezek 9:4, NIV), coupled with the very conspicuous omission of Dan and Ephraim from the list of tribes, tribes that were known for their idolatry and assimilation (see Chapter 5), reinforce for Christians in Thyatira the call to repent of the assimilation that Jezebel was promoting.

The beautiful picture of the redeemed standing in the presence of God and the Lamb in Revelation and praising him for their salvation (7:9) would have helped drive home for Christians in Thyatira what really matters. Yes, they may lose their livelihood and homes for following Jesus, but a day is soon coming when "they shall hunger no more, neither thirst anymore; the sun shall not strike them, nor any scorching heat" (7:16). Likewise, the picture of those who are "coming out of the great tribulation" and have "washed their robes and made them white in the blood of the Lamb" (7:14) would have reminded them of two things: (1) tribulation is to be expected, and it may be possible to escape the great tribulation only through their deaths; and (2) what is important is that they are washed in the blood of the Lamb and that they remember that those who have been purchased with the precious blood of Jesus must live as those who belong to him, knowing that he is the One "who searches mind and heart, and . . . will give to each of you according to your works" (2:23).

Like many Christians today, some of those in the church in Thyatira easily fell into the trap of living as functional atheists. They made decisions in life as if God did not exist, thinking that if no one else was aware of their spiritual adultery, they were safe. Jesus reminds them that he is fully aware of what goes on in the mind and heart as well as in outward actions, and each will receive what is due them for their thoughts and motives as well as what they do.

REVELATION 8–9: THE MESSAGE TO THYATIRA

We have seen that Jesus has threatened unrepentant Christians in Thyatira with "great tribulation" (2:22). In Rev 8–9, the nature of the ultimate "great tribulation" (7:14) and the "hour or trial" (3:10) is fleshed out in more detail in the trumpet judgments. Jesus has promised that he is going to strike the unrepentant Jezebel with serious sickness, and those who have been cavorting with her are going to suffer severely. In fact, many of them will die for their unfaithfulness (2:23). The trumpet judgments show these professing believers the danger of trying to "love God" and "love the world." We are told in 1 John 2:15 that "If anyone loves the world, the love of the Father is not in him." In Revelation, we learn that those who love the world will face the world's fate, which is vividly spelled out in the trumpet judgments.

Perhaps the most striking description is found in the fifth trumpet, where the suffering is so severe that unsealed inhabitants of this world will "long to die, but death will flee from them" (9:6). Those who "commit adultery" with Jezebel, i.e., follow her teachings and assimilate to the sinful practices of the culture around them, will not have the seal of God on their forehead (9:4), and will therefore be targets of attack by the demonic horde that will be released. The final words of the trumpet judgments particularly drive home the warning that Jesus gives to compromisers in Thyatira: "The rest of mankind, who were not killed by these plagues, did not repent of the works of their hands nor give up worshiping demons and idols of gold and silver and bronze and stone and wood, which cannot see or hear or walk, [21]nor did they repent of their murders or their sorceries or their sexual immorality or their thefts" (9:20–21). The pagan population of the earth will stubbornly refuse to repent of their sin even in the face of God's wrath being poured out on them. What will they refuse to repent of? Two of the sins that Jesus lists here are sins that he has staunchly warned professing Christians in Thyatira to repent of: idolatry and sexual immorality. For them to fail to repent and root out such cancers from the church would be to place themselves in league with the rest of the pagan world that was in rebellion against God and about to face his wrath.

REVELATION 10: THE MESSAGE TO THYATIRA

As the scene shifts in Rev 10, Christians in Thyatira would likely have noticed the similarities between the description of the mighty angel in 10:1 ("his feet were like pillars of fire," οἱ πόδες αὐτοῦ ὡς στῦλοι πυρός, *hoi podes autou hōs stuloi puros*) and the description of Jesus in 2:18 ("his feet were like burnished bronze," οἱ πόδες αὐτοῦ ὅμοιοι χαλκολιβάνῳ, *hoi podes autou homoioi chalkolibanō*). Although this does not imply that Jesus and the powerful angel of 10:1 are one and the same, it does help connect this part of Revelation to the message to Thyatira. The description of Jesus in 2:18 is likely intended to strike fear into the hearts of those in Thyatira who were professing allegiance to him while committing spiritual adultery. Jesus' warning to such compromisers is then reinforced with the announcement of the terrifying angel of 10:1 who announces "that there would be no more delay" (10:6). For those in Thyatira hesitating in their decision to abandon Jezebel and reaffirm their allegiance to Jesus, the reminder that God is on the verge of doing what he has promised through his prophets would have helped motivate them to act on what Jesus has said.

REVELATION 11: THE MESSAGE TO THYATIRA

The vision of the two prophets of God who come in the power of Moses and Elijah in Rev 11 would have stood in stark contrast to Jezebel, the self-styled prophetess in Thyatira. Jezebel preached compromise. Jezebel preached assimilation to the culture around them. Jezebel encouraged Christians not to be too concerned with blatant sin. In today's culture, she may have said something like, "We're all just sinners who happen to be saved by grace! You can't expect us to avoid the sins that are all around us, particularly if it's a question of making a living. We all sin a hundred times every day anyway! Besides, when God looks at us he sees Jesus! So, you're sin doesn't really matter in the end. After all, God will forgive you if you confess your sins." The two witnesses of Rev 11, on the other hand, are like the prophets of old. They preach repentance, symbolized by wearing sackcloth (11:3), and there is no compromise in their lifestyle or in their message. They are antitypes of Jezebel. Rather than proclaiming "deep things," which turn out to come from Satan rather than God anyway, they preach the clear and simple message of the gospel, calling all people to repent and bow the knee before the one true King of kings and Lord of lords and demonstrate their allegiance to him and him alone.

Like the two witnesses, God is calling Christians in Thyatira (and Christians today) to a life of obedience to Jesus, despite the earthly consequences of such obedience. Like the two witnesses, all followers of Jesus are impervious to the evil one's assaults for as long as God ordains. As emissaries of the Lord Jesus Christ the two witnesses are vehemently hated by the people of this world, and become targets of persecution. God, though, wants to make it very clear to Christians in Asia Minor that *being targets of persecution does not make them vulnerable*. God gives the two witnesses the ability to protect themselves, bringing death to those who would kill them (11:5). Divine protection, however, is not something God promises will last forever: "when they have finished their testimony, the beast that rises from the bottomless pit will make war on them and conquer them and kill them" (11:7). The key phrase here is "when they have finished their testimony." Just as God has determined a particular number of Christians who will die for their faith (6:11), so also he has determined the precise time of each of their deaths. The two witnesses are not killed because wicked men or the evil one caught God off guard and were therefore able to destroy his servants; they are killed because these servants have finished the work God gave them to do. God is now ready to take them home, and through their deaths he will receive greater glory (11:13). God makes it very clear through this passage that only he determines the time and circumstances of the death of his people. A follower of Christ, therefore, cannot argue, "I had to compromise my faith in order to feed my family; otherwise, we would have all starved to death." Those who faithfully follow Jesus can rest assured that God will meet their needs regardless of how things look, until he is ready to take them home. He is in control; no one else.

Before moving on, it is worth asking why the hatred for the two witnesses is portrayed in such strong terms: "those who dwell on the earth will rejoice over them and make merry and exchange presents" (11:10). The reason for the intense hatred of these two individuals and the celebration that is sparked by their deaths is the fact that "these two prophets had been a torment to those who dwell on the earth" (11:10). When we look at the nature of that torment, we find that "they have the power to shut the sky, that no rain may fall during the days of their prophesying, and they have power over the waters to turn them into blood and to strike the earth with every kind of plague, as often as they desire" (11:6). In other words, by their actions they bring drought and famine and plague throughout the course of their ministry, things that are similar to what is described in the third and fourth seal judgments. We also find curious statements at the end of the description of the seal judgments and the trumpet judgments, and after the fourth and fifth bowl judgments:

> Then the kings of the earth and the great ones and the generals and the rich and the powerful, and everyone, slave and free, hid themselves in the caves and among the rocks of the mountains, [16]calling to the mountains and rocks, "*Fall on us and hide us from the face of him who is seated on the throne, and from the wrath of the Lamb,* [17]*for the great day of their wrath has come, and who can stand?*" (6:15–17)

> The rest of mankind, who were not killed by these plagues, *did not repent* of the works of their hands nor give up worshiping demons and idols of gold and silver and bronze and stone and wood, which cannot see or hear or walk, [21]*nor did they repent* of their murders or their sorceries or their sexual immorality or their thefts. (9:20–21)

> The fourth angel poured out his bowl on the sun, and it was allowed to scorch people with fire. [9]They were scorched by the fierce heat, and *they cursed the name of God who had power over these plagues. They did not repent and give him glory.* (16:8–9)

The fifth angel poured out his bowl on the throne of the beast, and its king-dom was plunged into darkness. People gnawed their tongues in anguish [11]*and cursed the God of heaven for their pain and sores. They did not repent of their deeds.* (16:10–11)

How do they recognize the seal judgments as the outpouring of the wrath of God and the coming of the day of the Lord? Why do they curse God for these "natural" disasters (16:9, 11)? How do they know that they are supposed to repent (9:20; 16:9, 11)? The answer is almost certainly found in the ministry of the two witnesses. The 1260 days of their ministry (11:3) not only coincides with the time of the outpouring of the seal and trumpet judgments, but their message includes a call to repent or face the wrath of God; and that wrath, at least in part, is initiated by the two witnesses themselves as they call on God to stop the rain and send plagues upon the land. The people of the earth recognize the hand of God in what is happening precisely because the two witnesses have made it clear to them that God is the agent. And just as the darkness always hates the light, so the world will hate the two witnesses.

Those in Thyatira who cease to compromise their faith under the influence of Jezebel can expect retribution, but they dare not continue on their path to destruction. The urgency to repent is reinforced yet again with the vision of the seventh trumpet in 11:15–19. The twenty-four elders are once again center stage, this time to remind Christians in Asia Minor that not only will God's wrath come against the nations as they have seen in the seal and trumpet judgments thus far, but God will also soon reward his servants. It must be remembered, however, that his servants are those who fear his name (11:18); and those who fear his name will certainly heed the warning of Jesus and repent of their sin immediately.

REVELATION 12: THE MESSAGE TO THYATIRA

Revelation 12 takes readers in Thyatira in a different direction. Jesus' had already told them that the ultimate source of the teachings they have been seduced by is Satan himself (2:24). Now, he connects the "ministry" of Jezebel with the work of Satan once again. He had earlier described Jezebel as one who was "seducing" (ESV), or "leading astray" (πλανάω, *planaō*) his people (2:20). In Rev 12, the same verb is used for the first time since 2:20 to create another important intratextual connection, ef-fectively communicating that Jezebel is a pawn of Satan. This self-styled prophetess is not someone to be trusted; she is not someone to take you deeper spiritually; she is in league with the enemy of your souls. She is one of Satan's tools that he is using to lead the whole world astray (12:9, πλανάω, *planaō*).[1] Some in the church at Thyatira had been falling for the oldest trick in Satan's playbook: the twisting of the truth to suit his goal of leading people away from God (see Gen 3:1). The reason Jesus is so intent on

---

1. The ESV regrettably masks this connection by failing to translate the verb consistently.

communicating the need for these Christians to "hold fast what you have" (2:25) is because Satan is trying in every way he can to snatch it away from them. He is a con artist, and he will take them for everything they have if they are not careful.

Jezebel was telling Christians in Thyatira how to survive in the hostile environment in which they found themselves. Simply mix one cup of truth with one cup of compromise. That is all it will take to save your job, care for your family, and save your life. Jesus, on the other hand, makes it very clear that his prescription for survival is very different. They have an enemy of their souls who is full of "wrath, because he knows that his time is short" (12:12), and they, like Michael and his angels, must "overcome" and "conquer" him. How do they do that? The vision in Rev 12 makes it quite clear as a loud voice from heaven (12:10) announces that part of the prescription for survival is that they must live as those who "love not their lives even unto death" (12:11). Followers of Jesus must focus on preserving their true life—and thus avoiding the second death—rather than preserving their current physical life in this world, which is fleeting anyway.

Built into the visions of Rev 12 is another subtle positive reminder of what God has in store for those who fear him. In 12:1–5 we see the vivid but very concise picture of the incarnation and ascension of Jesus. And God has chosen to describe the incarnation in language that was tailor-made to capture the attention of Christians in Thyatira. These Christians were facing financial ruin because of their faith. "Thankfully," Jezebel had come to the rescue and showed them a way out whereby they could continue as Christians and also fulfill the requirements of being good citizens of their city. What appeared to be a "way out," however, was really a path to destruction. Jesus thus calls these Christians to repent and stop tolerating Jezebel's false teaching in their church; and to those who respond appropriately to his rebuke Jesus promises a wonderful reward: "The one who conquers and who keeps my works until the end, to him I will give authority over the nations, 27and he will rule them with a rod of iron, as when earthen pots are broken in pieces, even as I myself have received authority from my Father" (2:26–27). Now in 12:5 God takes Christians in Thyatira back to the first coming of Jesus when he came as the "one who is to rule all the nations with a rod of iron." This is the absolute authority that the Father has granted to the Son (2:27), and Jesus has chosen to share that authority with his faithful followers. Once again, Christians in Thyatira are being called to carefully consider what is at stake. Will they trade an eternal role of reigning with Jesus for temporary safety and security now, or will they patiently endure to the end like other overcomers?

REVELATION 13: THE MESSAGE TO THYATIRA

Although it can easily be missed in the ESV, there is an important connection between Jezebel and the beast in Rev 13. Jesus has described Jezebel as a false prophetess who "seduces" (2:20), or "leads astray" or "deceives" his servants. At the heart of false teaching is deception; and deception is the first agenda of the beast, for he is the emissary of "the deceiver of the whole world" (12:9). What is important about the description of the beast in Rev 13 for Christians in Thyatira is the beast's modus operandi. The beast uses recovery from a mortal wound (13:3) and other spectacular signs (13:13–15) to gain credibility with the masses and he thus "deceives those who dwell on earth" (13:14, the second use of the verb πλανάω/*planaō* since 2:20). He appears as a resurrected messiah figure, but his outward appearance like a lamb belies a heart that is controlled by Satan himself (13:11). Both he and Jezebel epitomize sheep in wolves' clothing (cf. Acts 20:29–30). They masquerade as angels of light, just as Satan himself does (2 Cor 11:13–14). Like Jezebel, the beast promotes an "if it works, it must be true" attitude. Jezebel proclaimed, "Compromise in these areas and you can go on with your lives and worship God as well." The beast proclaims, "I must be a god in light of the amazing miracles I am doing."

Perhaps most striking in the vision of Rev 13 for Christians in Thyatira would have been the ultimatum that is given in 13:16–17: "Also it causes all, both small and great, both rich and poor, both free and slave, to be marked on the right hand or the forehead, [17]so that no one can buy or sell unless he has the mark, that is, the name of the beast or the number of its name." Christians in Thyatira were being told by the trade guilds to participate as an active member of the guild or they would not be allowed to carry on business. They were being told that if they wanted to buy or sell, their lives must carry marks of devotion to the guild, including participation in guild functions where there was idolatry and sexual immorality. In Rev 13, Jesus effectively links the trade guilds to the beast and links participation in the guilds to taking the mark of the beast.[2] By doing so, he makes it clear that Jezebel's message of compromise comes straight from the devil.

Far too often modern readers get caught up in trying to identify the technology that will allow a world leader to force people to take his mark in order to buy or sell. The fact that we have such technology today makes a literal realization of the mark of the beast quite possible, and it is natural to make such connections in our minds. Focus on such realities, however, can have the unfortunate consequence of causing us to miss Jesus' point. His point is that Christians will have to compromise their faith in order to participate in the economy. This was happening in the first century through trade guilds, the imperial cult, and other civic institutions. Activities associated with these institutions forced Christians to choose to either be "marked" as on board with the emperor and with the city's or guild's commitment to particular deities or suffer the consequences.[3] Those wrestling with the temptation to give in to the trade guilds are reminded that the temptation will only get worse as the beast assumes his author-

---

2. Hemer (*Letters*, 127) also connects the mark of the beast with membership in the trade guilds, and goes on to suggest that the mark "on the right hand" symbolized one's working life.

3. As Ramsay (*Letters*, 77) notes, "in one way or another every Asian must stamp himself overtly and visibly as loyal, or be forthwith disqualified from participation in ordinary social life and trading."

ity over the world. If they are not resisting assimilation now, they will certainly fail when they are faced with the pressure the beast will bring to bear.

What about Christians today? Could there be "marks of the beast" in our own culture? Have we been duped into unwittingly taking these marks? Where the trade guilds dominated Thyatira, in North America today we live in a consumer culture. When "consumer confidence" is low, people become afraid. The American government, for example, encourages good citizens to keep on spending, and in times of economic crisis may even send out money for its citizens to spend more in order to stimulate the economy. How many Christians view it as their duty to buy more to help the economy? How many Christians who have received such checks have stopped to ask how to use the money for the glory of God? As mentioned above, in our culture, and increasingly on a global scale, the Economy has been deified and is regularly promoted as the patron god of the land who must be faithfully served by all good citizens.

Related to this is the question of how Christians are tempted to compromise in order to enjoy the fruit of the corrupt societies we live within. How often are we indulging ourselves at the expense of those who have been exploited for the sake of profit? On the one hand, we must be careful to avoid shutting down apparently unjust businesses operating international "sweatshops" because the wages they pay seem ridiculously low by our standards. At times, protest movements have shut down such businesses that were paying their employees many times what they could have earned at any other job in their region. In an effort to promote justice, we can easily do the exact opposite. Having said that, Christians need to educate themselves to ensure that they are not eating the fruit of the beast's wicked rule. We can "take the mark of the beast" by making choices that are driven by our own hedonistic desires without recognizing that the companies or even nations that we are receiving the goods from are in league with the evil one and oppressing their people.

REVELATION 14: THE MESSAGE TO THYATIRA

Six features of Rev 14 would have been particularly striking to Christians in Thyatira. First, the language of sexual purity in 14:4 provides a conspicuous contrast with the sexual immorality of those who had followed Jezebel's teachings. Some in Thyatira had defiled themselves with a woman (Jezebel) by committing adultery with her (2:22). In 14:4, Jesus reminds them that it is virgins "who have not defiled themselves with women . . . who follow the Lamb wherever he goes."

Second, an angel "with a loud voice" proclaims the eternal gospel to every corner of the globe, reminding every man, woman, boy, and girl that they must "Fear God and give him glory, because the hour of his judgment has come, and worship him who made heaven and earth, the sea and the springs of water" (14:7). To tolerate false teaching in the church out of fear of the consequences is absurd when people cannot escape being held accountable by the One who made everything. Fear of man cannot coexist with fear of God. In fact, to fear people is to demonstrate an inadequate fear of God.

Third, Babylon the great, which epitomizes evil and opposition to God, is described as a city that makes the "nations drink the wine of the passion of her sexual immorality" (14:8). With these words Jesus connects Jezebel, who has already been connected to Satan himself and Satan's emissary the beast, with Satan's city, Babylon, the chief promoter of sexual immorality. When Jezebel preaches accommodation to the culture around them in Thyatira she is preaching the values of Babylon. To give in to the teachings of Jezebel is to side with Satan, the beast, and Babylon, all of which are going to be destroyed.

Fourth, this part of the John's visions vividly portrays the end of those who associate with Babylon and the beast. Once again, an angel informs John "with a loud voice" in 14:9–11 that to worship the beast by following a false prophet's encouragement to assimilate to the culture around them will lead those who profess to belong to Jesus to be recipients of the full strength of God's wrath by being tormented forever and ever. Associating with the beast through assimilation is to be avoided at all costs. No price is too high to pay to remain (or become!) a pure virgin follower of Jesus.

Fifth, Jesus calls his followers to endurance by faithfully obeying the commands of God and clinging tenaciously to their faith in him (14:12). They are to expect to have to endure. It will not be easy, but their sure guide for staying on track is the unchanging commands of God. They need to know them and they need to meticulously obey them to avoid being led astray by the evil one and his emissaries. No one can claim to know God if they are not devoted to obeying his commands (see 1 John 2:3).

Sixth and finally, Jesus had earlier reminded them of his awareness that their "latter works exceed the first" (2:19) before he mentioned that he had something against them (2:20). Now, he reminds those who have resisted Jezebel's allure (2:24) and been urged to hold fast to what they have until he comes (2:25) that when he comes and they appear before him their deeds will follow them (14:13). Not a single one of their acts of devotion to Jesus in this world will be forgotten. Each one will be recognized and rewarded, and their struggle to resist the Jezebels of this world will give way to sweet rest in the presence of the One who redeemed them with his own blood. If allegiance to Jesus in this world results in the loss of one's livelihood or even life itself, they can take heart that those who "die in the Lord" will be blessed beyond measure (14:13).

REVELATION 15–16: THE MESSAGE TO THYATIRA

As Christians in Thyatira heard the words of Rev 15 they would have been gripped, once again, by the desire to be among the redeemed who stand before God and sing the song of Moses and the song of the Lamb. To participate in the wonderful celebration of God's redemption, though, they must first overcome "the beast and its image and the number of its name" (15:2). Those who are overcome by the beast and capitulate to the pressure to worship him and live by his values and for his glory will be forever lost. Perhaps most striking would have been the question that would be left ringing in their ears: "Who will not fear, O Lord, and glorify your name?" (15:4). Followers of Jesus are tempted to fear all sorts of people and things besides God. In many Western cultures today, the pressure to be "tolerant" is overwhelming. Jezebel presented herself as a prophetess and apparently had some outward means of validating her claim. Perhaps she was a woman of status; perhaps she had been successful in the world and was thus highly respected; perhaps she came from an important family in the church; or perhaps she was simply an effective charlatan like many today. Whatever the source of her influence, Jesus rebukes the church in Thyatira for listening to teaching that was obviously inconsistent with Scripture. Those who fear God and seek to glorify his name will always be quick to test all teachings against the sure and unchanging Word of God. Those who fear God and seek to glorify his name will put his honor above human relationships. God calls Christians in Thyatira to stop sleeping on the job and deal with the Jezebel problem (16:15).

As Christians in Thyatira were confronted with the "seven golden bowls full of the wrath of God" (15:7), which are described in detail in 16:1–21 and represent the last of the plagues God will pour out on the world (15:1), they should have been horrified at the thought of failing to heed God's warning to stop tolerating Jezebel's teaching. The problem was not that they would come under God's wrath if they allowed Jezebel to persist; the problem was that weaker members of their congregation were being deceived by this woman. Jesus is about to judge not only Jezebel, but also her children—all "those who commit adultery with her" (2:22). They will face "great tribulation" (2:22) and Jesus will strike them dead (2:23). Jesus is essentially warning the church in Thyatira that what is described in Num 25:1–9 is about to repeat itself. Jezebel, like the Nicolaitans, was peddling the teachings of Balaam. She was leading the people of God into sexual immorality and idolatry, and both she and her followers were about to be judged by God with sickness and death. The judgment that is described in Rev 16 is a judgment that those who follow Jezebel will face if they fail to repent.

REVELATION 17–18: THE MESSAGE TO THYATIRA

As Christians in the church in Thyatira continued to wrestle with the nature of Jezebel's teachings and the need to take action, the vision of the great prostitute and the fall of Babylon in Rev 17–18 would have helped remove any delusions about Jezebel. Many Christians today wrestle with the temptation to elevate a "positive" attitude to the epitome of godliness. In first-century Thyatira they would have been quick to urge Christians to focus on all the good that Jezebel was doing. "Sure, her teaching on sexual ethics and eating meat that has been offered to idols is off-base, but the vast majority of what she teaches is orthodox and helpful to the church. Stop picking on her; no one is perfect! Stop being so negative and so judgmental!" In response to such an expression of superficial piety God uses Rev 17–18 to call believers in Thyatira to recognize that which is of the devil and respond appropriately. To do so, Jesus paints a striking picture.

Rome, "the great city that rules over the kings of the earth," is portrayed as nothing more than a prostitute (17:18) who will be utterly annihilated by the Lord. Notice, though, the language that is used in 17:2: "with whom the kings of the earth have committed sexual immorality, and with the wine of whose sexual immorality the dwellers of the earth have become drunk." Similar language is used again in 18:3: "For all nations have drunk the wine of the passion of her sexual immorality, and the kings of the earth have committed immorality with her, and the merchants of the earth have grown rich from the power of her luxurious living." Christians in Thyatira could not have missed the parallels to the language Jesus had used in the first part of his message to them. In 2:20, he had told them that Jezebel was "teaching and seducing my servants to practice sexual immorality." He then went on to speak of Jezebel's followers as "those who commit adultery with her" (2:22). The picture of the great whore of Rev 17, then, would have made it infinitely clear that Jezebel was ultimately only a pawn of Satan who was the force behind the Roman Empire. For those in Thyatira, it would have been difficult to miss the fact that while those in the trade guilds may well be getting rich from Rome's luxuries (or simply continuing to have a livelihood) by going along with the system, that system was about to come crashing down. Any compromise, then, would ultimately only bring a temporary reprieve, because Babylon is going to burn. Christians in Thyatira were thus left with a clear choice: Enjoy the benefits of the Roman economy now and soon face Jesus' harsh judgment, or trust God to meet your needs even when you are staring economic ruin in the face, knowing that that choice will result in you being given authority over the nations and ruling with Jesus, the true King of kings and Lord of lords.

Any doubts about which choice was the right one would have been removed by the detailed picture of the destruction of the prostitute and the downfall of Babylon. To compromise their faith and participate in the trade guilds would have meant siding with Babylon and prostituting themselves. The folly of such action is evident in the violent and irrevocable end that Babylon will soon face. Through these visions Jesus calls his followers to make sure they have the right perspective on what this world has to offer. There *is* no security except in obedience to him. What appears to be an all-powerful world system that offers the good life, safety, and security to all who embrace it is actually a prostitute about to meet her end. And following Jezebel, who was seducing the people of God in Thyatira into sin, is no better than following the great city (17:18) that entices the world to turn from God and embrace idols.

The obvious response is to stop tolerating such evil among them; and this is exactly what Jesus calls Christians in Thyatira to in 18:4–5: "Come out of her, my people, lest you take part in her sins, lest you share in her plagues; [5]for her sins are heaped high as heaven, and God has remembered her iniquities." Just as God is well aware of the sins of Babylon and about to judge the evil city, so he is well aware of the sins of Jezebel and her followers and is about to judge them as well. Jezebel is a citizen and promoter of Babylon who has infiltrated the church. For Christians in Thyatira "coming out of Babylon" means rejecting the teachings of Jezebel, purging her and her teachings from the church, and insisting that all followers of Jesus refuse to participate in the sins that go along with trade guild membership.

REVELATION 19: THE MESSAGE TO THYATIRA

Christians in Thyatira are clearly being asked to choose sides. Will they side with the great prostitute, whom God is about to judge or will they side with the One who bought them with his precious blood (5:9)? These are the implicit questions that emerge as we listen to the great multitude in heaven shouting praise to God in Rev 19:1–3. Notice again that the great prostitute "corrupted the earth with her (sexual) immorality" (19:2), and that corruption has spread to the church through people like Jezebel. The great prostitute is about to go up in flames, and her destruction will be absolute (19:3). Babylon's end is sure, and so is the end of all those who attempt to "follow Jesus" and protect themselves from persecution in this world through compromise (2:22–23).

God's judgment on Babylon is in part an act of vengeance against her because of "the blood of his servants" that she had shed (19:2), since "in her was found the blood of prophets and of saints, and of all who have been slain on earth" (18:24). This is a sober reminder that Babylon and those who indulge in what she has to offer stand opposed to the people of God and will not permit those who resist her to live. Just as inhabitants of the cities of Asia Minor would have viewed those who followed Jesus as unpatriotic citizens or even treasonous, because their refusal to worship the gods of the city and the gods of the empire would bring divine retribution, so also in the Western world today if Christians truly choose to live as followers of Christ they will be branded "unpatriotic,"[4] "bad citizens," and even be held responsible for not doing their part to maintain the well-being and prosperity of the nation.

Revelation 19:5 then raises the question once again for the people of God: Whom will you fear? Will you fear the wrath of the beast for failing to live as a good citizen of "Rome" or "Thyatira" or whatever city or nation you inhabit? Or will you fear God? God's servants fear him, and fear of God drives out fear of anyone else. Only those who fear God will shun sexual immorality and idolatry, and only such people will be ready for the marriage feast of the Lamb. This is made remarkably clear in 19:6–9.

---

4. Although Jesus' messages to the seven churches of Revelation clearly draw on the local contexts, he does not encourage patriotism to one's city in any way; contra Ramsay (*Letters*, 201). On the contrary, the whole of Revelation vividly calls its readers to embrace their citizenship and inheritance in the New Jerusalem, recognizing that everything else will ultimately be destroyed.

Brides, until recently in the West, had always been associated with purity; and here in 19:7 we are told that the Lamb's bride "has made herself ready." As members of the church of Thyatira heard this passage and reflected on the state of some among them who were cavorting with Jezebel, the seriousness of their situation would have been driven home. It is not Jesus who has made his Bride ready, though without the shedding of his blood his Bride would have no righteousness. Instead, it is the Bride who has made *herself* ready. She has clothed "herself with fine linen, bright and pure" (19:8). The ESV's "it was granted her to clothe herself" is far better than the NIV's "was given her to wear" (19:8). The point is not that she is handed fine line to wear, but rather that she was given the privilege of clothing herself with fine linen, bright and pure. Why is that privilege given to her? The second part of 19:8 answers that question: "the fine linen is the righteous deeds of the saints." Jesus tells Christians in Thyatira that he is about to judge Jezebel and her followers and when he does, "all the churches will know that I am he who searches mind and heart, and I will give to each of you according to your works" (2:23). Those who live as faithful followers of Jesus will be given, in accord with their works, "fine linen, bright and pure" with which to clothe themselves (19:8). This is why it is so critical for the church to take action before more among them are led astray by Jezebel. And those who have been seduced by her need to be urged to repent before they are struck dead. They need to be reminded that no one will be blessed by an invitation to the marriage supper of the Lamb (19:9) who does not have proper clothes to wear (see also Matt 22:11–14).

He who is the Judge of all mankind is coming soon, riding on a white horse (19:11), and just as he is "Faithful and True," so he expects his followers to be faithful and true. There is no room for compromise among those who follow the Lord Jesus, and there is no room for persisting in sin. The description of Jesus in 19:12 would have shaken Christians in Thyatira to the core. Jesus, who presented himself to them as the One "who has eyes like a flame of fire" (2:18), is here again described as One whose "eyes are like a flame of fire" (19:12). If there was any question regarding what the vision of Jesus was supposed to communicate in 2:18, it has now been removed. This is not a tame Jesus who comes on a white pony, and it was not a tame Jesus who spoke words of warning to the church in Thyatira. His professing followers ignore his warnings at their own peril. Those among them who do not repent will face his fiery stare and firm judgment.

Although we suggested in our comments in Chapter 5 that Jesus' "robe dipped in blood" (19:13) may subtly remind his followers that their devotion to God may cost them their lives, just as it did in Jesus' case (see John 15:18–20), a second interpretation of this imagery likely would have been more obvious to Christians in first-century Asia Minor. Once again, the Old Testament provides crucial guidance (Reading Instruction #6). In Isa 63:1–6, we find blood stained clothing clearly associated with judgment. This suggests that the description of Jesus' clothing may well serve to highlight the purpose for which he is coming. He is coming as the Judge of the nations; he is coming in wrath. This is certainly made plain in what follows: "From his mouth comes a sharp sword with which to strike down the nations, and he will rule them with a rod of iron. He will tread the winepress of the fury of the wrath of God the Almighty" (19:15). It is no coincidence how Jesus' conquering of the nations is described. He will strike down the nations and rule them with a rod of iron, as he had promised overcomers in Thyatira (2:26–27). In Rev 19 we see Jesus asserting his authority, with his faithful and true followers "following him on white horses" (19:14). To shrink back from following Jesus in an effort to avoid persecution is to make one-self the object of Jesus' fiery eyes that portend his judgment, while to remain faithful and true to him despite being hated by the world is to clothe oneself in "fine linen, bright and pure" (19:8); and it is no coincidence that those who accompany Jesus at his glorious return in Rev 19 will be "arrayed in fine linen, white and pure" (19:14).

This glorious vision of Jesus, then, serves as another powerful exhortation for Christians in Thyatira and elsewhere to give their undivided allegiance to him, much like the exhortation that Joshua gave to the children of Israel in Josh 24:14–15: "choose this day whom you will serve, whether the gods your fathers served in the region be-yond the River, or the gods of the Amorites in whose land you dwell. But as for me and my house, we will serve the LORD." To refuse to repent is to side with the evil one and those who gather "to make war against him who was sitting on the horse and against his army" (19:19). Such people have nothing to look forward to but death and having their carcasses eaten by carrion (19:21). Like Moses so many years before, in some of his last words to the Israelites, Jesus is essentially telling believers in Asia Minor and throughout the centuries, "I call heaven and earth to witness against you today, that I have set before you life and death, blessing and curse. Therefore choose life" (Deut 30:19). He *will* strike Jezebel's children dead (2:23), but that is not his desire. His desire is for Jezebel's children to repent and become overcomers. That is the whole reason that he sent the book of Revelation to Christians in Thyatira.

SUMMARY: JESUS' MESSAGE TO CHRISTIANS IN THYATIRA

To Christians in Thyatira who have come under the spell of a false prophetess and compromised Jesus' call to walk in obedience to his commands and be holy as he is holy, Jesus has much to say in the rest of the story for this church. The best medicine for those who are wavering in their commitment to God and becoming ensnared by the wrong kind of love for this world is to stop and take a good look at a larger reality. The One to whom they belong is infinitely more glorious, infinitely more valuable, and infinitely more worthy of their devotion than anything this world has to offer (Rev 4–5). This positive encouragement to change their ways and stop tolerating the evil teachings among them is quickly followed by a negative encouragement as the reality of what it looks like to come under the judgment of Jesus (2:22–23) is vividly illustrated in Rev 6. The world out there is going to be soundly judged for its rebellion against God, but "it is time for judgment to begin at the household of God" (1 Pet 4:17). In light of that impending judgment, those in Thyatira need to ensure that they are not among those who are thrown "into great tribulation" (2:22; 7:14). They dare not end up like the tribes of Dan and Ephraim, who were infamous for their assimilation to the practices of Canaan and thus excluded from those who are sealed in Rev 7. And they dare not think that their unfaithfulness is beyond Jesus' notice; after all, he "searches mind and heart" and will repay each one according to their works (2:23). If they refuse to repent of their sexual immorality and idolatry like the rest of the world (9:20–21), they too can expect to face judgment from God.

The church at Thyatira had been tolerating a peddler of false teachings and Jesus is now urgently calling them to wake up and deal with the problem. They dare not delay in responding to his warning, for the time is short (10:6). Revelation presents them with a number of important questions: Will they continue to associate with Jezebel, the false prophetess, or will they instead reject her influence and associate themselves with the two witnesses (Rev 11). Will they heed Jesus' implicit call to repent and abandon Jezebel's "deep teachings" in favor of the pure and simple gospel? Will they become like the two witnesses who place their lives in the hands of God and live for his glory alone? Will they realize that love for God will often lead to hatred from the world (11:10), just as Jesus had warned elsewhere (John 14:18–20), and such an outcome should be expected by followers of Jesus (John 16:33)? Will they come to their senses and recognize that Jezebel is Satan's pawn in his game of leading the world (and the church) astray (12:9) and is nothing less than a tamer version of the beast who will do the same on a global scale (13:14)? Will they repent and thus reign with the one who was born "to rule all the nations with a rod of iron" (12:5)? Will they recognize that compromise with the idolatrous demands of the trade guilds, which Jezebel promoted, puts them in league with the beast who will ultimately make it impossible for those who refuse to take his mark throughout the world to feed their families? Will they turn from their sexual immorality and begin to live again as pure virgins betrothed to the Lamb (14:4)?

Christians in Thyatira needed to grapple with the fact that to give in to the teachings of Jezebel would be to side with Satan, the beast, and Babylon, all of which are going to be destroyed. They needed to realize that forfeiting rights and even their very lives in this world through their allegiance to Jesus would result in great reward in the coming age (14:13). To support the urgent exhortation to deal with Jezebel Jesus provides Christians in Thyatira with vivid visions of the downfall of the prostitute in Rev 17–18. Just as Jesus had earlier used a name associated with wickedness and leading God's people astray to characterize a self-styled prophetess in Thyatira (Jezebel), so here he uses language that closely links Jezebel with the great prostitute whom God will also destroy. Following her teachings, then, or even allowing her influence within the church, is the height of folly. Those in Thyatira who have not succumbed to her enticements must continue to stand firm, holding fast until Jesus returns (2:25). For only through doing so can they make themselves ready for the marriage supper of the Lamb (19:7).

10

Jesus' Message to the Church in Sardis

And to the angel of the church in Sardis write: The words of him who has the seven spirits of God and the seven stars. I know your works. You have the reputation of being alive, but you are dead. (3:1)

AS WE CONSIDER JESUS' message to the fifth group of Christians that he addresses, we need to once again remember that we are reading a message that was addressed to the "Wealthy East" of the first century. Sardis was the capital of the kingdom of Lydia and one of the more illustrious cities in ancient Anatolia.[1] It was home to a temple of Artemis, the fourth largest Ionic temple known to have been built in the ancient world, and had a population of 60,000–100,000. It had once been known as the greatest of all Greek cities.[2]

By the Roman period, however, Sardis had lost its ancient stature, and its reputation for greatness was based more on its past than its present.[3] In AD 17, the city had been almost completely destroyed by an earthquake, along with eleven other cities in the Lydian valley, including Philadelphia.[4] Pliny the Elder, writing about this earthquake, states that "the greatest earthquake which has occurred in our memory was in the reign of Tiberius, by which twelve cities of Asia were laid prostrate in one night."[5] Sardis was the most severely damaged of the cities in the region, and consequently, Tacitus notes, "it attracted to them the largest share of sympathy. The emperor

---

1. Hemer (*Letters*, 134–35) provides evidence suggesting that Sardis may have been the same as Sepharad, which is mentioned in Obad 20.

2. Ramsay, *Letters*, 259.

3. Ibid.

4. Ibid., 290.

5. Pliny the Elder, *Nat.* 2.86.

promised ten million sesterces, and remitted for five years all they paid to the exchequer or to the emperor's purse."[6] Given the fact that the city was rebuilt with aid from Rome, it is not surprising that the inhabitants of the Sardis had a very positive attitude toward Rome and were devoted to the imperial cult. Their gratitude and devotion is illustrated in coins from the period that show a woman, representing Sardis, kneeling before the emperor who is depicted as granting her favor. The city is also referred to as "Caesarean Sardis" on the coin.[7]

Even before Tiberius and later Claudius stepped in to help Sardis, however, the city had been devoted to Rome. It had unsuccessfully attempted to establish Asia's first temple to Caesar Augustus in 27 BC, and later built a local temple to Augustus (5 BC) and a cult statue to Augustus' son Gaius. Sardis went on to compete for the honor of building a temple to the emperor Tiberius in AD 26, but lost out to Smyrna. All of this points to a population in Sardis that was enthusiastic about the Roman Empire and eager to give their allegiance to the emperor.

To Christians in this city Jesus introduces himself as the one "who has the seven spirits of God and the seven stars." We have already been informed by Jesus in 1:20 that the "seven stars" represent angels. If we are correct in viewing the "seven spirits," first introduced in 1:4, as a symbol of the Holy Spirit, what is the significance of Jesus having, or perhaps better "holding," the Holy Spirit in his hand, along with the seven stars/angels? This imagery appears to portray Jesus as the dispenser of the Holy Spirit—the One who sends the Holy Spirit to his people (see John 15:26)—and the One who also sends his angels to minister to God's people (see Heb 1:14). Once again, Jesus has chosen his title to fit his audience's needs (Reading Instruction #4). The inhabitants of Sardis were well-accustomed to having the Roman emperor as the dispenser of aid when disaster struck, but Jesus is subtly calling believers in Sardis to recognize that he is the One to look to in time of need. The culture around them would pressure them to live lives that demonstrated allegiance to Rome, their benefactor. Jesus calls them to look to him who has infinitely more resources at his disposal than any Roman emperor. The emperor may give them a tax break, but Jesus gives them the Holy Spirit and sends his angels to help them as well.

The fact that Jesus holds the Holy Spirit, ready to lavish him upon his people, is also a timely reminder to the saints in Sardis. As Gordon Fee has rightly said, the Holy Spirit is "God's Empowering Presence" among God's people.[8] He enables followers of Jesus to lead holy lives that are pleasing to God and fruitful in his service. Jesus, who knows the needs of the church, sends the Holy Spirit to meet those needs. He does not do this in a piecemeal fashion, but rather sends the Spirit in all his fullness to each of the seven churches, as the symbolic "*seven* spirits" makes clear (Reading Instruction

---

6. Tacitus, *Ann.* 2.47.

7. Ramsay, *Letters*, 268.

8. Fee, *God's Empowering Presence*.

#5).[9] Thus, there is no need that Jesus is unable to meet through the sending of the Spirit.[10] Perhaps more important in the case of Christians in Sardis, whose garments had been soiled, the Holy Spirit's work is to make them holy, and it is critical that they cooperate with his work.

The exalted Jesus makes it clear to the church in Sardis that he not only walks among them and has knowledge of their behavior, but his knowledge extends even to the motives of their hearts. It is quite possible that part of the reason Jesus chose the title, "him who has . . . the seven stars," was to highlight the fact that he has placed angels over the churches who report to him how his people are doing. At any rate, the key point here is that Jesus will never be satisfied with superficial piety. Such was the piety of many of the Pharisees! While Christians today are often quick to brand the Pharisees as "legalists" and so seek to avoid falling into that same trap, we often neglect the fact that central to the sins of the Pharisees was their contentment with fostering a reputation for outward devotion to God while their hearts were actually far from him. They were first-class hypocrites. Jesus quotes Isa 29:13 to describe them, "You hypocrites! Well did Isaiah prophesy of you, when he said: [8]"This people honors me with their lips, but their heart is far from me; [9]in vain do they worship me, teaching as doctrines the commandments of men'" (Matt 15:7–9). It is this very hypocrisy that many Christians in Sardis had fallen into. Jesus knows all too well that while they may have been renowned for their spirituality, it was a superficial spirituality that masked a dead heart. Like the Christians at Ephesus, they had begun well, but things had gone sour.[11] They had a form of godliness, but were denying its power (2 Tim 3:5).[12]

As Ramsay argues, it is quite possible that once again Jesus is using the unique history and character of a city to communicate his message (Reading Instruction #4). Sardis had a reputation for greatness that was inconsistent with the reality of a city in decline. "No city of Asia at the time showed such a melancholy contrast between past splendor and present decay as Sardis."[13] Although Ramsay's description appears to be overstated, since Sardis remained an important city in some ways,[14] the contrast between the past and the present was nevertheless dramatic, as was the contrast between reputation and reality. Jesus' choice of words here to Christians in this city thus produces another rhetorical hotspot.

9. Cf. Ramsay, *Letters*, 272–73.

10. Cf. ibid., 143.

11. Ibid., 271.

12. Hemer, *Letters*, 143.

13. Ramsay, *Letters*, 275.

14. Hemer, *Letters*, 143.

*Wake up, and strengthen what remains and is about to die, for I have not found
your works complete in the sight of my God.* (3:2)

To a church that appeared to be alive but was really dead, Jesus has an urgent
wake up call. Fortunately, the church in Sardis was only "mostly dead"; it was not
"all dead." Consequently, Jesus can urge it to rouse itself from its spiritual stupor and
build upon "what remains," likely a reference to the limited spiritual vitality that was
still present within the church.[15] It is not a lost cause, but the church is on the verge of
destruction.

Notice also the way that Jesus contrasts appearances with reality. He says that he
has not found their works "complete in the sight of my God." From the perspective
of other churches in the region, the church in Sardis was likely doing quite well. They
had all of the signs of spiritual vitality. In our modern context we might say that they
were growing in number, had just completed a successful building program, their giving had doubled in the past three years, they were expanding their ministry to include
televised services, they were sending out ten teams on short term missions each year,
they were very involved in bettering life in their community, etc. All of these things
would lead many of us to conclude that we were dealing with a healthy church. The
church in Sardis had comparable markers of spiritual vitality; but while their works
may have passed muster with the people around them, they came up far short in God's
sight.[16] God was not impressed by their activity or by their superficial signs of growth
and "vibrant spirituality." He saw the deep recesses of their heart; and what he found
there was disease and imminent death. What masqueraded as a spiritually vibrant
congregation was a congregation that was actually spiritually comatose.

We dare not rush by the danger that Jesus is pointing to for us today. Consider
one typical criterion used to determine whether or not a church is alive: "vibrant worship." We tend to think that if there is lively singing—yes, we also have the problem of
viewing singing as the time when we "worship," when singing is just one of the many
ways we worship God when we gather together—then our church is alive. Passages
like Amos 5:21–24, however, make it clear that singing songs of praise to God do not
always please him. When songs of praise and other acts of so-called worship do not
flow out of a life of devotion to God—seeking first the kingdom of God and his righteousness—they become an offense to God because they serve as a regular reminder
of our hypocrisy. Those who are content to appear devoted to God when their hearts
are far from him will never please him. Instead, they will be stereotypical Pharisees
through and through; pious on the outside, self-centered and worldly on the inside.

In the case of Christians in Sardis, this state of affairs led Jesus to pronounce
them "dead." But what was causing their death? Notice how Jesus describes the problem: "I have not found your works complete in the sight of my God." The consistent

15. Aune (*Revelation 1–5*, 216) notes the use of the neuter for people in 1 Cor 1:27–28 and Heb 7:7.
16. Hemer, *Letters*, 144.

message of Scripture, which Jesus alludes to here, is this: faith that is genuine is faith that works. Although this message is rightly attributed to James, Paul actually makes clear throughout the book of Romans that "faith" and "obedience" are two sides of the same coin.[17] Spiritual life will always translate into godly action. The church in Sardis, though, was content as long as others thought well of them, and indifferent to what God thought. They were "asleep in the light."[18]

> Remember, then, what you received and heard. Keep it, and repent. If you will not wake up, I will come like a thief, and you will not know at what hour I will come against you. (3:3)

As we think about why the Christians in Sardis may have neglected God's good commands, it is worth noting that we find no indication in Jesus' words to them that they were struggling because of persecution. Nor does Jesus place any focus on false teaching within the church. Instead, there appears to be an utter lack of discernment in this church that led the majority to be content with how things were, content with an appearance of spirituality, even when the church was dead or dying. Like the other churches in Asia Minor, the church at Sardis was not faltering because it lacked a strong foundation of sound teaching. Believers in Sardis knew what God required of them, but they had either actively turned away from it or simply neglected to pay attention to it out of complacency. Either way, the call from Jesus is to remember what they have already received. They do not need new instructions; they simply need to obey what they have already been told.

It is interesting that this call to "remember" is given only to Christians in Ephesus and Sardis. With Ephesus, this makes very good sense, since Jesus is calling them back to what they had been and done (2:5). With Sardis, though, he is calling them back to what they had *received and heard*. They knew the teachings of Jesus, and had likely been taught by the Apostle John himself. They did not lack good, solid Bible teaching. What they lacked was the long-term commitment to follow what they had been taught. How easily followers of Jesus neglect the clear teachings of the Word of God and slowly drift away from an intimate relationship with God, while maintaining the outward trappings of spirituality. The ancient Christians at Sardis show us that such drift can be masked by truckloads of religious activity that give the illusion of spiritual life when the church is, in reality, slowly dying or already dead.

Jesus is calling these Christians to "keep" what they had received and heard. In other words, he is calling them to obedience, just as he had done at the beginning of Revelation (1:3). "Wait a minute," many might say today, "Christianity isn't about rules, it's about relationship!" This common way of thinking is actually severely flawed theologically. It draws a sharp distinction between rules and relationship, framing

---

17. Notice how he frames the entire letter with the phrase "the obedience of faith" (Rom 1:5; 16:26).

18. See the powerful song of this title by Keith Green.

them as an either/or proposition, when in fact Christianity is about both rules (God's good commands) and relationship. It may well be that the very thinking that is so prevalent today was at work in Sardis many years ago; and the result was a church on the brink of death.

Jesus actually makes it clear elsewhere that careful attention to knowing and following his commands is one of the surest ways to a *deeper* relationship with God. In the short span of less than ten verses in John 14, Jesus defines what it means to love him three times in the very same terms (John 14:15, 21, 23). To love Jesus is to obey his commands. All three times he uses the same word as in Rev 3:3; those who love him "keep" (τηρέω, *tēreō*) his commands. What Jesus wants us to see—and what the Christians in Sardis had likely missed—is that *his commands are not legalism, they are life*. When we devote ourselves to finding out what pleases the Lord (Eph 5:10) and doing it, we are able to enter into the abundant life that Jesus promised (John 10:10). It is a life where we enjoy the presence of the Holy Spirit living in us, helping us, and teaching us (John 14:16, 17, 26); it is a life of being showered with the love of the Father and the Son (John 14:21, 23); it is a life in which Jesus comes and actually reveals himself to us in ways we could never imagine (John 14:21); and it is a life of unthinkable intimacy with the Father and the Son as they come and live with us (John 14:23)—*if* we keep Jesus' commands.

So, are his commands a burden or a blessing? Listen to what John himself wrote likely to the very same churches on this issue: "this is the love of God, that we keep his commandments. And his commandments are not burdensome" (1 John 5:3). As with us, a warped view of "rules" (God's good commands) seems to have been a perennial problem with the Christians that John shepherded. So, he reminds them and us, "Stop thinking of God's commands as a burden. They are a blessing! They are the path to intimacy with God and fullness of joy, just as Jesus made clear when he was on earth."

This is why Jesus graciously calls on his followers in Sardis in Rev 3:3 to "Remember, then, what you received and heard. Keep it." In many North American churches today, if I were to stand up and say what Jesus says here, I would be branded a legalist. If I were to say, "Look at how God's Word tells us to live. Obey it and repent!" I would probably be shown the door after being told, "We have a grace-based ministry here. There is no place here for such negativity and legalism in this church." Those who take such a warped approach to the Christian life make Jesus unwelcome in the church. They abandon the Scriptures in favor of the latest traditions of men and consign themselves to the same fate as the church in Sardis. They may have an appearance of life, but they will really be dead.

So, what does Jesus say about repentance? Does he portray it as optional? Quite the contrary, he makes it clear that failure to repent will lead to judgment, judgment on the church. The spiritual stupor of believers in Sardis, if left unchecked, will render them unprepared for the coming of the Lord. His coming will be a shock and it will lead to shame. Christians sometimes think that Jesus' return is intended to be like a thief in the night, unexpected for everyone. Quite the contrary, Scripture makes it clear that his return will *not* be a surprise for those who are faithful and watchful (see, e.g., 1 Thess 5:4–11). It is only for those who are not eagerly looking forward to his return and living accordingly that his return will be unexpected.

Jesus' mention of coming unexpectedly, like a thief, clearly creates a powerful rhetorical hotspot given the history of Sardis (Reading Instruction #4).[19] Although most of the city was eventually built in the valley, the original city was built 1500 feet higher on a plateau at the top of a hill. Ramsay notes that "it was actually inaccessible except at one point, namely, the neck of land on the south, which still offers the only approach. On all other sides the rock walls were smooth, nearly perpendicular, and absolutely unscalable even without a defender."[20] The defensive position of Sardis was so perfect that one might speak of the impossible by proverbially referring to Sardis. Thus, Lucian, speaking of someone who has been most fortunate in every way wrote: "You have won, then, lucky man, and have gained the Olympic crown—nay, you have taken Babylon or stormed the citadel of Sardis."[21] Sardis had a history marked by frequent wars, and although its natural defenses made it virtually impregnable, on two occasions they were breached. King Cyrus of Persia and later Antiochus III in 214 BC each captured the city by sending soldiers up the cliff.[22] As Ramsay sums up, the leaders of the city "in careless confidence were content to guard the one known approach, and left the rest of the circuit unguarded, under the belief that it could not be scaled."[23]

Unfortunately, many of the Christians at Sardis seem to have been afflicted with the same case of over-confidence in their position before the Lord. "Surely, God would never judge *us*! After all, he is a God of love and grace. He would never do anything to upset us." This same kind of attitude reigned supreme in Jerusalem in the years leading up to its destruction by Nebuchadnezzar. The Israelites reasoned, "This is the temple of the LORD, the temple of the LORD, the temple of the LORD!" (Jer 7:4). In other words, "God would never destroy his temple or the city where it is located! As long as we're in Jerusalem, we're safe. Nothing can touch us!" The Israelites had a false sense of security that ultimately led to their destruction. The same was true of the history of Sardis, and everyone still knew those stories very well. Jesus' words, then, would have been a stark warning not to let it happen again; this time within the church. Appearances could be deceiving. Outward spiritual health could be a mere façade, much like Sardis's superficial invincibility. The Christians in Sardis, then, must be vigilant to guard against attacks, particularly the temptation to assimilate to the culture around them, which would soil them even more with the filth of the world.

---

19. As Hemer (*Letters*, 144) notes, the following historical context has long been recognized by commentators.

20. Ramsay, *Letters*, 260.

21. *On Salaried Posts in Great Houses*, 13.

22. See Herodotus, *Hist.* 1.84. See also Polybius, *Hist.* 7.15–18.

23. Ramsay, *Letters*, 265.

*Yet you have still a few names in Sardis, people who have not soiled their gar-
ments, and they will walk with me in white, for they are worthy.* (3:4)

Here, we find another metaphor with the reference to soiled clothes; and once
again there is clear guidance from the Old Testament to help us understand its significance (Reading Instruction #6), this time in the vivid vision of Zech 3:1–5. In
Zech 3:3–4, it is clear that Joshua's sinful state is being metaphorically depicted by his
filthy clothes. Replacing his filthy clothes with clean garments is used to symbolize
the cleansing of his sin. Jesus' language in Rev 3:4, then, points to the fact that most
of the Christians in Sardis were living in sin in some way, while there were a few
who had been careful to remain pure in the face of temptation. The latter were thus
"worthy" to walk with Jesus. But what was the temptation? We know that Sardis "was
a principal, and perhaps very early, centre of the Jewish Diaspora."[24] Although it was
likely not built until at least 100 years after Revelation was written, Sardis was also
home to the largest synagogue in the ancient world, a "mega-synagogue" that could
accommodate 1,000 people. Archaeological evidence suggests that unlike other cities
in Asia Minor, where there was tension between Jews and the rest of the population,
in Sardis Jews seem to have blended into city life "by accommodation to their pagan
surroundings."[25] It is quite possible that some of the Christians in Sardis had followed
the lead of their Jewish neighbors, perhaps through blending into the synagogue,
which was itself syncretistic (Reading Instruction #4).[26] If so, their "deadness" did
not simply stem from a lack of spiritual nourishment. Instead, it would have stemmed
from a slow surrender to the temptation to blend in to the society around them. Jesus
warned of the dangers of such assimilation, as we already saw in our discussion of his
words to the church in Ephesus. His words in Matt 24:12 serve as a stark reminder of
the way that assimilation will kill one's spiritual life: "And because lawlessness will be
increased, the love of many will grow cold." For those who enter into the wickedness
of the surrounding society, in small ways and large, their compromise slowly cools
their faith until it is all but frozen.

It is possible that when Jesus speaks of their works not being "complete" (3:2),
his concern is parallel to his concern with the Christians in Ephesus whom he exhorts
to "do the works you did at first" (2:5). If so, we have another church that has ceased
to be an overt witness for Christ.[27] Blending into society naturally requires that one
ceases to do those things that make you stand out the most. For Christians, that would
without doubt include, first and foremost, the preaching of the gospel. Supporting
this view is one of the promises that Jesus gives to Christian overcomers in Sardis in
verse 5: "I will confess his name before my Father and before his angels." Christians in

24. Hemer, *Letters*, 136.

25. Ibid., 137.

26. Cf. ibid., 149.

27. So Beale, *Revelation*, 275.

Sardis who had "received" the words of Jesus from the Apostle John and others could not help but notice the connection between this promise and the fuller versions of the promise he gives in the Gospels:

> So everyone who acknowledges me before men, I also will acknowledge before my Father who is in heaven, ³³but whoever denies me before men, I also will deny before my Father who is in heaven. (Matt 10:32–33)

> And I tell you, everyone who acknowledges me before men, the Son of Man also will acknowledge before the angels of God, ⁹but the one who denies me before men will be denied before the angels of God. (Luke 12:8–9)

Although the ESV is inconsistent here and uses "I will confess" in Rev 3:5 and "I will acknowledge" in Matthew and Luke, the word is the same in Greek. Jesus' acknowledgement of someone before his Father and the angels is dependent on that person's acknowledgement of him before people in this world. It is difficult, then, not to see at least part of the "incompleteness" of their works as relating to abandoning their central calling of being overt witnesses of Jesus.

The context, though, seems to suggest that more is involved here. Unlike those in Ephesus who had vigilantly guarded against evil creeping into the church, patiently endured trials that were associated with their status as followers of Christ, and yet slowly shrunk back from taking the gospel to the culture around them (likely out of fear of further reprisals), Christians in Sardis appear to have done the same thing, but for very different reasons. Part of the problem of their "works" involved activity that "soiled" their clothing, activity that stained them with sin. This was a church that had it altogether outwardly, with all the appearances of spiritual life, but had utterly compromised their integrity. In their effort to blend in with the culture around them they had likely not only ceased being an overt witness but had also willingly compromised their moral purity in a variety of ways. They had thus soiled their clothes.

Not everyone in Sardis, though, was clothed in filthy spiritual rags; and those who had not compromised would walk with Jesus, dressed in white, "for they are worthy." Ramsay notes that "white was widely considered among the ancient nations as the color of innocence and purity."[28] Again we note that this has traditionally been reflected in our own culture's practice of brides wearing white for their wedding. Ramsay goes on to point out that "all Roman citizens wore the pure white toga on holidays and at religious ceremonies, whether or not they wore it on ordinary days."[29] Thus, just as soiled clothing is used as a metaphor for spiritual impurity, so white clothing is used as a metaphor for spiritual purity.

It is noteworthy that elsewhere in Revelation, it is only God or Christ who is identified as "worthy" (4:11; 5:9). So, what makes a Christian in Sardis worthy of white

28. Ramsay, *Letters*, 282.
29. Ibid.

clothes? On the one hand, followers of Jesus can praise God that they are worthy by virtue of Christ's death for them; but that does not seem to be the point here, as the rest of Revelation makes clear. Here, the focus is on those who *by their own actions* do not soil their clothes and are therefore worthy. How exactly does this happen? By choosing moral purity in their lives and refusing to compromise. Such people are worthy. Those who are faithful to Jesus are worthy. And such people will enjoy the beautiful intimacy with God that is portrayed in language that is designed to draw our attention back to the Garden of Eden. As Adam and Eve walked with God in the Garden, so will those who choose to resist the pressure to live like the culture around them.

Once again, then, we find that God's grace does not preclude the absolute necessity of Christian faithfulness. The fact that followers of Jesus are saved by God's unilateral gracious act through Jesus Christ does not make living in the fear of the Lord an option for salvation. To profess faith without embracing God's call to holiness is to embrace a false gospel. Holiness is simply not optional.

> *The one who conquers will be clothed thus in white garments, and I will never blot his name out of the book of life. I will confess his name before my Father and before his angels.* [6]*He who has an ear, let him hear what the Spirit says to the churches.* (3:5–6)

Jesus' words in verse 5 are intended as a call to those who have soiled their clothes. It is a beautiful offer of grace to those who have compromised, as well as a promise of a sure reward to those who have not. To those in Sardis who will hear his words and "keep" them (1:3) Jesus holds out the promise of purified garments. As the high priest Joshua had his filthy garments exchanged for clean ones, so too can those in Sardis who have been seduced into compromise experience cleansing through repentance. A proper response to Jesus' exhortation to repent will restore their soiled clothing to the pure whiteness that it once had. What follows, though, also implicitly provides a strong warning to those who persist in lifestyles that soil their clothes.

Jesus tells those who overcome that he will never blot out their name from the book of life, but will acknowledge their name before his Father and the angels. The expression, "to have one's name erased/blotted out of the Book of Life," is a metaphor of severe judgment that frequently occurs in the Old Testament and other Jewish literature (Reading Instruction #6):[30]

> So Moses returned to the Lord and said, "Alas, this people has sinned a great sin. They have made for themselves gods of gold. [32]But now, if you will forgive their sin—but if not, please blot me out of your book that you have written." [33]But the Lord said to Moses, "Whoever has sinned against me, I will blot out of my book." (Exod 32:31–33)

---

30. Aune, *Revelation 1–5*, 223.

Add to them punishment upon punishment; may they have no acquittal from you. [28]Let them be blotted out of the book of the living; let them not be enrolled among the righteous. (Ps 69:27–28)

You who have done good will wait for those days until an end is made of those who work evil . . . Wait until sin has passed away, for their names will be blotted out of the book of life and out of the holy books, and their seed will be destroyed forever, and their spirits will be slain, and they will cry and make lamentation in a place that is a chaotic wilderness, and in the fire they will burn; for there is no earth there. (1 *En.* 108:1–4)

But if they transgress and work uncleanness in every way, they will be recorded on the heavenly tablets as adversaries, and they will be destroyed out of the book of life, and they will be recorded in the book of [23]those who will be destroyed and with those who will be rooted out of the earth. (*Jub.* 30:22–23)

Often, the metaphor simply meant, "to die." But in later periods, it was frequently used of eschatological judgment. Thus, in *Jos. Asen.* 15:3 we read, "Take heart, Aseneth, your name is written in the book of life, and it will never be blotted out." Similarly, in *T. Levi* 18:59–60 we find, "Your offspring will be recorded in the book of the remembrance of life, and your name will not be erased, nor the name of your offspring forever."[31]

Erasure of a name from a book, though, was not a distinctively Jewish practice. This same idea was common in secular Greco-Roman contexts as well (Reading Instruction #4): "in all Greek and Roman cities of that time there was kept a list of citizens, according to their class or tribe or *deme,* in which new citizens were entered and from which degraded citizens were expunged."[32] In ancient Athens, when a citizen was going to be executed for a crime, his name was first erased from the roll of citizens.[33] All of this suggests that having one's name erased from the book of life would not only imply death, but also the loss of rights as a citizen in the Kingdom of God. It is quite likely, then, that when Jesus says, "I will never blot his name out of the book of life," he is saying that overcomers will not experience the second death, but will instead enjoy all the benefits of citizenship in the coming messianic kingdom.

The use of this particular promise with the church of Sardis may also suggest that their accommodation to the surrounding culture came at least in part from a willingness to integrate into the synagogue. Just as earlier Jews had uttered curses against

---

31. See ibid., 225.

32. Ramsay, *Letters,* 281.

33. See Dio Chrysostom, *Or.* 31.84: ἐκεῖ γὰρ ὅταν δημοσίᾳ τινὰ δέῃ τῶν πολιτῶν ἀποθανεῖν ἐπ' ἀδικήματι, πρότερον αὐτοῦ τὸ ὄνομαἐξαλείφεται (*ekei gar hotan dēmosia tina deē tōn politōn apothanein ep' adikēmati proteron autou to onomaexaleiphetai*).

their enemies,[34] so also in the first century Jews recited curses against the enemies of Judaism, including Christians (Reading Instruction #4):

> For the apostates let there be no hope, and uproot the kingdom of arrogance, speedily and in our days. May the Nazarenes and the sectarians perish as in a moment. Let them be blotted out of the book of life, and not be written together with the righteous. You are praised, O Lord, who subdues the arrogant.[35]

A key part of the curse was the call upon God to blot Christians (Nazarenes) out of the book of life. In Jesus' promise to overcomers at Sardis, we find him assuring them that no such fate will ever befall them. Given the historical context, the use of this particular promise may (1) point to a willingness on the part of many Christians in Sardis to blend in to the synagogue where they were forced to recite a curse against themselves involving being blotted out of the book of life; (2) suggest that Jesus is subtly appealing to those who have not soiled their clothes to avoid giving in to the temptation to find refuge in the synagogue; or (3) simply serve as a figurative way of promising eternal life to overcomers. Whatever the specific circumstances, the promise not to blot out their name from the book of life clearly serves as another metaphor for eternal life.

Finally, Jesus also promises the overcomer that he will "confess his name before my Father and before his angels." As we have already seen, this promise is strongly reminiscent of Jesus' words in the Gospels (Matt 10:32; Luke 12:8). There is little question that Jesus is playing off his earlier statements here. He will acknowledge before his Father those who overcome, and such overcoming involves, in part, acknowledging him before people. This again raises the question of whether Christians in Sardis were trying to find refuge in the Jewish synagogue, a place where they not only would not dare acknowledge Jesus but would also be forced to recite, or pretend to recite, the "Curse Against the Heretics." They no doubt also faced the broader temptation to hide their faith in the midst of a hostile environment. It was dangerous to be a Christian in the first-century Greco-Roman world. To acknowledge Jesus as Lord was to imply that Caesar was not. Whatever the case, Jesus' tailor-made promise for Christians in Sardis suggests that unwillingness to acknowledge him publicly was likely an issue. And this is certainly a challenge that we face today, no matter what our cultural context.

SARDIS: PROFILE OF A CHURCH

Sardis was a church that was self-deceived. It was quite comfortable with the status quo, recognizing that they had all that mattered to them: a good reputation among

---

34. Some form of curse or "imprecation" occurs in at least twenty-eight of the psalms alone. For more, see Culy, "Do Psalmists who Curse Belong in the Church?," 35–60.

35. This is the *Birkat Ha-Minim*, or "Curse against the Heretics"; quoted from Aune, *Revelation 1–5*, 225. On its first-century dating, see Instone-Brewer, "The Eighteen Benedictions and the Minim before 70 CE."

the churches. Jesus reminds them, however, that it is not others' estimation of their spiritual status that was important; it was his. And he had found them wanting. Not only was he not impressed with their superficial piety, but he also saw their heart and knew that they were actually dead—or, at least, almost dead. Leaders in Sardis were like many church leaders today who are content to focus on the positive and take a "steady as she goes" approach to ministry, rather than asking the hard question, "Does Jesus have anything against us?" or "Is there anything we are doing or failing to do (2:2) that is displeasing to God?" These are questions that should be central to the regular reflection of church leaders, but are often swept away under the guise of keeping positive and not being judgmental. To those who embraced such an attitude in Sardis Jesus sounded a strong warning and urged them to go back to the basics of what they had been taught. The role of church leaders is not to make everything run smoothly so that people will be impressed with "our church." Rather, church leaders are called to "shepherd the flock of God that is among" them (1 Pet 5:2); they are called to pay careful attention to themselves and to all the flock knowing that fierce wolves will come, not sparing the flock, and even from among them "will arise men speaking twisted things, to draw away disciples after them" (Acts 20:28–30). Leaders in Sardis had apparently failed considerably in their role as shepherds, since there were only a few who had "not soiled their garments" (3:4). To overcome they must completely change their thinking. They must go back to the basics of what they had been taught. They must repent and follow the commands of Jesus, rather than compromising and continuing to soil their garments.

11

Jesus' Message to the Church in Sardis
The Rest of the Story

And to the angel of the church in Sardis write: The words of him who has the seven spirits of God and the seven stars. I know your works. You have the reputation of being alive, but you are dead. (3:1)

WE SAW EARLIER THAT Jesus' description of himself as the one who holds the seven spirits of God highlights the fact that he is the sender of the Holy Spirit. As we come to the throne room visions of Rev 4–5, however, we find that more is likely going on here than first meets the eye. We only find reference to "the seven spirits of God" twice more in Revelation after 3:1. In 4:5, we are reminded that the Holy Spirit dwells in the presence of God as well as among God's people. This means that God is at once both empowering his people through his Spirit and also being kept abreast of all that is going on among his people by his Spirit. The latter is particularly emphasized in the second reference, in 5:6, where the Lamb is described as having "seven eyes, which are the seven spirits of God sent out into all the earth." In other words, through the Holy Spirit Jesus has complete awareness of all that is going on in this world.

The church in Sardis had been behaving much like Babylon (Rev 17–18). They were going along their merry way to destruction, thinking that all was well, when in fact they were about to die. And when they died, they would find themselves in a difficult position. For, "the dead who die in the Lord" have "their deeds follow them" (14:13), and unfortunately most Christians in Sardis had incomplete deeds (3:2). Furthermore, when the time comes for the marriage supper of the Lamb, the saints of God will be clothed in "fine linen [which] is the righteous deeds of the saints" (19:8), but many of those in Sardis had "soiled their garments" (3:4), making them entirely inappropriate for access to the marriage supper of the Lamb. It is absolutely critical, then, that they wake up and address their dire problem immediately.

Christians in Sardis, more than any of their neighbors in Asia Minor, would have been particularly struck by later references to "works" in Revelation, given Jesus' words in 3:1 ("I know your works . . . you are dead"). As they came to the trumpet judgments in Rev 8–9 and the bowl judgments in Rev 16, the description of how the inhabitants of the world respond to the outpouring of God's wrath would have caught their attention: "The rest of mankind, who were not killed by these plagues, did not repent of *the works of their hands* nor give up worshiping demons and idols of gold and silver and bronze and stone and wood, which cannot see or hear or walk, [21]nor did they repent of their murders or their sorceries or their sexual immorality or their thefts" (9:20–21); "The fifth angel poured out his bowl on the throne of the beast, and its kingdom was plunged into darkness. People gnawed their tongues in anguish [11]and cursed the God of heaven for their pain and sores. *They did not repent of their deeds [works]*" (16:10–11).[1] These passages would have raised an important question: Will Christians in Sardis align themselves with unrepentant pagans who persist in works that displease the Lord, or will they change their ways?

Christians in Sardis were, like us, tempted to assimilate to the culture around them. Like many of us, they had become adept at playing the piety game, appearing devoted to God on the outside when there were all sorts of hidden sins in their lives. Their loyalties were mixed, and God knew it, even though everyone around them sang their praises. Like a skilled politician they may have been adept at "spinning" their reputation. Like the myriads who paint sugar-coated pictures of themselves on social media today, they were skilled in living a double-life. But such an approach to life could never fool Jesus. He identifies the church in Sardis as "dead." Coming from the lips of the Lord Jesus Christ, who perfectly knows the hearts of all people, this would have been shocking to any professing believer. They may well have known what Jesus had said in his vine metaphor: "I am the true vine, and my Father is the vinedresser. Every branch in me that does not bear fruit he takes away" (John 15:1–2); "If anyone does not abide in me he is thrown away like a branch and withers; and the branches are gathered, thrown into the fire, and burned" (John 15:6). Spiritual decline is not something to be toyed with; it must be recognized and repented of, lest one end up completely dead and worthy of being cut off.

> *Wake up, and strengthen what remains and is about to die, for I have not found your works complete in the sight of my God.* (3:2)

Jesus' words in 3:2 are intended to elicit a sense of urgency in Christians in Sardis. They are in an emergency room situation. He has described them in verse 1 as "dead," but here it becomes clear that they are only mostly dead. There is still the opportunity

---

1. The ESV's inconsistency in translating the same word here unfortunately masks the connection.

for revival, for a vibrant spiritual life of walking with Jesus; but for this to happen, they have to wake up, recognize their current state for what it is, and take action. Part of the challenge for those who are nearly comatose in their faith is the danger of deception. Christians of all ages have needed to wake up to avoid being deceived by the beast (13:14). For those who take the name of the beast (13:16–17) will suffer the fate of the beast (19:20; 14:9–10). We might argue in light of 17:8 that those who are deceived by the beast show that their names are not written in the book of life. Jesus' point, though, is to call those who profess to belong to him to make sure that they do not take the mark of the beast, i.e., give their allegiance to people or things in this world that are in league with Satan.

In Rev 14, we find that Jesus has again chosen the language of 14:11 very carefully in order to set up a striking contrast, although it is easily missed in our English translations. We read that worshipers of the beast "have no rest, day or night" (καὶ οὐκ ἔχουσιν ἀνάπαυσιν ἡμέρας καὶ νυκτὸς, *kai ouk exousin anapausin hēmeras kai nuktos*) from the torment of God's eternal judgment. This is precisely the same language that is used in 4:8 of a very different group of people: "And the four living creatures, each of them with six wings, are full of eyes all around and within, and day and night *they never cease to say*, 'Holy, holy, holy, is the Lord God Almighty, who was and is and is to come!'" (4:8). The italicized portion more literally reads, "and they have no rest day and night saying" (καὶ ἀνάπαυσιν οὐκ ἔχουσιν ἡμέρας καὶ νυκτὸς, *kai anapausin ouk exousin hēmeras kai nuktos*). The language is identical to 14:11, with just a minor difference in word order. This would not have been missed by the original readers, who would have been struck by the implicit question: Who are you going to join? Will you join the four living creatures in ceaseless worship, or will you join the enemies of God in ceaseless torment? The choice is yours!

The call to wake up, within the broader context of Revelation, is similar to what Paul urges in Rom 13:11–14. The eschatological reality of Jesus' imminent return leaves no question of how his followers should live their lives today. There is no time for spiritual laziness; there is no room for dabbling in sin; it makes no sense whatsoever to continue in the deeds of darkness. The day of the Lord is at hand. Jesus' followers should not be thinking about how to feed their flesh; they should be focused on how to please their Lord . . . and let their flesh starve.

That the works of Christians in the church of Sardis are incomplete shows a low view of God. Jesus reminds them in 11:18 that a reward is coming for those who fear the Lord (overcomers); but their spiritual stupor and incomplete works demonstrate a lack of the fear of the Lord. Instead, they had fallen into the fear of what people would do with them if they failed to blend in to the society around them. Unlike overcomers, who "loved not their lives even unto death" (12:11), they had shrunk back in the face of danger; and not without reason. Indeed, Rev 6:11—the only other place in Revelation where the verb "complete" (πληρόω, *pleroō*) is used—reminds them that those whose works Jesus finds "complete" may in fact be part of the complete number of those whom God has ordained for martyrdom! Keeping their works incomplete may well save them from an untimely death, but only at the cost of their soul.

When Jesus proclaims, "I have not found your works complete," his stark negative assessment is meant to motivate repentance. Their deeds, good or bad, are going to follow them (14:13); and Jesus is going to judge them according to what they have done (20:12). They do not want to be among those who are "saved, but only as through fire" (1 Cor 3:15), with nothing to show for a life that was supposed to be lived for God's glory. Jesus is thus graciously giving his followers in Sardis a mid-term exam to reveal their current problems so that when the time for the final exam comes they will be well prepared.

In addition to this gracious warning, we find an exhortation in 16:15 that could not have been missed by Christians in Sardis. In fact, I suspect that this verse would have stood out more than any other to Christians in Sardis because it was likely custom crafted to catch their attention: "Behold, I am coming like a thief! Blessed is the one who stays awake, keeping his garments on, that he may not go about naked and be seen exposed!" Given their city's history (Reading Instruction #4), the language here would have created a rhetorical hotspot that shook them to the core. The metaphor reminds them that alertness and preparedness are both critical if one is going to avoid shame at the coming of Christ. Within the context of Rev 16, staying awake and keeping your clothes involves avoiding the deception of the evil one, avoiding the temptation to change allegiances and join the side of the beast, whether explicitly through rejecting Jesus outright or implicitly through compromise and assimilation. "Wake up and stay awake!" Jesus exhorts the Christians in Sardis.

> *Remember, then, what you received and heard. Keep it, and repent. If you will not wake up, I will come like a thief, and you will not know at what hour I will come against you.* (3:3)

Jesus calls Christians in Sardis to remember. They had become disinterested in the teachings of Jesus and the apostles that had been faithfully passed on to them. Perhaps like many so-called "grace-oriented" churches today, thinking themselves to be more pious and "gospel-centered" by avoiding an emphasis on "rules," they had fallen into the trap of neglecting the commands of Jesus rather than "keeping" them. "Keep" language (the verb τηρέω, *tereō*) is very important in Revelation. Saints, by definition, are "those who keep the commandments of God" (14:12; see also 22:9). Saints obey what Jesus says. Period. His commands need not fit with their conception of what makes good sense to be obeyed. They do not have to be practical to be obeyed. Jesus' followers obey them because they are given by the Lord of the universe and they will all have to give an account to him for how they have responded to his commands.

Much of what follows in Revelation provides a terrifying picture of what it looks like for Jesus to "come like a thief" (3:3), effectively piling on motivation for Christians in Sardis to repent before it is too late. To come like a thief is not only to come unexpectedly, but also to come in judgment. In Old Testament prophetic passages that refer to God's imminent judgment, the prophecy is frequently expressed in terms of God "coming" to judge a nation. In each case, the prophecy refers not to God's literal coming, but rather to his use of other means or other nations to punish the nation the prophecy is spoken against. Thus when Isaiah predicts that the Assyrian armies will devastate Egypt he writes, "Behold, the LORD is riding on a swift cloud and comes to Egypt; and the idols of Egypt will tremble at his presence, and the heart of the Egyptians will melt within them" (19:1). The picture is one of terror for those who are unprepared for the arrival of the Lord. Other judgments that were clearly political and military in nature are described in similar terms: "Then shall all the trees of the forest sing for joy [13] before the LORD, for he comes, for he comes to judge the earth" (Ps 96:12–13; see also 98:9); "For behold, the LORD is coming out from his place to punish the inhabitants of the earth for their iniquity" (Isa 26:21); "For behold, the LORD is coming out of his place, and will come down and tread upon the high places of the earth" (Mic 1:3). All of these passages speak of God "coming" to earth, and in every case his coming involves judgment.

At the very beginning of Revelation, Christians in Sardis would have noticed the language of God "coming," and they would have recognized both the reference to the Father in 1:4 as the One "who is to come" and the announcement regarding the Lord Jesus in 1:7 ("Behold, he is coming with the clouds") as the language of coming judgment. As in 3:3, it would have been clear that both of these descriptions carry with them the implicit warning to prepare for the Coming One. Jesus does not just threaten to come like a thief; he threatens to "come against" them (3:3).

The terrifying visions that begin in Rev 6, then, would by no means have simply been read as the wicked pagan nations of this world finally getting what was due them. Instead, these visions of seven seals, and the visions that follow of seven trumpets and seven bowls, all flesh out in gory detail what will happen to those for whom Jesus comes as a thief. One does not want to be among the masses of people crying out in terror to find a way to hide "from the wrath of the Lamb" (Rev 6:16). The coming terror of that wrath is reinforced throughout Revelation through the repeated mention of earthquakes. In 6:12, John sees "a great earthquake." Just prior to the blowing of the seven trumpets we read that an "angel took the censer and filled it with fire from the altar and threw it on the earth, and there were peals of thunder, rumblings, flashes of lightning, and an earthquake" (8:5). Then, in Rev 11 we read of another "great earthquake" (11:13) that vividly portrays God's judgment on the city where the two witnesses were murdered. This is quickly followed in 11:19 with the blowing of the seventh trumpet, which leads to yet another earthquake, this one part of the standard physical phenomena that accompany an appearance of God Almighty. There is nothing "standard," however, about the final earthquake, which occurs with the seventh bowl judgment, the final outpouring of God's wrath: "a great earthquake such as there had never been since man was on the earth, so great was that earthquake" (Rev 16:18).

All of these earthquakes, but particularly the last, would have squarely struck home for Christians in Sardis and Philadelphia. As unsettling as this language is for all those who read it, for Christians in these cities it would have produced powerful rhetorical hotspots. The earthquake of AD 17 had been an utter catastrophe for Sardis (Reading Instruction #4). Neither the Christians nor the other inhabitants of the city would have been able to remember any earthquake or any other disaster equal to it. Thus, when they read in 11:13 that "at that hour there was a great earthquake, and a tenth of the city fell," they would have been able to visualize the type of destruction that was in view. And better than most, though they had not experienced the level of destruction described in 16:18–19, they could imagine what it would be like because of their own past experience. After all, they had the questionable boast of having received the worst damage during the worst earthquake in memory. That quake, however, could not compare to "the big one" that was coming. The coming earthquake would not just devastate Sardis and Philadelphia; it would destroy the great city and cause the rest of the cities on earth to collapse. The destruction would be absolute. This is the judgment that God is foretelling for all who oppose him. For Christians in Sardis who are being urged to remember what they had been taught and to repent and obey Jesus' teachings this threat of judgment would have been particularly poignant. The fate described in these passages is something to be avoided at all costs. Only repentance makes sense in light of Jesus' warning to wake up so that they do not experience him coming like a thief.

If we are left with any question on this issue, if we are still clinging to the misguided notion that the Jesus of the Bible is a pacifist through and through who would never harm a fly, we need only look at Rev 19, where Jesus' physical "coming" is finally vividly portrayed. Here, Jesus is not pictured as a gentle shepherd; he is portrayed as the Great King leading his armies into battle. He comes to "judge" (19:11); he comes to "make war" (19:11); he comes to "strike down the nations" and "rule them with a rod of iron" (19:15); he comes to "tread the winepress of the fury of the wrath of God the Almighty" (19:15). This is a Jesus to fear! He is a terrifying figure with eyes like flaming fire and clothing splattered with the blood of his enemies. This Jesus is not someone to be apathetic toward. And this clear biblical picture of Jesus should cause us to hang our heads in shame over the false Jesus we have created in our own image. Particularly in the popular thinking of the wealthy West, Jesus has been so domesticated that many would be shocked to learn that he actually "makes war." "Jesus is all about peace!" we are told. "Jesus is tolerant and would never force himself on anyone!" Such conventional wisdom, though, has nothing in common with the Jesus of the Bible. The true Jesus will come with the armies of heaven and will decimate the nations that are opposed to him and set up a kingdom where he will reign supreme. No one will be able to oppose him in any way. It will not be a democracy; and he does not plan to hold an election as soon as things are stabilized. Instead, he will rule with a rod of iron!

North American Christians tend to be particularly fond of claiming that Jesus is not someone Christians should be afraid of; but Revelation says exactly the opposite. Revelation has often been used as a tool for scaring people into the kingdom. Many today would reject such an approach to evangelism even though we see that part of the purpose of the plagues that are poured out in Revelation is to encourage repentance (this is implied, e.g., in 9:20–21). A significant purpose of the extensive description of judgment in Revelation, however, is actually to *scare Christians into staying in the kingdom*. Much of the terrifying details in passages like Rev 9:7–11 and 9:17–19 are there to bolster Christians' resolve not to become one of those who will come under the wrath of God. The detailed descriptions of the appearance of the locusts and the appearance of the horses and riders are both intended to terrify. You want to be among those who are sealed and thus protected from these terrifying creatures (9:4), not among those who are tormented by them for five months (9:5) to such a degree that they will want to die to escape their torture (9:6).

Years ago there was a documentary program called "Scared Straight," which was designed to scare juvenile delinquents into abandoning their life of petty crime before they did something more serious and it was too late to change their ways. The approach was to put a group of young offenders in prison with a group of hardened criminals who verbally abused the youth, screaming at them until they were scared out of their wits in an attempt to use terror to motivate them to change their ways, to scare them into leaving their lives of crime and "going straight." Whatever the value and appropriateness of this controversial program, the idea is largely consistent with what we find being done in Revelation: The terrifying visions recorded in Revelation are intended, in part, to shock the spiritual offenders in the seven churches of Asia Minor and within the church universal throughout the ages so that they will abandon their lives of sin, compromise, and assimilation before it is too late. The people of the world who have steadfastly stood opposed to God and his commands will not be swayed by the plagues that God pours out (9:20–21). Christians in Sardis are implicitly being asked as they come to these verses, "Will you too be obstinate, or will you repent, exchange your soiled clothes for white garments, and live?"

Along with this important question they are also being reminded of the terrible danger they are in. Both in Rev 9 and Rev 16 the danger of persisting in sin is vividly highlighted. Notice the response of mankind to the horrific suffering that the world had been facing, first through the trumpet judgments, then through the bowl judgments:

> The rest of mankind, who were not killed by these plagues, *did not repent* of the works of their hands *nor give up worshiping demons and idols* of gold and silver and bronze and stone and wood, which cannot see or hear or walk, [21]*nor did they repent* of their murders or their sorceries or their sexual immorality or their thefts. (9:20–21)

The fourth angel poured out his bowl on the sun, and it was allowed to scorch people with fire. [9]They were scorched by the fierce heat, and they cursed the name of God who had power over these plagues. *They did not repent and give him glory.* (16:8–9)

The fifth angel poured out his bowl on the throne of the beast, and its kingdom was plunged into darkness. People gnawed their tongues in anguish [11]and cursed the God of heaven for their pain and sores. *They did not repent of their deeds.* (16:10–11)

What happens to those who stubbornly refuse to repent? Sin hardens their heart and darkens their mind. No one can deny that it makes absolutely no sense that people would not be quick to repent in the face of such suffering and death; and yet they refuse. Why? They refuse because their persistent rebellion against God has so allowed the evil one to gain control of their thinking that they have literally lost their senses. *That* is the danger of persistent sin. We give the evil one an "opportunity" (Eph 4:27) or "foothold" (NIV) in our lives. That foothold can easily become a stronghold, and if we still do not take decisive action (pluck out our eye, cut off our hand; see Matt 5:29–30), the stronghold can easily become a stranglehold that robs us of our ability to see things as they are. Spiritually, we become comatose, though we go on living. We look alive, but we are dead. We cannot even see that God is graciously taking steps to get our attention and turn us from our sin. So, the church of Sardis was in extreme danger; and the same is true for Christians everywhere who take sin lightly. Jesus has issued them a clear warning. Will they repent? Or will they be like the pagans who cling to their rebellion in the face of utter destruction?

Yet you have a few people in Sardis who have not soiled their clothes. They will walk with me, dressed in white, for they are worthy. (3:4)

As we have seen, the lack of soiled clothes among "a few people" in Sardis refers to their moral purity. The picture of this group is reinforced in 14:4–5 in what at first glance can be a baffling passage. Before looking at that passage, though, it is important to note that we have here another example of Revelation using specific language to link portions of the book together (to form intratextual connections) and thus aid us in understanding Jesus' message to the church. The verb μολύνω (*molunō*) is used in both 3:4 and 14:4 (and elsewhere in the NT only in 1 Cor 8:7),[2] though regrettably it is translated "soiled" in 3:4 and "defiled" in 14:4 by the ESV, masking the connection. The use of the same language strongly suggests that Christians in Sardis would have seen in 14:4–5 further instructions on how to avoid soiled clothing.

In describing the 144,000, John writes: "It is these who have not defiled themselves with women, for they are virgins. It is these who follow the Lamb wherever he

2. Though rare in the New Testament, this verb is common enough, occurring 20 times in the LXX and regularly outside of Christian literature.

goes. These have been redeemed from mankind as firstfruits for God and the Lamb, [5]and in their mouth no lie was found, for they are blameless." At first glance, the statement that they "have not defiled themselves with women" (μετὰ γυναικῶν οὐκ ἐμολύνθησαν, *meta gunaikōn ouk emolunthēsan*) may seem sexist; but the language is simply symbolic of pure devotion to Jesus and a rejection of assimilation, as the following sentence makes clear: "It is these who follow the Lamb wherever he goes." Why, though, does he use such language? Very similar language is used in 1 *En.* 12:4 of the angels (or "the Watchers") who left heaven, took human wives, and thus "defiled themselves with women" (μετὰ τῶν γυναικῶν ἐμιάνθησαν, *meta tōn gunaikōn emianthēsan*).[3] This legendary account, which was likely quite well known in the late first century, may well have led Christians in Asia Minor to take the reference in 14:4 as an indication that unlike the Watchers, the 144,000 had carefully followed the commands of Christ and so avoided moral defilement. Similar language is found in two passages in Ezekiel:[4]

> that the house of Israel may no more go astray from me, nor *defile themselves* anymore with all their transgressions, but that they may be my people and I may be their God, declares the Lord God. (Ezek 14:11)

> They shall not *defile themselves* anymore with their idols and their detestable things, or with any of their transgressions. But I will save them from all the backslidings in which they have sinned, and will cleanse them; and they shall be my people, and I will be their God. (Ezek 37:23)

As we have seen, Ezekiel is very concerned with the issue of God's people assimilating to the nations around them. It is likely that the parallel language in Rev 14:4 serves to highlight the staunch devotion of the 144,000 to God. They refuse absolutely to pollute themselves in any way by assimilation. This point is strengthened by the more specific language of "defile themselves with women," which seems to have been distinctively used of the heinous sin of the angels who rejected their place in heaven to indulge themselves. The specific avoidance of defiling themselves with women, however, is likely also playing off another pivotal event in the history of Israel, an event that has already been alluded to through reference to "the teaching of Balaam" in Rev 2:14 (Reading Instruction #6). In Num 31, we find an account of the Lord's vengeance being executed on Midian (31:3). The Israelites kill all of the kings of Midian along with every male (31:7), but they take the women and children captive (31:9). In verses 15–17 we read Moses' response to the army commanders:

3. For more on the Watchers, see 1 *En.* 7, 9, 10, 15, 69.

4. As in 1 *En.* 12, the close synonym μιαίνω (*miainō*) is used in the Septuagint rather than μολύνω (*molunō*). The reason for this is simple. Both terms are used to refer to ceremonial defilement (see Louw and Nida 53.54), while only μολύνω (*molunō*) is also used of causing something to be dirty or soiled (see Louw and Nida 79.56). Thus, only μολύνω (*molunō*) works with the soiled clothing metaphor in Rev 3:4, and the same language is carefully chosen in 14:4 to link the two passages together.

Moses said to them, "Have you let all the women live? [16]Behold, these, on Balaam's advice, caused the people of Israel to act treacherously against the Lord in the incident of Peor, and so the plague came among the congregation of the Lord. [17]Now therefore, kill every male among the little ones, and kill every woman who has known man by lying with him." (Num 31:15–17)

What is Moses referring to? We have an account of the events at Peor in Num 25:1–3. As was noted above, it was apparently Balaam who told the Moabites that if they wanted to overcome the Israelites they would need to bring them under God's wrath. To do that they enticed them with Moabite women who led them into sexual immorality and idolatry, the same two sins that are front and center throughout Revelation.

It is quite likely, then, that one of Jesus' primary points in portraying the 144,000 as those who "have not defiled themselves with women" was to characterize them as the antithesis of the Israelites at Peor. Faced with the temptation to assimilate to the nations around them and indulge in sexual immorality and idolatry, the Israelites failed miserably. The same will not be true of the 144,000. Their lives will be marked by absolute purity and devotion to Jesus. They will not give in to the intense pressure to compromise their devotion to God and assimilate. The emphasis on purity would have spoken particularly strongly to Christians in Sardis, where most had "soiled their garments" (3:4). Just as the 144,000 in Rev 14 who had kept themselves pure are with the Lamb (14:1) and "follow the Lamb wherever he goes" (14:4), so Jesus promises those who have not soiled their clothes in Sardis that they "they will walk with me in white, for they are worthy" (3:4).

In a church context where Christianity is often portrayed in highly passive terms ("Just step back and let Jesus live his life through you!"), we need to consider carefully the implicit responsibility that is placed on believers in Rev 3:4. Just as many in Sardis had soiled their clothes *by their own actions*, so a few had kept their clothes clean, and thus were worthy *by their own actions*. The actions of the people of God and of the inhabitants of the earth who do not follow Jesus are both given great significance throughout the book of Revelation. That his followers' actions are important to Jesus is strongly emphasized by the five-fold repetition in Rev 2–3 of the words, "I know your works" (2:3, 19; 3:1, 8, 15). Jesus promises Christians in Thyatira (and all other Christians) that he will "give to each of you according to your works" (2:23). In 19:8, the saints prepare for their wedding to the Lamb by *clothing themselves* in righteous deeds. What Jesus is getting at by connecting preparation for the wedding feast of the Lamb with righteous living mirrors what the writer of Hebrews says: "Strive for peace with everyone, and for the holiness without which no one will see the Lord" (Heb 12:14). Christians are commanded to make every effort to live holy lives. The writer is not talking about "imputed" holiness, that is, a holiness that is credited to our account through faith in what Jesus has done for us. Instead, he is talking about a day by day holiness that requires human effort in the power of the Holy Spirit to live in obedience to the commands of Christ. To take such holiness lightly is to live with a false sense of security, since without this practical daily holiness "no one will see the Lord." That is Jesus' message to Christians in Sardis.

This, in fact, is what is regularly in mind as Paul exhorts followers of Jesus to live lives that are "worthy of the calling to which you have been called" (Eph 4:1), "worthy of the gospel of Christ" (Phil 1:27), "worthy of the Lord" (Col 1:10), and "worthy of God" (1 Thess 2:12; see also 2 Thess 1:5, 11). It is through taking these exhortations seriously that the people of God, in utter dependence on the Holy Spirit, can become "worthy." As they choose to live in obedience to the Lord Jesus Christ their lives are filled with righteous deeds and they are dressed in fine white linen; for they are worthy. This is also what Paul is alluding to at the end of his life when he writes, "I have fought the good fight, I have finished the race, I have kept the faith. [8]Henceforth there is laid up for me the crown of righteousness, which the Lord, the righteous judge, will award to me on that Day, and not only to me but also to all who have loved his appearing" (2 Tim 4:7–8). The crown, or reward, that Paul is talking about here comes as a result of fighting the good fight and keeping the faith to the end. It is the result of living this life in light of Jesus' imminent Second Coming. God will reward such people with righteousness, or in the language of Revelation, God will clothe them in their righteous deeds.

As if to drive that point home for the church in Sardis there is also a striking parallel in language between 3:4 and 16:6 where the exact same phrase is used of very different groups of people: ἄξιοί εἰσιν (axioi eisin, "they are worthy"). In 3:4, those with unsoiled clothes enjoy intimate communion with Jesus because "they are worthy" of such communion. In 16:6, God pours out his judgment on those who have persecuted his people because "they are worthy" of such judgment.[5] Revelation thus puts forward the proposition that all are either worthy of walking with Jesus or worthy of facing God's wrath, and implicitly raises the question: Which will be true of us and our church today?

> The one who conquers will be clothed thus in white garments, and I will never blot his name out of the book of life. I will confess his name before my Father and before his angels. (3:5)

Jesus' promise to overcomers includes being clothed in white garments, just as a few in Sardis already are. The promise, like the other promises to the seven churches, offers deep encouragement to those who hear Jesus' message and keep it (1:3). Though their clothes are currently soiled, those who repent will "conquer" and likewise be clothed in white garments. What incredible grace permeates Jesus' words here. We have already read in 3:4 that the faithful in Sardis will walk with Jesus in white. This reality is beautifully reinforced in Rev 7:9–10. Those who are clothed with white will

---

5. Regrettably, the ESV translates the same phrase "they are worthy" in 3:4 and "It is what they deserve!" in 16:6. Although the latter is a good functional equivalent, it obscures the connection between the two passages that Jesus almost certainly intended readers to see.

stand before the very throne upon which the Lamb of God now reigns as the King of kings and Lord of lords. They alone will be able to cry out in praise to the Father and the Son for their salvation, which was purchased with the blood of the Lamb. But those who wear white robes will not find life in this world easy:

> Then one of the elders addressed me, saying, "Who are these, clothed in white robes, and from where have they come?" [14]I said to him, "Sir, you know." And he said to me, "These are the ones coming out of the great tribulation. They have washed their robes and made them white in the blood of the Lamb." (7:13–14)

To wear a white robe as a faithful follower of Jesus would be to be marked as an enemy of the State, an enemy of the evil one. We saw in 19:8 that the fine linen that the saints are clothed in when they enter the presence of the Lamb represents "the righteous deeds of the saints." In 7:14 we see that one of those righteous deeds is remaining faithful even in the face of death (cf. 2:10). This reality is further driven home in the description of the fifth seal:

> When he opened the fifth seal, I saw under the altar the souls of those who had been slain for the word of God and for the witness they had borne. [10]They cried out with a loud voice, "O Sovereign Lord, holy and true, how long before you will judge and avenge our blood on those who dwell on the earth?" [11]Then they were each given a white robe and told to rest a little longer, until the number of their fellow servants and their brothers should be complete, who were to be killed as they themselves had been. (6:9–11)

That it is martyrs who are given a white robe is not to say that martyrdom is the only way to receive such attire. Rather, it drives home the point that overcomers' refusal to assimilate and "soil their clothes" will lead to the death of many of them.

So, being clothed in white requires action on the part of God's people. It is those who "conquer" or "overcome" who will be clothed in white. For those whose clothes are currently soiled "overcoming" requires repentance from compromise and rejection of assimilation. It calls for taking active steps to clean one's clothes, even as we see in 22:14: "Blessed are those who wash their robes, so that they may have the right to the tree of life and that they may enter the city by the gates." Christians rightly ask in song, "Are you washed in the blood of the Lamb?" because this question reflects the language of 7:14; but in Revelation Jesus suggests that we should also be asking one another, "Have you washed your robe (22:14) through devotion to righteous deeds (19:8)?"

Jesus' promise, "I will confess his name before my Father and before his angels," is strikingly reinforced by the awe-inspiring vision in Rev 4–5. We see the overwhelming majesty of the Father's throne room where all the host of heaven worships him incessantly. This is the place of greatest glory because it is the place where the Father himself dwells in inapproachable light; but it is in this very context that Jesus will declare for all to hear that every overcomer belongs to him. Each will be acknowledged by name in the hearing of the Father and all his angels. Just as Christians should tremble at the thought of standing wearing soiled clothes before the majestic God described in Rev 4–5 —a God who is holy, holy, holy—so also we should be overjoyed by the thought of having our name confessed in God's throne room.

Even more striking, perhaps, is the parallel language that Jesus uses in 14:10 to drive home the urgent need for repentance. He leaves no question that those who take the name of the beast (13:16–17) will not have Jesus confess their name before his Father and before his angels (3:5), but will instead face God's fury and "be tormented with fire and sulfur before the holy angels and before the Lamb" (14:10; my translation here shows the parallel language in the Greek that is masked in the ESV).[6] As we look at the picture of God's terrifying judgment announced by the third angel in Rev 14:9–11, we find that this is not some idle threat that has no significance for Christians. The very next verse says, "Here is a call for the endurance of the saints, those who keep the commandments of God and their faith in Jesus" (14:12). Jesus was warning *Christians* in Asia Minor and Christians in all the centuries to follow. He has again intentionally chosen language in two passages to set up a clear contrast and a clear choice: Do you want to be faithful to Jesus and have him confess your name before the Father and his angels, or do you want to compromise, soil your clothes, and end up having a very different outcome?

That eternal destruction is in view for those who merely profess to belong to Jesus is made clear through the alternative to Jesus' promise to overcomers: having one's name blotted out of the book of life. Jesus' promise is powerful in the Greek: "I will *certainly not* erase his name from the book of life." But it is a promise for overcomers, not for all professing "Christians." The tendency among Christians today is to ignore statements like this, which occur throughout Revelation. After all, Jesus would never blot out a true believer's name. Once saved, always saved! Right? This type of thinking has not only served to all but neuter the message of Revelation, but it has also nullified the message of the entire book of Hebrews and many other passages in the New Testament. Such a common approach to this significant teaching in the New Testament likely reflects the same tendency that Jesus rebukes the Pharisees for: "You are 'making void the word of God by your tradition that you have handed down'" (Mark 7:13)? God's people have always struggled with the temptation to get so wrapped up in

6. There is another striking parallel in language in this passage that is masked in most English translations. Just as Babylon "made all nations drink from the wine of the 'wrath' of her sexual immorality" (14:8, ἐκ τοῦ οἴνου τοῦ θυμοῦ τῆς πορνείας αὐτῆς, *ek tou oinou tou thumou tēs porneias autēs*), so the Lord will make all followers of Babylon and the beast "drink from the wine of the wrath of God" (14:10, ἐκ τοῦ οἴνου τοῦ θυμοῦ τοῦ θεοῦ, *ek tou oinou tou thumou tou theou*). The unusual choice to use τοῦ θυμοῦ (*tou thumou*, "the wrath") in connection with τῆς πορνείας αὐτῆς (*tēs porneias autēs*, "her sexual immorality") in verse 8 strongly suggests that Jesus intends readers to draw a link between verses 8 and 10.

their favorite doctrines, including the so-called "doctrines of grace," that they dismiss passages that do not fit with their preconceived notions.

So what do we do (and what should Christians in Sardis have done) with the fact that the New Testament teaches, on the one hand, that nothing can separate us from the love of God and nothing can snatch us out of the Father's hands (Rom 8:38–39; John 10:29); and affirms, on the other hand, that only those who persevere to the end (overcome) will be saved (Matt 24:13; Mark 13:13)? First, we must humbly acknowledge that *both* are true. This is beautifully illustrated in the book of Jude where we first read, "keep yourselves in the love of God, waiting for the mercy of our Lord Jesus Christ that leads to eternal life" (v. 21); and then just a few verses later we read, "Now to him who is able to keep you from stumbling and to present you blameless before the presence of his glory with great joy" (v. 24). Who does the keeping, the Father or us? The answer to that question, of course, is we both have a role. Our role does not in any way diminish God's glory or downplay his unilateral action in saving us. Quite the contrary, it forces us to choose not to be like Israel and recognize that covenants bring responsibilities as well as rights. Following Christ is not a passive "resting" in Jesus until God takes us home; Revelation calls us to "conquer," "overcome," or "be victorious" in the power of the Spirit through patient endurance, faithfulness to Jesus, and keeping his word.

Second, we must try to put together the reality of God's keeping with our responsibility to endure to the end in a way that does justice to both biblical teachings. There are three primary possible ways of doing this: (1) The most obvious way, perhaps, is to say that although the Bible clearly states that no outside force can separate us from God's love or snatch us from his hands, it does not say that *we* cannot separate *ourselves*. Such willful separation from God, in fact, seems to be implied by the second part of 2 Tim 2:12: "The saying is trustworthy, for: If we have died with him, we will also live with him; [12]if we endure, we will also reign with him; *if we deny him, he also will deny us*; [13] if we are faithless, he remains faithful—for he cannot deny himself" (2 Tim 2:11–13). This passage very closely mirrors the message of Revelation. Those who overcome, or patiently endure, will reign with Jesus. Those who abandon their allegiance to Jesus and deny him—something that faithful Christians in Philadelphia had refused to do despite all that was against them (3:8)—will be denied by Jesus. Again, this should not surprise us, since it is perfectly consistent with what Jesus had said in the Gospels: "So everyone who acknowledges me before men, I also will acknowledge before my Father who is in heaven, [33]but whoever denies me before men, I also will deny before my Father who is in heaven" (Matt 10:32–33). There is no ambiguity there. In 2 Tim 2:13, though, God graciously reminds us through Paul's words that temporary faithlessness does not equal denying Christ. Sin, or "backsliding," is quite different than denying Jesus, though persistent sin may be a slippery slope to denying him. That is what makes repentance so urgent. At any rate, this is one way to acknowledge both God's role in keeping us and our role in keeping ourselves in the faith; and it is the best explanation from what most would call an Arminian perspective, which holds that it is possible for a genuine believer to renounce his or her salvation (notice that I did not say "lose," as if you can accidentally lose it).[7]

This, of course, is not the only way to reconcile these two teachings. The best Reformed handling of this issue, in my view, which affirms that all those who are elect will persevere to the end and be saved, takes passages like this and acknowledges the warnings of destruction to be directed at genuine Christians, but maintains that these warnings do not imply that a genuine believer can lose or abandon his or her salvation. Rather, the warnings simply function as God's means of insuring that Christians will in fact persevere to the end. In his treatment of the warning passages in Hebrews,[8] Schreiner illustrates this view by pointing to the account in Acts 27. Paul is on board a ship bound for Rome that encounters a terrible storm and it looks like there is no hope left for those onboard to survive. In the night, though, an angel of God appears to Paul and tells him "Do not be afraid, Paul; you must stand before Caesar. And behold, God has granted you all those who sail with you" (27:24). In other words, by God's sovereign decree, as in election, no one is going to die. Just a few verses later, however, we find that when some of the sailors try to escape from the ship in an effort to save their own lives, Paul tells the centurion and soldiers onboard, "Unless these men stay in the ship, you cannot be saved" (27:31). God had promised that all would survive, but Paul now insists that they will *not* all survive unless everyone stays together on the ship! How can both statements be true? Schreiner maintains that the first statement represents God's sovereign will, which will certainly come to pass, while the second one represents a genuine warning that serves as the means of God accomplishing that sovereign, preordained plan. If this is correct—and it is not the only way to read the two statements in Acts 27[9]—then Jesus' implicit warning to those who do not overcome in Revelation may simply be the means of assuring that they do, in the end, overcome.

While I find much to commend Schreiner's arguments, I do not think he goes far enough in explaining the warning passages in Hebrews, and by implication dealing with the warnings in Revelation. Let me suggest a way to strengthen the Reformed

---

7. For the best treatment from this perspective, see McKnight, "Warning Passages."

8. Schreiner, "Perseverance and Assurance." For a fuller treatment from the same perspective, see Schreiner and Caneday, *Race Set before Us*.

9. Schreiner, who does a masterful job of presenting this argument, does not appear to consider an obvious alternative reading of Acts 27. Recall that when Jonah was sent to proclaim God's coming judgment to the inhabitants of Nineveh, he chose to run in the other direction. Why? He answers that question himself Jonah 4:2. God had told him to go preach a message announcing the destruction of Nineveh, but he knew that God's promise to judge Nineveh was *conditional*. If they repented, they would be spared. It is quite possible that the same thing is going on in Acts 27. Paul knows that God's promise to save everyone on board is conditional, and he is simply repeating that condition to the centurion and soldiers that God had told him but that he had not mentioned in verse 24. We find clear evidence of partial quotations elsewhere in Acts such as in the repeated accounts of the same events in Acts 10:1—11:18.

reading. Recall what we have said about the imminent return of Jesus. We know that it has been a long time since Jesus said that he would soon be returning, and yet as Christians we are called to live with the orientation that Jesus could come at any moment and we need to be prepared. That is a necessary feature of a biblical worldview for every Christian. Regardless of how Reformed we might be in our theology, Scripture calls us to live with an orientation that recognizes our urgent need to do all that we can to ensure that we do not fall away or deny Jesus. It calls us to hold to the belief that if we reject Christ as the one sacrifice for our sins we will be eternally lost. Period. That is why we need to keep a close watch on ourselves and what we teach and believe (1 Tim 4:16a). Paul goes on to tell Timothy to take this exhortation seriously because it is a matter of life and death: "Persist in this, for by so doing you will *save both yourself and your hearers*" (1 Tim 4:16b). That is why we need to "be all the more diligent to confirm [our] calling and election" (2 Pet 1:10). That is why we need to "continue to work out [our] salvation with fear and trembling" (Phil 2:12). As we look forward to the culmination of the ages or the culmination of our life we need to "make every effort to be found spotless, blameless and at peace with him" (2 Pet 3:14); and "knowing this beforehand," not least through the book of Revelation, we need to "take care that [we] are not carried away with the error of lawless people and lose [our] own stability [better: our 'own place of security']" (2 Pet 3:17). We need to "abide in him, so that when he appears we may have confidence and not shrink from him in shame at his coming" (1 John 2:28), knowing that everyone who has the hope that Revelation puts forward for overcomers "*purifies himself* as he is pure" (1 John 3:3). This is precisely what Jesus is calling Christians in Sardis to do. It is a call to repentance, a call to action.

This message would have been reinforced as Christians in Sardis came to Rev 13 and read concerning the beast that "all who dwell on earth will worship it, everyone whose name has not been written before the foundation of the world in the book of life of the Lamb who was slain" (13:8). Given the promise that is given to overcomers in Sardis, this statement would not only have served as a description of what *would* be true, but also as a strong exhortation about what *must* be true of them. Overcomers will never have their names blotted out of the book of life. What a promise! How do they overcome? In part, by not joining with the inhabitants of the earth in worshiping the beast. For only those whose names are not found in the book of life engage in such worship.

The message is clear: Be very careful to ensure that you are not being sucked into worshiping the beast. In the late first century, the superficial meaning would have been quite clear. Jesus is calling upon his followers to resist the temptation to burn incense to Caesar or to participate in trade guilds and other civic activities in order to save their lives or their livelihoods. More than that, though, "worshiping the beast" should likely be connected more broadly to assimilating to the beast's kingdom. Living like the world around us is how we soil our clothes. It is a world where the "the prince of the power of the air, the spirit that is now at work in the sons of disobedience" (Eph

2:2) is actively blinding "the minds of the unbelievers, to keep them from seeing the light of the gospel of the glory of Christ, who is the image of God" (2 Cor 4:4). The spiritual blindness he brings leads to assimilation to the ways of this world. That was how Christians of Asia had once lived. That is how all of us once lived when we followed "the course of this world" (Eph 2:2). When we lived in this way, "carrying out the desires of the body and the mind," we "were by nature children of wrath, like the rest of mankind" (Eph 2:3); we brought glory to the evil one, by living in accord with his purposes and his nature. We worshiped the beast, as it were. Now, our names are written in the book of life and we have no business having anything to do with the beast. Instead, we must steadfastly be those who overcome this temptation so that we will be clothed in white garments on that final day, and rather than having our name blotted out of the book of life we will have Jesus announce before the Father and his angels, "This one belongs to me!"

SUMMARY: JESUS' MESSAGE TO CHRISTIANS IN SARDIS

Like far too many Christians today, believers in ancient Sardis had fallen into the trap of being content to present an outward façade of spirituality when their hearts were full of sin. Just as Jesus was not fooled by the Pharisees' superficial piety, so he was not fooled by the grand reputation that the church of Sardis enjoyed. For a church that thought it had it altogether learning that when weighed in the scale their measure of works had come up wanting would have been sobering. The gravitas of Jesus' words would have been heightened by the emphasis on the wicked works of pagans who come under God's judgment throughout Revelation. Could those with soiled garments, clothing that identifies them as friends of the world (see 1 John 2:15), hope for anything less than judgment from God? Knowing that Jesus will judge each one according to his or her works (20:12), and that their works, which will "follow them" (14:13) in the next life, were incomplete in God's sight should provide the necessary shock to jolt their collective heart into beating again. Whether or not it was enough we do not know, but we must ask ourselves whether an awareness of these profound theological truths is sufficient to keep us tenaciously pursuing obedience to the commands of Christ ourselves. Will we heed Jesus' call to stay awake and alert as we await his return? His words in 16:15 could not have been more carefully chosen for Christians living in a city that had on two occasions been caught relaxing with a false sense of security and been overcome by the enemy. If the thought of Jesus "coming like a thief" were not enough to motivate them to change their ways, then perhaps the visions of what his coming would look like might do the trick. The seal, trumpet, and bowl judgments all provide vivid pictures of what it looks like to face the wrath of the Lamb. This is not someone you want to have come against you (3:3). Jesus is thus graciously trying to "scare" those who profess to belong to him into making the right decision by highlighting the consequences of compromise. He is calling them to change their ways so that they can avoid the same sin that Israel committed at Peor, and the same fate. Those who would walk with Jesus must be worthy to do so, and their worthiness will be directly connected to the choices they make regarding how they relate to the world around them. Will they choose to reject assimilation and so replace their soiled clothes with fresh white clothes? That is clearly the right choice, but they also need to recognize that such garb will not only mark them as belonging among those at the marriage supper of the Lamb but will also mark them now as enemies of the State. Those who would be faithful to Jesus, however, will be willing to pay whatever the price might be. For, it is only those who overcome who can expect to have a place in the coming kingdom where Jesus' faithful followers will walk with him dressed in white.

12

Jesus' Message to the Church in Philadelphia

And to the angel of the church in Philadelphia write: The words of the holy one, the true one, who has the key of David, who opens and no one will shut, who shuts and no one opens. (3:7)

As MENTIONED ABOVE, THE earthquake of AD 17 had virtually destroyed twelve cities in the Lydian valley, including Philadelphia and Sardis.[1] What set Philadelphia apart was the fact that it not only suffered from the frequent aftershocks that followed, but was plagued by frequent tremors in general. Strabo reported that the city was subject to so many earthquakes that new cracks appeared in the city wall on a daily basis and few citizens actually lived within the walls. Instead, they tended to live in huts or other crude shelters outside of the city.[2]

Life in Philadelphia was thus difficult compared to other cities in Asia Minor, and the economic toll that the great earthquake had taken on the city made living there that much more challenging.[3] Nevertheless, Philadelphia benefitted significantly from imperial aid during this difficult time, and like Sardis enjoyed an exemption from Roman taxes for five years.[4] This imperial generosity no doubt led to great gratitude toward the emperor, as is evident in the city's choice to assume the name "Neocaesarea"

1. Ramsay, *Letters*, 290.

2. *Geogr.* 12.8.18; 13.4.10.

3. Ramsay (*Letters*, 299) points out that during the twenty years following the great earthquake, no new coins were minted in Philadelphia, apparently as a result of its depressed economy. Hemer (*Letters*, 157), however, suggests that this is likely reading too much into the scanty available numismatic evidence.

4. Hemer, *Letters*, 156.

during this period.[5] The fact that Philadelphia also assumed a second imperial title during the reign of Vespasian (AD 69–79), calling itself "Flavia"[6] after the Flavian dynasty of Roman emperors, further demonstrates its devotion to the imperial system, though we will see later that this devotion had begun to wane significantly in the years leading up to the sending of the book of Revelation.

As in the other letters, Jesus' choice of titles in his opening words is again handpicked to address the needs of this specific congregation. His use of "the holy one, the true one" is almost certainly intended to reassure Christians who have been denounced as heretics who embrace a false messiah. Contrary to such claims by the synagogue of Satan, Jesus is the "Holy One" who was foretold by the prophets, the Messiah. Here, the ESV is superior to the NIV's "These are the words of him who is holy and true," though we can still miss the point in the ESV's translation. The Greek phrase ὁ ἅγιος ὁ ἀληθινός (ho hagios ho alēthinos) should be translated either, "the Holy One, the True One" or better "the true Holy One."[7] Jesus' point in using this title is almost certainly to respond to the Jews who were cursing him as a fraud ("the fake holy one" or "the fake messiah") and cursing all those who followed him. To Christians in Philadelphia suffering such slander from the powerful synagogue, he reminds them that he is indeed the Messiah the Jews had been waiting for all these years. He is the true Messiah.

As the genuine Messiah, Jesus "has the key of David" and he is the one "who opens and no one will shut, who shuts and no one opens." Here we find a fairly transparent allusion to Isa 22:22. In the context of Isaiah, this prophecy clearly refers to Eliakim who is to replace Shebna as palace administrator/prime minister, a prophecy that had come to pass by the time Isa 36:3 was written (see also 2 Kgs 18:18). In Revelation, Jesus applies this language to himself. Where Eliakim was given control of the administration of the Davidic throne (and the royal treasury) for a brief time and with certain restrictions, Jesus is the absolute ruler, who alone decides who is permitted entrance into his kingdom.[8] Jesus meant what he said in Matt 28:18: "All authority in heaven and on earth has been given to me." We will return to the language of "opening" and "shutting" below.

---

5. Ramsay, *Letters*, 291.

6. Ibid., 292.

7. ὁ ἀληθινός (ho alēthinos) should be taken as an attributive modifier of ὁ ἅγιος (ho hagios), just as ὁ πιστὸς καὶ ἀληθινός (ho pistos kai alēthinos) is an attributive modifier of ὁ μάρτυς (ho martus) in 3:14. If Jesus had intended to employ two titles for himself, the author likely would have used a conjunction between them.

8. Thus we see an Old Testament symbol or text that is taken and reapplied to Jesus.

I know your works. Behold, I have set before you an open door, which no one is able to shut. I know that you have but little power, and yet you have kept my word and have not denied my name. (3:8)

In the second part of verse 8, we learn that Christians in Philadelphia had little strength or "power" (δύναμιν, *dunamin*). While some have taken this as an indication of limited spiritual vitality among the Philadelphians, such a reading does not fit with the positive tone of Jesus' message to this church. Jesus makes no claim to have anything whatsoever against the church in Philadelphia. Like the church in Smyrna they were faithfully following him despite their difficult circumstances. Their lack of power more likely refers to the limited influence and resources these Christians possessed, particularly in contrast to their Jewish opponents. As we will see in our discussion of the next verse, Christians in Philadelphia found themselves with no good options. On one side they were facing the might of Rome, which threatened the existence of any who would not renounce their allegiance to the Lord Jesus and worship the emperor. On the other side were Jewish opponents who were intent on rooting out followers of Jesus and likely handing them over to the Roman authorities as they had done with Jesus himself.

Jesus' use of "little power" also draws a correlation between Christians in Philadelphia and the city of Philadelphia itself (Reading Instruction #4). Although Philadelphia had a history of good relations with Rome and devotion to the emperor, in recent years that relationship had begun to sour. "In AD 92 [likely just a few years before Revelation was written] Domitian issued an edict requiring at least half the vineyards in the provinces to be cut down and no new ones planted . . . an act bitterly unpopular in Asia and not rigorously enforced" anywhere.[9] Indeed, "literary sources suggest that the act was an unprecedented outrage."[10] Although there is no evidence that Philadelphia cultivated olive trees, there was an unwritten rule in eastern warfare that olive trees and grapevines must be spared during war because they took so long to mature.[11] Domitian, in another delusional moment, chose to spurn this common sense policy, effectively undoing the bonds of devotion that had formed between Philadelphia and Rome over the course of the first century, since there was perhaps no city in Asia Minor that was more dependent on viticulture than Philadelphia.[12] Indeed, its vines were its most significant source of revenue, making Domitian's edict that much more maddening. The city itself, then, would have felt that it had "little power" to resist the maniacal policies of an emperor who could not even remain true to established policy and common sense. This sense of helplessness on the part of the city was strongly parallel to what Christians in Philadelphia would have faced as their

9. Hemer, *Letters*, 158.
10. Ibid., 158n22.
11. Ibid., 158n25.
12. Ibid., 158.

"little power" came up against the significant influence of local Jewish leaders (the synagogue of Satan) and the might of Rome itself.

Although it happened more than half a century after Revelation was written, *Mart. Pol.* 19:1 refers to eleven believers from Philadelphia who had been martyred in Smyrna prior to Polycarp's execution there (mid-second century AD).[13] Regardless of the precise dating of this event, it provides a helpful window into the level of pressure that was likely being exerted on Christians in Philadelphia to renounce their faith in Jesus Christ. Following Jesus was a life and death proposition for these Christians, and they had very limited resources for withstanding the threat. In fact, their only resources appear to have been their faith in Jesus and the grace of God. This, of course, makes the fact that they have kept Jesus' word and not denied his name all the more commendable. These beleaguered Christians had refused to compromise their faith in order to save their own skins. They faithfully followed Jesus' teachings no matter what it cost them.[14]

Notice that Jesus did not ask them—and he does not ask us—to change the world. That is his job. He asked them to be faithful, regardless of their circumstances. He asks us to obey all that he commanded and to live for his glory. It is that simple obedience from people with "little power" that pleases him. And Jesus is very pleased with these Christians who though they have nothing to fall back on other than their trust in God, have continued to live as his visible followers and have refused to deny their allegiance to him. Consequently, he has rewarded them; he has placed an open door before them that no one can shut. Although there has been some debate regarding what Jesus means by the "open door" metaphor here, this debate largely appears to be a product of failing to read the expression in context. Many look to the use of this phrase elsewhere in the New Testament and contend that it refers to opportunities for effective evangelism.[15] Although there is no question that "open door" language is frequently used in this way in the New Testament (see 1 Cor 16:9; 2 Cor 2:12; Col 4:3), we actually need not look elsewhere for help in understanding the significance of the "open door," since its meaning is rather obvious from the context. Jesus is the one who holds the key of David (3:7); he is the one who alone decides who is permitted entrance into the Messianic kingdom. Because he is pleased with the works of the Christians in Philadelphia he wants to assure them that he has granted them eschatological salvation and no one can take it away, not even those of the synagogue of Satan who were opposing them.[16]

13. Or perhaps *with* Polycarp, whose death we can plausibly date to February 23, 155.

14. It is well worth noting that once again there is an interesting correlation between local Christians' status and the status of their city. Philadelphia had become a city of "little strength" as a result of its frequent earthquakes. "The world in general thought, like Strabo, that Philadelphia was unsafe to enter, that only a rash person would live in it, and that only fools could have ever founded it." Ramsay, *Letters*, 299, 298.

15. See, e.g., Charles, *Revelation*, 87; Swete, *The Apocalypse*, 54.

16. Hemer (*Letters*, 162) falls into the trap of a both/and interpretation here.

Jesus is essentially telling them that they have "reserved seats" in the kingdom.[17] They have an inheritance that is kept for them by the one who alone holds the keys to the messianic kingdom. Any denunciation by the Jews of the city, then, needs to be received in light of the fact that Jesus is "the *true* Holy One" who determines their destiny. No one has the power to close the door on those for whom he has opened it. Faithful Christians in Philadelphia have thus been given a wonderful gift. Though they are weak in themselves, Jesus is strong; and he has set an open door to the kingdom before them. They do not need to try to keep it open; that is Jesus' job, and he is omnipotent. No misguided Jewish opponents can resist his will. Their ultimate fate is thus assured, regardless of what those from the synagogue might insist. For those being tempted to join the synagogue so that they can be "the true people of God," Jesus reminds them that that path leads away from the open door to the kingdom that he has placed before them and into a community that is doing the work of Satan, not the work of God.

> *Behold, I will make those of the synagogue of Satan who say that they are Jews and are not, but lie—behold, I will make them come and bow down before your feet, and they will learn that I have loved you.* (3:9)

As was the case with the church in Smyrna, the church in Philadelphia had Jewish opponents—opponents who believed that they were doing God a favor by persecuting followers of Jesus, but who were actually acting as Satan's agents instead. Jesus makes it clear here that such ethnic Jews were not true Jews. In fact, they were not the people of God at all; they were imposters and liars.

The reference to "the synagogue of Satan" here may have had one of two realities in view. First, it may have been a reference to Judaizers, i.e., teachers who were emphasizing that Gentiles, in order to be full-fledged Christians, had to be circumcised and observe the Law of Moses. It is quite likely that certain Gentile converts to Judaism were actively seeking to proselytize Gentile Christians and urge them to join the synagogue. This appears to be what is in view in Ignatius's letter to Christians in Philadelphia not many years later (ca. AD 107):

> But if any one preaches the Jewish law to you, do not listen to him. For it is better to listen to Christian doctrine from a man who has been circumcised,

---

17. Although this reading is almost certainly correct, Ramsay may well be right in arguing that the "open door" metaphor would have been particularly meaningful to those living in Philadelphia: "Philadelphia lay at the upper extremity of a long valley, which opens back from the sea. After passing Philadelphia the road along this valley ascends to the Phrygian land and the great central plateau, the main mass of Asia Minor. This road was the one which led from the harbor of Smyrna to the northeastern pats [*sic.*] of Asia Minor and the East in general, the one rival to the great route connecting Ephesus with the East, and the greatest Asian trade route of medieval times" (*Letters*, 296). Philadelphia was thus the "door" to the plateau (ibid., 297). If ancient readers understood Philadelphia in this way (Reading Instruction #4), Jesus' words would have once again highlighted the way in which his kingdom blessings infinitely surpassed the benefits of living as a citizen of Philadelphia, and his use of "open door" would have functioned as another rhetorical hotspot.

than to Judaism from one uncircumcised. But if they do not speak about Jesus Christ, they are monuments and tombs of the dead to me, upon which are written only the names of men. (Ignatius, *Phil.* 6.1)

Alternatively, or perhaps in addition, Jesus may be alluding to the *Birkat Ha-Minim*, or "Curse against the Heretics," which we alluded to in our discussion of the message to Sardis. This curse was likely written in the late first century around the time Revelation was written or perhaps earlier:[18]

> For the apostates let there be no hope, and uproot the kingdom of arrogance, speedily and in our days. May the Nazarenes and the sectarians [*minim*] perish as in a moment. Let them be blotted out of the book of life, and not be written together with the righteous. You are praised, O Lord, who subdues the arrogant.[19]

What is particularly important about the "Curse against the Heretics" is the tool it provided for detecting Christians trying to surreptitiously find a place of safety within the synagogue:

> The Christian was faced with a cruel dilemma. His safety was assured only by preparedness, in time of need, to identify himself either with pagan society, by sacrifice to the emperor and the expected participation in the religious aspects of guilds and social life (the 'Nicolaitan' answer), or with Judaism on whatever terms would gain him acceptance in the synagogue, that is, probably, at least an implicit denial of his Lord.[20]

As Hemer goes on to note, the first temptation would have been "strongest in those places where the pressures of authority and pagan society were most direct (Pergamum and Thyatira, and also Ephesus, where it was steadfastly rejected)."[21] In such cities, the temptation was more singular: conform to Rome and embrace its idolatry or face the consequences. In other contexts, however, there was a potential way out for those who refused to compromise with Rome. In places with a synagogue community (especially Smyrna and Philadelphia), one had the option of gaining the legal protections afforded to Jews within the Roman Empire by joining (or rejoining) the synagogue community. With the "Curse against the Heretics" forming a part of synagogue worship, however, the synagogue provided only superficial safety, since the price of membership was denying Jesus. As with the crucifixion of Jesus Christ,

---

18. The *Birkat Ha-Minim* was apparently written by Samuel the Little during Gamaliel's tenure of leadership (who died ca. AD 117), likely around AD 90, according to Hemer (*Letters*, 9); but see also Instone-Brewer, "The Eighteen Benedictions and the Minim before 70 CE."

19. Quoted in Aune, *Revelation 1–5*, 225.

20. Hemer, *Letters*, 10.

21. Ibid.

the Roman Empire, which is "the ultimate antagonist throughout Revelation,"[22] once again provided Jewish unbelievers with an opportunity to vanquish their foes.[23]

The second half of 3:9 implies that Jews in Philadelphia were attempting to discredit Christians' relationship with God. It is likely that they were claiming that the Christians in Philadelphia were not the people of God, since they were not Jews. As we saw above, at least by the time that Ignatius wrote perhaps a dozen or so years later, there were apparently Gentile converts to Judaism who were trying to evangelize other Gentiles. They would have then been appealing to the Philadelphia Christians as fellow Gentiles to take the "right" path to becoming the people of God, the path that also led to peace and security within the Roman Empire. "If acceptance in the synagogue offered a status of exemption from . . . [participation in the] imperial cult, this was a standing inducement to the weaker Christian."[24]

Jesus, however, puts things in perspective for the harassed believers in Philadelphia. The very ones who were denouncing them as being outside of God's people would be made to come and bow down at their feet and acknowledge them as the object of God's love. There is rich irony in this statement, since throughout Jewish tradition it is clear that the Jews expected the Gentiles to eventually grovel before Israel (Reading Instruction #6). The Jews looked forward to the day that Israel, Jerusalem, and her people would be acknowledged by the nations (Isa 49:22–23; see also 60:14). From the perspective of at least some of the Philadelphian Jews, Christian "heretics" would be among those who would bow down to them. Jesus, though, makes it clear that just the opposite is true. To emphasize this point it is quite likely that he draws on more language from the Old Testament. Jesus has already identified himself as "the true Holy One." Now, with the words "I have loved you" he seems to be pointing readers back to one of the most beautiful promises of protection that God gave to his old covenant people:

> But now thus says the Lord, he who created you, O Jacob, he who formed you, O Israel: "Fear not, for I have redeemed you; I have called you by name, you are mine. ²When you pass through the waters, I will be with you; and through the rivers, they shall not overwhelm you; when you walk through fire you shall not be burned, and the flame shall not consume you. ³For I am the Lord your God, *the Holy One* of Israel, your Savior. I give Egypt as your ransom, Cush and Seba in exchange for you. ⁴Because you are precious in my eyes, and honored, and *I love you*, I give men in return for you, peoples in exchange for your life." (Isa 43:1–4)

22. Ibid., 12.

23. Hemer (ibid.) notes that "It is only through the policy of Rome that the Jewish opposition has received its temporary power."

24. Ibid., 169. Hemer (ibid., 169–73) goes on to argue that part of the challenge to the Christians in Philadelphia related to the Scriptures. As eyewitnesses to the resurrection died off, Christians may have been under greater pressure to prove the viability of Jesus' messianic credentials from the Old Testament.

In both Rev 3:7 and LXX Isa 43:3, the speaker identifies himself as "the Holy One" (ὁ ἅγιος, *ho hagios*). In Rev 3:9, Jesus goes on the declare to/of his people "I have loved you" using virtually identical language to what is found in LXX Isa 43:4.[25] This suggests, though we cannot assume that most readers would have made this specific connection, that Jesus is laying the irony on even thicker. It is Christians in Philadelphia who have been redeemed. They are the ones whom Jesus has loved. They are the ones who are precious to him. Things may seem bleak now, but as is frequently done throughout the New Testament these Christians are being urged to persevere in light of the reversal of roles that is coming.

> *Because you have kept my word about patient endurance, I will keep you from the hour of trial that is coming on the whole world, to try those who dwell on the earth.* (3:10)

As we saw in our discussion of the church at Sardis, "keep" language is very important in Revelation. Here, this theme is used to draw a striking connection between *keeping* Jesus' command and *being kept* by God from the hour of trial. Before considering what it means to be kept from the hour of trial, which we will examine at length in the next chapter, we need to first address the question of what Jesus is referring to when he mentions his word about "patient endurance" (τῆς ὑπομονῆς, *tēs hupomonēs*). Jesus had left no doubt that his followers would be required to patiently endure. In Luke 8:15, he made it clear that such endurance was necessary evidence that his seed had fallen on good soil: "As for that in the good soil, they are those who, hearing the word, hold it fast in an honest and good heart, and bear fruit with patience" (ἐν ὑπομονῃ, *en hupomonē*). In Luke 21:19, in the context of describing the coming persecution of God's people, Jesus declares "By your endurance (ἐν τῇ ὑπομονῇ ὑμῶν, *en tē hupomonē humōn*) you will gain your lives." It is worth noting that the language here for "gain" (κτάομαι, *ktaomai*) shows that Jesus is not opposed to implying necessary activity on the part of those who would be saved, even though salvation is "through grace alone by faith alone in Christ alone." Nor is Paul reticent to use such language: "He will render to each one according to his works: ⁷to those who by patience (καθ' ὑπομονὴν, *kath hupomonēn*) in well-doing seek for glory and honor and immortality, he will give eternal life" (Rom 2:6–7). The writer of Hebrews similarly reminds us of the connection between patient endurance and receiving what God has promised: "For you have need of endurance (ὑπομονῆς, *hupomonēs*), so that when you have done the will of God you may receive what is promised" (Heb 10:36). Here again the writer has used a word translated "receive" in the ESV (the middle form of κομίζω, *komizō*) that means "to come into possession of someth. or experience someth., *get back, recover*."[26] And, of course, we have already seen that John essentially makes patient endurance a

25. The text reads ἐγὼ ἠγάπησά σε (*ego ēgapēsa se*) in Rev 3 and κἀγώ σε ἠγάπησα (*kago se ēgapēsa*) in LXX Isa 43:4.

26. BDAG, 557.2.

defining characteristic of a follower of Jesus: "I, John, your brother and partner in the tribulation and the kingdom and the patient endurance that are in Jesus (ὑπομονῇ ἐν Ἰησοῦ, *hupomonē en Iesou*)" (Rev 1:9); and this key term (ὑπομονή, *hupomonē*) is used a total of seven times in Revelation. The church in Ephesus is twice commended for its patient endurance (2:2, 3), as are the churches in Thyatira (2:19) and Philadelphia (3:10). Jesus then strongly urges all seven churches of Asia Minor—and all Christians of all times—to embrace his call to patient endurance (13:10; 14:12). Patient endurance—persistently and tenaciously refusing to compromise one's devotion to Jesus over the course of a lifetime—is central to the calling of every Christian. And those who embrace that calling and live it out, find favor with the Lord. That is what we see in Rev 3:10; the King of kings and Lord of lords is pleased with this seemingly insignificant group of Christians in Philadelphia and so he gives them a wonderful promise, a promise that naturally extends to all those who patiently endure.

As we think about what patient endurance entails, it is important to ask ourselves: How often do we plead with God or even demand that God change our circumstances rather than patiently enduring in the midst of the trial? There is nothing wrong with asking God to spare us from a particular trial. There is nothing wrong with asking God to heal someone you love who has cancer. God gives us the right and even the responsibility to bring our needs before him. And there is nothing wrong with asking God to deliver us from persecution. That is, in fact, part of what Jesus had in mind when he taught his disciples to pray "deliver us from evil" (Matt 6:13). What *is* wrong is insisting that God do as *we* wish, as if we knew what were best for us. What *is* wrong is thinking that we deserve a pain free life, when our Lord was met with ridicule, torture, and death. How often is God trying to tell us in the trials of life to endure the trial quietly and patiently in order to bring honor to him, but we instead are spending all of our energy trying to get out of the trial? We need to let God decide when we are to be exempt from a particular trial and when, contrary to conventional wisdom, that particular trial is his very best for us. In the case of the Philadelphians, exemption from the greatest of all trials is precisely what he has in mind for them. They will not have to face, Jesus tells them, "the hour of trial that is coming on the whole world, to try those who dwell on the earth." This raises two very important questions: (1) What is the trial of which Jesus is speaking; and (2) What does it mean for the Philadelphians and perhaps other Christians to be spared from this trial?

Many believe that "the hour of trial" in Rev 3:10 refers to the final period of tribulation described in Rev 6–19 and specifically named in 7:14. This makes very good sense in the narrative world of Revelation. This period of suffering is first referred to here in 3:10 and then immediately after the final message to the seven churches the nature of the hour of trial is spelled out.[27] John is called up to heaven so that God can

---

27. Jesus' language here ("the hour of trial that is coming on the whole world, to try those who dwell on the earth") is similar to his language in Luke 21:34–35 ("that day . . . will come upon all who dwell on the face of the whole earth").

show him "what must take place after this" (4:1).[28] And while the throne room visions of Rev 4–5 provide a stunning revelation of the majesty of the Father and the Lamb, in the narrative they also serve the important purpose of introducing the One who is able to open the seven seals (Rev 6), through which Jesus will begin to spell out in great detail what "the hour of trial" will look like.

What, then, does Jesus' promise to Christians in Philadelphia entail? Many North American Christians would maintain that Jesus is referring to the Rapture, and Jesus' words here are thus a promise to remove all Christians from the world before the Great Tribulation begins. In order to determine whether this is what Jesus was promising we will need to read this verse in the context of all of Revelation. So, we will save that discussion for the next chapter. For now we should simply recognize that Jesus goes beyond promising blessing in his messianic kingdom to the Christians in Philadelphia and also includes a beautiful promise of protection from the coming cataclysmic suffering that "those who dwell on the earth" will experience. Whatever he is referring to, any sane person should also want to be the recipient of this promise.

> *I am coming soon. Hold fast what you have, so that no one may seize your crown.* (3:11)

After the wonderful promise of 3:10, Jesus turns to exhortation. He tells Christians in Philadelphia to "hold fast" to what they have. The phrase, "what you have," could be taken in one of two ways. It could be viewed as a subtle reminder that though they are weak and lack influence, they have been graciously given a wonderful inheritance through Jesus Christ. This seems to fit with the reference to "your crown" in this verse. Jesus' words could also, though, be referring back to the "little power" that they have (2:8). In this case, he is simply telling them not to give up. He is reminding them that they do have *some* power and they should not abandon it. Either way, Jesus is clearly calling them to persevere, to tenaciously cling to their devotion to him; but how are they to do that? The answer is found in the first part of the verse: "I am coming soon." Ultimately, much of our ability to persevere through the challenges of this life depends on the degree to which we cling to Jesus' imminent return as a reality. Whether he returns in our lifetime or not, it is absolutely imperative that we realize that this life is a short part of our overall existence. Our trials will soon be over and we will have all eternity to spend in God's presence. This should help us to hold on to what we have and not deny Jesus.

Jesus is frequently said to be "coming soon" in Revelation (3:11; 22:7, 12, 20). As we saw earlier, this is also true elsewhere in the New Testament. I have suggested that every Christian in all places and at all times has been called to live with a mindset that Jesus' return could happen at any moment. The purpose of letting God work that

---

28. John likely weeps loudly (5:4) because he knows the scroll contains the revelation of "what must take place after this" (4:1), and he is aghast at the thought that the amazing revelation he was invited to receive is going to be short-circuited by a scroll that cannot be opened.

into the fabric of our identity is so that it will shape our daily lives. When we really believe at a heart level that Jesus' return could happen at any time, it impacts every area of our lives; it determines our priorities. This does not mean that Christians stop "living" because Jesus is coming soon. Quite the contrary, the reality of Jesus' imminent return *frees* Christians to live as God intended, to live for him who saved them. For the Philadelphians this meant that when things were really difficult they could remind themselves that their trials would soon be over. They only needed to hold on until Jesus returned or until they left this life and entered his presence through death. Either way, they would soon be with him and therefore could take heart and continue to persevere.

Why do we need to persevere according to Jesus? Jesus' final statement implies that our reward is vulnerable: "so that no one will seize your crown," (or better, "so that no one will take your crown"). The expression, "to take away someone's crown" was probably a metaphor that indicated being disqualified in a contest and thus losing out on one's reward. Paul expresses the same idea in 1 Cor 9:25–27. He recognized that missing out on the prize was something that he, the great Apostle Paul, needed to guard against. Jesus' next words to the Christians in Philadelphia make it clear that the choice is between failing to "hold fast" and thus losing one's crown, and overcoming and thus being rewarded.

> *The one who conquers, I will make him a pillar in the temple of my God. Never shall he go out of it, and I will write on him the name of my God, and the name of the city of my God, the new Jerusalem, which comes down from my God out of heaven, and my own new name.* [13]*He who has an ear, let him hear what the Spirit says to the churches.* (3:12–13)

Those who overcome are promised that they will be pillars in God's temple. What does this imagery indicate? It appears to be another fairly transparent metaphor for eschatological salvation. In 21:22, John notes that he "saw no temple in the city, for its temple is the Lord God the Almighty and the Lamb." The city of God does not need a temple because it is a place where God lives among his people. So why does Jesus choose this particular metaphor for these particular Christians?

First of all, the metaphor points to the fact that Philadelphian Christians will have a permanent place in God's kingdom. This is made clear in the following statement: "Never again will he leave it."[29] Jesus is painting a word picture of security and stability.[30] Remember that at the time when Jesus was writing to them Christians in Philadelphia had "little power" (3:8).[31] It was very difficult for them not to be moved

---

29. The fact that overcomers will never go outside of the temple of God or the New Jerusalem stands in stark contrast to those who are refused entry (21:27).

30. Hemer, *Letters*, 166.

31. Note also the names of the pillars in 1 Kgs 7:21.

by the forces around them; but all that would change forever when Jesus returned. Then they would become immovable pillars in God's temple forever.[32]

Second, it is very likely that we are dealing with another rhetorical hotspot here. Notice Jesus' promise: "Never again will he leave it."[33] Remember that Philadelphia was a city plagued by earthquakes, to such a degree that most of the inhabitants had been forced to leave the city and live outside in makeshift shelters. Jesus, who knows their hearts and everything about their day to day lives, is thus, in a very vivid manner, using their present experience to highlight the goodness and security of his coming kingdom (Reading Instruction #4). His kingdom is an unshakeable kingdom (Heb 12:28)! Although they lived in a city where no one ever knew when the next earthquake was going to level the place, Jesus promised them that they would be "pillars" in his temple, permanent fixtures in his unending kingdom. No need to leave the city to be safe anymore, for now they would be living in the city of God under his protection forever.

But wait, there's more. Jesus also promises overcomers that they will wear God's name, the name of his city, and his own name. They will be marked irrevocably as belonging to the Father, the Lamb, and the city of God.[34] This visible marker of belonging to God would have been particularly encouraging to those who were being denounced by the synagogue of Satan as losers whom God had rejected. No doubt as another verbal jab against those who "say that they are Jews and are not, but lie" (3:9), Jesus draws his metaphor of ownership and belonging out of the Old Testament (Reading Instruction #6), where it is expressed in a variety of related ways (see Num 6:27; Deut 28:10; Isa 43:6–7; 44:5; 48:1; 62:2; 63:19). In each case, the point seems to be analogous to what Jesus is saying in Rev 3:12; God's people bear his name, they belong to him. And this belonging is something that is to be obvious to others around them (as in Deut 28:10). What is distinctive about the promise in Rev 3:12 is that it heralds a day when the fact that followers of the Lamb belong to God will be visible to all creation, including the members of the "synagogue of Satan," who will at that time learn that God has loved the Philadelphian Christians (3:9). This promise to the Philadelphians is thus very close to Jesus' promise to overcomers in Sardis: "I will confess his name before my Father and before his angels" (3:5). It is focused on Jesus acknowledging that these badgered Christians belong to him and the Father, and have a permanent place in God's kingdom. With such a wonderful status in Christ the response is obvious: Don't assimilate! Don't take the mark of the beast by compromising

---

32. The language here is clearly figurative. The focus is on security and stability, not on a literal pillar or a literal temple. So there is no contradiction with the later revelation that there will be no temple in the New Jerusalem.

33. Ramsay, *Letters*, 298–99.

34. Swete (*The Apocalypse*, 58) rightly points out that the language suggests that "their lives and characters are to be dominated by the sense of their consecration to the service of God as He is revealed in Christ."

either to benefit from the beast's kingdom, which is all around you, or to spare yourself from further persecution. Stand fast and overcome!

Finally, we should say something about Jesus' "own new name." This is likely another rhetorical hotspot, where Jesus is playing off of local realities. The taking of the name of a ruler to show a special relationship to that ruler would have been quite familiar in Philadelphia, which had first taken the name Neocaesarea, not long after the earthquake of AD 17 when they received imperial aid from Tiberias, and later also took the name Flavia during the reign of Vespasian (AD 69–79).[35] Hemer points out that "it was a great honour for a city to be permitted to assume such titles, and they bound it closely to the imperial service."[36] Jesus thus appears to once again be choosing words that will resonate with the inhabitants of this particular city (Reading Instruction #4). Those who overcome will not be called by the name of one who usurps titles like "ruler of kings on earth," "savior," and even "god." Instead, they will wear the name of the true Ruler of the kings of the earth, the only God and Savior, Jesus Christ.

PHILADELPHIA: PROFILE OF A CHURCH

Christians in Philadelphia lived in very unstable circumstances, in more ways than one. On the one hand, their city could have been called "Earthquake Central." This had led most of the inhabitants to make use of temporary shelters outside of the city for their own safety. On the other hand, their status within the city was tenuous at best. They were denounced by some within the synagogue as followers of a false messiah and they had very little power to withstand this assault. Despite the persecution, however, they had been completely faithful to Jesus. Indeed, Jesus offers them no words of rebuke whatsoever. Instead, he presents not just a final promise, but a series of promises.

First, he reminds them that he in fact is the genuine Holy One, the Messiah that Israel had been awaiting for centuries. As the true Davidic Messiah he alone controls access to his kingdom; and he had chosen to put an open door to that kingdom before the Philadelphia Christians, a door that no man or power on earth could ever close.

Second, Jesus promises that these suffering Christians who had refused to deny his name and had instead heeded his call to patient endurance would be spared the coming hour of trial. What must they do then? They must simply continue to do what they have been doing, holding on to what they have, clinging to their relationship with the Lord Jesus so that their reward will not be stolen from them.

Third, to those who do so Jesus promises that the daily instability of life in Philadelphia will give way to the absolute stability and security of life in God's presence. They will go from being exiles from their own city to being pillars in God's temple, with no need to ever leave God's presence.

35. Ramsay, *Letters*, 292, 301.
36. Hemer, *Letters*, 158.

Finally, Jesus will indelibly mark them as belonging to himself, to God, and to the new Jerusalem. Everyone in heaven and on earth will know that they are children of God. All of this will be theirs if they overcome by clinging to what God has given them and continuing to refuse to deny Jesus' name.

13

Jesus' Message to the Church in Philadelphia
The Rest of the Story

And to the angel of the church in Philadelphia write: 'The words of the holy one,
the true one, who has the key of David, who opens and no one will shut, who
shuts and no one opens.' (3:7)

LIKE THE CHURCH IN Smyrna, the church in Philadelphia was under siege. Where
Christians in Smyrna were living in poverty because of their faith, Christians in Philadelphia were living with "little power." In both cases, Jesus essentially calls on his followers to "hold on" a little while longer; and he presents them with a description of
the glorious reward that is in store for all those who patiently endure. Christians in
Philadelphia would have been particularly encouraged by the promises that Jesus had
given to overcomers in the other churches of Asia Minor. Yes, they were suffering now,
but things were about to change. The King was coming soon and they would be richly
rewarded for their faithfulness if they continued to live as overcomers.

When Christians in Philadelphia heard the words of Rev 4–5, they would have
been struck by the wonder of the door that Jesus had opened for them (3:8). The messianic kingdom, where they will dwell in the very presence of God, is a place where
the most glorious creatures in the entire universe incessantly worship the One on the
throne and the Lamb. As the one "who opens and no one will shut," Jesus is able to
invite his followers in Philadelphia to join in that worship now and to rest assured of
their place before the throne in the age to come.[1]

---

1. While the function of "a door standing open" in 4:1 is not the same as "an open door" in
3:8—John actually sees an open door, which symbolizes the invitation he is being given to see what is
going on in heaven—the parallel language would have naturally led the church of Philadelphia to pay

Although Jesus' title "the holy one, the true one," or better "the true Holy One," has no parallel in Rev 1 like the titles that he uses with the other churches, his titles here are not unusual. The "Holy One" is used of the Father in 4:8 and 6:10; and throughout the New and Old Testaments "Holy One" is a common title for the Messiah (see Mark 1:24; Luke 1:35; 4:34; John 6:69; Acts 4:27, 30; 1 John 1:20; Ps 16:10; Isa 40:25; Hab 3:3). Jesus' use of this title here, then, both closely connects him with the Father and more importantly identifies him as the one who has been specially set apart by the Father to serve as the Messiah.

There are a number of ways that Jesus expands and fleshes out these words later in Revelation. First, his role as the Messiah, the "Holy One," is beautifully portrayed in Rev 5, where we see him appearing as "a Lamb standing, as though it had been slain" (5:6) and later described as the one who by his blood "ransomed people for God from every tribe and language and people and nation" (5:9). His messianic credentials are put forward as he is described as the "Lion of the tribe of Judah" and the "Root of David" in 5:5. We then learn that as the Davidic king he has subjects who are not only redeemed through his own sacrificial death, but who will also reign with him in his earthly kingdom (5:10). In the meantime, as the one who has the key of David he is able to protect those who belong to him (the "Israel of God") by sealing them so that they do not face God's wrath (7:3). As the true Holy One he is also worthy of worship (5:8–14) and he is uniquely qualified to unleash the hour of trial that is coming upon the people of this world through the opening of the seven seals (3:10; 5:5; 6:1–17; 8:1). In the midst of the sixth seal, the "holy and true" character of the One who will judge is reaffirmed (6:10). The delay in bringing judgment does not make him less holy or less reliable; judgment *will* come in his perfect timing. Indeed, through both the Lamb being the one who opens the seals and the Sovereign Lord being the one ordaining martyrdom for many of the saints (6:10–11), the fact that God is in absolute control is clearly highlighted.

Jesus' nature as the true Holy One is further reinforced in the vision of heaven in 7:9–10. Once again he is portrayed as the sacrificial lamb who takes away the sin of the world (see also John 1:29, 36), who is thus rightly worshipped as the one from whom salvation comes (7:10). And his people, who can only be described as "a great multitude that no one could number, from every nation, from all tribes and peoples and languages" (7:9), are pictured "standing before the throne and before the Lamb" (7:9). The vision in this part of Rev 7 represents the first "fast-forward" to the end of the story and serves to reorient Christians in Asia Minor to recognize what is at stake and what God has in store for them. For the Philadelphian Christians it is a beautiful picture of Jesus' promise of "an open door, which no one is able to shut" (3:7) being realized. For those who lived in a city that was constantly shaken by earthquakes, the question that concludes the description of the seal judgments in Rev 6 would have particularly resonated: "for the great day of their wrath has come, and who can stand?"

---

particular attention to how the throne room visions relate to them.

(6:17). That question, however, is immediately answered in Rev 7 as they encounter the spectacular vision of heaven where the great multitude of God's redeemed people is "*standing* before the throne and before the Lamb, clothed in white robes, with palm branches in their hands" (7:9).

We have already seen that by taking the title "the *true* Holy One" Jesus is contradicting claims made by the "synagogue of Satan" that he is not the Messiah. His identity as the true Davidic Messiah is reinforced in Rev 12, where he is described as the "male child . . . who is to rule all the nations with a rod of iron" (12:5), and where it is also made clear that he has been "caught up to God and to his throne" (12:5), where he now reigns. His genuine messianic status stands in stark contrast to the false messiah of Rev 13, the beast, who likewise received a fatal wound from which he was healed, thus deceiving the entire world (13:3, 12, 14).

Since Jesus is "the true Holy One," his followers can rest assured that he is coming soon to rescue them and to right all wrongs. The use of the same language, "true" and "holy," in 15:3–4 reinforces the surety of God bringing justice in due course through Jesus who "is called Faithful and True, and in righteousness . . . judges and makes war" (19:11). As the one with the key of David, he will rule the nations with a rod of iron (19:15), and he will consign the false messiah and his false prophet to the lake of fire (19:20). And those who had died as his faithful followers, though they might have little power now, will be raised to life to *reign* with him in his coming kingdom (20:4–6), because what he opens no one can shut (3:7), including the gates of death. Those who have the privilege of living in the New Jerusalem with God himself can rest assured that "its gates will never be shut" (21:25). Access to the kingdom for those who overcome will be absolute and will never be revoked or limited in any way. The surety of Jesus' coming judgment upon his enemies and reward for his followers, which reinforces his status as "the true Holy One," is likely highlighted further by the name he is given for the first and only time in Revelation in 19:13: "the Word of God." He is the expression of all that God is, "the radiance of the glory of God and the exact imprint of his nature" (Heb 1:3). He is the One who carries out all that is in the Father's mind to do, as the one who "upholds the universe by the word of his power" (Heb 1:3).

> 'I know your works. Behold, I have set before you an open door, which no one
> is able to shut. I know that you have but little power, and yet you have kept my
> word and have not denied my name.' (3:8)

Jesus is clearly pleased with the "works" of the Philadelphian Christians, despite the fact that they have little power. Their lack of power stood in stark contrast to the beast, whose ten horns (13:1) symbolize his extreme power, and whose ten diadems (13:1) symbolize his extreme authority (Reading Instruction #5). The fact that he is a combination of Daniel's four powerful beasts, and thus a single Uberbeast (Reading Instruction #6), makes the contrast with the almost powerless Philadelphians that much starker. Indeed, the fact that the beast is given power by the dragon himself

(13:2) and then allowed to force everyone to take his mark (13:16) would have been sobering for Christians with "little power." This striking contrast, however, serves to remind the Philadelphians of the urgency to hold on to what they have (3:11) so that their crown, i.e., their reward, is not taken, knowing that their "works," of which Jesus is well aware, will follow them (14:13),[2] and they will be rewarded. To such beleaguered Christians facing the might of the beast, Jesus' two-fold reminder would have been particularly important: "Here is a call for the endurance and faith of the saints" (13:10); "Here is a call for the endurance of the saints, those who keep the commandments of God and their faith in Jesus" (14:12). Both statements strongly echo and reinforce Jesus' call to "hold fast" (3:11).

Although Christians tend to guard against any connection between works and salvation, the New Testament in many places uses language that portrays the kingdom as a reward (Heb 10:36; 11:39; 1 Pet 1:9; 5:4; cf. 2 Cor 5:10), as we saw in the last chapter. Here, Jesus' beautiful promise of an open door (to the messianic kingdom) is given in response to his knowledge of their works, which are further specified as keeping his word and not denying his name. His promise here is thus parallel to the promises to overcomers at the end of each of the seven messages. Those who overcome will experience all of the joys of his coming kingdom. This does not mean that they have earned their salvation, but it does mean that God rewards faithfulness (a central part of Revelation's message). The Christian life is not a passive existence. Jesus makes the necessary marriage of Christian responsibility and divine action clear to Christians in Philadelphia by commending them for "keeping" his words (3:8) and then giving them the promise that he will "keep" them from the hour of trial that is coming (3:10). In this case, Jesus' "keeping" is portrayed as a reward for their "keeping," much as "the righteous deeds of the saints" (19:8) are the means by which the bride of Christ clothes herself in fine linen in order to make herself ready for the marriage of the Lamb (19:7).

As the Philadelphian Christians encountered the rest of Revelation they would have seen that their limited power could never be an excuse for failure to keep Jesus' words or for denying his name. Throughout Revelation overcomers are frequently defined as those who "have" or "keep" Jesus' words or their testimony (6:9; 12:11, 17; 19:10; 20:4; cf. 1:2, 9; 11:7). Overcomers do not deny Jesus' name, even in the face of death (12:11). Instead, they are those who bear witness to Jesus (17:6) and remain faithful to him (14:12). Overcomers are the ones who, as "faithful followers," can expect to accompany him when he returns in glory (19:14). Yes, God has ordained that many of them will be killed for their faith (6:11), and the beast will be "allowed to make war on the saints and to conquer them" (13:7), but that reality simply strengthens the "call for the endurance and faith of the saints" (13:10). For, those who give in and take the mark of the beast "will drink the wine of God's wrath, poured full strength into the cup of his anger, and . . . will be tormented with fire and sulfur in the presence of

---

2. Unfortunately, the ESV translates the same expression (τὰ ἔργα, *ta erga*) "works" in 3:8 and "deeds" in 14:13.

the holy angels and in the presence of the Lamb" (14:10). The only sensible response, then, for Christians in Philadelphia is to continue in their faithfulness in the midst of facing the hostility of the society around them with their limited power.

Finally, the portrayal of the two witnesses in Rev 11 would have also been a powerful word of encouragement to the powerless Christians in Philadelphia. The fact that the two witnesses exercise miraculous powers reminiscent of Moses and Elijah (11:6) would have reminded them that those who have little strength (3:7) by the world's standards can be mighty men of valor when empowered by the Holy Spirit. Thus, as they faced the might of Rome and the oppression that came from the local synagogue of Satan, they could rest assured that he who is in them is "greater than he who is in the world" (1 John 4:4).

> *Behold, I will make those of the synagogue of Satan who say that they are Jews and are not, but lie—behold, I will make them come and bow down before your feet, and they will learn that I have loved you.* (3:9)

Jesus reminds the saints in Philadelphia that those who are oppressing them through their claims of being God's true people are actually liars. They are in league with the one who is the great deceiver of the whole world, Satan (12:9). But Satan, their chief accuser, has been cast out of heaven. He no longer has the ability to accuse the people of God before God. He has lost his voice. All he can do now is try to harass the people of God during the little time that he has left (12:12). He is filled with fury—and Christians must expect to be the target of that fury—and he is working through the synagogue in Philadelphia, the Roman government of the late first century, and many societal institutions today in his war against the saints (12:17). But the ultimate "resting" place for Satan will be in the lake of fire (20:10), and each member of the synagogue of Satan and others who oppose the believers in Philadelphia will one day stand before the great white throne of God (20:11) where they will be judged "according to what they had done" (20:12). It is quite likely that it is at this judgment that they will not only bow down before the One on the throne, but also before overcomers who will reign with him (20:4, 6); and before they too are consigned to the lake of fire (20:15) they will recognize all too clearly that Jesus loved the Philadelphians (and all overcomers). Indeed, like a church full of wedding guests grows mute and cranes their necks to see the beauty of the bride as she walks down the aisle, so will the whole universe see the Bride of Christ, clothed in "fine linen, bright and pure" (19:9) for who she is. And all those who make up the Bride, each of whom is invited to the marriage supper of the Lamb, will be blessed (19:9).

The Philadelphians are reminded that they can bank on this promise because it is the true Holy One who has revealed it to them, and he speaks "the true words of God" (19:10) and will certainly come to mete out justice on his enemies as the rider on the white horse who is called "Faithful and True" (19:11). As the two banquets of Rev 19 are juxtaposed for Christians of all ages, it becomes strikingly clear that all will either be invited to "the marriage supper of the Lamb" (19:9) or be served up as supper for vultures at "the great supper of God" (19:17) where all of God's enemies will be consumed (19:17–18, 21). The synagogue of Satan may appear to be winning now, but in the end God will show them to be liars and will give them what they deserve. The synagogue of Satan may be denying Jesus' followers access to the synagogue—the supposed meeting place of the people of God for worship—but a day is coming when God's temple in heaven will be opened to his people and they will have access to the very Holy of Holies (pictured in 11:19). All of this, of course, also helps reinforce Jesus' call to Christians in Philadelphia to hold fast to what they have (3:11) and not give in to the temptation to switch sides under pressure. For it is only those who stand firm to the end, in whose mouth "no lie was found" (14:5), who will be "redeemed from the earth" (14:3)—unlike the Jewish imposters in the synagogue in Philadelphia.

> *Because you have kept my word about patient endurance, I will keep you from the hour of trial that is coming on the whole world, to try those who dwell on the earth.* (3:10)

In the last chapter, we left open the question of what exactly Jesus meant by keeping the Philadelphian Christians "from the hour of trial that is coming on the whole world." Like many debated passages, the debate here appears to stem in large part from a failure to read the passage in context. In this case, each part of this verse is important for determining what Jesus is referring to, as is the rest of the book of Revelation.

First, we need to grapple with the significance of Jesus' reference to their patient endurance. It is important to remember that just as John used "patient endurance" as a defining characteristic of a believer's life in 1:9, so also in the same passage he includes "tribulation" (τῇ θλίψει, *tē thlipsei*) as a second defining characteristic. This is perfectly consistent with what Jesus had told his disciples many years before: "In the world you will have tribulation (θλῖψιν, *thlipsin*). But take heart; I have overcome the world" (John 16:33).[3] Jesus goes on in Revelation to describe such "tribulation" as part of both the present and coming experience of the church in Smyrna (2:9, 10). It is not a stretch, then, to see the mention of "the great tribulation" (τῆς θλίψεως τῆς μεγάλης, *tēs thlipseōs tēs megalēs*) in 7:14 as something Christians should expect to face, at least at some level. Interestingly, the only other use of the noun "tribulation" (θλίψις) in Revelation is in 2:22, where Jesus warns of the "great tribulation" that is coming to those *in the church of Thyatira* who follow the message of assimilation being promoted by Jezebel (2:22). Thus, those who patiently endure are promised exemption from "great tribulation" and those who do not are promised "great tribulation." But what does the exemption entail?

Many have argued over the past 100 years or so that Jesus' promise to these believers indicates that he will protect Christians from the hour of trial by "rapturing" them out of the world prior to the onset of the Great Tribulation. The Pre-Tribulation

---

3. Christians can "overcome" in the midst of tribulation because Jesus has "overcome."

Rapture view relies heavily on the reference to Jesus *keeping* them *from* (σε τηρήσω ἐκ, *se tērēsō ek*) the hour or trial in Rev 3:10, with the claim being that the Greek preposition ἐκ (*ek*) suggests "removal from." As John 17:15 makes clear, however, "keeping someone from something" does not always indicate *removal* from that circumstance: "I do not ask that you take them out of the world, but that you keep them from the evil one." The language here for "keep them from" (τηρήσῃς αὐτοὺς ἐκ, *tērēsēs autous ek*) is identical to the language in Rev 3:10. Both use the verb τηρέω (*tereō*, "keep") plus the preposition ἐκ (*ek*, "from"). Yet, Jesus explicitly states in John 17:15 that he is *not* asking God to "take them out of the world." The language in Rev 3:10, then, is far from sufficient to establish the Pre-Tribulation Rapture view.

There are a variety of other factors that should actually put a nail in the coffin of the Pre-Tribulation Rapture view. We have already seen that Jesus makes it clear in Revelation that Christians suffer. What should be painfully obvious to even a casual reader of Revelation is that Christians are portrayed as suffering *throughout this book*. The saints never disappear from the scene as advocates of the Pre-Tribulation Rapture view maintain. In the midst of the seal judgments of Rev 6, where are Christians? Are they watching from heaven? Well, actually some of them are in heaven, but they are waiting for the rest of their fellow believers "to be killed as they themselves had been" (6:11). In the midst of the trumpet judgments of Rev 8 and 9, where are Christians? They are praying to God from the earth (8:3–4), where they are protected from his outpoured wrath (9:4) through being sealed and thus marked as belonging to him (7:3). Indeed, the detailed description of the sealing of the 144,000 in 7:1–8 is intended to vividly portray just how Jesus will keep his people from the hour of trial. The coming cataclysm described in 8:6–12 would have made the Philadelphians' experience of earthquakes seem quite tame by comparison, but they could rest assured that God would spare them from those plagues and from the torment of the locusts (9:4–6), even though these things will affect the world around them. In the midst of the bowl judgments of Rev 16, where are Christians? They are there on earth being exhorted by Jesus in language that he had earlier used to address Christians in Sardis: "Behold, I am coming like a thief! Blessed is the one who stays awake, keeping his garments on, that he may not go about naked and be seen exposed!" (16:15). The saints of God are clearly present throughout all three cycles of judgment that Revelation describes, with no indication that they have ever left the scene, except through their death.

Notice, though, that although they are protected from God's wrath they are pursued by the evil one who is actively making war against "those who keep the commandments of God and hold to the testimony of Jesus" (12:17). This was no new revelation to the saints in Asia Minor, particularly those in Smyrna, Pergamum, and Philadelphia. They were all too familiar with persecution before Jesus sent them the message of Revelation. Now, though, they will expect that things will get worse before Jesus returns to reign supreme. After all, when the beast appears and begins his reign of terror, where are Christians? They are the only ones who do not worship the beast (13:8).

Remember that Revelation is addressed to seven actual churches in Asia Minor, some of whom Jesus calls to repentance and all of whom he calls to patient endurance. In the midst of his description of the beast Jesus first in 13:10 says, "Here is a call for the endurance and faith of the saints," and then in the next chapter when he returns to the pressure that people will feel to take the mark of the beast and the wrath of God that will come upon all who do so (14:9–11), he does not say, "No worries! Christians will be watching the action from heaven!" Instead, he says once again, "Here is a call for the endurance of the saints, those who keep the commandments of God and their faith in Jesus" (14:12). And he does so to make it absolutely clear that *a major function of his overall message in Revelation is to prepare Christians to face the coming great tribulation,* or whatever challenges they are currently facing as his followers in their particular historical and cultural context. This is further driven home in 14:13, which implies that Christians should not only expect to die in the great tribulation, but that they can rest assured that their deaths will bring heavenly rewards: "And I heard a voice from heaven saying, 'Write this: Blessed are the dead who die in the Lord from now on.' 'Blessed indeed,' says the Spirit, 'that they may rest from their labors, for their deeds follow them!'" God will indeed take them out of the Great Tribulation (this is implied in the harvest vision of 14:14–16), but their exit will come through being faithful to death (2:10). This is likely what is intended in the description of 7:13–14. When Jesus recounts in great detail the downfall of "Babylon" in Revelation 17–18, which chronologically occurs at the very end of the outpouring of God's wrath on the earth, where are Christians? They are being urged, as Jesus has been urging the saints in Asia Minor from the very beginning of Revelation: "Come out of her, my people, lest you take part in her sins, lest you share in her plagues; ⁵for her sins are heaped high as heaven, and God has remembered her iniquities" (18:4–5). When God judges the world for its sin, the saints will still be in the world throughout that period of terrifying judgment. They will be protected from God's wrath, but not immune to the wrath of the beast.

The fact that the saints are protected from God's wrath is actually made clear in Rev 3:10 itself. It is "those who dwell on the earth" who are the target of the coming trial. At first glance, this expression might be assumed to be all inclusive: all those who live on earth will face this great tribulation. When we look at how the phrase is used throughout the book of Revelation, however, we find that "those who dwell on the earth" is a technical expression used to distinguish those who stand opposed to God from the saints of God (see 6:10; 8:13; 11:10; 13:8, 12, 14; 17:2, 8). This distinction is quite obvious in 6:9–10: "When he opened the fifth seal, I saw under the altar the souls of those who had been slain for the word of God and for the witness they had borne. ¹⁰They cried out with a loud voice, 'O Sovereign Lord, holy and true, how long before you will judge and avenge our blood on *those who dwell on the earth*?'" It is also evident in 11:10, where it is "those who dwell on the earth" who are tormented by the two witnesses and celebrate when they die; in 13:8 and 13:12, where it is "all who dwell on earth" who worship the beast; in 13:14, where it is "those who dwell on earth" who are deceived by the beast; in 17:2, where it is "the dwellers on earth" who have become drunk with the wine of the great prostitute's sexual immorality; and in 17:8, where "the dwellers on earth" are those whose names have not been written in the book of life from the foundation of the world" and who thus "will marvel to see the beast." The hour of trial that is coming on the whole world, then, is not intended to *directly* impact the people of God. It is intended for those whom God created to live in this world and worship him alone, but who have persisted in rebellion against him even in the face of his wrath and their imminent demise.

Although the common view—at least in North America—that God will use the Rapture to remove Christians from this world before he pours out his wrath is appealing, it suffers from two major liabilities. First, it does not have a biblical basis. We have seen that the saints of God are present throughout the period of tribulation described in Revelation. And although advocates of the Pre-Tribulation Rapture view often point to 4:1 as a reference to that event ("Come up here"), such a reading is contrived at best. John is simply saying that after Jesus had given him messages for the seven churches he heard a voice inviting *him* to come up to heaven so that God could show him "what must take place after this." There is simply no way that the original readers of Revelation could have heard any indication of a Rapture of the church here.

Second, the Rapture view is, plain and simple, a modern Western invention. It was first taught by John Nelson Darby in the mid-1800s and popularized in North America in the early 1900s. It is not surprising that a view that holds that Christians will be graciously removed from the scene by God prior to the worst period of suffering the world will ever know would be popular in a society that strives to avoid suffering. But we should always be suspicious of a theological innovation that brings Scripture into line with our own sensibilities.

We should also note that although the primary significance of the "keeping" language in 3:10 may relate to being exempt from the wrath of God that is coming, more may be going on here when we read this passage in light of what Jesus prayed in John 17:15: "I do not ask that you take them out of the world, but that you keep them from the evil one." Jesus' high priestly prayer in John 17 is focused on protection from the evil one so that his followers can live as overcomers while in this world. It is quite possible that when Jesus promises to keep the Philadelphian Christians—and by application all other Christians—"from the hour of trial that is coming on the whole world" he is including in that promise a commitment to give them power to endure the backlash from the evil one and from the people of the world that Christians will face as God pours out his wrath on "those who dwell on the earth." Whatever the case, the focus of the "keeping" language here is clearly on seeing them *through* "the hour of trial," rather than removing them *from* that trial.

Within the context of suffering and persecution, part of what Jesus' promise would have done was to remind them of truth of his words in John 16:33: "I have said these things to you, that in me you may have peace. In the world you will have tribulation. But take heart; I have overcome the world."[4] Just as Jesus had revealed to his first disciples what was to come so that they could have peace, so Jesus in Revelation is making known to his followers at the end of the first century, and every century since, that trouble is coming, but that trouble need not rob us of peace. We should expect trouble. We should expect suffering in this world. But that is not the end of the story. Jesus has overcome the world.

Jesus prayed for his disciples, "I do not ask that you take them out of the world, but that you keep them from the evil one" (John 17:15), and we know that the Father *always* hears Jesus and answers his prayers. But we also know that not many years later James, the brother of John, was murdered by Herod (Acts 12:2). Indeed, tradition holds that ultimately almost all of the twelve apostles were martyred. Does this mean that God did not "keep them from the evil one"? Or does it show us that protection from the evil one does not mean protection from suffering and even violent death? As we think about the significance of Rev 3:10, and the popular interpretation of that passage that has spread widely in North American churches, it is important to consider how Revelation as a whole describes the people of God and what they can expect to face. In Rev 13:10 and 14:12, part of a book that as a whole is addressed to *Christians* living in seven cities of Asia Minor, God tells those saints that the people of God will need to patiently endure what is being described and continue to be faithful to Jesus come what may.

This is perfectly consistent with the message thus far. Remember that God had already revealed to these Christians that martyred believers would have to wait "until the number of their fellow servants and brothers who were to be killed as they had been was completed" (6:11). In 7:3, we were told that the servants of God on earth would be sealed so that his wrath would not affect them. In 7:14, Jesus had implied that his people would exit the great tribulation through their deaths. In the midst of God's wrath being poured out on the pagan inhabitants of the earth, we are told that the prayers of the saints continue going up to God (8:4), again indicating that God's people are still on earth. In 9:4, we are once again reminded in the midst of God's wrath being poured out—in this case the fifth trumpet—that God's people are present but sealed to protect them from that wrath. In chapter 11, we found that during the beast's reign of terror God will have witnesses testifying of the Good News (however we interpret the two witnesses). In Rev 12, we found that ever since Jesus' ascension Satan has been filled with fury (12:12) and very actively engaged in fighting against followers of Jesus (12:17). Then in Rev 13, we saw that the beast's war will only intensify for Christians in the coming years as the beast cracks down on all dissent

---

4. The word translated "overcome" here is the same word that the ESV renders "conquered" throughout Revelation.

against his rule and any refusal to worship him. In short, followers of Jesus will need to patiently endure and be sure to be faithful to Jesus because they will face the wrath of the beast. What God promises to "keep" the Philadelphian Christians from, then, is not any and all suffering during the great tribulation, but rather the plagues that he will pour out on the unbelieving world.

Just as the plagues in Revelation, particularly in Rev 16, are intended to remind readers of the plagues God poured out on Egypt, so also the promise in 3:10 and the parallel symbol of God's people being sealed prior to the outpouring of his wrath (7:3) are intended to remind readers of the distinction God made between the Egyptians and the Israelites. The Israelites were living in Egypt, the target of God's wrath, but the plagues did not touch them:

> But on that day I will set apart the land of Goshen, where my people dwell, so that no swarms of flies shall be there, that you may know that I am the Lord in the midst of the earth. 23Thus I will put a division between my people and your people. Tomorrow this sign shall happen. (Exod 8:22–23)

> But the Lord will make a distinction between the livestock of Israel and the livestock of Egypt, so that nothing of all that belongs to the people of Israel shall die. 5And the Lord set a time, saying, "Tomorrow the Lord will do this thing in the land." 6And the next day the Lord did this thing. All the livestock of the Egyptians died, but not one of the livestock of the people of Israel died. 7And Pharaoh sent, and behold, not one of the livestock of Israel was dead. But the heart of Pharaoh was hardened, and he did not let the people go. (Exod 9:4–7)

> Then the Lord said to Moses, "Stretch out your hand toward heaven, so that there may be hail in all the land of Egypt, on man and beast and every plant of the field, in the land of Egypt." 23Then Moses stretched out his staff toward heaven, and the Lord sent thunder and hail, and fire ran down to the earth. And the Lord rained hail upon the land of Egypt. 24There was hail and fire flashing continually in the midst of the hail, very heavy hail, such as had never been in all the land of Egypt since it became a nation. 25The hail struck down everything that was in the field in all the land of Egypt, both man and beast. And the hail struck down every plant of the field and broke every tree of the field. 26Only in the land of Goshen, where the people of Israel were, was there no hail. (Exod 9:22–26)

> Then Moses called all the elders of Israel and said to them, "Go and select lambs for yourselves according to your clans, and kill the Passover lamb. 22Take a bunch of hyssop and dip it in the blood that is in the basin, and touch the lintel and the two doorposts with the blood that is in the basin. None of you shall go out of the door of his house until the morning. 23For the Lord will

pass through to strike the Egyptians, and when he sees the blood on the lintel and on the two doorposts, the Lord will pass over the door and will not allow the destroyer to enter your houses to strike you." (12:21–23)

Although only in the case of the Passover plague do the Israelites have some sort of literal mark (on their homes), in each case they were "sealed" against the plagues God was sending on the land in which they were living. God made a distinction between his people and the pagans they were living among. And the same is true for Christians facing the great tribulation; God promises to keep them from that trial by protecting them from "the fury of his wrath" (16:19).

It is important to recognize that through the plagues themselves and through the reference to the song of Moses and the song of the Lamb (15:3) Jesus is drawing a correlation between two events: the redemption of Israel out of Egypt and the redemption of the new covenant people of God out of "Babylon." In both cases, God accomplishes his mighty rescue by pouring out his wrath on the oppressor nation *while the people of God are still suffering under an evil ruler.* In the case of Revelation, the oppressor nation is the entire world, which is under the power of the evil one (1 John 5:19). Just as in Egypt many centuries before, the plagues in Revelation bring a backlash against God's people; but in the end, God is victorious and his people are set free. And just as was the case in Egypt, it is only the enemies of God and of his people, "who bore the mark of the beast and worshiped its image" (16:2) rather than being sealed by God (7:3), who face his wrath and get what they deserve (16:6). The repeated portrayal of those affected by the plagues cursing God (16:9, 11, 21) reinforces the fact that God's people are not touched by them. God keeps them from the hour of trial as he kept the Israelites from the plagues that were poured out on Egypt; but this does not mean that they are not present when all of this is going on. Quite the contrary, in the midst of the horrible suffering the people of this world will face who are in rebellion against their Creator, Jesus reminds his people to hold on and "stay awake" so that they will be prepared to meet him when he returns (16:15).

> *I am coming soon. Hold fast what you have, so that no one may seize your crown.* (3:11)

Jesus exhorts the believers in Philadelphia to hang in there. They have a reward coming, but it is a reward that can be lost through failing to continue in faithful devotion to him. Yes, an hour of trial is coming; but Jesus is also coming . . . and soon. So, hold on, Jesus says, knowing that you will come out of the hour of trial, the great tribulation (7:14), wearing a white robe that has been washed in the blood of the Lamb (7:13–14); and you will enjoy perfect peace and joy in God's presence forever (7:15–17). Hold on, knowing that your prayers are being heard (8:4–5). God will answer. Yes, you must be faithful witnesses to the point of death, because the beast will be given power to conquer the saints and kill them just as he does the two witnesses (11:7); but hold on nevertheless because your resurrection is sure to follow (11:11–12).

Yes, you will face great shame and humiliation in this world (3:9; 11:8–10), but glory is sure to follow. God will reward you for your faithfulness (11:18) and bring judgment on your enemies (11:18).

This promised reward is reinforced in what follows in Revelation in a variety of ways. One of the most beautiful is the simple statement concerning the saints who die in the Lord that "their deeds follow them" (14:13). In other words, when this life comes to an end, what we have done in serving the Lord will be remembered by God and rewarded. Rest may only come through martyrdom, but Jesus' followers are assured that a glorious rest will be the reward of all overcomers. Here, we see a striking contrast to what early Old Testament saints faced as followers of God with very little sense of anything beyond this life. This is why the author of Ecclesiastes can say, "As he came from his mother's womb he shall go again, naked as he came, and shall take nothing for his toil that he may carry away in his hand" (Eccl 5:11). For him, because God had not revealed more at that point, when this life was over, it was over. That is why the writer was so despondent throughout Ecclesiastes. He reasoned that no matter what you do and however good this life can be, when you die you are no better than a dead dog. The New Testament, and Revelation most prominently, reveals quite another story. This life is not all there is; in fact, it is merely the prelude to true life in the presence of God under the absolute rule of the Lamb. More than that, it becomes crystal clear throughout the New Testament, but again particularly in Revelation, that what we do in this life has a major impact on what happens after we die. Overcomers can rest assured that their faithful devotion to Jesus will "follow them" and they will be rewarded according to what they have done (2 Cor 5:10). This life is not "meaningless" or "vanity" now that Christ has come.

While all of Rev 4–22 is designed to encourage overcomers in Philadelphia to hold on, it still only provides a partial picture. Jesus is careful only to reveal so much (10:4), because he still expects his followers to walk by faith not by sight; the life of the overcomer is the life of faith.

> *The one who conquers, I will make him a pillar in the temple of my God. Never shall he go out of it, and I will write on him the name of my God, and the name of the city of my God, the new Jerusalem, which comes down from my God out of heaven, and my own new name.* (3:12)

We have seen that Jesus' promise to make the Philadelphian Christians pillars in the temple of God, and his promise that they would never have to go out of the temple would have stood in stark contrast to their current situation. They had "little power" (3:8) and their lives lacked stability. Not only were they targets of persecution, but they also faced the daily realities of life in Philadelphia where people had to live outside of the city in order to be safe from the constant earthquakes. To such people Jesus promises safety and security. When the "big one" to end all big ones strikes this world, causing the nations of this world to collapse (16:17–19), Christians can know that their future is to be permanent pillars in God's temple.

Although the promise of having the name of God, the New Jerusalem, and Jesus' own name written on them is primarily a promise that they will be marked as belonging to God the Father, Jesus the Son, and the city of the Great King in the coming kingdom, it also has implications for the here and now. Jesus has bought us with his own blood. We have been redeemed. We are *now* "called children of God" (1 John 3:1). This picture of belonging to God is reinforced in 7:2–8 with the account of the sealing of the 144,000. What greater comfort could there be in the midst of a hostile culture than to know that you belong to God, are citizens of his kingdom, and will be totally protected from his wrath both in this world and in the world to come?

As Christians in Philadelphia came to 7:15–17 they would have been struck by the way the words of the elder reinforce Jesus' promise in 3:12. Yes, Christians will go through the Great Tribulation, but they will come out of it (many through death) with robes "made white in the blood of the Lamb" (7:14), and their new reality will be very different (7:15–17). Suffering will be over. There will be no more exposure to the elements (7:16) like the inhabitants of Philadelphia regularly faced, and particularly those who were persecuted because of their devotion to Jesus; for God will now shelter them with his own amazing presence (7:15). No more hunger and thirst, like they had suffered as outcasts in their own hometown; for Jesus, the Lamb who was slain to redeem them, will now guide them as their Good Shepherd "to springs of living water" (7:17). The pain of their suffering will come to an end as God himself wipes "away every tear from their eyes" (7:17). How Christians in Philadelphia would have latched on to these wonderful promises in Rev 7! What hope the words of the elder would have brought them in their distress!

Jesus, though, promises them even more; he promises that as overcomers they will have new names written on them. Now, remember that overcomers, by definition, are those who reject the name of the beast and instead bear the name of the Lamb and the Father. This name, we learn later, is on the forehead of the people of God (14:1; 22:4). In other words, overcomers *visibly* display their allegiance to Jesus. When Christians in Philadelphia came to the description of the 144,000 in 14:1 with the name of the Lamb and the name of the Father clearly written on their foreheads, they could not have missed the striking contrast set up between Rev 13 and Rev 14. Either one visibly displays the name of the beast on their forehead (or right hand), or they visibly display the name of the Lamb and the Father. No one is allowed to exist without one or the other. As Bob Dylan sang, "You're gonna have to serve somebody." And Revelation makes it clear that in the final analysis you will not be able to hide whose side you are on. To understand what Jesus is promising here and the description of the 144,000 in Rev 14, we need to understand what is going on with the reference to the mark of the beast in Rev 13.

In Rev 13, we find the second beast "causes all, both small and great, both rich and poor, both free and slave, to be marked on the right hand or the forehead, [17]so that no one can buy or sell unless he has the mark, that is, the name of the beast or the number of its name" (13:16–17). This effectively places a spotlight on the saints, who will refuse to take that mark; and their refusal will lead to their deaths. Like armies of old who laid siege to enemy cities in an effort to starve their enemies into surrender, so the beast will make it difficult or even impossible for Christian families to get access to food and other necessities unless they compromise and demonstrate their allegiance to the beast.

The language of "the right hand or the forehead" is important here. Christians in Asia Minor, who would have been well acquainted with at least key parts of the Old Testament (Reading Instruction #6), would have quickly caught the significance of the picture Jesus has painted for them. As we noted in Chapter 3, they would have been drawn back to the central confession of every pious Jew: the *Shema* (Deut 6:4–9). The fact that the same idea is repeated four times in Exodus and Deuteronomy makes the connection to Rev 13 that much more obvious (see also Exod 13:9, 16; Deut 11:18). In each case, the point appears to be that Jews are to be visible, obvious followers of Yahweh; through obedience to God's commands their lives are to leave no question of where their allegiance lies. Particularly important is Exod 13, where the language is found twice and each time it is preceded by a reference to the observance of the Passover. God specifically says that "it," that is the Passover observance, "shall be to you as a sign on your hand and as a memorial between your eyes" (13:9). This is repeated in 13:16. What is God saying? He is saying that the outward observance of the Passover Feast was to function as a clear and visible symbol of their devotion to Yahweh. It was to be as obvious to those around them as a mark on their hand or in the middle of their forehead. This same idea of visible allegiance to God is reinforced in the context of Deut 6 and 11 where Moses goes on to write two times: "You shall write them on the doorposts of your house and on your gates" (6:9; 11:20). While Jews might respond to this by literally writing God's laws on their house—and this can only be a good thing—what the command points to is God's call to his people to live a life that is, to even a casual observer, devoted to him and thus very different from the society around them.

What does all this have to do with the mark of the beast? Everything! In our technological age, it is very easy for us to get caught up in whether the mark of the beast will be a tattooed bar-code, a microchip implanted under the skin, or some other high-tech wizardry. It may, in fact, end up being a high-tech mark, just as Jews literally wrote God's laws on their doorposts and gates; but the point of those actions is what we need to focus on. Otherwise, we run the risk of missing the significance of the message in Rev 13 and thus put ourselves in grave danger. Think about it. It is quite easy to guard yourself from accepting a microchip or a barcode tattoo; and if we think that that is all this passage is calling us to do, we will feel safe. "I will never take the mark of the beast!" we tell ourselves.[5] What Rev 13 is describing, however, is something far more subtle. Using the language of Exodus and Deuteronomy, which called the old covenant people of God to vibrant, visible devotion to him, Rev 13 is calling the new covenant people of God to avoid giving their devotion to the beast. The beast will demand that all people visibly give their allegiance to him. Christians in Philadelphia would not have been left scratching their heads over the mark of the beast just because they lived long before the computer age. Instead, they would have seen Rev 13 as a call to guard their thoughts and actions from being shaped by the beast's agenda. They would have recognized that the mark of the beast leaves no room for compromise. Indeed, the stark juxtaposition of 13:16–18 (the mark of the beast) with 14:1 (where the 144,000 have the name of the Lamb and the Father's name written on their foreheads) would have reminded them that there never has been and never will be any middle ground. You either are devoted to God or you are devoted to Satan. You either give your allegiance to the Lamb or you give your allegiance to the beast. We must thus ask ourselves: Does my lifestyle serve as a clear indicator that I belong to God—as clearly as if I had his holy name tattooed in the middle of my forehead? Or does my life instead serve like a giant tattoo proclaiming that I am devoted to the beast and his kingdom?

As Christians from Philadelphia came to Rev 14, they would have seen for the first time the realization of Jesus' promise to overcomers in 3:12. Here are all overcomers (the 144,000) standing with the Lamb himself on Mount Zion with his name and the Father's name written on their foreheads. They are in *their* new city, the city of which they are citizens, in the presence of the Father and the Lamb, and marked as clearly belonging to the Father, the Lamb, and the New Jerusalem (3:12). The correspondence between 14:1 and 3:12 reinforces the conclusion that the 144,000 in some way refers to the true people of God. This is further supported by 14:4, where they are described as those who have been "redeemed," just as the Lamb has "ransomed" (5:9, the same word in Greek[6]) people from every ethnic group on earth for God. What would have been particularly encouraging for Christians in Philadelphia is the fact that the 144,000 are portrayed singing a new song before the throne and before the very ones they first saw in Rev 4–5, the four living creatures and the elders. The "new song" is sung when there is a new powerful deliverance of God, as was the case when the Israelites were magnificently rescued from slavery in Egypt and then sang the song of Moses (Exod 15). They can sing the song because they have been "kept from" the hour of trial by the mighty power of God, and unlike their opponents in Philadelphia—the members of the synagogue of Satan who lie about being Jews—no lie was found in their mouths (14:5). Along with this strong encouragement, though, comes a subtle reminder. The 144,000 are those who "hold fast" (3:11) and remain pure (14:4).

5. Actually, most North American Christians tell themselves that they won't be around to face the pressure to take the mark of the beast anyway; but that's another story.

6. It is again regrettable that the lack of consistency in the ESV masks the connection here.

SUMMARY: JESUS' MESSAGE TO CHRISTIANS IN PHILADELPHIA

Christians in Philadelphia had the dual challenge of living in a city that had been devastated by frequent earthquakes and being targets for persecution from the local synagogue. Their lives were anything but stable or secure. Jesus, though, has a message of hope and encouragement for these Christians. He gives them a spectacular vision of what the "open door" entails that he has placed before them, providing a glimpse of what is in store for those who hold fast to what they have. He reminds them that he, in fact, is the true Holy One, despite what their opponents from the local synagogue might be saying. He came, he lived, he died, he was raised from the dead, and he is now seated at the right hand of God. One day soon he will come in glory and bring judgment to those who oppose him and his people. He recognizes that they have "little power," and yet he calls them to patient endurance and faithfulness regardless of their circumstances. They must keep his word, and in return they can expect that he will keep them from the hour of trial that is coming upon the whole world. Such "keeping" does not indicate that they will not face continued suffering. On the contrary, the book of Revelation vividly shows that God's people will face increasing pressure to submit to the demands of the world around them, which is living in active rebellion against God. Indeed, the people of God are going to face the wrath of the beast during the coming hour of trial. At each stage of the ultimate conflict between good and evil that is recorded in Revelation, God's people are clearly on the scene. And as participants in those ultimate events, they must continue to refuse to deny Jesus' name even if it costs them their very lives. Jesus' promise to keep them assures them that he will give them the power they need to patiently endure to the very end. And as they do so, they can rest assured that like the two witnesses of Rev 11, nothing will be able to touch them without God's prior approval. In the end, those who have opposed them will be forced to acknowledge that it is they who belong to God and are loved by him. All that Jesus has promised them will come to pass; for nothing can nullify his promises (19:10, 11). They will be marked with God's name through all of eternity; but the name of God, and Jesus' own new name, and the name of the New Jerusalem will only be written on those who have steadfastly refused to bear the name of the beast. And avoiding the "mark of the beast" cannot simply be relegated to avoiding being physically branded with his number. Just as God commanded Israel to tie his words on their hand and foreheads, using figurative language to speak of the visible and obvious devotion to him that their lives must demonstrate, so here taking of the mark of the beast on the right hand or forehead is all about visible devotion to the beast. Such devotion would have been demonstrated in the first century through burning incense to the Roman emperor, participation in the idolatry and immorality that was a part of everyday life in the cities of Asia Minor, or simply actively pursuing the values of the Roman Empire rather than living as a citizen of the New Jerusalem.

In other words, wearing the mark of the beast would have most likely been associated with adopting a particular lifestyle; and it is no different for us today.

14

Jesus' Message to the Church in Laodicea

And to the angel of the church in Laodicea write: The words of the Amen, the faithful and true witness, the beginning of God's creation. (3:14)

JESUS' MESSAGE TO THE church in Laodicea brings us to the last of his seven messages, a message that brings his words of encouragement and warning to Christians in Asia Minor to a crescendo. In the church at Laodicea we find the epitome of compromise, to which Jesus responds with a very strong and vivid threat.

Verse 14 is the only place in the New Testament where "Amen" is used as a title, and likely reflects an allusion to Isa 65:16: "So that he who blesses himself in the land shall bless himself by the God of truth (Hebrew: *amen*), and he who takes an oath in the land shall swear by the God of truth (*amen*); because the former troubles are forgotten and are hidden from my eyes." It is interesting that the LXX translates "the God of Amen" in Isa 65:16 as "the true God" (τὸν θεὸν τὸν ἀληθινόν, *ton theon ton alethinon*). Jesus' use of both "amen" and "true" in his titles here makes the connection to Isa 65 even more likely by encompassing both the Hebrew original and the Greek translation. Revelation 3:14 thus appears once again to assign a title to Jesus that had previously been used only of God, a title that highlights Jesus as the one with whom there is absolute certainty.

The meaning of "the Amen" is fleshed out in what follows: he is the "faithful and true witness" who is fully trustworthy. It is noteworthy that the message to the church in Laodicea is the only one in which none of Jesus' titles is drawn from the description or words of Jesus recorded in 1:14–18. Instead, his titles take us back to the introductory words of 1:5, where he is referred to as "the faithful witness." Jesus is the One who remained a faithful witness, glorifying God regardless of his circumstances. When the devil tempted him with comfort (food), status (protection by angels), and worldly power, he stood on the Word of God and did not waver. This, of course, sharply contrasts with the track record of Christians in Laodicea.

Jesus is not only the Amen and the faithful and true witness, but he is also "the beginning of God's creation" (ESV).[1] Similar language is found in Paul's letter to the Colossians, a letter that he instructed the Colossians to share with the church in Laodicea (Col 4:16). In Col 1:15, Jesus is described as "the image of the invisible God, the firstborn over all creation." A few verses later, he is called "the beginning" (1:18). It is likely that Jesus' words in Rev 3:14 have a similar function to Paul's words in Colossians. Both highlight the uniqueness of Jesus as the Creator and ultimate authority to counteract those who were seeking to deny his deity.[2] He is the starting point of all things, for "All things were made through him, and without him was not any thing made that was made" (John 1:3).

For Christians in Laodicea who had been anything but "faithful" or "true" in their "witness" for Jesus, Jesus' use of titles would have served as an implicit rebuke. They were supposed to be devoted to the one who was the beginning of God's creation, the one through whom all things existed, but instead they were living a life of self-indulgence and self-sufficiency.

> *I know your works: you are neither cold nor hot. Would that you were either cold or hot!* [16]*So, because you are lukewarm, and neither hot nor cold, I will spit you out of my mouth.* (3:15–16)

Jesus, of course, is well aware of the conduct of believers in Laodicea, and in this case he will make it clear that he is well aware of their attitudes as well. What is striking in this final message is the fact that Jesus has nothing good whatsoever to say about this church. It was a church that viewed itself as fabulously rich, and yet Jesus' assessment of them is wholly negative. It is summed up in a single word: "lukewarm." His charge that they were lukewarm has often been taken to mean that their "passion" for Jesus had waned, leaving them with a lukewarm faith that was not yet cold, but was certainly not hot. When we look at known characteristics of Laodicea (Reading Instruction #4), however, it becomes quite obvious that Jesus has something entirely different in mind. Not only does he call them lukewarm, but three times in a row he refers to them as "neither hot nor cold," with slightly different phrasing each time. Jesus is emphatically contrasting them with something that is hot and something else that is cold.

The city of Laodicea was located on a trade route on a plateau in the fertile valley of the Lycus River. It was six miles south of Hierapolis, about ten miles west of Colossae, and about 100 miles east of Ephesus. Colossae to the east had a pure supply of cold

1. This is preferable to the NIV's "the ruler of God's creation" given the similarities to Col 1 noted below.

2. Others have noted additional correspondences between the letters to the church at Laodicea and Paul's letters to the Colossians and Ephesians (churches in the Lycus valley): Rev 3:21 corresponds to Col 3:1 and Eph 2:6; and Rev 3:17–19 corresponds to Col 1:27; 2:8, 18, 23.

water. Hierapolis to the north, on the other hand, was renowned for its healing hot springs (said to be 95°F), whose medicinal virtues were widely lauded and reflected in the local religion.[3] Hemer notes that the springs had "formed spectacular petrified cascades almost unique in the world,"[4] leaving a 300–foot cliff covered with white mineral deposits (calcium carbonate), which was clearly visible from Laodicea.[5] In contrast to Colossae and Hierapolis, Laodicea possessed no springs of its own and the Lycus River dried up in the summer, and thus could only supply the city with water during part of the year.[6] Archaeologists have found the remains of an aqueduct at Laodicea that probably carried water from springs that were located about five or six miles south of the city.[7] The thick layer of incrustation in these pipes clearly reveals the poor quality of the water. Worse than that, by the time it arrived, the water would have been lukewarm. What Jesus appears to be doing, then, by calling them "lukewarm" is creating a rhetorical hotspot. He is pointing out that they are not cold like the refreshing water of Colossae, or hot like the medicinal waters of Hierapolis—*both of which are good*—but rather they are just as offensive to him as their lukewarm water is to those who had to drink it.[8]

Once again, Jesus does not mince words. He does not say that they could use a bit of improvement. He does not commend them for all of the good things in their church and then gently encourage them to work on this or that. Instead, he tells them that he is about to spit them out of his mouth! No other church in Asia Minor is so strongly condemned. It is important to note that the ESV is less than ideal in this passage. Jesus does not say "I will spit you out," he says, "I am about to spit you out." He is giving them a powerful warning, not declaring what he is going to do. The threat to "spit them out" does not suggest a slap on the wrist; instead, it likely reflects a warning that he is about to utterly reject them. Similar language was used of what God did to the inhabitants of Canaan whom the Israelites displaced, and also of what he warned that he would do to the Israelites if they did not obey him (see Lev 18:24–30). It is not coincidental that Lev 18 deals with assimilation and its consequences. Just as God called the nation of Israel to be distinct from the nations around them, so he called the Laodicean Christians to cease living like the society around them. Jesus' stark warning here is reminiscent of his warning to the church at Ephesus, who risked losing their lampstand (2:5)—their very existence—if they did not repent. So what exactly was wrong with the church at Laodicea?

3. Hemer, *Letters*, 187–88.

4. Ibid., 182.

5. Ibid., 187.

6. Rudwick and Green, "Laodicean Lukewarmness," 177.

7. Ramsay, *Letters*, 305; Hemer (*Letters*, 188) points to hot springs near the modern town of Denizli as the likely source.

8. This interpretation appears to have been first set out in detail by Rudwick and Green, "Laodicean Lukewarmness," 176–78. Some argue that the unpleasant nature of the Laodicean water related to its impurity rather than its temperature. See Hemer, *Letters*, 189.

*For you say, I am rich, I have prospered, and I need nothing, not realizing that
you are wretched, pitiable, poor, blind, and naked.* (3:17)

The "for" or "because" (ὅτι, *hoti*) at the beginning of this sentence should not be
ignored, as is unfortunately done in the NIV. Essentially, this is short for, "*I am saying
this* because you say . . ." In other words, verse 17 is intended to outline the specific
nature of their lukewarmness. What has made them so offensive to Jesus? The offense
comes from their attitude of utter self-sufficiency, an attitude that is on par with overt
rebellion against God because it fails to recognize him as God, glorify him, and give
him thanks (Rom 1:21). What can be worse than for Christians to be slowly deceived
into utterly ignoring the One through whom and for whom all things were created?

Understanding the city these Christians lived in is of particular importance
for understanding the church's sin. Laodicea was an extremely wealthy city. It was
a banking center[9] and some of its citizens had enormous wealth by any standard.[10]
Like the other cities of Asia Minor, Laodicea had regularly suffered from the frequent
earthquakes in the region; but while the others were dependent on Rome for aid in
rebuilding after the devastating earthquake of AD 60, Laodicea was able to refuse
imperial financial assistance. It could say to Rome, "Thanks, but no thanks! We don't
need your charity. We're doing just fine on our own!" It was a city that not only possessed great wealth but also prided itself on its self-sufficiency. Indeed, to demonstrate
their self-sufficiency and wealth in the face of a catastrophic earthquake, they not only
rebuilt their city at their own expense but also made it bigger and better.[11] Hemer, for
example, cites the massive amphitheater that was built by a generous citizen. It had
an arena that was "900 feet long, semicircular at both ends, with continuous seating
round the whole circumference."[12] There are other examples of generous individual
donations to the rebuilding and improvement of the city during this period, which
show the extreme level of wealth that some individuals possessed in this city.

Laodicea's wealth was largely due to its strategic location at the crossroads where
the route from Ephesus to the east intersected the route from Pergumum and Sardis
that ran to the south coast.[13] This helped make it a natural center of trade for the
region. It was also a center for manufacturing.[14] In contrast, although Hierapolis continued to be a center for religion, medicine, and a wool industry, Colossae was on the
decline and may have never recovered from the earthquake of AD 60.

---

9. Ramsay, *Letters*, 307.

10. Hemer (*Letters*, 192) points to Hiero, who in the first century BC "bequeathed to the city more
than 2,000 talents and embellished it with many public works."

11. Ibid., 194–95. It is quite possible that their independent nature stemmed in part from past
Roman abuse and oppressive taxation (see ibid., 202–3).

12. Ibid., 194.

13. Ibid., 179–80.

14. Cf. ibid., 181.

As we examine Jesus' charge against the Christians in Laodicea, we find that as with the church at Sardis there was a fundamental contrast between appearances and reality. The Laodicean Christians viewed themselves as rich, like the city around them. They lived in the greatest city in the Lycus Valley[15] and had all that they could possibly need. Like the other inhabitants of their city, they were living the good life. Ramsay notes that Laodicea was a "successful trading city, the city of bankers and finance, which could adapt itself to the needs and wishes of others, ever pliable and accommodating, full of the spirit of compromise."[16] Pride in riches and commitment to self-reliance had not been abandoned when these Christians professed allegiance to Jesus Christ. Their culture had been brought into the church, and apparently was even being celebrated with great pride. They had assimilated without realizing how grossly offensive this was to Jesus. They had convinced themselves that they could swear allegiance to Jesus and continue with business as usual, that they could follow Jesus while continuing to pursue the "Laodicean Dream." Like many of us, though, the Laodiceans were suffering from a serious case of self-deception. As Jesus' stark warning to this group of believers makes clear, such a mindset, which is rampant in North American Christianity, is ultimately fatal. In reality, the Laodicean believers were "wretched, pitiable, poor, blind, and naked." They were actually in desperate straits. They had exchanged the wealth of God's kingdom for the superficial riches of this life. Thus, Jesus has a word of counsel for them in verse 18.

> *I counsel you to buy from me gold refined by fire, so that you may be rich, and white garments so that you may clothe yourself and the shame of your nakedness may not be seen, and salve to anoint your eyes, so that you may see.* (3:18)

Jesus' prescription for spiritual health responds directly to his diagnosis in the previous verse. He has just told them that they are poor, blind, and naked. Now, he exhorts them to come to him for true riches to solve their poverty problem, to come to him for white clothes to address their nakedness, and to come to him for eye salve to address their blindness. But what does Jesus mean by the counsel that he gives to the Laodiceans? He appears to be drawing on well-known local realities once again (Reading Instruction #4) to create a rhetorical hotspot that will make his exhortation more forceful.

Yes, Laodicea was a city with ample supplies of gold, but its banks were filled with the gold of this world, and such gold brought with it all sorts of temptations, some of which had ensnared the Laodicean Christians. This is why Jesus counsels them not just to come to him for gold, but for "gold refined in the fire." Worldly riches pollute; riches from Jesus have been refined and are pure. Those who pursue the former will find destruction; those who pursue the latter will find life and communion with the One whose reign will never end.

15. Ibid., 178.
16. Ramsay, *Letters*, 312.

Laodicea was also well known for the distinctive wool that it produced, which had a glossy black color that made it particularly appealing: "The area around Laodicea produces excellent sheep, remarkable not only for the softness of their wool, in which they surpass even those of Miletus, but also for their raven color. And they make a great deal of revenue from them."[17] It would have been difficult to miss the contrast Jesus draws between Laodicea's famous black clothing and the white clothes that he offers. The white clothes, then, not only represent purity, but also represent being clothed in the attire of a citizen of heaven rather than the attire of a wealthy citizen of Laodicea. He is thus calling this church to stop being infatuated by what the culture around them had to offer and look to him both to satisfy them and to define their identity.

Finally, Laodicea was known for its famous school of medicine[18] that utilized, among other things, a powder (more likely than an ointment)[19] for treating ears and eyes.[20] Residents of the city, then, including Christians, would have typically looked to local doctors to treat eye problems. With the resources of their impressive city they had an answer for everything. Jesus, though, makes it clear that the type of vision problem that they have cannot be cured by anyone but him. They need to abandon their self-sufficiency and humbly come to him for help.

We should not be surprised that Jesus' exhortation is somewhat paradoxical if read literally. How can the Laodiceans buy anything—let alone gold—if they are as poor as he says? The answer should be obvious by now. As we have encountered the repeated exhortations to be "overcomers," nowhere has there been any indication that Jesus' followers can achieve such status through wealth or any worldly asset. This does not mean, however, that real wealth, real honor, and real health cannot be obtained from Jesus. To "buy" real wealth his followers must be faithful to him, stalwart in their devotion to him even in the face of economic ruin or death. The price may seem high, but only when one fails to recognize the priceless nature of that which is obtained from the hand of Jesus and the horrific nature of the alternative, both of which are vividly described at the end of Revelation.

> *Those whom I love, I reprove and discipline, so be zealous and repent.* [20]*Behold, I stand at the door and knock. If anyone hears my voice and opens the door, I will come in to him and eat with him, and he with me.* (3:19–20)

In the midst of Jesus' stinging denunciation of the Laodicean church's present state, he extends a gracious opportunity to repent. Indeed, that is his whole reason for

---

17. Strabo, *Geogr.* 12.8.16; my translation.

18. See ibid., 12.8.20.

19. Ramsay, *Letters*, 317.

20. Ibid., 309. Hemer (*Letters*, 196–99) notes that although the use of eye salve at Laodicea is an inference rather than something clearly referred to in the literature of the time, there is strong evidence for this inference.

exposing their self-deception in the first place. He deeply cares for them and therefore he rebukes them. At the beginning of this book we considered the question of whether our typical understanding of Rev 3:20 is appropriate. Is Jesus calling unbelievers to open the door of their hearts to him? If not, what does Jesus really mean here? The answer is quite simple when this verse is read within the context of the message to the church in Laodicea. Jesus is painting a picture of the preceding words in verse 19 and reinforcing his exhortation to "be zealous and repent." In another shocking indictment he implies that the Laodiceans have become so deluded that they do not even recognize that he is no longer among them when they gather together to worship him. He is outside waiting to be let back in. That is a desperate situation that requires urgent and decisive countermeasures.

What will it take for the Laodicean Christians to repent? They must "be zealous" or "be earnest" (NIV), which involves changing their desires; and they must change their ways. They must stop seeking the pleasures that Laodicean culture affords them, stop celebrating their self-sufficiency that has led them to be oblivious to God's absence, and turn to Jesus as the one who is to shape and control every area of their lives. They need to confess anew that "Jesus is Lord," acknowledge their utter dependence on him, and turn from following their own path. A veneer of devotion to Jesus is simply not enough; in fact, it cannot mask the idolatry of trying to love the world and love God at the same time. If, though, the Laodiceans would repent of their self-sufficiency (and hedonism) and humbly invite Jesus to reign in their lives, the result would be sweet fellowship, which is pictured here as sharing a meal together.[21] The language in verse 20 thus echoes what we read in the beautiful promise found in 1:3. Hearing is not enough. One must hear and respond accordingly. For the Laodiceans, keeping Jesus' words is portrayed as opening the door and letting him back into the church where he can reign as its rightful king.

> *The one who conquers, I will grant him to sit with me on my throne, as I also conquered and sat down with my Father on his throne.* [22]*He who has an ear, let him hear what the Spirit says to the churches.* (3:21–22)

The message to Laodicea, and the messages to the seven churches as a whole, ends with one final promise to overcomers, a promise that is very similar to the promise given to overcomers in Thyatira (2:26–27). The distinctive prerogative of the Messiah (ruling the nations with a rod of iron) is to be shared with faithful followers of the Messiah. Two things are distinctive about the way Jesus presents his promise to overcomers in Laodicea. First, he specifically refers to them sitting with him on his throne. As we will see in the next chapter, Jesus' reference to the throne in this final

---

21. "Particularly in the Roman period, there was a strong link between meals (*convivia*) and friendship (*amicitia*). Philo viewed meals as a sign of 'genuine friendship,' while Cato the Elder considered meals 'the very best promoter of friendship' (Plutarch, *Cat. Maj.* 25.2). For Seneca, having a meal without the company of friends was unthinkable (*Ep.* 19.10)." See Culy, *Echoes of Friendship*, 142.

promise to overcomers is strategically located here because it allows him to bridge into the throne-room scene of Rev 4–5 and use those chapters to make the profundity of his promise to this church that much more stark. Jesus' promise to overcomers, however, also draws a clear correlation between faithfulness to God and the reward that follows. Just as Jesus, "who for the joy that was set before him endured the cross, despising the shame, and is seated at the right hand of the throne of God" (Heb 12:2), so his followers, though they rightly despise the shame that they will face in this world if they live lives of devotion to him, are called to endure in light of the reward that is to follow, here expressed as sitting with him on his throne, reigning with him.

Jesus has likely also created another rhetorical hotspot here. Hemer points out that in 40 BC, when Labienus Parthicus invaded Asia, no city was able to resist his power until he reached Laodicea, where under the leadership of the orator Zeno and his son Polemo, the city stood firm against him. As a result Polemo was granted a throne.[22] Jesus thus draws on a key feature of the civic identity of Laodiceans (Reading Instruction #4) to strengthen his call for them to overcome. "The general appropriateness of Rev. 3.21 to the church in a city which had provided a dynasty of kings is apparent, especially as we have reason to think that its character was much influenced by this family."[23]

LAODICEA: PROFILE OF A CHURCH

To the last of the seven churches of Asia Minor Jesus identifies himself as the faithful and true witness, setting himself in stark contrast to a church that had utterly failed to live as his faithful witnesses. Although he is the one with whom there is certainty ("the Amen"), these Christians had chosen to put their stock in what their city had to offer instead. Like their fellow citizens in Laodicea they wore their self-sufficiency as a badge of honor and viewed it as one of their highest values. The very ones who viewed themselves as rich beyond measure, however, were actually spiritual skid row bums. Consequently, Jesus sharply rebukes them, essentially telling them that their utter disregard for him makes him want to vomit. His rebuke, though, does not simply speak to his feelings toward them; rather, it threatens them with utter rejection if they do not repent of their self-sufficiency and self-centeredness. They desperately needed to recognize their spiritual poverty and humbly come to him so that they could be truly rich. They needed to recognize that they had relegated him to the church parking lot, all the while pretending that they were pleasing him through their "worship." In an amazing offer of grace, despite this horrible mistreatment and the fact that these Christians had come to value the "stuff" of this world far more than Jesus himself, Jesus offers to come and commune with these believers anew if they will simply turn from their self-seeking lives and re-embrace his lordship. To such overcomers Jesus

22. Hemer, *Letters*, 205.
23. Ibid., 206.

also offers the unthinkable: they will sit with him on his throne. The letter to the church in Laodicea is thus a message that carries the harshest condemnation *and* the most striking statement of grace, reminding us that what Jesus says here is true: "Those whom I love, I reprove and discipline" (3:19).

15

Jesus' Message to the Church in Laodicea
The Rest of the Story

Christians in Laodicea no doubt would have been shocked by the contrast between their message and the messages to the other six churches of Asia Minor. Jesus seemed downright gentle with the earlier churches by comparison; they themselves are not commended for anything! They would have also, though, been able to glean from the earlier messages what their repentance must look like. Each of the other churches in some way illustrated a life centered on devotion to Jesus. Such a life will be characterized by "toil" and "patient endurance" (2:2; 3:10), guarding against false teachers (2:2, 14–16, 20–24) and clinging to Jesus' teachings (2:25; 3:3), bearing up for the sake of Jesus' name (2:3), and hating the practices of those who promote assimilation (2:6). It will be characterized by faith and service and growth in their impact for God's glory (2:19). It will be characterized by willingness to pay the price for devotion to Jesus and resist the temptation to deny your faith in him (2:13) even if it costs you your life (2:10). It will be characterized by a commitment not to soil your clothes through assimilating to the culture around you (3:4–5).

In short, the commendations that Jesus gives to the other churches of Asia Minor would have served as powerful reminders of the type of life to which followers of Christ are called. They are called to live lives that are distinct from the world around them and centered on bringing glory to the One who appeared to John on the island of Patmos in terrifying glory (1:12–16) and was now speaking directly to them. That the risen Christ is alone worthy of such devotion is then reinforced in the visions that follow.

REVELATION 4–5: THE MESSAGE TO LAODICEA

As we move from the final initial message to the seven churches in Rev 3 into Rev 4–5 we encounter one of the most obvious examples of the careful literary craftsmanship (specifically, intratextual connections) that is evident throughout Revelation. It is not to the church in Sardis that Jesus promises the right to sit with him on his throne; this promise is reserved for overcomers in Laodicea. And while it likely is chosen in part because it would have resonated deeply with citizens of a city who had experienced an "overcomer" in their civic history being granted a throne (Polemo), it also meshed nicely with what is coming next in Revelation. Jesus first promises a throne to overcomers in 3:21, and then unveils a spectacular vision of what the throne looks like in Rev 4–5.

As was noted earlier, the word "throne" (θρόνος, *thronos*) occurs nineteen times in these two chapters alone. There is no question that Rev 4–5, along with the rest of the book, are intended to remind God's people that he is the One who is seated on the throne reigning supreme. While Christians in Smyrna would have been encouraged by the reminder of God's absolute sovereignty in the midst of a world where it appears that Caesar wields absolute power, those in Laodicea would have taken something very different from these chapters. Revelation 4–5 portrays God in all of his regal splendor. His throne room makes Caesar's magnificent throne room in the greatest city on earth look like a garbage dump. The One seated on the throne in heaven can barely be described with human words. His appearance can only be compared to sparkling precious gems, and he gives off an aura like a bright green rainbow (4:3). He is surrounded by twenty-four noble rulers wearing brilliant garments and golden crowns, who are seated on their own thrones (4:4), and they cast their crowns before the One on the ultimate throne and worship him (4:10–11). With them are four majestic creatures, unlike anything in this world, who incessantly worship the One on the throne (4:6–8). God's throne is a place that inspires awe and fear as "flashes of lightning, and rumblings and peals of thunder" (4:5) emanate from it. The Laodiceans would have been left with no question that the throne at the center of the vision is a throne like no other, and the One who is seated on it is One who is like no other. And yet, Jesus promises overcomers in Laodicea that they will sit with him on his throne (3:21)! How can this be? How indeed, particularly for those who have sunk so far into their self-sufficiency that they had been living as if this Glorious One did not even exist?

The throne room scene in Rev 4–5 thus serves to overwhelm the senses of those who have been given such a shocking promise. He through whom all things were made (3:14; John 1:3; Heb 1:2) actually promises an infinitesimal part of the universe he created—Christians in Laodicea who overcome—that they will reign with him. This is an astounding promise intended to shake these Christians out of their self-reliance and apathy toward God. And it is a promise of astounding grace, because it is offered to Christians in Asia Minor of whom Jesus had nothing good to say and yet to whom he offers the richest of rewards if they will but repent of their sin.

Although it is impossible to be certain what precisely Jesus was intending to communicate through the vision of the twenty-four elders in Rev 4, 5, 7, 11, 14, and 19, the description of these individuals would have likely spoke most powerfully to Christians in Laodicea. Just as Jesus promises overcomers in Laodicea that they will sit with him on his throne (3:21), so the twenty-four elders are each seated on their own thrones (4:4; 11:16), which surround the throne of God (4:4), and each of them wears a crown (4:4, 10). These two images both speak of the elders' position of authority. It would have been difficult not to think back to Jesus' words to the twelve apostles in Matt 19:28: "Truly, I say to you, in the new world, when the Son of Man will sit on his glorious throne, you who have followed me will also sit on twelve thrones, judging the twelve tribes of Israel" (see also Luke 22:30). It is possible, then, that the twenty-four elders represent a combination of the twelve apostles and the twelve patriarchs, the leaders of God's new and old covenant people now united into one people worshiping the one true God.

There is more, though, in these chapters for Christians in Laodicea. Revelation 5 provides a vivid picture of how Jesus overcame. He is the divine Lamb who is worthy of worship along with the Father (5:12–13), who overcame (5:5) by denying himself, taking up his cross, and giving his life to ransom "people for God from every tribe and language and people and nation" (5:9). Moreover, Revelation goes on to make clear that the whole purpose in redeeming the Laodiceans is so that they might become "a kingdom and priests to our God, and . . . reign on the earth" (5:10). Again, Jesus not only invites his followers to reign with him in the age to come, but he also establishes for them a clear path to the throne, a path that requires self-denial and self-sacrifice rather than the self-indulgence and self-sufficiency that were characteristic of life in the church in Laodicea and are far too often characteristic of life in the church today. Jesus ransomed a people for God so that they can serve the One who is on the throne as his priests and faithful subjects.

REVELATION 6: THE MESSAGE TO LAODICEA

The vivid description of the suffering that is coming in Rev 6 would have been a wake-up call to those in the church in Laodicea who were quite content with the good life their city had to offer them and had thus grown complacent in their relationship with God. They thought they had everything they needed, and far more; but all that they had and all that they owned was subject to their city remaining at peace. A day was coming, Jesus reminds them, when foreign conquering armies would disrupt their lives of ease and self-indulgence (6:1–2), when enjoying the pleasures of Laodicea would be replaced with bloodshed (6:3–4, 7–8), when full bellies and tables loaded with the finest foods would be replaced with famine (6:5–6, 7–8), and when their robust health and world's best medical care would be replaced with pestilence and plague (6:7–8). Their apparent control over their own lives would be so undone that they would even be at the mercy of marauding wild beasts (6:8). Their self-sufficiency would be replaced with ever present questions of where their next meal would come from, how they would evade the sword, how they would avoid the epidemic diseases that were spreading like wildfire, and how they could hide from the wild animals stalking whoever had survived the other threats. Revelation 6, thus, would have provided Christians in Laodicea with the realization that the fairytale lives that many in their city were living were tenuous at best. An hour of trial was coming, and they needed to stop living like Laodiceans and start living as followers of the Lamb. God's judgment was coming on a world that was in rebellion against him, and those who professed to be his people but lived like he did not even exist could expect no better.

REVELATION 7: THE MESSAGE TO LAODICEA

This message would have been reinforced by the account of the sealing of the 144,000. Catastrophe is coming to this world, but before it comes God will graciously seal "the servants of our God" (7:3). For many in the churches in Asia Minor this promise would have been reassuring, but for a church where Jesus had been relegated to the church parking lot and was waiting for an invitation to come back inside (3:20), it was difficult to make a case that they were currently servants of God. In fact, they were a people who were proud to declare that they "need nothing" (3:17), God included. Such self-sufficient, independent, God-ignoring people could hardly call themselves "servants of God" in any practical sense, though Revelation as a whole is a call to them to re-embrace their God-given identity as his servants. Even the most deluded church that has slowly squeezed God out of their corporate life can come to its senses, hear Jesus knocking on the door, and through repentance invite him back in to reign where he belongs. The result will be incredible intimacy with him, which is pictured as sitting down for a meal together in 3:20. Turning to him will also result in their ability to gain white garments, the very garments of those who will spend eternity in the very presence of God (7:13–17). Those are the garments they should desire, not the fashionable black garments of the Laodicean elite.

REVELATION 8–9: THE MESSAGE TO LAODICEA

As Rev 7 raised sobering questions ("Are we servants of God?" "Will we be sealed to protect us from God's coming wrath given the fact that Jesus is currently about to spit us out of his mouth?"), so the beginning of Rev 8 forces the question of whether or not Christians in Laodicea are on the right side as the hour of trial approaches. The beginning of Rev 8 provides a vivid picture of God hearing and attending to the prayers of his people. The "prayers of all the saints" are pictured rising up before God in 8:3–4.

Again, for Christians in most of the churches of Asia Minor this would have been comforting and reassuring, but for the First Church of Self-Sufficiency in Laodicea, they would have recognized that prayer had long since become obsolete for them. Those who need nothing have no need to turn to God. And so, once again they would have been faced with the stark reality that as Jesus visually and verbally portrays "the saints" throughout Revelation, the descriptions he uses do not fit with their lifestyle. This, of course, would have reinforced why he is ready to spit them out of his mouth (3:16).

Like the vision of the seals, the portrayal of the destruction that will come through the seven trumpet judgments would have reminded Christians in Laodicea that the things they value so much, the "stuff" that has come to define who they are, were temporary at best. It would all go up in smoke one day very soon. It was part of this world's system on which God was going to pour out his wrath; and all of the wealth that they possessed would not be able to protect them from the global catastrophe that was coming. There would be no rebuilding this time for those who stood opposed to God or for those who professed to be his children but who lived as functional atheists. This is why it was so critical that they reassess their values and come to Jesus in humility to get "gold refined in the fire," riches that will last. For this to happen, though, Christians in Laodicea would need to separate themselves from the culture around them. Although they did not likely literally worship "idols of gold and silver and bronze and stone and wood" (9:20), like the other citizens of Laodicea, riches had certainly become an idol for them that had replaced their devotion to Jesus Christ in such subtle yet profound ways that they were not even aware that he was no longer present among them when they gathered to worship him.

In the "wealthy West" we certainly face the same temptation. In churches where the Bible is actually preached we frequently hear warnings against all sorts of sins, particularly the sexual varieties, but we rarely hear exhortations to deal drastically with the greed that not only pervades our society, but has also gained a solid foothold within the church. We are not often reminded that the one sin that is explicitly associated with idolatry in the New Testament is the sin of greed (Col 3:5). We live as if ten percent—at best—of what we have belongs to God and the rest can be freely used for our own self-indulgence. We give more to those who serve us our food in restaurants than to God! "God is clearly 'blessing' us, so we had better enjoy that blessing to the fullest," is our motto. Such thinking, though, flies in the face of Jesus' clear command that if anyone would be his follower, he must deny himself and take up his cross daily and follow him (Luke 9:23). Self-denial is central to the life of a Christian. Yet, although there is no way around that, it is rarely preached in our self-sufficient, self-centered, self-indulgent churches. Both at a corporate and at an individual level we need to ask whether Jesus is outside of our life and/or outside of our church knocking and waiting to be invited back in where he belongs.

Revelation is written, in part, to those who are facing intense persecution and need to be warned not to give in and abandon their allegiance to Jesus. Far more Christians in Asia Minor in the first century, however, were facing temptation from a considerably more subtle source. They were living in the "Wealthy East" of their day. Life was good; they had everything they needed; and they, like the Israelites before them, faced the temptation of forgetting God as a result (see Deut 8:11–20). Most Christians are quick to turn to God in their time of need; but what happens in times of plenty? What happens when everything is going well? In such times, being careful to seek God with all our might does not seem nearly so urgent. This, of course, is why we find in Proverbs a prayer that every Christian should have the courage to pray, "give me neither poverty nor riches; feed me with the food that is needful for me, ⁹lest I be full and deny you and say, 'Who is the LORD?' or lest I be poor and steal and profane the name of my God" (Prov 30:8–9). This, in fact, is the essence of the prayer Jesus taught to his disciples: "Give us this day our daily bread" (Matt 6:11). It is not "Give us today a high paying job" or "Give us this day a million dollars to put in our bank account so that we can feel secure." Instead, it is the prayer of one who is "taking care" lest he forget the LORD his God when he has far more than he actually needs (Deut 8:14). Christians in Laodicea appear to have ignored the strong warnings in Deut 8. They viewed themselves as rich and in need of nothing. And just as Deut 8:19–20 strongly warned the nation of Israel that if they became self-sufficient and began trusting in their wealth, which had ultimately come from the Lord rather than their own ingenuity and hard work, they would face destruction, so Jesus warns the Laodicean Christians who had succumbed to this very temptation that he is about to spit them out of his mouth (3:16).

REVELATION 10: THE MESSAGE TO LAODICEA

The words of the mighty angel in 10:6 would have helped convey the sense of urgency that Jesus had already communicated to Christians in Laodicea. They need to "be zealous and repent" because a time is soon coming when there will be no more delay (10:6). The vision of the sweet and sour scroll, on the other hand, would have been a subtle reminder to Christians living the high life in Laodicea that Jesus' followers cannot expect a life of ease. To follow him does bring incredible blessing. Indeed, life in Christ is as "sweet as honey" (10:10); but it also consists of suffering. To follow Jesus will bring a backlash from the society around you rather than affirmation that you are a valued member of the community. Without embracing these twin effects of embracing the gospel in this life, no one can be an effective witness for Christ; nor can they expect to be an overcomer.

REVELATION 11: THE MESSAGE TO LAODICEA

As Christians in Laodicea listened to the words of Rev 11, they would have likely first been struck by the significance of the counting of the worshipers in the temple of God (11:1). They had been told by the Lord Jesus himself that when they gather together to worship him, he was not even present. He was outside knocking on the door and asking to be let back in (3:20). Christians today are far too quick to use passages like Matt 18:20 as proof texts to insist that whenever Christians gather together God is there with them: "For where two or three are gathered in my name, there am I among them." And so we sing "God is here, God is here" in an effort to convince ourselves that we are in the presence of God; but are we? The Laodiceans certainly may have sung songs celebrating God's presence among them, but Jesus was not among them as they were singing. If Jesus promises to be present when two or three believers are gathered, how could he be absent when the entire church in Laodicea gathered? The answer is found in the little phrase Jesus uses in Matt 18:20: "in my name." When his followers gather to worship, they need to gather in a way that is consistent with his name, i.e., in a manner that is consistent with his character. When they gather together to worship, they need to come in the fear of the Lord, seeking his glory rather than coming with their own selfish motives. Those who come with lives that grieve the Holy Spirit and show no hint of repentance should not expect to meet with God. Those who come quenching the Holy Spirit should not expect to meet with God. And those who come with utter disregard for their fellow believers, as the Corinthians were doing at times when they celebrated the Lord's Supper, should only expect to meet with God's strong judgment rather than experience his sweet presence (see 1 Cor 11:30–31). Like the Corinthians, the Laodiceans needed to take a careful look in the mirror and gain a right perspective on their spiritual state before it was too late.

Ultimately, the church in Laodicea appears to have been very closely aligned with the city of Laodicea. Christians in this church looked very much like the world around them: prosperous, self-sufficient, and living the good life. There was nothing in their lifestyle that led the citizens of Laodicea to mark them out as different. Sure, they gathered for a meeting once a week, sang songs, and listened to someone give a lecture, but that was not uncommon among other groups in the city as well. There is an important lesson here. When the world is comfortable having us around, we need to ask whether we are living as overcomers, and indeed whether we are followers of Jesus at all. Remember the words of Jesus: "If you were of the world, the world would love you as its own; but because you are not of the world, but I chose you out of the world, therefore the world hates you" (John 15:19). Jesus drives home this point to Christians in Laodicea with the vision of the two witnesses. These prophets of God cannot be tolerated by a world that they are calling to repentance. Indeed, the world hates them so much that when they are finally killed by the beast (11:7) they throw a party (11:10)! This is not a picture of Christians meeting their community on their own turf and thus being warmly welcomed. Instead, it is a picture of those who live lives worthy of the gospel bearing faithful witness to Jesus and as a result being rejected, persecuted, and killed.

To be loved and accepted by the society around us is usually evidence that we belong to the world rather than to Jesus. Jesus clearly told his followers that they would "be hated by all for my name's sake" (Matt 10:22 || Mark 13:13 || Luke 21:17). The world will hate Jesus' followers because they do not belong to the world even as he did not belong to the world and was therefore hated and killed (John 17:14). Followers of Jesus cannot expect to enjoy the benefits of a world that is under the control of the evil one (1 John 5:19), but must rather expect to endure suffering at the hands of the world. This is the message of Revelation, as is the reminder that "the one who endures to the end will be saved" (Matt 10:22 || Mark 13:13). Suffering and endurance will culminate in a future reward, just as Jesus had promised earlier: "Blessed are you when people hate you and when they exclude you and revile you and spurn your name as evil, on account of the Son of Man! [23]Rejoice in that day, and leap for joy, for behold, your reward is great in heaven; for so their fathers did to the prophets" (Luke 6:22–23).

For Christians in Laodicea the question was simple: Are you viewed by the society around you like the two witnesses of God, or are you viewed as good hedonistic Laodiceans who fit right in with the society around you? And Jesus reminds them that they dare not put off answering that question because the day was soon coming when all would recognize that "The kingdom of the world has become the kingdom of our Lord and of his Christ, and he shall reign forever and ever" (11:15). On that day, people will either sit with Jesus on his throne (3:21), or will be excluded from his presence, since, as Jesus makes clear elsewhere, "Not everyone who says to me, 'Lord, Lord,' will enter the kingdom of heaven, but the one who does the will of my Father who is in heaven" (Matt 7:21). To be about our own business rather than our Father's business, to be pursuing our own pleasures rather than our Father's pleasure is to be excluded from the kingdom as those who make claims of belonging to Jesus but show the contrary to be true by being disinterested in the will of the Father. How easy it is to fall into this very trap when we live in a society like Laodicea, where we have very few real practical needs and an abundance of disposable wealth! A reward is coming to those who fear God's name (11:18), but for those who have turned their backs on God within the church itself, Jesus only holds out the prospect of being spit out of his mouth.

REVELATION 12: THE MESSAGE TO LAODICEA

To Christians in Laodicea who had been promised the incredible privilege of sitting with Jesus on his throne if they lived as overcomers (3:21), Rev 12 would have reminded them that after his resurrection Jesus was "was caught up to God and to his throne" (12:5), and Satan was cast down to earth where he established his throne (2:13) and now actively leads the whole world astray (12:9), even attempting to deceive the people of God. For Christians in Laodicea who had failed to grapple with the reality that "the love of money is a root of all kinds of evils" (1 Tim 6:10), Satan's job was much easier. He was actively engaged in making war against God's people (12:17), but for those whom he can dupe into a life of self-indulgence and self-sufficiency he has little need to make war, because he has already achieved his goal of turning them away from God.

REVELATION 13: THE MESSAGE TO LAODICEA

Those who resist the temptation to be swallowed up by all that the culture around them has to offer, on the other hand, will face the wrath of the dragon and the beast. Satan will take drastic measures to snuff out "those who keep the commandments of God and hold to the testimony of Jesus" (12:17); and his emissary, the beast, will be "allowed to make war on the saints and to conquer them" (13:7). The Laodicean Christians need to be reminded that the day has come to make a choice. Will they selfishly pursue their own comfort, pleasure, and security by compromising their devotion to Jesus so that they can continue to enjoy the "Laodicean Dream"? Or will they choose lives of devotion to the Lord Jesus that mark them as belonging to him just as clearly as a tattoo in the middle of their forehead? Those who associate with the beast and the society around them that is under the control of the evil one (1 John 5:19) will be able to enjoy the benefits of that society. Those who refuse to do so will not even be able to buy food and clothing (13:17), let alone enjoy what their city has to offer. One is left wondering how many people in the church in Laodicea after hearing Jesus' words of correction "went away sorrowful" like the rich young ruler (see Matt 19:16–22) because they could not bear the thought of trading in all their stuff for a life in which they would be locked out of the economy because of their devotion to Jesus.

REVELATION 14: THE MESSAGE TO LAODICEA

As we have already seen, the vision of the 144,000 in Rev 14 highlights the fact that the blessing this group enjoys is a result of the lives of purity they had lived in this world (14:4). They had refused to assimilate to the world around them, steadfastly repudiating their culture's call to indulge in what it had to offer. Consequently, they had "been redeemed from mankind as firstfruits for God and the Lamb" (14:4). This is a message that Christians in Laodicean needed to hear: God had purchased them with the precious blood of Jesus. They were no longer their own; so it was absurd to think that they could go on living for themselves. They belonged to Jesus; but had failed to grapple with this fundamental truth of the faith (1 Cor 6:19–20). Jesus did not just purchase their salvation; he purchased them. And as Paul goes on to make clear, the only logical response is to "glorify God in your body" (1 Cor 6:20). Those who recognize they have been purchased by God will never embrace an attitude of self-sufficiency. Nor will they live their lives pursuing their own pleasures. A slave relies every day on his master to supply food, clothing, housing, etc. A slave does not pursue his own agenda, but is set on carrying out the wishes of his master. A slave does not seek to please himself, but rather to please his master. So also, we are to rely fully on God to meet all of our needs as we steadfastly focus our lives on being about our Father's business rather than pursuing our own agenda.

After all, the "eternal gospel" is a call to "fear God and give him glory" (14:6), not ignore God and be apathetic toward his absence from our church. Our lives are to be fixed on worshiping the One who made heaven and earth (14:7), not indulging ourselves in what the evil one's realm has to offer. For that realm, symbolized by Babylon, is going to be destroyed (14:8), and those who give allegiance to the beast who rules that realm will also be condemned to eternal torment (14:11). Thus, Christians in Laodicea needed to be careful to pay attention to the "call for the endurance of the saints, those who keep the commandments of God and their faith in Jesus" (14:12). Those who keep their faith in Jesus will not be embraced by the culture around them. Instead, they will be persecuted and will thus need to endure as they await his return in glory.

REVELATION 15–16: THE MESSAGE TO LAODICEA

As Christians in Laodicea grappled with the importance of abandoning assimilation to their culture's hedonism and self-sufficiency, their attention would have been drawn to the picture in Rev 15 of "those who had conquered the beast and its image and the number of its name, standing beside the sea of glass with harps of God in their hands" (15:2) singing songs of praise to the One who had delivered them. This picture of victorious Christians enjoying God's presence would be encouraging, but to be among this group of people the Laodiceans would have to repent of their association with the beast and their current apathy toward God's absence among them. Their self-indulgence and self-sufficiency spoke loudly of their willingness to compromise in their engagement with their city so that they could enjoy the wealth and benefits it had to offer. Their behavior raised very real questions of where their allegiance was located. Was it with Jesus, the Lamb who was slain, the one whose followers were hated by this world? Or was it with the beast who from the beginning of time has led people to think that they can get by just fine without God. Those who bore the mark of the beast would face the wrath of God, this time in the form of painful sores (16:2). And while the Laodicean Christians were likely not overtly participating in idolatry or emperor worship, their lives appear to have "marked" them as being in league with the Satanic powers that ruled their city. They were getting along very well in their city, even though faithful followers of Jesus elsewhere were being persecuted and even losing their lives (16:6). Repentance was urgently needed for these deceived Christians. To be among those who sang, "Who will not fear, O Lord, and glorify your name?"

(15:4), they would need first to repent of their apathetic attitude toward God that led to an astounding ignorance of his absence among them. To be blessed with those who stay awake as they await Jesus' return (16:15), they would first need to wake up and realize their desperate condition. Jesus, in his grace, tells it like it is. They thought they were rich, but their type of wealth would get them nowhere in the end. This would have become particularly clear as they moved into Rev 17 and 18.

REVELATION 17–18: THE MESSAGE TO LAODICEA

Perhaps no church in the "Wealthy East" of Asia Minor had more richly benefited from the wealth of their city than Christians in Laodicea. In contrast to wealthy individuals like Barnabas in the early years of the church, who willingly liquidated assets in order to help care for those in need (see Acts 4:36–37), Christians in Laodicea appear to have been eager to grow increasingly wealthy without any concern for being good stewards of what God had entrusted to them. They were proud to be rich, and proud of the independence their wealth brought them. Revelation 17–18 provides the Laodicean Christians with a picture of what it has taken to achieve their wealth—they have been cavorting with a prostitute—and then sketches a vivid picture of what is going to happen to the Babylons of this world.

First, we see a vivid picture of the great prostitute's opulence. She flaunts her wealth, dressed in purple and scarlet (royal colors), dazzling with gold, jewels, and pearls, and parading her extravagance by drinking from a cup of gold (17:4). This "if-you've-got-it-flaunt-it" attitude likely would have struck very close to home with many of the Christians in Laodicea. Indeed, the extravagant show of wealth displayed in the vision of the great prostitute bears striking similarities to the extravagant wealth of Laodicea, wealth that not only captivated the populace in general but also had ensnared Christians. What Christians in Laodicea needed to be reminded of was that the great prostitute's opulence was connected to her blatant opposition to God. Instead of God's seal on her forehead like the 144,000 (7:3), which may well have read, as with the high priest of old, "Holy to the Lord" (Exod 28:36–38), her forehead had written on it "Babylon the great, mother of prostitutes and of earth's abominations" (17:5). Who did the Laodiceans want to associate with, the great prostitute or the 144,000?

The prostitute is portrayed as a global Roman-like Empire (*seven* kings represent universal authority, 17:7), with the use of "seven hills" (17:9) being a transparent reference to the city of Rome[1] and the reference to "peoples and multitudes and nations and languages" (17:15) making the imperial nature of the prostitute's authority clear. The beast comes from this empire and is allied with it (he is an eighth king who "belongs to the seven," 17:11), but he will seize power along with some other leaders (ten kings, 17:12). They will not only rebel against the Lamb and his followers (17:14),

---

1. Both in Roman literature and on Roman coins we find frequent references to Rome as the city on seven hills.

but will also turn on the prostitute and destroy her (17:16).[2] The language here is reminiscent of Nero burning Rome, apparently to make a bigger and better city for himself. Here, too, in Rev 17 we find Satanic mimicry, as the beast seizes power and then attempts to "rule all the nations with a rod of iron" (12:5).

As we move into Rev 18 and the more detailed description of Babylon's destruction, we find language that would have been particularly poignant for Christians in Laodicea. This picture of Babylon bears a striking resemblance to what some have called "unfettered capitalism" in our own day, an approach to acquiring wealth that shows no regard for who it might hurt.[3] Notice the emphasis in Rev 18 on how the merchants and kings of the earth grieve over the destruction of Babylon because through her "excessive luxuries" (NIV) they had grown fabulously wealthy (18:3; 9, 11–19). Indeed, we find repeated references to Babylon's hedonism in this chapter. Mention of the fact that "the merchants of the earth have grown rich from the power of her luxurious living" (18:3) points to Babylon's insatiable appetite for anything that will gratify its fleshly desires. This picture of a society that gives free rein to its sinful desires is reinforced in verses 7 and 9 where the verbal form of the noun used in verse 3 is utilized. In each case, it would likely be better to translate the term "hedonism" rather than "luxury."

In first century Asia Minor such hedonism was rampant. Those who embraced Rome and its ways also embraced "conspicuous consumption" ("If you've got it, flaunt it"). They were a nation of consumers that helped drive the global economy, to the degree that a global economy existed. The city of Laodicea was particularly wealthy as we have seen, and Christians in that city seem to have marched in line with the society around them, viewing themselves as rich and self-sufficient, and likely indulging in what their city, aligned with "Babylon," had to offer. The picture in Rev 17–18 of what God has in store for what they have come to value could not be more sobering. And Jesus' warning that he is about to spit them out of his mouth, much like the sudden destruction that is coming for Babylon, serves to reinforce his clarion call to "Come out of her, my people, lest you take part in her sins, lest you share in her plagues" (18:4). It is not only through avoiding sexual immorality and blatant idolatry that God's people are to be distinctive (holy), but also in how they treat wealth. Self-indulgence, hedonism, and "excessive luxuries" (18:4, NIV) do not go along with following Christ. Overcomers will never be "good consumers."

---

2. Ramsay (*Letters*, 68) argues that the reference here is to the Roman emperors who "were no true friends to Rome; they feared it, and therefore hated it, curtailed its liberties, deprived it of all its power, murdered its citizens and all its leading men, wished (like Caligula) that the whole Roman people had one single neck, and (like Nero) burned the city to the ground."

3. Note the reference to "bodies and souls of men" (my translation) in 18:13.

REVELATION 19: THE MESSAGE TO LAODICEA

Finally, we come to the glorious appearing of the Lord Jesus Christ in Rev 19 where Laodicean Christians would have once again been reminded that "the great prostitute . . . corrupted the earth by her adulteries" (19:2). The benefits that the Roman Empire offered them through participation in the life of their city invariably involved spiritual adultery. Laodicean Christians had fallen into the trap of being good citizens. They hung their Roman flag on holidays to show their patriotism, showed up for city festivals, and were on board with their city's pursuit of a better life for its citizens. What they failed to recognize was that their hearts had been corrupted by a society that was not neutral, but rather was driven by the agenda of Satan himself.

The wedding feast of the Lamb was coming and they had been caught in the very act of spiritual adultery. It was very difficult for them to claim the title of "God's holy people" (19:8) or point to righteous acts (19:8), when they had been pursuing their own comfort rather than God's purposes. They had been neither "faithful" nor "true" to Jesus, the "Faithful and True" rider on a white horse who is coming to judge and wage war (19:11). Jesus has already warned the Laodicean Christians that were he to judge them at that point, they would be found wanting. Repentance is urgently called for. For the beast, the false prophet, and all those associated with them are about to meet their end (19:19–21).

SUMMARY: JESUS' MESSAGE TO CHRISTIANS IN LAODICEA

As Christians in Laodicea encountered the "rest of the story" of Jesus' message to them in Rev 4–22, they would have no doubt been more than a little shell-shocked by his seemingly harsh indictment of their current state. "Doesn't Jesus have anything good to say about us," they may have wondered. The appropriateness of Jesus' strong rebuke, however, would have become quickly apparent as they gazed in wonder on the majesty of the One whom they had been neglecting to the extent that he had been effectively locked out of their gathering. The most spectacular beings in the universe and all the host of heaven worship the One who is seated on the throne of heaven day and night, and the church in Laodicea had not even noticed that this Glorious One was absent when they gathered together ostensibly to worship him. They had forgotten that they had been saved "to be a kingdom and priests to our God" (5:10), not to live like the world around them. They had failed to recognize how tenuous was their hold on the good life in Laodicea; for the wrath of God was about to be poured out, and all that made Laodicea "the place to be" in the Roman Empire would be taken away. And when that wrath came, it was critical that those who professed to be God's people would be found to be servants of God, since only his servants would be marked as exempt from his wrath. Revelation provides a clear picture of what it looks like to live as servants of God ("the saints"), and the contrast with those in Laodicea could not have been starker.

Urgent change was needed, change that would begin with humble confession of their sin and a fresh acknowledgment that Jesus is Lord. Their lives must begin to demonstrate that they exist to please their Master, not to please themselves. They must repent of the flagrant idolatry, otherwise known as greed, that summed up their current lifestyle. They had gained everything they could want, but in the process they had forgotten the Lord their God (cf. Deut 8:12–14). They had embraced a perspective on the Christian life that had some strong similarities to modern false gospels that promise health and wealth to God's people. They believed that following Christ would be the "sweet" life—with sweet defined in material terms—with no "bitter" element included (Rev 10:10). They had come to believe that they could live like their non-Christian neighbors and simply incorporate Jesus into the good lives that they had been enjoying. The vision of the two witnesses in Rev 11 makes it clear, though, that those who are faithful ambassadors of Christ in this world—every Christian's calling—can expect to be rejected, reviled, persecuted, and even killed. If their city accepted them because they did not see any difference in them, such acceptance provided strong evidence that they were not living for Jesus, and perhaps did not belong to him in the first place. Genuine Christians live a life in which they "fear God and give him glory" (14:6), not a life of ignoring God and indulging themselves. For, those who would enjoy God's presence later must live in God's presence now. Such people, rather than flaunting their wealth like the great prostitute of Rev 17, will relish their relationship with the King of kings and Lord of lords and boast in the eternal inheritance that awaits them. For the Laodiceans, this mean that rather than aligning themselves with their city—which bore a striking resemblance to Babylon in Rev 18—and all that it had to offer, they must "come out from her" (18:4) and live with the values of the kingdom of the Great King. To fail to do so would be to continue in spiritual adultery, a sure path to destruction.

16

Revelation 20
The Millennium in Context

ANYONE WHO HAS STUDIED the book of Revelation is well aware of the endless debates surrounding the nature of the Millennium and its relationship to the Second
Coming of Jesus Christ. At the risk of oversimplifying a complex set of issues, in my
view these debates have stemmed largely from a failure to read Rev 20 in context.
Revelation 20 is part of a larger whole, and we cannot determine what Jesus is saying
here without situating it within its context, which clearly includes a narrative chronology that runs from Rev 4–22. Beyond this, it is also crucial that we continue to ask
what this particular portion of Revelation would have meant to the original readers,
Christians living in late first-century Asia Minor. All of Revelation is a message to the
seven churches, with Rev 20, like the rest of Rev 4–22, reinforcing and driving home
the specific messages to each of the churches found in Rev 2–3. In this chapter, we
will attempt to navigate the troubled waters of the Millennium debate by using the
sure rudder of the context of Revelation. Then, in the next chapter, we will examine
more closely what Rev 20 would have meant to Christians in the seven churches of
first-century Asia Minor.

There are three primary views of the Millennium (premillennialism, postmillennialism, and amillennialism), each of which has had significant support at different
points in church history and each of which has advocates today, though premillennialism and amillennialism are the more dominant views currently. Ultimately, the
question we need to ask is not who supports which view today, but rather, which of
these views, if any, the original readers could have plausibly embraced as they read Rev
20. In Chapter 13, we examined how the book of Revelation fits, or rather does *not* fit,
with the common belief that the Rapture will precede the Great Tribulation. This view

is one form of premillennialism, typically referred to as dispensational premillennial-ism or pre-tribulational premillenialism. It not only maintains that Jesus will return in glory prior to the Millennium, but also that Jesus' Second Coming will be a two-part affair, with Second Coming Part 1 being a secret return to take his people to heaven prior to the onset of the Great Tribulation, and Second Coming Part 2 being his visible return in glory with his people accompanying him as he comes to set up his Millennial reign on earth.[1]

As I attempted to demonstrate in Chapter 13, the view that believers are removed from the action described in Rev 6–19 is completely foreign to the book of Revelation. The same believers addressed in Rev 1–3 are consistently called upon to endure what they will face under the tyrannical rule of the beast. They are called to be ready to suf-fer and to be faithful to the end. They are told that some of them will be put in prison (2:10) and many of them will suffer martyrdom (6:11). There is absolutely no indica-tion of a get-out-of-town-before-the-showdown pass that will be given to Christians. Quite the contrary, Revelation clearly called first-century Christians, and calls us, to faithful endurance in the midst of the beast's reign (13:10; 14:12); and it reminded them to be vigilant and faithful in the midst of the outpouring of God's wrath on a rebellious world with the sure knowledge that Jesus is coming soon (16:15). In short, dispensational pretribulationalism not only suffers from being a novel teaching that has only been around for the past 150 years or so, but it is heavily based on a theologi-cal system that would have been completely foreign to the original readers and does not mesh with what the book of Revelation actually says.[2]

How about postmillennialism? Based on what we know of Christians in Asia Minor in the first century, would the original readers have likely heard the book of Revelation pointing to an increasingly Christianized world leading up to the Second Coming of Jesus? In other words, does Revelation suggest that as a result of successful global evangelism society will more and more function according to God's standards, with a "millennial age" of peace and righteousness gradually being ushered in on the earth, which will then be followed by the return of Christ? If we read Rev 20 in con-text, we see just the opposite. We see frequent warnings against the insidious and se-ductive effects of a corrupt world on the church and warnings not to give in and deny the faith in the face of persecution. Jesus does not promise Christians in Smyrna that the world will soon become a better place; he promises prison and death. He does not promise the martyrs in 6:9–11 that they were among a select few who would be killed for their faith; he instead makes it clear that there is a "full number" of saints whom God has ordained to face death as followers of Jesus. He does not show Satan's power

1. Dispensational premillennialism essentially posits both a Second Coming and a Third Com-ing of Jesus that are separated by a seven-year Great Tribulation period.

2. With this statement I do not intend to dismiss dispensationalism outright. There are cer-tainly ways in which this theological system sheds important light on what God has revealed in the Scriptures.

being slowly curtailed as the world becomes more and more Christian; he shows the devil going off in a rage to wage war against followers of Jesus (12:17), ultimately culminating in his agent, the beast—the epitome of earthly evil—gaining control of the whole world and forcing the whole world, except for the elect, to rebel against God and worship him instead (13:1–17). We see a clear indication of the world becoming increasingly opposed to God and standing firm against him in their rebellion. Revelation does not paint a picture of an increasingly Christianized world at all. Instead, it paints a vivid picture of an increasingly defiant world that refuses to repent even in the face of its absolute destruction by God.

This picture is consistent with the rest of the New Testament. When asked, "Lord, will those who are saved be few?" Jesus replied, "Strive to enter through the narrow door. For many, I tell you, will seek to enter and will not be able" (Luke 13:24). Similarly, he told people that "the gate is narrow and the way is hard that leads to life, and those who find it are few" (Matt 7:14). This does not appear to fit with the notion that the world will become more and more filled with Christians leading up to the return of Christ. Likewise, the Greek text of Jesus' question in Luke 18:8 ("when the Son of Man comes, will he find faith on the earth?") expects a negative answer, not implying that there will be *no* faith on earth, but suggesting that Jesus does not expect the earth to be filled with faith when he returns. Paul clearly tells us regarding the return of Christ, "For that day will not come, unless the rebellion comes first, and the man of lawlessness is revealed, the son of destruction, [4]who opposes and exalts himself against every so-called god or object of worship, so that he takes his seat in the temple of God, proclaiming himself to be God" (2 Thess 2:3–4). This is fully consistent with the picture we find in Rev 13, but not consistent with a golden age that culminates with the Second Coming. Similarly, in 2 Tim 3:1–5, the descriptions of people "in the last days" do not reflect those who have been saved and are now living in harmony with God's purposes. Instead, this passage depicts the people of this world broadly standing in willful rebellion against God. Likewise, Jesus' words in the Gospels, just like the words of Revelation, portray a world in chaos prior to his Second Coming. In Matt 24:21–22, 29–31, for example, he does not paint a picture of a utopian society that has left the evil of its past behind as it has embraced him as Lord, and is now calmly awaiting his coming to reign on earth now that everything has been prepared for him. Instead, passages such as this picture a world of great evil and great suffering, with tribulation that exceeds all previous periods of suffering on earth.

This, in fact, is precisely what Revelation itself depicts, but in far greater detail. It begins by reminding Christians in Asia Minor that suffering is part of their calling (1:9). It then specifically predicts more suffering for some of them (2:10), reminds them of the death of Antipas (2:13), and acknowledges the frightful influence of Satan in Pergamum (2:13) and the persecution by the "synagogue of Satan" in both Smyrna (2:9) and Philadelphia (3:9). In all of this there is absolutely no indication that Christians should hold on "because things are going to get better." Instead, we find repeated calls to be prepared to endure even unto death. The rebellion is coming. The beast is waiting in the wings. Life is going to get much worse than it is now for followers of Jesus, to the point of not only being unable to buy the necessities of life or make a living (13:17), but also to the point where followers of Jesus will be conquered by the beast and killed (13:7). How are they to respond? Their lives must be characterized by endurance and faith (13:10). That the endurance Jesus calls them to is absolute in nature is driven home not only by the repetition of the call to endurance in 14:12, but also by the not so subtle reminder that follows in 14:13: "And I heard a voice from heaven saying, 'Write this: Blessed are the dead who die in the Lord from now on.'"

All of this is clearly portrayed in Revelation as the period of time leading up to the return of Jesus Christ. It is a time when followers of Jesus, rather than being embraced by a Christianized world, can expect rejection, suffering, and even death. Indeed, the world will have a global party to celebrate when two prominent followers of Jesus are murdered (11:10)! It is a time of utter faithlessness when God's people are called to separate themselves from the wickedness that pervades the world (18:4–5). It is only after God has destroyed "Babylon," the persecutor of the saints (18:20, 24), that Jesus will return (Rev 19), avenge the blood of his servants (19:2), and set up his millennial reign (Rev 20). And when he returns, he will not be greeted with open arms, but rather with a "final" rebellion (19:19).[3]

Plain and simple, in the book of Revelation Jesus does not hold out for his followers in Asia Minor hope for a brighter tomorrow in which this world comes to its senses and gladly bows before him and joins the church. Instead, he makes it crystal clear that Satan will fight with all his might, right to the bitter end, to turn this world away from God (Rev 13) and attempt to destroy the people of God (12:17). Ultimately, he will have great success on both counts (13:7–8), but only for a short time (12:12).

Postmillennialism, then, like dispensational premillennialism, is simply not a plausible way to understand Rev 20, at least not if you believe that this chapter of Revelation must be read in the context of the entire book and interpreted in a manner that is consistent with how the original readers could have understood it. So how about amillennialism, the view that there is no future Millennium because the 1,000 years mentioned in Rev 20 is a figurative way of referring to the lengthy period of time that we know as the "church age," during which Jesus, having ascended to the right hand of God, is currently reigning with his followers who have already died? Could the original readers have believed, given their current reality, or understood, given their reading of the rest of Revelation, that they were currently living in the Millennium? Could they have plausibly believed that Revelation taught that Satan had already been bound (20:1–3)? Look at Jesus' words to the Christians in Pergamum: "I know where you live—where Satan has his throne" (2:13). This church was feeling the brunt of Satan's considerable power in the late first century. One of their own had suffered martyrdom in their city "where Satan lives" (2:13). Satan was not bound; he was quite

---

3. There is actually one last rebellion, which is depicted in 20:7–9.

active and issuing orders from his throne. Indeed, Revelation portrays him as actively seducing the nations, attempting to destroy God's people, and doing so with the sure knowledge that his time is short (12:12).

For these dear Christians in Asia Minor the idea that they were *currently* living in the Millennium would have come as a slap in the face. The idea that Satan was currently bound "to keep him from deceiving the nations anymore until the thousand years were ended" (20:3) would have been utterly absurd. John himself notes in his first letter that "the whole world lies in the power of the evil one" (1 John 5:19). He repeatedly records Jesus referring to Satan as "the ruler of this world" in his gospel (John 12:31; 14:30; 16:11). Paul describes him as the "god of this world" (2 Cor 4:4) and the "the prince of the power of the air" (Eph 2:2). Beyond all this, the narrative chronology of Revelation flies in the face of amillennialism.

If we read Rev 1–19 before we read Rev 20, part of what we encounter is the visionary account of Jesus' incarnation in 12:1–5 (briefly encapsulated through reference to the beginning and end of his time on earth—his birth and ascension). This is *chronologically* clearly followed by Satan being hurled to the earth (12:9a). It is at that point in the chronology, after Jesus' ascension (when the Millennium begins according to amillennialists), that Satan is described as "the deceiver of the whole world" (12:9b). It is also clear in 12:13–17 that *after this* Satan "went off to make war on the rest of her offspring, on those who keep the commandments of God and hold to the testimony of Jesus" (12:17). Again, these are actions of Satan that chronologically clearly occur after the incarnation, resurrection, and ascension. There is also a clear distinction that is made between what Satan was doing at the time Revelation was written ("the deceiver of the whole world," 12:9) and what he will be *prevented* from doing during the Millennium ("so that he might not deceive the nations any longer," 20:3). Then in Rev 13, which is post ascension by any interpretation I have ever heard, we have Satan deceiving the whole world (13:3, 14) and all the inhabitants of the world consequently worshiping the beast (13:8).

Thus, the context of the Christians in Asia Minor, even without the context of Rev 12–13, makes it impossible that they could have read Rev 20 as amillennialists do. It simply makes no sense to believe that they would understand the reference to Satan being bound "so that he might not deceive the nations any longer, until the thousand years were ended" as a reference to their current reality, particularly given the current assaults from the synagogue of Satan in Smyrna and Philadelphia (2:9; 3:9), Jesus' promise that Satan is going to put some Christians in Smyrna in prison and they need to be faithful even to death (2:10), and what appears to be a clear chronology in Rev 12–13 in which Satan's worldwide deception and battle against the saints comes after Jesus supposedly binding him for the Millennium (i.e., church age). Furthermore, the notion that believers' reign with Jesus is a spiritual reign in heaven would have not computed for believers who are promised that they will be given "authority over the nations" (2:26), and "will rule them with a rod of iron" (2:27), clearly implying an earthly reign. And if that were not clear enough, followers of Jesus are later told that they will reign "on the earth" (5:10). This promise is then fleshed out in more detail in 20:4–6. There can be no question that believers in Thyatira would have read this passage in relation to the promise that Jesus made to them in 2:26–27. When we read Rev 20 in context, then, many of the common arguments regarding amillennialism are simply not tenable.

But wait, there's more. In the narrative world of the text, at the end of Rev 19, following the glorious Second Coming of Jesus Christ, the beast and the false prophet are "thrown alive into the lake of fire that burns with sulfur" (19:20). This naturally leaves readers asking: What about the dragon? Revelation 20 then presents *the next chronological event*: dealing with the dragon. He is not thrown into the lake of fire. Instead, he is bound for 1,000 years. Notice that if we were living in the "Millennium" now, as the amillennial view maintains, then the beast and the false prophet would have had to have been thrown into the lake of fire prior to Satan being bound (at the resurrection of Jesus). This makes absolutely no sense, since much of Revelation is warning about present and future circumstances from the perspective of the original recipients of Revelation as the church in the late first century faces the beast and false prophet who are both puppets of a very active dragon, and Jesus is warning his followers of the need to resist the temptation to give in to pressure from the beast and compromise their faith to save their skin. Thus, even though the amillennial view is quite popular among many Christians today and has a long historical pedigree, it is highly implausible when Rev 20 is read within the context of the whole of Revelation.

Where does that leave us? I have suggested that dispensational premillenialism is a novel doctrine that does not fit with Revelation's portrayal of the saints enduring the coming chaos that is described from the beginning to end of Revelation. We have examined the commendable optimism of postmillennialism, which sees the world becoming a better and better place as the gospel advances until a golden age (Millennium) is ushered in, culminating in the return of Christ. Although being "positive" is often viewed as being "next to godliness," this view is simply not consistent with the New Testament's regular portrayal of increasing wickedness prevailing on earth in the years leading up to the return of Christ. Furthermore, it is utterly out of step with Revelation itself, which portrays a time of great tribulation when the people of God will face the wrath of the beast, though they are protected from the outpouring of the wrath of God. Finally, I have suggested that amillennialism also fails to adequately consider the context of Revelation, in which Jesus warns real Christians in Asia Minor, long after his ascension to the right hand of God, that they are going to suffer incredibly under the attack of the devil and his earthly followers but they must endure to the end to enjoy the coming blessings of his reign.

We might seem to be out of options, but there is actually one more. Long before dispensational premillennialism was invented, another form of premillennialism, which dates back to the earliest years of the church, was well-known. This view, known as classic or historic premillennialism is the same as dispensational premillennialism but with the notable difference that it does not include a pre-tribulation Rapture in the equation. How does such a view fit with the message of Revelation? Would this have likely been the way the original readers would have heard Revelation 20?

Notice that at the end of Rev 19 we read about the Battle of Armaggedon (actually, the Massacre of Armaggedon, since there is no battle involved!), at the end of which the beast and false prophet are thrown into the lake of fire (19:20). We are left wondering what happens to Satan. For amillennialism to work, Rev 20 would have to represent a flashback to the time of Jesus' incarnation or ascension when Satan was supposedly bound. What we find instead is not only the next event that we expect after the destruction of the other two members of the "satanic trinity," but explicit chronological markers as well. We are told that Satan is bound "for a thousand years" (20:2) and that "after that" he would be released "for a little while" (20:3). We then read of the resurrection of the saints and their reign with Jesus while Satan is bound (20:4–6). We are then told that "when the thousand years are ended, Satan will be released from his prison" for a time (20:7), but will quickly and finally be thrown into the lake of fire (20:10). Only then will the resurrection of the wicked and the second death take place.

The original readers of Revelation, then, almost certainly would have understood the reference to a thousand year reign of Christ as an indication that when Jesus returns at his Second Coming he will not only destroy his enemies (Rev 19), but will also establish his kingdom here on earth. And his reign will last for a long period of time. Given the fact that numbers are usually symbolic in Revelation, the length of the Millennium need not be a precise one thousand years, though it could be. During this Millennial period some of the promises made to overcomers will be fulfilled along with a number of Old Testament prophecies. The pictures of the apostles judging the twelve tribes of Israel and reigning with Jesus (Matt 19:28; Luke 13:29–30; 22:28–30) fit best in a millennial kingdom,[4] as do the descriptions in a number of Old Testament passages that do not seem to fit either in the present age or in the new heavens and new earth where there will be no more death (Ps 72:8–14; Isa 11:2–9; 65:20; Zech 14:6–21).

Although this chapter does not do justice to any of the four views of the Millennium that it discusses, I hope that it has shown the value of reading Rev 20 within the broader context of Revelation as a whole. If we leave behind our prior understandings of Rev 20 and attempt to read the passage through the eyes of the first-century readers to whom it was originally addressed, it is difficult to avoid the conclusion that Jesus is pointing Christians in Asia Minor to his coming earthly reign, which will follow his Second Coming and be enjoyed by all those who have overcome throughout the centuries.

---

4. Blomberg, "The Posttribulationalism of the New Testament," 67–69.

17

Revelation 20

The Millennium for the Seven Churches

WHAT DETAILS OF REV 20 would have been particularly important to Christians in first century Asia Minor? Revelation 20:1–3 would have been a powerful word of encouragement to believers in Smyrna who were about to face a greater measure of Satan's wrath. Jesus had earlier directly warned them that more suffering was coming (2:10). He softened the blow by noting that their trial would last just "ten days," while at the same time he forced them to face the reality that the reason for the brevity of their trial may be that some would quickly be put to death. Christians in Smyrna were left with no doubts about who their real enemy was. Although some from the synagogue were persecuting them, behind this persecution was one who raged with fury and made war against God's people because he knows his time is short (12:12, 17). In Rev 20, Jesus directs their attention to the end of Satan's activity in this world, and the end of Satan himself. When Jesus returns the beast and the false prophet will be quickly dispensed with in the lake of fire (19:20). Satan, however, will be given a temporary stay of execution. He will be bound and thrown into the Abyss for the full duration of Jesus' earthly reign so that he will have absolutely no influence over the nations. This is "pay back." Christians in Smyrna may be persecuted and imprisoned for "ten days" by the devil, but their tormentor will be thrown into the deepest, darkest prison of all for a thousand years! And when he gets paroled, it will only be for a short time in anticipation of being thrown into the lake of fire for all eternity (20:10). God *will* bring justice.

More than that, the "ten days" of persecution that Christians in Smyrna were about to face must be viewed within the context of their lofty status when the King of kings comes to rule. Ten days of suffering does not sound quite so bad when compared to 365,000 days of reigning with Christ (20:4)! And that does not even take eternity into consideration. Jesus' message to Christians in Smyrna, then, is sobering, but it also calls them to face the challenges ahead with a larger reality firmly in mind. This world is not all there is; a day is soon coming when they will reign with Jesus and their adversary will be vanquished once and for all. Jesus has already promised them, "Be faithful unto death, and I will give you the crown of life" (2:10); now, he vividly shows them the realization of that promise.

As with Christians in Smyrna, Christians in Philadelphia, who were facing the wrath of the synagogue of Satan with almost no earthly resources to defend themselves, would have been relieved by the reminder of what was coming for Satan. The same would have been true for those living in Pergamum, the place where Satan kept his earthly residence (2:13b) and where his throne was located (2:13a). He would soon be exchanging his throne in Pergamum for a massive set of chains that would bind him securely (20:1), and he would be relocating once again, this time from Pergamum to a dark home in the Abyss (20:3) for a thousand years or so. All of this would have reminded the stressed Christians in these cities of Asia Minor that it was God who was in control of this world and their fate, not Satan.

This, of course, raises two important questions: (1) Why in the world would God bind Satan for one thousand years and then set him free again for a short time? (2) Who are the nations who are referred to in verses 3 and 8? It is quite natural to read "the nations," whose number is ultimately once again "like the sand of the sea" (20:8), as a reference to those who survive the hour of trial and repopulate the earth during the "one thousand year" reign of Christ. This is a necessary part of God's plan since Jesus promises overcomers that they will be given "authority over the nations, [27]and ... [they] will rule them with a rod of iron, as when earthen pots are broken in pieces, even as I myself have received authority from my Father" (2:26–27). For this prophecy to be fulfilled there must be nations to be ruled. This points us to an earthly rather than a heavenly rule, as was made explicit in 5:10. The same is true of Jesus' promise to his apostles: "Truly, I say to you, in the new world, when the Son of Man will sit on his glorious throne, you who have followed me will also sit on twelve thrones, judging the twelve tribes of Israel" (Matt 19:28). We find a similar promise in Luke 22:30. In each case, Jesus seems to be pointing to an earthly kingdom in which his apostles have a leadership role related to the twelve tribes of Israel. As overcomers in the churches of Asia Minor read Rev 20, then, they would have been reminded of the coming role they would have of governing the nations under the reign of the Lord Jesus himself on this earth.

Why, though, would Satan not be destroyed with his earthly pawns, the beast and the false prophet? Why lock him up for a thousand years, only to give him one more chance to deceive those who had been created in the image of God? The answer is found in both the amazing grace of God and the utter depravity of humankind. Those who survive and live on earth during the millennial period will experience all the benefits of a perfectly beneficent Ruler. There will be no hint of injustice. Life will be *almost* as God intended it to be in the Garden of Eden. The only difference will be that the earth will still include sinful human beings among its population, though they will not have the devil to deceive them and they will have the benefit of godly rulers (the Lord Jesus himself and overcomers who reign with him). And although God in his great grace offers to all of the surviving inhabitants of earth and their descendants the choice of coming freely under his rule and enjoying all of the benefits of his kingdom, because of their depraved hearts at least many of them will choose rebellion instead.

What we see in 20:7–10, then, is a repeat of what took place in the Garden of Eden in the very beginning. Despite the idyllic earth that they will inhabit under the just and true reign of the Lord Jesus, when given the chance to choose between voluntary allegiance to Jesus and rebellion against him, a great masse will side with Satan and attempt to overthrow Jesus. This demonic delusion will end in their utter destruction. Just as the inhabitants of the earth had steadfastly refused to repent throughout the seal, trumpet, and bowl judgments of God, even in the face of their annihilation, we find the same insanity being described in 20:7–10, as people who now have everything they could possibly need under the reign of Jesus (just as Adam and Eve had before them) insist on the one thing God did not create human beings to have: autonomy. He made us for himself, but the nations in Rev 20:7–10 want nothing to do with his absolute rule. How can this be? Their hearts are still steeped in sin and thus susceptible to the deception of the evil one. Their delusion serves as a powerful reminder to Christians in the churches of Asia Minor that Satan is the deceiver par excellence. He is not to be trifled with. Vigilance is needed. Patient endurance is required. Faithfulness must be clung to at all costs.

To bolster his call to patient endurance and faithfulness Jesus provides a beautiful description of what is in store for his followers during the Millennium in 20:4–6. It is critical that we read these verses in light of all that has gone before. The glorious future that Jesus says is in store for those who overcome not only includes a rich inheritance in the "by and by" of heaven, but also involves a complete reversal of fortunes in the "here and now" of earth under the rule of the Lord Jesus himself. For Christians in Smyrna facing death at the hands of Satan himself the reminder that Satan would be bound and thrown into the Abyss for a thousand years while they themselves were raised from the dead (i.e., receive the "crown of life," 2:10) to reign with Jesus would have helped bolster their resolve to stand firm and "be faithful unto death" (2:10). Jesus does not whitewash what they are about to face. Just as he had told them to expect prison and even death in 2:10, so now he reinforces that in 20:4: "Also I saw the souls of those who had been beheaded for the testimony of Jesus and for the word of God." Jesus' faithful followers can expect to face death because of their faith, but he makes it very clear that death is not the end of the story. Indeed, he calls his followers not to fear death, but rather to fear the second death, the lake of fire. The fact that Jesus specifically says that "Over such the second death has no power" (20:6) would not have been lost on Christians in Smyrna to whom he had already promised, "The one who conquers will not be hurt by the second death" (2:11).

Christians in Laodicea, on the other hand, who had become apathetic toward Jesus as they lived lives of self-sufficiency, would have seen with greater clarity what was at stake. Jesus had already called them to repentance and then assured them that "The one who conquers, I will grant him to sit with me on my throne, as I also conquered and sat down with my Father on his throne" (3:21). Now he vividly shows them what that will look like as he reveals not a single throne in the Millennium, but many (20:4). Thus, the vision of the thrones in Rev 20 provides positive motivation to Christians in Laodicea to turn from their sinful ways, cease living like the society around them, and embrace their calling as God's holy people who are to be visibly distinct from the inhabitants of this world who are in rebellion against God and living for themselves. God's people are destined to reign; clinging to the stuff this world has to offer at the expense of losing that inheritance is the height of foolishness.

Similarly, believers in Thyatira would have readily connected Jesus' language in 20:4 ("seated on them were those to whom the authority to judge was committed") with the promise he gives to overcomers in their city: "The one who conquers and who keeps my works until the end, to him I will give authority over the nations" (2:26). To be recipients of the authority promised to overcomers in the Millennium, though, Christians in Thyatira needed to abandon their commitment to tolerance and actively purge their church of false teaching even as they held fast to right teaching (2:25).

The church in Ephesus had succumbed to the temptation to cease being overt witnesses for Jesus in their city, some likely in an effort to maintain their jobs or live the good life that Ephesus offered to those who went along with the Roman program and others out of fear for their lives. Revelation 20 reminds these Christians again that Jesus is making no effort to sugarcoat the realities that his faithful followers can expect. In 20:4, John sees a vision of people "who had been beheaded for the testimony of Jesus and for the word of God." What is particularly important here, as we think back to the nature of the mark of the beast, is the way that "their testimony of Jesus" and holding to "the word of God" are set up as the alternative to worshiping the beast, worshiping his image, and receiving his mark on their foreheads or hands (20:4b). In other words, there are two choices facing Christians in Ephesus—and only two—be visibly identified with Jesus or be visibly identified with the beast. There is no fence to sit on, no middle ground. To identify with the beast is to face the same fate that he will face. Those who continue to proclaim their testimony about Jesus, on the other hand, will be raised from the dead and will reign with him for a thousand years. All opposition will be removed, and life on earth will be as God intended.

Finally, we find that Jesus' promise to overcomers in Sardis, "I will never blot his name out of the book of life" (3:5), is vividly reinforced in the final chapters of Revelation. First, we find a description of what will happen to those whose names are not found in the book of life. They will receive the ultimate judgment, being thrown into the lake of fire (Rev 20:11–15). The description at the end of Rev 20 issues a clarion call, "Be sure that your name is written in the book of life! If it is there, don't let it be blotted out!" To avoid the lake of fire one must live as an overcomer. Knowing the stakes, Christians in Sardis should be living with tunnel vision that tunes out anything that distracts them from overcoming. More specifically, they must guard against the temptation to allow their clothes to be soiled by assimilation to the culture around them.

Indeed, Rev 20 strongly reinforces the call of Jesus in Revelation to resist assimilation at all costs. Who is it that comes to life in the first resurrection and reigns with Jesus? It is "those who had not worshiped the beast or its image and had not received its mark on their foreheads or their hands" (20:4). Those who try to love God and love the world (i.e., the beast) at the same time may seem to have it all in this world, but they are in for a rude awakening when Jesus returns. To give allegiance to the beast, and the societies of this world that are under the control of the evil one, is to reject allegiance to Jesus and purchase a one-way ticket to the lake of fire. To refuse to assimilate and instead be faithful to Jesus even unto death, on the other hand, is to enjoy all the blessings of the first resurrection.

Ultimately, all of those who reject the lordship of Jesus Christ will face both physical death and the second death. Those who are killed as the wrath of God and the Lamb are poured out in the great tribulation will have to wait through the Millennium for their resurrection and subsequent judgment. At the end of the millennial period, after Satan has been released and allowed to deceive the nations for one last brief time, all of those who foolishly follow his leading will also face physical death as they are consumed by fire from heaven (20:9). At that point Satan will finally be condemned to the lake of fire once and for all (20:10). For those suffering under his oppressive hand in Asia Minor these would have been words of great encouragement and vindication. Justice is coming; they need only be faithful in the face of whatever comes.

The fearsome nature of that coming judgment is portrayed in 20:11: "Then I saw a great white throne and him who was seated on it. From his presence earth and sky fled away, and no place was found for them." Earth and sky are personified here and pictured as running in terror from the prospect of standing before the Creator and Judge of all things. If there is ever anything that someone should want to avoid, it is the great white throne judgment that is coming. Whatever it costs to guarantee that you do not end up there, it is well worth paying. Why? Look again at what that judgment entails according to Rev 20:12–15. First, those who stand before the great white throne to face God's judgment in this passage are those who were not raised in the first resurrection. This is clear both from John's language ("And I saw the dead") and from the chronology that has already been established in this passage. We have been told that Satan would be bound for one thousand years (20:2). At the beginning of that period followers of Jesus ("the dead in Christ," 1 Thess 4:16) are resurrected (20:4). This is described as the first resurrection (20:5), implying that there will be a second resurrection, which is connected with the second death (20:6). At the end of the thousand years Satan is released, rallies the nations to rebel against God and the people of God, and is defeated and destroyed along with all those who joined with him (20:7–9). Satan is then thrown into the lake of fire (20:10). All that remains now is for God to deal with human beings who have rebelled against him and steadfastly rejected his rule. This is the focus of 20:12–15. It is concerned with those who have chosen in this life to reject Jesus. Along with them, if we read Revelation rightly, are all those who have claimed to be followers of Jesus in this life but whose allegiance was mixed. Those who chose compromise and assimilation over devotion to the One True Lord have no hope of sharing in the first resurrection and avoiding the second death. These are the types of people to whom Jesus will say, even though they claim to have been his followers, "I never knew you; depart from me, you workers of lawlessness" (Matt 7:23). It is to overcomers that Jesus promises the right to reign with him in the Millennium (2:26–27; 3:21) and avoid the horrible fate of the second death (2:11). Thus, the positive reinforcement of 20:4–6, in which faithful followers of Jesus see the glorious future in store for them, is coupled with the negative reinforcement of 20:12–15, where Christians in Asia Minor would have been reminded of the horrible future in store for those who reject Jesus or take him lightly.

Second, this passage emphasizes the fact that no one will be able to escape this judgment: "And I saw the dead, great and small, standing before the throne" (20:12). "Great and small" is a way of using both ends of the spectrum to emphasize that no one is left out. No matter how wealthy, how high one's status, how highly esteemed a person is in this world, everyone without exception who does not share in the first resurrection will stand before the great white throne of God to be judged for their rebellion against him. And that also includes the "small." We live in an age where many are arguing that God is on the side of the poor and that following Jesus is all about caring for the poor and fighting injustice. The reality is that on Judgment Day those who have not given their allegiance to Jesus Christ in this life, however poor and oppressed they may have been in this world, will face the great white throne judgment and end up in the lake of fire. Heaven is not a consolation prize for the poor and oppressed of this world.

Third, a day is coming when the books will be opened. This should be utterly terrifying for those who have not been washed in the blood of the Lamb. This reality again reminds us that God is not someone to trifle with. Those who play games with him and think they are able not only to fool others into thinking they are devoted to him but also to fool God himself need to have their heads examined. Nothing we ever do, say, or think is beyond God's awareness (Heb 4:13). It is all recorded in the books of God, which will one day be opened for those who have rejected him so that all that they have ever done is revealed (20:12). This reality would have added significant force to Jesus' rebuke of Christians in Sardis. As those whose works were not complete in the sight of God (3:2), they would have not only been sobered by the reality of what happens to those whose names are blotted out of the book of life, but they also would have been scared stiff at the prospect of being judged "according to what they had done" (20:12, lit. "according to their works").[1]

Fourth, God's judgment will be absolutely fair and just. Everyone who is forced to stand before the great white throne of God will be judged "according to what they had done" (20:12, 13). The fact that it is repeated twice drives home the point for those in the churches of Asia Minor in the first century and for us today that *if* we are judged according to what we have done, we are utterly lost. "None is righteous, no, not one" (Rom 3:10); "all have sinned and fall short of the glory of God" (3:23); and "the wages of sin is death" (6:23), a death that is described in terrifying terms in Rev 20:15: "And if anyone's name was not found written in the book of life, he was thrown into the lake of fire."

As we contemplate the fate of unbelievers, we need to remember that this portion of Revelation, like all the rest, was addressed to *believers* in Asia Minor. It is a message to God's servants, those who believe that Jesus died for their sins, was raised that they might have life, and have confessed that Jesus is Lord. On the one hand, it brings great hope. A day is coming when even Death is going to be thrown into the lake of fire, along with Hades (20:14). All that is wrong with this world will be done away with. All creation will be able to declare with absolute finality, "Death is swallowed up in victory" (1 Cor 15:54–55). On the other hand, it also reminds us that we dare not take Jesus lightly. The original readers of Revelation were facing the twin temptations either to turn back from following Jesus in order to save their lives or to compromise their devotion to Jesus in order to share in what the wicked society around them had to offer. Giving in to either temptation is portrayed as a one-way ticket to the great white throne judgment and the lake of fire that follows. So, Jesus is using yet another vision that he gives to John to pass on to his followers as a tool for further motivating Christians to endure patiently and make sure that they are living lives of faithful devotion to him. He is reminding us that no sacrifice is too great—even losing your livelihood (13:17) or your life itself (13:7)—to ensure that you escape the coming judgment that is depicted in Rev 20:11–15.

Before concluding our discussion of Rev 20, I want to briefly consider the fate of the wicked: "And if anyone's name was not found written in the book of life, he was thrown into the lake of fire" (20:15). What would this verse have meant to the original readers? It clearly answers the question of 6:10: "O Sovereign Lord, holy and true, how long before you will judge and avenge our blood on those who dwell on the earth?" God will bring justice. Some have asked how God could be fair to send people to an eternity in the lake of fire when they have only sinned for ninety or one hundred years at most. Does Revelation speak to this question? Revelation actually portrays rebellious human beings who have countless opportunities to repent still choosing to curse God and still refusing to bow the knee to Jesus. Revelation portrays sin as costly.

---

1. Once again the ESV is regrettably inconsistent in how it translates the same word.

The very blood of the Lamb of God is used to purchase our salvation. Sin is no small matter. The lake of fire is a fitting place for those who live in sin and refuse to repent.

While the thought of God's justice on the wicked would have been encouraging for those suffering under the oppression of wicked men who opposed God in Smyrna, Pergamum, and Philadelphia in particular, for Christians in Ephesus this description would have been a sober reminder of what happens to those who do not embrace the Good News of Jesus Christ. As Paul reminds us in Rom 10:14, "How then will they call on him in whom they have not believed? And how are they to believe in him of whom they have never heard? And how are they to hear without someone preaching?" To believe that "Whoever has the Son has life; whoever does not have the Son of God does not have life" (1 John 5:12) and yet shrink back from or be apathetic about taking the gospel to the society around us is to live a contradiction. It is to remove our reason for existing as a people of God; and the only thing we can expect in such circumstances, if we do not repent, is for Jesus to come and remove our lampstand (2:5).

18

Revelation 21–22
Final Words to the Seven Churches

REVELATION 21–22 REPRESENTS A fitting end to this amazing book for more reasons than we often recognize. As we have seen, the messages to the seven churches provide a necessary grid through which the remainder of Revelation should be read. As we arrive at the end of the book, we find that these vivid chapters bring to consummation the grand message introduced in Rev 2–3. More than that, these chapters form a natural and yet carefully crafted conclusion to what began in Gen 1, and they sum up God's grand message to both those who confess "Jesus is Lord" and those who do not.

First and foremost, they represent the fulfillment of the remainder of the promises that Jesus makes in Rev 2–3 to those who overcome. Beyond that, they describe the final undoing of the Fall. Adam's sin had not only corrupted the human race—right down to the last man, woman, boy, and girl—it had also corrupted the good creation that God had spoken into existence. This is perhaps why we find that same corrupted creation fleeing from the presence of the one who is about to pass judgment on sin in 20:11. It is conceivable at that point that the words of 2 Pet 3:10 are realized, where we read of the dissolution of this world, indeed this material universe, likely right down to the elemental level.[1] The death of this universe, though, will give way to new life as the new heaven and new earth burst forth in all of their unsullied glory. The language of 21:1 ("for the first heaven and the first earth had passed away") leaves little doubt that God is replacing the old creation with a new one.

This beautiful picture would have reminded the original readers that all of the pervasive evil that they have known and suffered under in this world will be utterly

---

1. What the ESV has translated "heavenly bodies" in 2 Pet 3:10 may perhaps better be rendered, "the elements."

done away with in the future as God unveils a new heaven and a new earth. Revelation drives home this point in 21:1 with the simple statement: "and the sea was no more." For those who love the ocean, as I do, the point here is not the lack of material oceans on the new earth; instead, the point is that chaos and evil, which are symbolized by the sea, will have no place in God's new creation. Indeed, Revelation connects "the sea" with "the Abyss" by stating that the beast will come up "out of the sea" in 13:1 while stating that the beast "rises from the Abyss"[2] in 11:7–8 and 17:8. The sea was the place from which the beast emerged, but with no more sea in the new earth there can be no more beasts to come. Satan and all of his allies have been vanquished once and for all. Jesus reminds the original readers that that day is coming soon. In light of that sure reality they must press on to know him and to live in light of his coming.

Jerusalem, the city of God under the old covenant, which was utterly defiled by the people of God through their idolatry and assimilation (recall, e.g., Ezek 5:5–12; 8:1–18), is now replaced with a New Jerusalem, which is radiant and pure like a "bride adorned for her husband" (21:2). While it is likely inappropriate to associate the New Jerusalem with the people of God simply because they are both described as a "bride"—the people of God in 19:7–8, and the New Jerusalem in 21:2 and 21:9—followers of Christ in Asia Minor would have been quick to notice the parallel language. Just as the city itself is "prepared as a bride adorned for her husband" (21:2), so the people of God who will inhabit that city need to be properly dressed to enter it. For Christians in Sardis who had soiled their clothes (3:4), this would have driven home Jesus' call to wake up (3:2), repent (3:3), and live as overcomers so that they will be clothed in white garments (3:5). For Christians in Laodicea who through their lifestyle of assimilation had become more enamored with what their city had to offer—including its distinctive black wool clothing—than with following Jesus, this would have driven home Jesus' call to be earnest and repent (3:19), to reaffirm their allegiance to him (3:20), and to come to him for "white clothes to wear" (3:18). For the "fine linen, bright and pure" that is the distinctive attire of the people of God was merely a symbol for "the righteous deeds of the saints" (19:8). The people of God must prepare themselves appropriately to dwell in the city of God.

While the picture of the New Jerusalem perfectly prepared to meet her husband would have strengthened Jesus' exhortations to some within Asia Minor to repent, the description that follows in 21:3–4 would have brought much needed comfort and hope to those who were suffering in Smyrna, Pergamum, and Philadelphia. What God intended in creating this world in the first place and making a Garden where he walked with Adam and Eve "in the cool of the day" (Gen 3:8) is now fully realized in the New Jerusalem where God and those he created live together. The statement, "they will be his people," should not be overlooked. Throughout the Old Testament[3] we are

2. My translation. The ESV is inconsistent once again, this time translating the same word "bottomless pit" in 11:7, 8, but translating it "Abyss" in 20:1, 3.

3. See, e.g., Exod 29:46; Lev 11:45; 22:31–33; 25:38, 55; 26:13; Num 15:41.

told that God rescued Israel out of Egypt in order to create a people for himself; but time and time again they refused to embrace that high calling. Enslaved to sin, they could not live as the people of God. A new redemption was needed; a new covenant was needed, a covenant that could only come through the blood of a better sacrifice than the bulls and goats that were offered in the Temple, endless sacrifices that could never take away sin (Heb 10:4). Through the blood of Jesus our eternal redemption has been secured (Heb 9:12) and we can now live as the people of God devoted to God, living forever with him in his very presence.

More than that, with the coming of God to dwell among his people "the former things" will finally pass away (21:4). Jesus reminds those who have been experiencing mourning, pain, and death that a day is soon coming when all of these will be forever a thing of the past, because they are features of "the former things." They are features of this sin-infected world where everything is broken and decaying, but in the new heaven and the new earth sin will have no place whatsoever, nor will its abhorrent offspring: suffering and death. Why? Because God, who is "seated on the throne," exercising absolute control over his kingdom, declares, "Behold, I am making all things new" (21:5). He will not be content with patching up or renovating the old creation. The first earth is gone (21:1), never to be seen again, never to be remembered given the magnificence of the new creation (Isa 65:17). God is making *all* things new. And what God declares is absolutely certain to come about, for his "words are trustworthy and true" (21:5). What great words of hope for those who are suffering! What an important reminder that just as this life is not all there is (20:5), so also this world is not all there is; a new, better, and perfect world is coming soon where all of the evils and suffering of this world will be things of the past. Those tempted to compromise their faith in order to enjoy what Satan's kingdom has to offer in this world by assimilating to the culture around them need to take note of the fact that this world is about to pass away and be replaced with something infinitely better. Which will they choose?

As if God's first declaration were not enough, he adds another one out of compassion for the faint of heart: "And he said to me, 'It is done! I am the Alpha and the Omega, the beginning and the end. To the thirsty I will give from the spring of the water of life without payment. [7]The one who conquers will have this heritage, and I will be his God and he will be my son'" (21:6–7). All that God had promised to do will be done. For, he is the One who shapes all of human history from beginning to end and his purposes cannot be thwarted. He is the One who offers free access to the spring of the water of life to all of his followers. For those who were "parched" by the challenges of living in a world hostile to the people of God, this promise would have come as a breath of fresh air that invigorated them and bolstered their resolve to press on and be faithful to the end. In the context of Revelation and the rest of Scripture, they would have quickly recognized that "without payment" does not mean that the water of life is "free for the taking." Verse 7 makes it clear that access to this glorious spring, as well as enjoying all of the other promises God has made, is restricted to those who overcome or "conquer" (21:7). Revelation thus effectively drives home Jesus' calls to each of the seven churches to live as overcomers so that they may enjoy all of the benefits of living in his coming kingdom, which includes an unthinkable level of intimacy between Creator and created, a relationship that can only be captured by comparing it to a Father-son relationship. Whether tempted to walk away from one's faith in order to avoid persecution, suffering, and death, or tempted to assimilate to the culture around us in order to share in its "ill-gotten gain" (Prov 1:19; 10:2), the words of 21:1–7 are a sober reminder of what is at stake.

In the midst of the beautiful visions of what is in store for overcomers, God pauses to remind Christians in Asia Minor of the alternative: "But as for the cowardly, the faithless, the detestable, as for murderers, the sexually immoral, sorcerers, idolaters, and all liars, their portion will be in the lake that burns with fire and sulfur, which is the second death" (21:8). A couple of features of this verse would have stood out as if they had a spotlight illuminating them. First, while one might expect "murderers, the sexually immoral, sorcerers, idolaters, and all liars" to end up in the lake of fire, the words that are placed first and second in the list could not have been more striking to the original readers. Following Jesus is not for wimps; it is not for cowards; and it is not for the faithless. When Jesus says, "the one who endures to the end will be saved" (Matt 24:13), he actually means it. When Jesus says, "For whoever would save his life will lose it, but whoever loses his life for my sake will find it" (Matt 16:25), he actually means it. When Jesus says, "Be faithful unto death, and I will give you the crown of life" (Rev 2:10), he actually means it. Jesus knows exactly how hard life will be for his followers. He knows that the emissary of Satan himself is coming, and this beast will rob them of their ability to make a living (13:17) and kill anyone who refuses to worship him (13:15); but this is still no excuse for compromise. The only way to overcome the beast is to refuse to love your life "even unto death" (12:11). Yes, the beast will inspire genuine fear on the part of followers of Jesus, but they dare not let fear lead them to becoming cowards. Instead, they must choose to fear God more than they fear the beast. They must remind themselves both of what God has in store for overcomers and also what he has in store for those who succumb to the Satanic pressure to assimilate to the ways of this world and worship the beast. For God has already told them that anyone who worships the beast "will drink the wine of God's wrath, poured full strength into the cup of his anger, and he will be tormented with fire and sulfur in the presence of the holy angels and in the presence of the Lamb" (14:10). If that is God's expectations for Christians who face the full force of the beast's reign of terror, what are his expectations for us? Dare we shrink back or assimilate to the ways of this world when we are facing such insignificant pressures compared to what is described in Revelation?

While the mention of cowards in 21:8 would have shaken many in Asia Minor who were rationalizing their compromise or giving in to the seductive teachings of the Nicolaitans and Jezebel, both of whom insisted that such compromise was really "not that bad," it would have also shaken the Christians in Ephesus and should shake many of us today. Christians in Ephesus appear to have retreated in fear from their first love of taking the gospel to the culture around them. They were doing very well in every other way, but in this foundational feature of what it means to be a follower of Jesus they appear to have become cowards. They had ceased to be faithful to that central calling of every Christian to be Christ's visible ambassadors in this world. Given the fate of cowards expressed in 21:8, it is not surprising that Jesus uses such strong language to warn the Ephesian Christians. Far too much is at stake to mince words.

Despite these warnings many today are attempting to hide their cowardice by claiming that they are doing gospel ministry by "showing Jesus' love" rather than "cramming the gospel down people's throats." Our churches need to reexamine what the mission of God really is. Jesus has called us to "make disciples of all nations, baptizing them in the name of the Father and of the Son and of the Holy Spirit, [20]teaching them to observe all that I have commanded you" (Matt 28:19–20). To baptize someone you must first verbally share the gospel with them and they in turn must embrace it. And embracing it includes embracing Jesus as Lord and covenanting to learn what he has commanded so that you can live a life of obedience to him. The Great Commission is not a call to raise the standard of living of the poor or bring a little sunshine to the lives of those who are suffering. Our churches today need to ask the question, "Have we sold out the gospel in order to look good to the world around us and feel good about ourselves without actually paying the price of allegiance to Jesus?" There is no place for cowards in the New Jerusalem; "their portion will be in the lake that burns with fire and sulfur, which is the second death" (21:8).

To overcome and enter into all of the blessings of the coming kingdom of God, then, followers of Jesus must stand firm to the end, rather than becoming cowards and faithlessly abandoning their allegiance to Jesus. It is not simply the temptation to reject Jesus in the face of persecution and death that they must beware of, however; God also reminds them that the sexually immoral and idolaters will end up in the lake of fire. This is why it was so imperative that Christians in Pergamum reject the teachings of Balaam and the teachings of the Nicolaitans, both of which advocated compromise with the culture around them in areas of sexuality and involvement in events connected with idolatry. This is why it was so important for Christians in Thyatira to cease tolerating Jezebel, for she was "teaching and seducing [Jesus'] servants to practice sexual immorality and to eat food sacrificed to idols" (2:20). This is why it was so important for Christians in Sardis who had soiled their clothes to repent so that they could once again "be clothed . . . in white garments" (3:5). And this is why it was so important for Christians in Laodicea who had embraced the idol of hedonism and been ensnared by the love of money to repent of their sin and once again bow before Jesus alone.

Finally, we should note the word of encouragement in 21:8, particularly to Christians in Philadelphia and Smyrna who were being oppressed by the synagogue of Satan. Within those cities there were ethnic Jews who were apparently reviling Christians as a bunch of losers who were under God's wrath, as was evidenced by what they were suffering. Jesus, however, has reminded these Christians that although such people say they are Jews, they actually are not the people of God at all (2:9; 3:9). Instead, they "lie" (3:9) and "all liars" have a one-way ticket to "the lake that burns with fire and sulfur" (21:8). So, these oppressed Christians can take heart, because justice is coming to those who do not repent of persecuting the true people of God.

The vision in Rev 21 then shifts to a fuller revelation of the nature and glory of the New Jerusalem in 21:9–27. As readers in Smyrna came to this part of Revelation, they would have been overwhelmed by the reality that what Jesus said was eminently true: As citizens of the amazing New Jerusalem, they were indeed rich (2:9). There are, in fact, a number of features of this vision that would have stood out to Christians in Asia Minor, but before considering them, let us attempt to answer the question: What is the purpose of this particular vision? Why does "one of the seven angels who had the seven bowls full of the seven last plagues" now tell John, "Come, I will show you the Bride, the wife of the Lamb" (21:10)?

First, we need to recognize the important parallel in Ezek 40–43. In Ezek 40–42 we find an extended description of a new temple. This is then followed by an account of the glory of God filling the temple (43:1–5) and an exhortation to the people of God to respond appropriately to the vision (43:6–9). The exhortation of Ezek 43:9 appears to be central to the purpose of Rev 21: "Now let them put away their whoring and the dead bodies of their kings far from me, and I will dwell in their midst forever." God is displaying the wonder and glory of the New Jerusalem in order to further urge his people to be ashamed of their sins and abandon them once and for all. What sin? In Ezekiel it is described in two ways, both of which are consistent with the sins Jesus is confronting in the churches of Asia Minor. The first one the ESV translates "their whoring." Block notes that while this "word may denote spiritual infidelity in general (Num. 14:33), in Ezekiel this unfaithfulness is expressed in illicit affairs with other gods and political powers."[4] Indeed, in Ezek 43:10–12 the purpose of the extended visions of the coming temple is made clear:

> Son of man, describe the temple to the people of Israel, *that they may be ashamed of their sins*. Let them consider its perfection, [11]and if they are ashamed of all they have done, make known to them the design of the temple—its arrangement, its exits and entrances—its whole design and all its regulations and laws. Write these down before them so that they may be faithful to its design and follow all its regulations.

Just as the beauty and glory and wonder of the temple in Ezekiel was intended to bring Israel to its senses by showing them what they were abandoning in their pursuit of being like the nations around them, so too the vivid description of the New Jerusalem

4. Block, *Ezekiel 25–48*, 582.

in Rev 21–22 spotlights for Christians in Asia Minor the stark contrast between the temporary pleasures and comforts of this world and the eternal joy of having a place in the New Jerusalem. How can followers of Jesus feel anything less than abject shame when they consider how easily they are enticed by that which is dung in comparison to the glories of the New Jerusalem?

Although the magnificent description of the New Jerusalem in Rev 21 would have arrested the attention of Christians in all seven churches, certain portions of it would have particularly resonated with Christians in Philadelphia. The overwhelming beauty and symmetry of the New Jerusalem stood in stark contrast to Philadelphia, where the buildings and city walls were cracked and crumbling and where it was not even safe to live. For those living a precarious existence in Philadelphia, the promise of the New Jerusalem would have been particularly poignant.[5] A city with twelve foundations will never be shaken. A city wall that was approximately 200 feet thick and made of jasper would never be breached and would never crack.

Within the description of the New Jerusalem a number of other details would have been important to Christians in Asia Minor. Beyond the dazzling beauty of the city—which is made of pure gold with a wall of jasper (21:18), gates made of giant pearls (21:21), multiple foundations made of twelve precious stones (21:19–20), and the main street made of pure gold like transparent glass (21:21)—the original readers would have quickly noted that the number twelve is written all over the New Jerusalem (Reading Instruction #5). It has twelve gates, made of twelve pearls and with the names of the twelve tribes of Israel written on them, which are guarded by twelve angels (21:12, 21). The wall of the city is built on twelve foundations upon which are written the names of the twelve apostles of the Lamb. The wall itself is 144 cubits thick (12 x 12 cubits), and the size of the city is 12,000 stadia long, 12,000 stadia wide, and 12,000 stadia high. Thus, the New Jerusalem may be summed up with the number twelve—the number of the people of God. This is not only the city of God; it is also the city of the people of God, a place where they will live forever in his presence. It is a city that is massive in size and built in the shape of a cube, just like the Holy of Holies (see 1 Kgs 6:20), thus effectively symbolizing a place that is large enough for all of the people of God, "from every tribe and language and people and nation" (5:9) to dwell in the very presence of God forever, with no barriers whatsoever remaining between them.

The intimacy that the people of God will enjoy with the One who created them is vividly portrayed in 21:22–23. Unlike the old Jerusalem, where the focal point of the city was its glorious temple, the New Jerusalem will not have a temple, "for its temple is the Lord God the Almighty and the Lamb" (21:22). In other words, there will be absolutely nothing to separate God from his people. For those overcomers in Philadelphia who had been promised that they would be pillars in the temple of God (3:12), here they discover that Jesus' promise was even better than it first appeared. They will

5. Cf. Hemer, *Letters*, 167.

not simply have a permanent place in God's temple; they will have a permanent place in God's presence where a temple to divide sacred from profane is no longer needed because all sin and uncleanness will have forever been done away with. In the New Jerusalem the people of God will see and worship the One on the Throne and the Lamb in all of their glory; and with their glory on display for all to see there will be no more need of a sun or a moon (21:23).

The story has thus finally come full circle. In the beginning, God had said, "'Let there be light,' and there was light" (Gen 1:3), light that was present before the sun, moon, and stars were created (Gen 1:14–18). It should not surprise us, then, that Jesus, who is the light of the world (John 8:12), would light this world with his glory, rendering the sun and the moon completely unnecessary in the new earth. As the universe began, so it will begin anew, with the light of God's glory serving as its only illumination (21:23) and night having no place at all (21:25). "By its light will the nations walk, and the kings of the earth will bring their glory into it" (21:24; cf. 21:26). In other words, those "from every tribe and language and people and nation" (5:9), who have been ransomed for God will bring the glory they share with the Lord (Rom 8:17) into the city of God as an act of worship.[6] The "nations" thus will no longer pollute the city of God by their presence, but rather as those who "have washed their robes and made them white in the blood of the Lamb" (7:14), who have now had the process completed of being transformed "from one degree of glory to another" (2 Cor 3:18), and who now possess "an eternal weight of glory beyond all comparison" to the "light afflictions" (2 Cor 4:17) they faced in this world, they are now prepared to bring glory rather than dishonor into the presence of God as they come without shame before him as his sons and daughters. They will be welcome in the New Jerusalem, while "nothing unclean will ever enter it, nor anyone who does what is detestable or false" (21:27). No such people will be able to enter the New Jerusalem because they will have already been consigned to the lake of fire. This is another subtle reminder to Christians in Asia Minor to be sure that they are living worthy of the gospel and not becoming unclean through following the teachings of Balaam, the Nicolaitans, and Jezebel. Those in the church in Sardis likely would have been particularly affected by the language here. With "nothing unclean" entering the city it would be critical for them to repent from those sins that had soiled their clothes. They needed to overcome their sin to enjoy Jesus' promise to each overcomer that he would "never blot his name out of the book of life" (3:5), for the only ones allowed in the New Jerusalem are those whose names "are written in the Lamb's book of life" (21:27). They needed to flee from impurity, shun what is shameful, renounce all deceit, and not be lulled into a sense of false security by merely thinking, in modern terms, that a prayer once prayed could save them.

6. Note that the glory that is spoken about in Rom 8:18 is not a glory that is "revealed *to* us" (contra the ESV), but rather a glory that is "revealed *in* us" (Greek: ἐν, *en*), paralleling the statement in 8:17 that we will be "glorified with him."

Jesus' earlier words in the Gospels are important here: "If your right eye causes you to sin, tear it out and throw it away. For it is better that you lose one of your members than that your whole body be thrown into hell. [30]And if your right hand causes you to sin, cut it off and throw it away. For it is better that you lose one of your members than that your whole body go into hell" (Matt 5:29–30). When it is about life and death, heaven and hell, no price is too high to pay to deal with sin now. God saves people to reconcile them to himself and to make them holy. To think that he would save anyone so that they could get on with their life of sin or go forward with a life of compromise with the culture around them is to embrace a gospel that cannot save anyone. No one who accepts such a false picture of Jesus will have his or her name written in the book of life.

As we move into Rev 22, the description of the New Jerusalem continues. Here, though, there is a shift to imagery that evokes the Garden of Eden. We thus find the biblical story of God and his people begins (see Gen 2:10) and ends in a garden/city that has a river flowing out of it and the tree of life within it. In the New Jerusalem, though, the river is "the river of the water of life" (22:1) and it is "bright as crystal, flowing from the throne of God and of the Lamb [2]through the middle of the street of the city" (22:1–2). Flanking "the river of the water of life" on both sides is the most unique species of plant life that God ever created: "the tree of life" (22:2); and it produces twelve crops every year. In other words, it is always bearing fruit and its fruit is commensurate with the full number of the people of God.

The imagery in this passage clearly is intended to draw readers' attention back to Ezek 47, where we find an earlier vision of the temple with a river flowing out of the temple: "And on the banks, on both sides of the river, there will grow all kinds of trees for food. Their leaves will not wither, nor their fruit fail, but they will bear fresh fruit every month, because the water for them flows from the sanctuary. Their fruit will be for food, and their leaves for healing" (Ezek 47:12). The primary differences between the two visions are (1) the fact that the water flows from the sanctuary in Ezekiel but flows "from the throne of God and of the Lamb" in Revelation (22:1), with Revelation highlighting the visible presence of God reigning among his people; and (2) the variety of trees along the river in Ezekiel give way to the tree of life in Revelation. The two differences highlight the nullification of the curse. All that was lost through Adam's sin so many years ago has now been undone. As God makes clear to John in Rev 22:3–5:

> No longer will there be anything accursed, but the throne of God and of the Lamb will be in it, and his servants will worship him. [4]They will see his face, and his name will be on their foreheads. [5]And night will be no more. They will need no light of lamp or sun, for the Lord God will be their light, and they will reign forever and ever.

The curse of sin had left those created in God's image separated from him, but in the New Jerusalem every cursed thing will be gone and God and the Lamb will be where they belong, with their servants doing what they were created to do: worshiping them. Where once no one could see the face of God and live (Exod 33:20) because of their sin and his holiness, now all of God's servants will see his face and thrive (22:4). What promises are given to the people of God! But they are promises exclusively for overcomers. This is implied by the statement, "and his name will be on their foreheads" (22:4), which corresponds to the promise given to overcomers in Philadelphia (3:12) and the picture of the 144,000 who are sealed by God (7:3; 14:1). So, once again the hope that is held out in the visions of Revelation carries with it a subtle exhortation to overcome. A time is coming when "night will be no more" and God's people "will reign forever and ever" (22:5), and those struggling against the temptation to either compromise their faith to avoid persecution or to indulge in what the society around them has to offer need to be reminded that

> The night is far gone; the day is at hand. So then let us cast off the works of darkness and put on the armor of light. [13]Let us walk properly as in the daytime, not in orgies and drunkenness, not in sexual immorality and sensuality, not in quarreling and jealousy. [14]But put on the Lord Jesus Christ, and make no provision for the flesh, to gratify its desires." (Rom 13:12–14)

In light of all that is coming, the only proper response, the only sane response can be to "cast off the works of darkness . . . walk properly as in the daytime . . . and make no provision for the flesh." Those being enticed by all that the world around them has to offer, if they will just cut a few corners in their faith, need to be reminded that "If anyone loves the world, the love of the Father is not in him. [16]For all that is in the world—the desires of the flesh and the desires of the eyes and pride of life—is not from the Father but is from the world. [17]And the world is passing away along with its desires, but whoever does the will of God abides forever" (1 John 2:15–17).

What God has revealed in the book of Revelation is "trustworthy and true" (22:6). There is no chance of any other outcome than the one God has revealed to us, both for the faithful and for the faithless. Jesus wanted to remind the original readers that these events were on their near horizon; they would "soon take place" (22:6). All Christians live one step away from eternity and need to allow that truth to shape their lives. Jesus is coming soon (22:7), and the only ones who will receive the blessings he promises are those who keep "the words of the prophecy of this book" (22:7). Once again, those words drive home the point that the message of Revelation, which was delivered to real people facing real challenges in first-century Asia Minor, was intended to be understood and obeyed.

Before leaving 22:7, it is worth pointing out that there is another important intratextual connection here. Jesus' words here would have served as a powerful motivation to all of the churches to persevere, knowing that his return is imminent, but they would have been particularly important for Christians in Philadelphia. Jesus makes the same statement four times in Revelation ("I am coming soon"). Three of them are found in rapid succession here in Rev 22: verses 7, 12, and 20. The only other use of this phrase is found in 3:11 addressed to the church in Philadelphia. With their "little power" (3:8), this church appeared to be hanging by a thread. So, Jesus encourages them with the thought that their struggle will not last much longer. Now, at the end of Revelation, Jesus fleshes out that word of encouragement by first highlighting the stark reality of what his coming will bring (the new heavens and new earth with the spectacular New Jerusalem), and then three times urging them again to hold on just a little bit longer ("Hold fast what you have, so that no one may seize your crown," 3:11) because he is coming soon.

With the call to keep "the words of the prophecy of this book" (22:7) still ringing in our ears, we come to 22:8 where for the second time in a short span (see 19:10) John is tempted to worship the angel who had been showing him the visions (22:8) and is once again reminded to "Worship God" (22:9). The recording of these parallel events serves to highlight this as an important part of the message of Revelation. Allegiance and worship belongs to God alone. The call to keep "the words of the prophecy of this book" (22:7) is actually summed up in the command to "worship God" alone. Indeed, the words of the angel in 22:9 once again drive home the point that servants of God are defined as "those who keep the words of this book" (22:9)—or those "who hold to the testimony of Jesus" (19:10)—and worship God. In other words, God's servants are not simply the sum total of those who have at some distant point in their lives prayed to "invite Jesus into their heart" and then gotten on with their lives now that the eternal destination question had been dealt with decisively. Instead, God's servants are overcomers, i.e., those who "hear" and "keep" what is written in the book of Revelation (1:3). Serving God, or being a "slave" of God, is not a passive existence in which we simply bask in God's grace and ignore the responsibilities that come with being a new covenant member of the people of God. Worshiping God is not something that is to be done in secret; our allegiance to him should be obvious to those around us.

In 22:10–11, the words of the angel echo two Old Testament passages. The first one stands in stark contrast to Dan 12:9: "He said, 'Go your way, Daniel, for the words are shut up and sealed until the time of the end.'" Where Daniel is explicitly told that the visions he has been given do not predict events on his near horizon, readers of Revelation are told precisely the opposite. For Daniel, "the end," when the Messiah would come and set up his kingdom, was still in the distant future. With Jesus' death and resurrection, however, the "beginning of the end" had arrived. From the moment of his resurrection and ascension, Christians have been living in "the last days." The fact that the last days have been a more prolonged period than first-century Christians would have anticipated does not change the fact that all Christians have lived on the brink of the culmination of the ages. Thus, Revelation continues to emphasize that "the time is near" (22:10). This is reinforced by 22:11 ("Let the evildoer still do evil, and the filthy still be filthy, and the righteous still do right, and the holy still be holy."), which echoes Dan 12:10 ("Many shall purify themselves and make themselves white and be refined, but the wicked shall act wickedly") and perhaps Ezek 3:27 ("Thus says the Lord GOD. He who will hear, let him hear; and he who will refuse to hear, let him refuse, for they are a rebellious house"). The point of Rev 22:11 is to reinforce the urgent call to repent and live like overcomers by underscoring that time has run out. This would have made this part of Revelation particularly striking to those in Thyatira who had been told that time had run out for Jezebel and her followers (2:21–23). The choice is simple: Choose allegiance to Jesus and live a life of doing right and being holy, or choose allegiance to the beast and settle in to a short life of doing evil and being filthy in anticipation of being thrown into the lake of fire.

This urgent imperative from Jesus is once again driven home in 22:12 with yet another reminder that he is "coming soon," and when he comes he will "repay each one for what he has done." Jesus' absolute control of all of human history is emphatically reiterated with the threefold title in 22:13: "I am the Alpha and the Omega, the first and the last, the beginning and the end." He is the creator and sustainer of all life and will one day soon be the judge of all mankind. Jesus' choice of titles here would have caused Christians in Smyrna, in particular, to sit up and take notice. They were facing current suffering for their faith, and Jesus had promised them that still worse suffering, prison, and death was on their near horizon. To be a Christian in Smyrna was to put one's life on the line. Jesus had already encouraged them to "Be faithful unto death" (2:10) by reminding them of the reward that will follow such faithfulness: "and I will give you the crown of life" (2:10). Death is not the end of the story! Here, the same "first and the last" who spoke to them in Rev 2 reiterates his promise while also adding a warning. He is coming soon! Whether we experience death in this life or are alive at Jesus' return, our suffering will soon be over. Those who die as faithful followers of Jesus will return with him to receive their resurrection bodies (see 1 Thess 4:13) and will share in the glory of the Second Coming. So, take heart! But that's not all; Jesus also tells Christians in Smyrna that he will "repay each one for what he has done." This would have brought both encouragement and a not so subtle warning.

First, it would have reminded them that those who were oppressing them and who were about to throw them in prison and have them executed would not get away with it. They would be judged by the King of kings and Lord of lords. They would be held accountable for all that they had done. Justice would come in the end. That is good news! But the accountability Jesus speaks of here will also extend to Christians in Smyrna, throughout the churches of Asia Minor, and to Christians at all times and in all places. Jesus will also repay each of us according to what we have done. The message to Christians in Smyrna would have been crystal clear: Choose correctly! Choose the crown of life by being faithful even to the point of death! Recognize the temporary nature of your present suffering and continue to embrace the one who is "the Alpha and the Omega, the first and the last, the beginning and the end." Only he has the power to write the final chapter of history; and at the end of all things he, along with his faithful followers, will triumph. Jesus' words in 22:12 would, of course, have also driven home his warning to Christians in Thyatira that he "will give to each of you according to your works" (2:23).

Revelation 22:12 also makes it clear that nothing will be hidden from Jesus' eyes when he returns; everyone will receive what is due them. And only one category of people can expect to escape the just and horrible fate that all deserve in the lake of fire: "Blessed are those who wash their robes, so that they may have the right to the tree of life and that they may enter the city by the gates" (22:14). How does one wash his or her robe? This question has been answered more than once in Revelation. Christians in Sardis would have been quick to recall that Jesus first calls them to account for having soiled their robes and then calls them to repentance so that they may be clothed in white garments again (3:5). Then, we see the vivid picture of those who have come out of the great tribulation who "have washed their robes and made them white in the blood of the Lamb" (7:14). One cannot have a clean robe without the cleansing blood of the Lamb; but the cleansing blood of the Lamb, Revelation makes clear, necessarily leads to a changed life, the life of an overcomer. Thus, we saw in 19:7–8 that the Bride of the Lamb, the church, had made herself ready. How had she done that? She had prepared herself by clothing "herself with fine linen, bright and pure—for the fine linen is the righteous deeds of the saints" (19:8). In other words, the blessing pronounced in 22:14 to "have the right to the tree of life and that they may enter the city by the gates" is for those who have believed that Jesus died on the cross for their sins and was raised from the dead that they might have life, *and* have lived out their professed allegiance to Jesus (Rom 10:9) in a life of righteous deeds, enduring to the end. This is not earning one's salvation; this is merely living out the implications of the new covenant relationship that a person enters with God through Jesus Christ, and allowing the Holy Spirit to do his work of sanctification.

To underscore the importance of ongoing visible allegiance to Jesus we are told in verse 15: "Outside are the dogs and sorcerers and the sexually immoral and murderers and idolaters, and everyone who loves and practices falsehood." Once again, those in Sardis and Philadelphia in particular would have been reassured that the liars (3:9) from the synagogue of Satan who were oppressing them would receive justice one day soon, along with all others who practice falsehood. But those within the churches of Pergamum, Thyatira, and Sardis who had given in to the false teachings of the Nicolaitans and Jezebel and indulged in sexual immorality and idolatry would have been once again reminded that to persist in such assimilation and compromise would leave them excluded from the city of God, the New Jerusalem, with others who were sexually immoral and idolaters.

As at the beginning of this marvelous book, so at the end, Jesus leaves no doubt that the message of Revelation comes from him. He has sent his angel "to testify . . . about these things for the churches" (22:16). The angel has faithfully carried out his role and now Jesus asks those in the churches of Asia Minor to do the same. As he had done with the angel, so he has done with all of his earthly followers: he has given them the task of being his ambassadors and testifying to all he has said and done. They are not to shy away from this central calling, as those in Ephesus had apparently done. For as was already made clear in 5:5, Jesus is "the root and the descendant of David" (22:16); he is the one whom Isaiah foretold would come: "There shall come forth a shoot from the stump of Jesse, and a branch from his roots shall bear fruit" (Isa 11:1); "In that day the root of Jesse, who shall stand as a signal for the peoples—of him shall the nations inquire, and his resting place shall be glorious" (Isa 11:10). He is the Davidic Messiah who will reign forever. And he is also the "bright morning star" (22:16), a title that makes clear to those in Thyatira who overcome by holding on to what they have until Jesus returns (2:25) and refusing to embrace Jezebel's call to compromise their devotion to Jesus or learn "what some call the deep things of Satan" (2:24) that Jesus promises them not just authority over the nations (2:26) but also himself, "the morning star" (2:28). The ultimate reward in the new heaven and new earth is not the spectacular New Jerusalem, with its streets of gold, or even the absence of death, pain, and suffering; the ultimate reward is God himself. He is our inheritance.

As Revelation comes to a conclusion, Jesus has one final invitation and one final warning for Christians in Asia Minor. This passage can easily be taken out of context and read as a universal invitation to all to "come" and "take the water of life without price" (22:17). The invitation to those who are thirsty clearly echoes Isa 55:1–3, and the context there is instructive:

> Come, everyone who thirsts, come to the waters; and he who has no money, come, buy and eat! Come, buy wine and milk without money and without price. ²Why do you spend your money for that which is not bread, and your labor for that which does not satisfy? Listen diligently to me, and eat what is good, and delight yourselves in rich food. ³Incline your ear, and come to me; hear, that your soul may live . . ."

Jesus exhorted Christians in Laodicea, whom he identified as "wretched, pitiable, poor, blind, and naked" (3:17), to buy from him "gold refined by fire, so that you may be rich, and white garments so that you may clothe yourself and the shame of your nakedness may not be seen, and salve to anoint your eyes, so that you may see" (3:18). Those who had nothing in their pockets were still exhorted to come and buy what matters from Jesus. So Yahweh in Isa 55 calls on his people: "come," and "he who has no money, come, buy and eat!" (Isa 55:1). But the invitation is not "come, just as you are." Instead, it is "listen diligently to me," "incline your ear," and "hear" (Isa 55:2–3). As in Revelation, the only way to receive the free blessing is both to "hear" and "keep" (1:3) what God has said. In 22:17, Jesus' invitation to come and drink freely is not an indiscriminant encouragement to those who are in rebellion against him to come and freely receive life from him. Rather, it is a beautiful promise to overcomers that their thirst will finally be satisfied when they enter into the joy of their Lord and drink from "the water of life without price" (22:17).

The narrow focus of his invitation to overcomers is made clear in verses 18–19. At first glance, we might take Jesus' words as a simple warning to be careful not to cut pages out of our Bible or add pages to our Bible. We might even say that the Judaizers exemplify adding to what God has said, by insisting that Gentile followers of Christ be circumcised and keep the Law of Moses (see Acts 15 where this view was debated and rejected by the leaders of the early church). Those who propagate such a message are preaching another gospel and are to be pronounced "accursed" (Gal 1:8–9), and "God will add to him the plagues described in this book" (Rev 22:18). The Nicolaitans and Jezebel, on the other hand, would exemplify taking "away from the words of the book of this prophecy" (22:19), for they advocated and encouraged Christians to lighten up on the issue of holiness. Where God says, "You shall be holy, for I am holy" (1 Pet 1:16), they said, "Don't be 'holier than thou'! We all sin thousands of times every day anyway; so what does a couple of extra sins in order to keep your job, avoid persecution, or save your life really matter? God will forgive you. Everything you ever do is covered by the blood of Jesus." Where God says to have nothing to do with behaviors that are an offense to him (Eph 5:3), these false teachers downplayed the seriousness of sin. As a result, "God will take away [their] share in the tree of life and in the holy city, which are described in this book" (22:19).

It is quite likely that there is more going on here, however. In fact, what we have in 22:17–19 is likely the second half of an often overlooked "inclusio," a bookend construction that is used to highlight the central message of the book. In 1:3, we were told, "Blessed is the one who reads aloud the words of this prophecy, and *blessed are those who hear, and who keep what is written in it*, for the time is near." Now, at the very end of Revelation this promise and implicit warning is reiterated. The blessing is elaborated in 22:17 and the implied warning (those who do not keep what is written in this prophecy will not receive the blessing) is elaborated in 22:18–19. How do we know this? To see what Jesus is doing here we need to recognize the intertextual connection with Deut 4 and 12 (Reading Instruction #6):

> And now, O Israel, *listen* to the statutes and the rules that I am teaching you, and *do them, that you may live*, and go in and take possession of the land that the Lord, the God of your fathers, is giving you. ²*You shall not add to the word that I command you, nor take from it, that you may keep the commandments of the Lord your God that I command you.* (Deut 4:1–2)

As Deuteronomy continues, there is a repeated call to "be careful" (NIV) to obey everything God has commanded (see, e.g., 4:9, 23; 5:32; 6:3, 12; 8:1, 11; 11:16; 12:1). These warnings culminate in Deut 12:32 where we read: "Everything that I command you, you shall be careful to do. You shall not add to it or take from it." Taken together Deut 4:2 and 12:32 strongly suggest that Jesus' words in Rev 22:18–19 serve primarily as one final exhortation to hear and obey the message of Revelation in all of its detail. It is a final call to live under the lordship of Jesus now, so that in the coming kingdom you will also live under the lordship of Jesus then, rather than being consigned to the lake of fire. For, to fail to be careful to do all that Jesus has commanded (Matt 28:20; cf. Deut 12:32) is to demonstrate one's lack of allegiance to Jesus and to come under the curses that are described in this book.

As he concludes the revelations given to John in 22:20–21, Jesus reminds his people one final time: "He who testifies to these things says, 'Surely I am coming soon'" (22:21). We are to live in light of his imminent return so that we are not caught off guard and found unprepared to meet him. For when he said, "Behold, I am coming like a thief! Blessed is the one who stays awake, keeping his garments on, that he may not go about naked and be seen exposed!" (16:15), he meant it. Revelation leaves professing followers of Jesus with no room for apathy, no room for doublemindedness, and no room for mixed allegiance. He is coming soon, and when he comes we will "all appear before the judgment seat of Christ, so that each one may receive what is due for what he has done in the body, *whether good or evil*" (2 Cor 5:10). To Jesus' final words, the apostle John can only respond "Amen. Come, Lord Jesus!" Those in Asia Minor who had compromised or who were faltering in their faith under the onslaught of the evil one were not prepared to meet the coming King of kings and Lord of lords. What about us? Can we say, "Amen. Come Lord Jesus"?

John concludes Revelation as he began it, like a letter: "The grace of the Lord Jesus be with all. Amen" (22:21). This is more than a simple "Sincerely, John." It also serves as a reminder to those who have been rebuked, corrected, or called to persevere in their faithfulness that they are not being left to pull themselves up by their bootstraps. Wherever they find themselves, if they are genuine children of God, the grace of the Lord Jesus is available to them. The somewhat peculiar use of "all" or "everyone," rather than, e.g., "all the saints" as we find in some later manuscripts, is not intended to suggest that the grace of Jesus is available to believers and unbelievers alike. Rather, here the point seems to be that whatever the challenge that was facing Christians in Asia Minor, whatever means of attack the evil one was using in an effort to turn believers from their faith, the grace of the Lord Jesus was both desperately needed and readily available. For, "His divine power has granted to us all things that pertain to life and godliness" (1 Pet 1:3). Amen.

Revelation

Jesus' Message to the Church . . . Today

As we come to the end of our study of Revelation, it is important to remember that by choosing to address this extended message to *seven* actual churches in first-century Asia Minor Jesus was symbolically sending a message to the church universal. Revelation was and is Jesus' message to the church; and if you have not noticed already, one of the things that Revelation teaches us is that there is nothing new under the sun. The entire Old Testament is an account of God redeeming a people (Israel), making a covenant with them—a covenant that carried with it both rights and responsibilities—and then repeatedly urging them to live within the conditions of that covenant, to worship and honor the God who had redeemed them. Often, those exhortations, which over the centuries were frequently delivered by God's faithful prophets, took the form of dire warnings: warnings of plagues, warnings of famines, warnings of attacks by wild animals, and warnings of falling before their enemies and being taken away into exile.

Revelation continues this same pattern, but with an important difference. Although many Christians over the years, particularly in the wealthy West, have simply taken Revelation as a comforting reminder that "in the end God wins," it is far more responsible to recognize that Revelation functions much like the prophetic warnings of the past that were directed at Israel. Now, though, it is the new covenant people of God who are being called to remain faithful even in the face of intense persecution, to repent of their sins, to reject assimilation to the societies in which they live, and to live each day in anticipation of the glorious return of the Lord Jesus Christ. Like the Israelites of old, the church today struggles to live in conformity with the covenant God has made with us. Like Israel of old, many Christians today have a false sense of security and are apathetic toward the demands of God on their life as expressed in the New Testament. They wrongly believe that they are safe and secure from the wrath of God regardless of how they live. To such foolish people Revelation sounds a clarion call to think again. Those who live in self-sufficiency, carrying on their outward spiritual practices without recognizing the absence of God in their lives or in their "worship," like the church of Laodicea are in very real danger of being spat out of the mouth of Jesus like the foulest, rankest water.

To those who are already seeking first God's kingdom and his righteousness Jesus warns them to expect to endure hardship for his name. The visions of Revelation were given, in part, to drive home the truth of 2 Tim 3:12: "everyone who wants to live a godly life in Christ Jesus will be persecuted." For followers of Jesus Christ there simply is no safe and easy pathway through this life. When the light shines in the darkness some will embrace it and come out of the darkness, but the majority will be offended by the light and will seek to snuff it out. Those in Pergamum had witnessed this firsthand with the martyrdom of Antipas; those in Philadelphia had wrestled with the helpless feeling that came with being an oppressed minority in their city where they had little power; and those in Smyrna now knew that prison, suffering, and even death were lurking on their near horizon as they became a primary target for the devil. For these threatened Christians—and for all who are suffering today because of their uncompromising faith in the Lord—Jesus paints a realistic picture of what is to come. Yes, they will face the wrath of the beast; but they will not only be exempt from the wrath of God and the wrath of the Lamb, but will also share in all the blessings of the coming kingdom of God as they reign for a thousand years with the King of kings and Lord of lords on this planet and then enjoy all of the benefits and wonders of the new heaven and new earth that will be completely and forever free from any of the horrible effects of human sin.

For those suffering today, Jesus calls us to take heart because our suffering is not the end of the story. Yes, God has ordained that many of his people will lose their lives because of their allegiance to him (6:11), but a day is soon coming when death itself will be thrown into the lake of fire never to touch any of God's people again. So, take heart and continue to stay awake and remain dressed for the daily battle so that you will not be caught with your pants down and be ashamed when the Lord returns (16:15). He is coming soon, and he will catch many by surprise. Don't find yourself among the many. Remember that Jesus warned you ahead of time what to expect and called you to endurance, faithfulness, and obedience to God's commands (13:10; 14:12). Fear of losing your livelihood is no excuse for abandoning your devotion to God; and neither is fear of losing your life. Blessed is he who is not touched by the second death.

All of this, we have seen, is accomplished through twenty-two chapters of carefully interwoven visions, dialogue, and reporting from the Apostle John. While some scholars have noticed the important connections, e.g., between Rev 21–22 and the seven letters,[1] none to my knowledge has adequately explored the pervasive connections between Rev 4–22 and the seven letters.[2] Indeed, Hemer claims that any such parallels have little if any significance: "They are just echoes of symbols and expressions which appear in the letters or which suggest that the circumstances of those churches were present to John's mind. A few of the correspondences are close and illuminating, but in general the reminiscences are elusive and marginal."[3] Perhaps if we were to focus merely on the specific language and imagery in the seven letters we might reach this conclusion. When we focus on the message to each of the churches, and each church's distinctive characteristics, however, the profound correspondences between the seven letters and the rest of Revelation become readily apparent.

As a whole, Revelation reveals the multi-pronged attack of Satan on the churches of Asia Minor. In some cases, the churches were simply being tempted to enjoy the prosperity of the Roman Empire. They would have been quite comfortable today wearing the badge "consumer" and living in as much comfort as possible. Other churches would not have viewed the Roman Empire so positively. Some Christians in Asia Minor were facing economic ruin or even a violent death if they refused to worship the emperor. For these, the temptation was to abandon their faith in order to save their lives. Still others were being tempted to find ways to have their cake and eat it too. These Christians were being enticed through the Nicolaitans and Jezebel to embrace as many aspects of Greco-Roman culture as possible so as to blend in better to society and enjoy its bounty. Finally, there were yet others who, in the face of pressure to participate in the imperial cult, were being tempted to find protection from prison and death by entering or reentering Judaism, which was granted certain religious concessions by Rome. In this case, the Christians would not have to worship idols; they would "only" have to renounce Jesus as Messiah and Lord. Whatever the means that was being used to lure them away from faithful devotion to God, Jesus urges his followers to remember his words in 16:15, "Behold, I come like a thief! Blessed is he who stays awake and keeps his clothes with him, so that he may not go naked and be shamefully exposed." Without vigilance followers of Jesus risk being "overcome" by Satan rather than "overcoming."

The seven churches of Asia Minor, then, were left with a fundamental choice that we too have to make. To whom or to what will we give our allegiance? Will we, like many in Asia Minor, make commitments to other masters, like the emperor? Or will our sole devotion be to the Lord Jesus Christ. In the ancient world, when people heard Jesus' declaration, "If anyone would come after me, let him deny himself and

---

1. See Hemer, *Letters*, 16.

2. Charles (*Revelation*, lxxxviii) and Swete (*The Apocalypse*, xlvi–xlviii), for example, highlight some important linguistic correspondences between various parts of Revelation, but do not reflect in detail on the significance of these correspondences other than to rightly argue that they point to the unity of the work.

3. Hemer, *Letters*, 16.

take up his cross daily and follow me" (Luke 9:23), the radical commitment that his vivid language pointed to would not have been particularly shocking, though it was certainly very serious. We find similar expressions of devotion to the emperor:

> I swear . . . that I will support Caesar Augustus, his children and descendants, throughout my life, in word, deed and thought . . . that in whatsoever concerns them I will spare neither body nor soul nor life nor children . . . that whenever I see or hear of anything being said, planned or done against them I will report it . . . And whomsoever they regard as enemies I will attack and pursue with arms and the sword by land and by sea.[4]

If the Roman emperor, a mere man, could elicit such absolute devotion, what should that tell us about the King of kings and Lord of lord who holds the keys of Death and Hades, is worshiped by all the host of heaven, and is coming to judge the living and the dead? He will not content himself with simply "coming into our lives"; he is Lord and must be acknowledged as Lord and served as Lord by everyone who would overcome and enjoy the benefits of his coming kingdom. Revelation, then, calls out to those in the wealthy West today, who profess to follow Jesus but take a very casual approach to relating to God, to think again about where we stand in God's eyes.

So, what have we discovered in our study of Revelation? We have seen that Jesus graciously delivered a powerful message to Christians in seven churches in Asia Minor to call some to perseverance, to call many to repentance, and to call all to radical devotion to him. He reminded them that being his servant is not for the fainthearted. It is not something to be taken lightly. Our relationship with Jesus cannot be viewed as simply a part of our life; Jesus must be our life. For, without that attitude toward him we will easily fall prey to the one who deceives the whole world, and we will become spiritual adulterers whose soiled clothes will make us unfit for the marriage feast of the Lamb. Ultimately, I am convinced that the original audience would have understood the vast majority of what is contained in this book in ways similar to what I have outlined in the preceding chapters. Whether or not they responded as Jesus intended is another question, a question that also faces readers of Revelation today: What will we do with Revelation now that we have heard the rest of the story?

---

4. An oath used by citizens of Paphlagonia to swear their allegiance to Caesar dating to 3 BC. See Judge, "Decrees of Caesar," 6.

Bibliography

Aune, David E. *Revelation 1–5*. Word Biblical Commentary. Dallas: Word, 1997.

Bauckham, Richard. *The Theology of the Book of Revelation*. New Testament Theology. Cambridge: Cambridge University Press, 1993.

Beale, G. K. *The Book of Revelation: A Commentary on the Greek Text*. The New International Greek Testament Commentary. Grand Rapids: Eerdmans, 1999.

Block, Daniel I. *Ezekiel 25–48*. The New International Commentary on the Old Testament. Grand Rapids: Eerdmans, 1998.

Blomberg, Craig L. "The Posttribulationalism of the New Testament." In *A Case for Historic Premillenialism: An Alternative to "Left Behind" Eschatology*, edited by Craig L. Blomberg and Sung Wok Chung, 61–87. Grand Rapids: Baker Academic, 2009.

Champlin, Edward. *Nero*. Cambridge, MA: Harvard University Press, 2003.

Charles, R. H. *A Critical and Exegetical Commentary on the Revelation of St. John*. International Critical Commentary. Edinburgh: T. & T. Clark, 1920.

Chesterton, G. K. *Orthodoxy: The Romance of Faith*. New York: Doubleday, 1990.

Collins, Adela Yarbro. *Crisis & Catharsis: The Power of the Apocalypse*. Philadelphia: Westminster, 1984.

Collins, John J. "Introduction: Toward a Morphology of a Genre." *Semeia* 14 (1979) 1–20.

———. *The Sceptre and the Star: The Messiahs of the Dead Sea Scrolls and Other Ancient Literature*. New York: Doubleday, 1995.

Culy, Martin M. "Do Psalmists Who Curse Belong in the Church? Understanding and Embracing the Imprecatory Psalms." *Canadian Evangelical Review* 32–33 (2006/2007) 35–60.

———. *Echoes of Friendship in the Gospel of John*. New Testament Monographs 30. Sheffield: Sheffield Phoenix, 2010.

Danker, Frederick W., ed. *A Greek-English Lexicon of the New Testament and Other Early Christian Literature*. 3rd ed. Based on Walter Bauer's *Griechisch-Deutsches Wörterbuch zu den Schriften des Neuen Testaments und der Frühchristlichen Literatur*, 6th ed., and on previous English editions by William F. Arndt, F. Wilbur Gingrich, and F. W. Danker. Chicago: University of Chicago, 2000. [BDAG]

Davis, John J. *Biblical Numerology: A Basic Study of the Use of Numbers in the Bible*. Grand Rapids: Baker, 1968.

Dmitriev, Sviatoslav. *City Government in Hellenistic and Roman Asia Minor*. Oxford: Oxford University Press, 2005.

Fee, Gordon D. *God's Empowering Presence: The Holy Spirit in the Letters of Paul*. Peabody, MA: Hendrickson, 1994.

Hemer, Colin J. *The Letters to the Seven Churches of Asia in Their Local Setting*. Journal for the Study of the New Testament Supplement Series 11. Grand Rapids: Eerdmans, 2001.

Hess, Richard S. "The Future Written in the Past: The Old Testament and the Millennium." In *A Case for Historic Premillenialism: An Alternative to "Left Behind" Eschatology*, edited by Craig. L. Blomberg and Sung Wok Chung, 23–36. Grand Rapids: Baker Academic, 2009.

Howard-Brook, Wes, and Anthony Gwyther. *Unveiling Empire: Reading Revelation Then and Now*. Maryknoll, NY: Orbis, 1999.

Instone-Brewer, David. "The Eighteen Benedictions and the Minim before 70 CE." *Journal of Theological Studies* 54 (2003) 25–44.

Judge, E. A. "The Decrees of Caesar at Thessalonica." *Reformed Theological Review* 30 (1971) 1–7.

Keener, Craig S. *The IVP Bible Background Commentary: New Testament*. Downers Grove, IL: InterVarsity, 1993.

———. *Revelation*. The NIV Application Commentary. Grand Rapids: Zondervan, 2000.

Louw, Johannes P., and Eugene A. Nida, eds. *Greek-English Lexicon of the New Testament Based on Semantic Domains*. 2 vols. 2nd ed. New York: United Bible Societies, 1988, 1989.

McKnight, Scot. "The Warning Passages of Hebrews: A Formal Analysis and Theological Conclusions." *Trinity Journal* 13 (1992) 21–59.

Osborne, Grant R. *Revelation*. Baker Exegetical Commentary on the New Testament. Grand Rapids: Baker, 2002.

Prigent, Pierre. *L'Apocalypse de Saint Jean*. 2nd ed. Geneva: Labor et Fides, 1988.

Ramsay, W. M. *The Letters to the Seven Churches*. Updated ed. Peabody, MA: Hendrickson, 1994.

Rapske, Brian. *The Book of Acts and Paul in Roman Custody*. Grand Rapids: Eerdmans, 1994.

Robinson, J. A. T. *Redating the New Testament*. Philadelphia: Westminster, 1976.

Rudwick, M. J. S., and E. M. B. Green. "The Laodicean Lukewarmness." *Expository Times* 69 (1957–1958) 176–78.

Sanders, J. N. "John on Patmos." *New Testament Studies* 9 (1962–63) 75–85.

Schreiner, Thomas R. "Perseverance and Assurance: A Survey and Proposal." *Southern Baptist Journal of Theology* 2 (1998) 32–62.

Schreiner, Thomas R., and Ardel B. Caneday. *The Race Set before Us: A Biblical Theology of Perseverance and Assurance*. Downers Grove, IL: IVP Academic, 2001.

Schüssler Fiorenza, Elisabeth. *The Book of Revelation: Justice and Judgment*. Philadelphia: Fortress, 1985.

———. "Revelation." In *The New Testament and Its Modern Interpreters*, edited by Jay Eldon Epp and George W. MacRae, 407–27. Atlanta: Scholars, 1989.

Smalley, Stephen S. *The Revelation to John: A Commentary on the Greek Text of the Apocalypse*. Downers Grove, IL: InterVarsity, 2005.

Swete, H. B. *The Apocalypse of St. John*. 3rd ed. London: Macmillan, 1911.

Talbert, Charles H. *The Apocalypse: A Reading of the Revelation of John*. Louisville: Westminster John Knox, 1994.

Thompson, Leonard L. *The Book of Revelation: Apocalypse and Empire*. New York: Oxford University Press, 1990.

Worth, Roland H., Jr. *The Seven Cities of the Apocalypse and Greco-Asian Culture*. New York: Paulist, 1999.

Author Index

Aune, David E., 55, 58, 106, 146, 152, 154, 179

Bauckham, Richard, 14
Beale, G. K., 30, 94, 150
Block, Daniel I., 249
Blomberg, Craig L., 235

Caneday, Ardel B., 170
Champlin, Edward, 19
Charles, R. H., 2, 114, 177, 262
Chesterton, G. K., 1
Collins, Adela Yarbro, 13
Collins, John J., 10, 121
Culy, Martin M., 154, 212

Davis, John J., 18
Dmitriev, Sviatoslav, 56

Fee, Gordon D., 144

Green, E. M. B., 208
Green, Keith, 50, 147
Gwyther, Anthony, 13, 14

Harris, Murray, 4
Hemer, Colin J., 2, 11, 32, 34, 36, 55, 56, 57, 58,
    59, 63, 86, 88, 93, 94, 95, 116, 117, 120,
    121, 122, 133, 143, 145, 146, 149, 150,
    174, 176, 177, 179, 180, 184, 186, 208,
    209, 211, 213, 250, 262
Hess, Richard S., 4
Howard-Brook, Wes, 13, 14

Instone-Brewer, David, 154, 179

Judge, E. A., 263

Keener, Craig S., 13, 20, 75

Louw, Johannes P., 119, 164

McKnight, Scot, 170

Nida, Eugene A., 119, 164

Osborne, Grant R., 92, 94, 105

Prigent, Pierre, 2

Ramsay, W. M., vii, 2, 17, 19, 31, 32, 55, 57, 58,
    60, 63, 85, 86, 91, 94, 95, 116, 120, 121,
    133, 138, 143, 144, 145, 149, 151, 153,
    174, 175, 177, 178, 185, 186, 208, 209,
    210, 211, 226
Rapske, Brian, 60
Robinson, J. A. T., 13
Rudwick, M. J. S., 208

Sanders, J. N., 2
Schreiner, Thomas R., 170
Schüssler Fiorenza, Elisabeth, 13, 14
Smalley, Stephen S., 44
Swete, H. B., 2, 34, 177, 185, 262

Talbert, Charles H., vii, 13, 14
Thompson, Leonard L., 13

Worth, Roland H., Jr., 2, 25, 26, 32, 52

Scripture Index

Genesis

1–3	37
1	244
1:3	251
1:14–18	251
2:10	252
3:1	131
3:8	245
3:24	36
35:17	93
37	74
39–50	74

Exodus

8:22–23	198
9:4–7	198
9:22–26	198
12:21–23	198–199
13:9	202
13:16	202
15	50, 203
16:4–36	92
16:32–36	93
19:16	17
20:18	17
28:36–38	225
29:46	245
32:31–33	152
33:20	253

Leviticus

11:45	245
18:24–30	208
22:31–33	245
25:38	245
25:55	245
26:13	245

Numbers

6:27	185
14:33	249
15:41	245
18:20–24	73
22–24	89
24:17	121
25:1–9	136
25:1–3	89, 165
31	164
31:3	164
31:7	164
31:9	164
31:15–17	164, 165
31:15–16	89

Deuteronomy

4	258
4:2	258
4:9	258
4:23	258
5:32	258
6	202
6:3	258
6:4–9	47, 202
6:8	47
6:12	258
8	220
8:1	258
8:11–20	220
8:11	258
8:12–14	228
8:14	220
8:19–20	220
11	202
11:16	258
11:18	202
12	258
12:1	258